DOCUMENTS OF KOREAN COMMUNISM
1918-1948

STUDIES OF THE EAST ASIAN INSTITUTE
COLUMBIA UNIVERSITY

DOCUMENTS
OF KOREAN
COMMUNISM
1918-1948

DAE-SOOK SUH

PRINCETON UNIVERSITY PRESS

PRINCETON, NEW JERSEY

1970

The East Asian Institute at Columbia

THE EAST ASIAN INSTITUTE was established by Columbia University in 1949 to prepare graduate students for careers dealing with East Asia, and to aid research and publication on East Asia during the modern period. The research program of the East Asian Institute is conducted or directed by faculty members of the University, by other scholars invited to participate in the program of the Institute, and by candidates for the Certificate of the Institute or the degree of Doctor of Philosophy. Some of the products of the research program are published as Studies of the East Asian Institute. The faculty of the Institute, without necessarily agreeing with the conclusions reached in the Studies, hope with their publication to perform a national service by increasing American understanding of the peoples of East Asia, the development of their societies, and their current problems.

The faculty of the East Asian Institute are grateful to the Rockefeller Foundation and the Ford Foundation for the financial assistance which they have given to the program of research and publication.

This book is one of the Studies of the East Asian Institute, Columbia University. Other books in the series are:

The Ladder of Success in Imperial China by Ping-ti Ho, New York, Columbia University Press, 1962; John Wiley, 1964.

The Chinese Inflation, 1937-49 by Shun-hsin Chou. New York, Columbia University Press, 1963.

Reformer in Modern China: Chang Chien, 1853-1926 by Samuel Chu. New York, Columbia University Press, 1965.

Research in Japanese Sources: A Guide by Herschel Webb with the assistance of Marleigh Ryan. New York, Columbia University Press, 1965.

Society and Education in Japan by Herbert Passin. New York, Bureau of Publications, Teachers College, Columbia University, 1965.

Agricultural Production and the Economic Development of Japan, 1873-1922 by James I. Nakamura. Princeton, Princeton University Press, 1966.

The Korean Communist Movement, 1918-1948 by Dae-Sook Suh. Princeton, Princeton University Press, 1967.

The First Vietnam Crisis by Melvin Gurtov. New York, Columbia University Press, 1967.

Japan's First Modern Novel: Ukigumo of Futabatei Shimei by Marleigh Grayer Ryan. New York, Columbia University Press, 1967.

Cadres, Bureaucracy, and Political Power in Communist China by A. Doak Barnett with a contribution by Ezra Vogel. New York, Columbia University Press, 1967.

The Japanese Imperial Institution in the Tokugawa Period by Herschel Webb. New York, Columbia University Press, 1968.

Higher Education and Business Recruitment in Japan by Koya Azumi. New York, Teachers College Press, Columbia University, 1969.

The Communists and Chinese Peasant Rebellions: A Study in the Rewriting of Chinese History by James P. Harrison, Jr. New York, Atheneum Publishers, 1969.

The Kemmu Restoration by Paul Varley. New York, Columbia University Press, 1969.

How the Conservatives Rule Japan by Nathaniel B. Thayer. Princeton, Princeton University Press, 1969.

Aspects of Chinese Education, edited by C. T. Hu. New York, Teachers College Press, 1970.

Economic Development and the Labor Market in Japan by Koji Taira. New York, Columbia University Press, 1970.

The Japanese Oligarchy and the Russo-Japanese War by Shumpei Okamoto. New York, Columbia University Press (forthcoming).

To Maurice Min-ho

PREFACE

THIS STUDY is an effort to present the much neglected but important documents of Korean communism, selected and translated from a collection of documents covering some thirty years of the Korean Communist movement. In view of their long and arduous struggle, the old Korean Communists left relatively few documents of their movement. Compared to the Communists of other movements, whose writings in general are prolific and often prolix, the Korean Communists did little to document their tortured movement. Constant involvement in action-oriented operations; the secrecy connected with underground organizational undertakings at home; the scattered and sporadic nature of activities abroad, uncontrolled and uncoordinated by a central organ; and the relative absence of polemics and discourses on the theoretical basis of the movement—all contributed to the relative scarcity of documents on Korean communism. In addition, because of the efficient suppression by the Japanese police forces, including the publication police, the appearance of documents on various phases of the movement often fluctuated with the severity of police surveillance of the party organization and its leadership.

In the study of the documents of Korean communism, perhaps more important than their relative scarcity are the problems arising from the political division of Korea today. The fiercely anti-Communist South condemns communism in Korea, past and present alike, and does little to study communism; the scholars of the South are little inclined to uncover the documents of the old Communists. The Communists in the North, without ties to the old Korean Communist movement, dismiss their predecessors' efforts as paltry, having little or no significance for the present. They utilize only those materials of the old Communists that appear to justify and enhance their rule in the North. In past studies by the Koreans and the Japanese, only two or three documents, usually of Comintern origin, were appended either to condemn or to glorify communism in Korea.

Despite the scarcity of documents in general and the
indifference of the scholars in presently divided Korea, it has
been possible to uncover and collect some 124 documents for
this study. Out of this collection, 66 documents have been
selected, translated and compiled here. Admittedly some key
documents known to exist are not yet available, and a few
documents introduced here are of dubious authenticity, but the
documents presented do represent the essential and by far the
major part of the basic documents of the old Korean Communist movement. Many hitherto obscure and secret documents
that shed much light on details of the movement are introduced
here.

From the first speech of Pak Chin-sun at the Comintern in
1920 to the speech of Kim Ha-il in the session presided over by
Comrade Ercoli (Togliati) at the Seventh Congress of the
Comintern in 1935, there are included important documents
that shed much light on details of the first Socialist party and
the relations between the Korean Communists and the Comintern. There are other obscure yet important documents, such as
the unconfirmed reports of the Korean Communists to the
Comintern, the theses of their regional movements at home, the
dissolution resolutions of their bureaus abroad, and several
original documents of the Korean Fatherland Restoration
Association in Manchuria clarifying the role of Kim Il-sŏng and
his partisans in Manchuria. Better known but often misunder-
stood and misinterpreted documents, such as the December
Theses on the expulsion of the Korean section from the
Comintern and Kuusinen's letter on Korean factionalism, are
also presented here in entirety.

The choice of documents compiled needs but little explanation. The choice has been made on the basis of contextual
importance to the movement as a whole. No effort has been
made to select documents to support a particular thesis or to
emphasize a specific period, but rather the selections are meant
to treat the period comprehensively. The selected documents
are grouped into six sections, with a commentary to each
section explaining each document. In order to demonstrate the

relevance of the documents grouped under each heading, a succinct summary is given of Communist activities during the period in question. For more details of any particular incident referred to by these documents or any specific subject in the context of the Korean Communist movement as a whole, the reader may consult my earlier study, *The Korean Communist Movement, 1918-1948* (Princeton University Press, 1967). Most of the documents collected but not included in this study, as well as those documents not yet available, are also briefly discussed in the commentaries.

It is hoped that the importance of this study will lie not merely in the presentation in English of hitherto unavailable documents of Korean communism, but rather in the formulation of a broad framework of inquiry upon which scholars can better interpret the existing documents, uncover as yet unavailable key documents and analyze in detail various segments and phases of the Korean Communist movement, and thus enhance the understanding of communism in Korea. Particularly fascinating for further study would be the polemics on the "Two-Party" and "Liquidation" theories, the response of different Korean Communist groups to the Comintern directives, a comparison of such regional Communist activities as those of Chŏlla and P'yŏngan provinces, a comparison of the various overseas bureaus of the Korean Communist party, the writings of Communist apostates and their motives, and the extent of external influences on the development and failure of the Korean Communist movement.

There were numerous problems and difficulties in preparing this study, but three are most important and need to be explained in some detail. The first concerns the authenticity of the documents. Although this is an important and persistent problem until an authentic document is found and verified, the problem is most acute in respect to only a small number of documents in Part I. These five documents of somewhat dubious authenticity can be divided into two groups. One is a selection of three agreements between the Bolsheviks and the Korean revolutionaries in Siberia and the Russian Maritime

Province, toward the end of the Russian revolution, when the Korean revolutionaries began to participate in Communist activities and accept communism; the other is the group of two documents allegedly written by a three-man committee of the Comintern concerning the Alexeyevsk Incident involving the Korear. Communists.

Although the authenticity of these documents is difficult to verify, such alleged agreements between the Korean Communists and the Russian Bolsheviks are available in abundance, and there are also numerous references, in other writings independent of bias, to the alleged decisions of the Comintern on the Alexeyevsk Incident. It is clear from the study of the origin of the Korean Communist movement that these agreements and directives are not fabrications and they are included here to shed light on the early stages of the Korean Communist movement. Where appropriate, each document of dubious authenticity is explained and the credibility of other documents of similar nature is also assessed in the commentaries.

The second major problem concerns the originality of the documents. Just as the operations of the Korean Communists were scattered in several countries, so are their documents also available in many languages, and at times it is difficult to ascertain in what language a particular document was originally written. Although the documents pertaining to the movement within Korea were written in Korean, there are many documents emanating from the Japanese bureau of the Korean Communists that were originally written in Japanese by Korean Communists. There are other documents that were written in English by Koreans abroad and some in Russian written by Korean emigrants to Russia and by the Russians and the Comintern. Many reports of the apostates were written originally in Japanese by these Communists in Korea.

Some translations have been made from English or Russian into Japanese or Korean, but till now there has not been any effort to collect these documents in their original languages or to translate them into one language, not even Korean. On the contrary, some of the documents written originally in Korean are not available. Those originally available in Korean and seized by the Japanese publication police were later translated into Japanese. The Japanese authorities, in an effort to uproot the Communist activities of the Korean recalcitrants, frantically translated from Korean and other languages those documents that could be useful in prosecuting the Communists. Some documents are available in two or three languages in translation, but not in the original, and others are available only in one language, sometimes in the original and sometimes in translation. An effort has been made both to collect the original documents and to verify the language in which they were originally written, but it has been necessary, in some cases, to retranslate the translation when the original documents were unavailable.

The third problem is that of translation itself. When a document was available in two or three languages, both the original and the translations were studied. However, a new translation of the original document was made so as to preserve in English as much of the original context as possible. A new translation was made even when an earlier translation was more readable than the badly written and often awkward original. When a document was available only in non-English translation, an almost verbatim translation was made, so not to burden the English translation with more errors than those of the earlier translation. It should be noted that, taking the example of those documents that are available in both the original and in translation, the essential meaning of any specific document generally is conveyed in translation. There is no doubt that in retranslating a document much sacrifice is made in terms of style, precision and wording, but a conscious effort has been made not only to avoid egregiously wrong translations, but also to maintain the essential meaning of the original documents. Footnotes have been inserted to explain special problems of translation, as well as to discuss particular persons, incidents or organizations not specifically treated in the Commentary. Those documents available in English translation or as English originals have been edited to conform in style to the other documents.

Perhaps the greatest problem in the translation of Korean Communist documents concerns not the translation or retranslation into English of translated documents, but the handling of badly written documents in the original Korean or Japanese, documents often expressing a passionate advocation of their cause by the action-oriented and the uneducated. In contrast to the documents written by Kuusinen or the directives from the Comintern, for example, the documents written by the Koreans are less doctrinaire and polemical, and these were, in general, written by men of little education. In addition they wrote under constant surveillance and frequently in haste, thus producing more prescriptive documents for action than discourses on Korean communism. Except in only a few cases, such as Kim Kyu-sik's writings in English and Kim Ha-il's writings in Russian, most of the documents written by the Koreans in non-Korean languages were done with but a cursory knowledge of the foreign language and thus are of marginal quality.

Several transliteration systems are followed: the modified Hepburn system for Japanese, the Wade-Giles system for Chinese, the system used by the Library of Congress for Russian, and the McCune-Reischauer system for Korean. For those who insist upon perfection of the imperfect Korean transliteration system, greater patience is asked.

To many scholars and colleagues who assisted me during various stages of this study, I am grateful. I am particularly grateful to Professor James William Morley, Professor of Government at Columbia and former director of the East Asian Institute, who guided this study from the very beginning and gave me timely advice and assistance. It was the Japan Foreign Relations Project under his direction which funded this project when I needed support to collect most of the documents compiled here. I am also indebted to Professor C. Martin Wilbur, George Sansom Professor of Chinese History at Columbia, who gave me valuable advice and encouragement. The Korea Committee of the Institute under his chairmanship continuously supported this project. To Dr. John M. H.

Lindbeck, Director of the East Asian Institute at Columbia, who nursed this study to completion and who also undertook the painstaking task of having the appropriate people check my translations, I am deeply grateful. I have also received a summer research grant from the Office of Research at the University of Houston, in support of this project, and I express my appreciation.

Among those who read portions of this study and gave me valuable assistance, I am particularly grateful to Dr. Harris H. Tallan and Professor James E. Anderson. I am also indebted to Professors Glenn D. Paige and Joseph L. Nogee, who translated two Russian documents, items 34 and 9, into English. Since I have altered their original translations freely and since all other translations are mine, I am solely responsible for this study. I also express my appreciation to Mrs. Sharon Baron, who typed most of these documents more than once, and Miss Jeanne E. Schoch for the final typing.

New York   D.S.S.
July 1968

CONTENTS

DOCUMENTS OF KOREAN COMMUNISM

1918-1948

ABBREVIATIONS USED

CY	Communist Youth
ECCI	Executive Committee of the Communist International
FCTFE	First Congress of the Toilers of the Far East
JANA	Japanese Army and Navy Archives
JFMA	Japanese Foreign Ministry Archives
KCP	Korean Communist Party
KCYA	Korean Communist Youth Association
KIM	Kommunisticheskogo Internatsionala Molodezhe [Communist Youth International]
KFRAM	Korean Fatherland Restoration Association in Manchuria
KUTV	Kommunisticheskii Universitet Trudiashchikhsia Vostoka [Communist University of the Toilers of the East]
MGB	Manchurian General Bureau
M.L.	Marxist-Leninist
MOPR	Mezhdunarodnoe Obshchestvo Pomoshchi Revoliuchii [International Revolutionary Fighters' Relief Society]
MPC	Manchurian Provincial Committee
NCKIL	North China Korean Independence League
NEAJUA	Northeast Anti-Japanese United Army
NKWP	North Korean Workers' Party
RILU	Red International of Labor Union
SKWP	South Korean Workers' Party
SPA	Supreme People's Assembly
WPK	Workers' Party of Korea
YCL	Young Communist League

PART I

THE EARLY STAGE

1919-25

COMMENTARY

The Early Stage, 1919-25

UNLIKE the beginnings of some Communist parties and movements which were inspired by indigenous intellectuals, the Korean movement was started by Korean revolutionaries and immigrants abroad who accepted and fought for the cause of bolshevism at the time of the Russian revolution without fully understanding and appreciating its impact upon Korea. Much of the early Korean movement was characterized by a general lack of discussion of communism as a political ideology contrasting and competing with other political ideas for the future of Korea. It was also characterized by intense and enthusiastic support for anything that was anti-Japanese, which attracted them rather blindly to bolshevism. Because of effective Japanese rule in Korea, the numerous and diverse centers of the Korean communism abroad did not converge into Korea until after some six years of trial and frustration abroad, including fierce factional strife between the two leading groups.

The movements' origins abroad, the lack of discernment about the nature of communism, the fervor of anti-Japanese attitudes combined with efficient Japanese suppression, contribute generally to the lack of documents of any value pertaining to the activities of early Korean Communists. This lack is further complicated by the fact that very few of the documents which did exist are available today, and those available are often not in their original languages.

The early centers of the Korean movement were in the Russian Maritime Province and in Siberia. One of the two dominant groups, the Shanghai group, later joined the Korean national revolutionary movement, unsuccessfully attempting to influence the Korean Provisional Government in Shanghai. They then began the movement in Shanghai with the help of the Comintern in which their representative was active. The Shanghai group soon was challenged by another group originating in Irkutsk. The two factions fought at Alexeyevsk, with the

Irkutsk group subsequently representing the Korean Communists at the First Congress of the Toilers of the Far East. The Congress did influence the Korean Nationalists but an attempted coalition of the two factions failed.

The documents of this period are presented under five headings: A) early agreements between the Korean revolutionaries and the Russians, under various titles but mostly the Bolshevik Army; B) documents of the Korean Communist Party in Shanghai; C) documents relating to their representation to the Comintern; D) materials pertaining to the Alexeyevsk Incident; and E) documents of the First Congress of the Toilers of the Far East.

A. *The Early Agreements, 1920-21*

Various agreements between the Russian bolsheviks and the Korean revolutionaries in Siberia and Manchuria are available particularly those made during the early 1920's. Although they are reported in numerous Japanese official records, the authenticity of many of these documents is quite dubious, not only because the agreements were secretly concluded between the Korean revolutionaries and the bolsheviks in Siberia, far removed from the centers of the Comintern and the Russian Communist Party, but also because the agreements were generally of such a nature that the Korean revolutionaries were guaranteed of their revolutionary, mostly anti-Japanese activities in Siberia upon their pledge to bolshevism. Also casting doubt on their authenticity is the fact that these secret agreements were reported by Japanese garrison army's intelligence group, which sought to discourage and prevent the Korean revolutionaries engaging anti-Japanese activities.

The three agreements included here are selected on the basis of their importance, as determined from the record of Korean participants to the agreements. The first one, item 1, is said to have been concluded by Pak Chin-sun, representing Yi Tong-hwi's Shanghai group; the second one, item 2, is by Mun Ch'ang-bom representing the Chita Korean Communist Party

Council (the Irkutsk group); and third, item 3, is an agreement made by a group from the Korean independence movement with the Bolsheviks. The credibility of some specific provisions, particularly those involving payment of money (item 1, article 4) and the supply of arms (item 3, article 1) are dubious, and the Russian counterparts to these agreements are difficult to identify because they are often referred to as the Russian government (items 2 and 3) and the Asian Bureau of the Russian Communist Party (item 1). These were all secret agreements, and perhaps the secrecy may account for some complicity. However, these documents provide some information on the circumstances under which the Koreans began their Communist activities, the origin of these activities abroad, and the beginning of the Korean movement by revolutionary leaders and groups who had fled abroad.

There are other similar agreements such as the "Agreement Between the Red Army Officer Corps Stationed at Vladivostok and the Korean Communist Party in the Maritime Province on November 17, 1922";[1] "Secret Agreement Between Kim Kyu-sik and the Russian Government";[2] and "Agreement Between the Russian Government and the Representative of the (Korean) Independence Corps of Blagoveschensk."[3]

These agreements are very short three-point to six-point documents with many of their provisions being similar in nature to the items 1, 2 and 3. The agreements usually provide for the support of the Russians and propagation of communism by the Korean revolutionaries in return for financial aid and the privilege to maintain arms to fight the Japanese in Siberia and Manchuria.

[1] "Nihon kyōsan-tō kankei zakken, Chōsen kyōsan-tō kankei, 1" [Miscellaneous Documents concerning the Japanese Communist Party, Korean Communist Party, 1]. *JFMA* (Japanese Foreign Ministry Archives), reel S 721 (S.9.4.5.2-30).

[2] Kim Kyu-sik cited here is not the same person as the more well-known Korean Nationalist leader. For this document see, "Taishō jūichinen Chōsen chian jōkyō, sono ni, kokugai," [The State of Public Peace and Order in Korea in 1922, Section 2, abroad]. *JFMA*, reel SP 46 (sp. 150), 364-71.

[3] See, *JANA* (Japanese Army and Navy Archives), reel 117 (T1,058), 29,132.

B. *The Korean Communist Party in Shanghai, 1921-22*

Although the first organization of the Korean Communists, the Korean Socialist Party of Yi Tong-hwi, can be dated as early as June 25, 1918 at Khabarovsk, it was not until August 1919 after their move to China in conjunction with their abortive participation in the Korean Provisional Government in Shanghai that the Korean Communists were reorganized as the Korean Communist Party and began active Communist programs. This first group was called the Shanghai group. Another group, composed mostly of the Korean emigrants in Russia and organized with the aid of a Comintern agent named Shumi-atsky, was known as the Irkutsk group. It later came into direct confrontation with the Shanghai group. Much of the early Korean Communist activity was the work of the Shanghai group, which was depicted by the Irkutsk group as feigning communism for the cause of the Korean national independence. The Shanghai group also was criticized by the Korean Provisional Government for an alleged usurpation of government funds for the cause of communism.

The documents presented in this section are primarily involved with the Shanghai group. The manifesto of the Korean Communist Party, item 4, is the first of its kind by the Koreans. Together with its platform, item 5, the two documents leave little doubt that the Shanghai group are Communists striving for the establishment of a government in Korea under proletarian dictatorship. Charges alleging their feigning communism can be largely dismissed on the basis of these documents, particularly the endorsement of the Communist International and the thoughts expressed in the platform of their five-point slogans about the problems of national emancipation, education, and religion. The by-laws of the party, item 6, although relatively short (7 Chapters and 36 Articles) and cursory, are also introduced here because they give some indication of the dimension of the group's operation from China inclusive of the Russian Maritime Province, Manchuria, Japan, and Korea. In addition many of the by-laws of the later parties within Korea seem to be patterned after these.

Perhaps the most controversial issue among the early Korean revolutionaries and Communists was the question involving funds from the Comintern. The exact amount promised by the Comintern, the sum actually received by the Korean Communists, and its value in terms of a particular currency at the time, are all important questions that remain to be clarified. However, the document of income and expenditure of the Korean Communist Party, item 7, indicates, if not in exact value, how the fund was allocated and spent. It is important to note that the money was spent not solely on the Korean movement, but also on the Chinese, Formosan, and Japanese Communist movements. The receipt of this money by the Japanese agent reported that he received 6,000 yen (approximately $3,000), although this document indicates some 11,000 yen was spent for the Japanese party. The fund caused a significant uproar from the Korean Nationalists, and the Korean Provisional Government's declaration, item 8, gives their version of the controversy in condemnation of the Korean Communist Party.

There are also other documents dealing with this phase, and especially with the activities of the Irkutsk group. Examples include the Irkutsk group's declaration in the name of the Korean National Council,[4] the temporary platform and by-laws of the youth organization in Shanghai,[5] their propaganda programs of August 6, 1921,[6] and others. Although the Irkutsk group did much to attract the Korean revolutionaries abroad to the Communist movement, they also contributed to the enervation of the movement by their intense factional opposition to the Shanghai group. Most importantly, the majority of

[4] "Zengoku Chōsen gikai sengen" [The Declaration of the All Korean National Council]. *JANA,* reel 117 (T1,084), 29,626-28. Some portion of this document is also available in Russian, see Ivan Gozhenskii, "Uchastie Koreiskoi semigratsii v revoliutsionnom dvizhenii na Dal'nem Vostoke," [Participation of Korean Immigrants in the Revolutionary Movement in the Far East], *Revoliutsiia na Dal'nem Vostoke,* 1923, pp. 359-374.

[5] See the Temporary Platform and By-laws of the Korean Communist Youth Corps in "Futei Senjinto kagekiha tono kankei" [Relationship Between the Recalcitrant Koreans and the Bolshevists], *JANA,* reel 122 (T1,186), 36,501-02.

[6] See the Propaganda Programs of the Korean Communist Party, *Ibid.,* 36,502-03.

the leaders in the Irkutsk group were Russian subjects and remained such even after the Communists' penetration into Korea.

C. *Pak Chin-sun in the Comintern, 1919-20*

The extent of Korean participation in the Communist International in its early years is not well known. The first manifesto of the Korean Communist Party (that of the Shanghai group in May, 1921) stated that "our party is an independent Korean section of the Communist International (item 4)." It is clear that the Korean Communist Party did not officially become a member, or a section, of the Communist International until 1928 (item 31). Whatever the extent of its participation, Korean representation was dominated by one man, Pak Chin-sun (see below for biographical information.)

Pak represented the first Korean Socialist party to the Comintern sometime in between the first and the second congresses of the Comintern in mid-1919. There was a Korean named Kain, representing Korean Workers' League, present at the first congress of the Comintern. This person or the organization that he represented had no connection with either the Korean Socialist Party or Pak Chin-sun. Pak makes it clear in the first document presented here, item 9, that the Korean Socialist Party was not aware of the founding of the Comintern and its first congress. Pak actively participated in the second congress in July, 1920.

The second congress of the Comintern turned its attention to the problems of Communist tactics and strategies among the colonial and dependent nations of the East. The second congress also featured a heated polemic on the question of the temporary alliance of Communists and bourgeois elements in the colonies between Lenin and M. N. Roy, an Indian representative at the Congress. Roy was opposed to Lenin's belief that the Communists in the East should make temporary alliances with bourgeois democratic movements. He contended that the bourgeois democratic national movement was directed toward the establishment of a bourgeois order while the Communist vanguard movement organized and developed class-consciousness among the masses preparatory to the revolutionary establishment of Soviet republics. These were two separate movements which could not form a workable alliance of any significance in the East. He also advanced the contention that the communism in the East is important because the success of the communism in the West depended largely upon the development of communism in the East. Much discussion ensued, but the controversy resulted only in modification of the wordings of the Lenin's thesis from that of "the bourgeois democratic movements" to that of "national revolutionary movements." Although a separate supplementary thesis by M. N. Roy was also adopted in the congress, the controversy was not a significant factor to subsequent Communist movements in the East.[7]

There were a few who attempted to conciliate the controversy; among these were Maring of Indonesia, Sultan-Zade of Persia, and Pak Chin-sun of Korea. The second document introduced here, item 10, is Pak's thesis concerning his effort at the conciliation. Pak reflected Lenin's contention when he stated the necessity of cooperation between the Communist vanguards and the bourgeois elements in the East were on the side of the revolution. He further stated that the Communists must utilize the revolutionary zeal of the bourgeois Nationalist elements but that the Communists should know when to turn their arms against their "quandum ally."

Item 9 is perhaps the first speech delivered at the Comintern by a Korean. This recounts the origin of the Korean Communist movement and their effort to affiliate themselves with the Comintern. It also gives a detailed account of the activities of

[7] See the Thesis on the National and Colonial Questions by Lenin and also the Supplementary Thesis by M. N. Roy in *The Second Congress of the Communist International,* Report of Proceedings of Petrograd Session of July 17th and of Moscow Session of July 19th- August 7th 1920 (Communist International, 1921), pp. 571-79. See the Russian version of these theses in *Vtoroi kongress Kominterna, iiul-avgust, 1920 g.* [Second Congress of the Comintern, July-August 1920] (Moskva 1934), pp. 491-99.

the Korean Socialist Party in Siberia, with less emphasis on the activities at Khabarovsk than at Vladivostok congress and the actions of the Communists of the Korean Socialist Party taken against the Korean Nationalist elements there. The importance of these documents is not so much in the fact that they are the first speech and the thesis reflecting conciliatory views on the dispute between Lenin and Roy by a Korean delegate, but because they indicate that Pak's early participation in the Comintern was an important factor in the origin of the Korean Communist movement, particularly in its early development and the perpetuation of communism among the Korean revolutionaries abroad. Available information on the Korean representations and participations in the Comintern lends credence to the view that his representation was perhaps not surpassed in effectiveness by his numerous successors.

Pak Chin-sun

Very little biographical information on Pak is available, although his activities in the early Korean Communist movement were prevalent. One explanation of his obscurity is the fact that he was one of those revolutionaries who conducted their activities not within but primarily outside of Korea. In various Comintern materials, Pak is generally known as Din'shun'Pak. His Russian name is Ilia Pak. Pak was born in Hoeryŏng, Hamkyŏng Pukto, and seemed to have left Korea in his youth for Russia. He is reported to have finished a college in Moscow studying politics before the Russian Revolution. At the wake of the Russian Revolution Pak joined forces with the Korean Nationalists in Siberia and the Russian Maritime Province, later becoming a personal secretary to and perhaps the closest comrade of Yi Tong-hwi, the founder of the Korean Communist Party. Pak served as the first secretary of the Korean Socialist Party of 1918 in Khabarovsk, and represented the party to the Second Congress of the Comintern. Pak was very active in the Comintern and served in the Executive Committee of the Communist International in early 1920's.

Involved in the dispute with the Irkutsk group on the fund from the Comintern, Pak lost much influence after the Alexeyevsk Incident and the First Congress of the Toilers of the Far East. There are scattered reports of Pak's activities in Russia after his fall. Pak was once reported to have been seen by a Korean in Moscow peddling for daily sustenance, and another Korean reported that Pak later in early 1930's was reported to have been employed as a teacher at the KUTV.* Pak was later openly denounced by the more doctrinaire Korean Communists in Russia, such as Tsoy Shenu (Ch'oe Sŏng-u) and Kim Sŏng-t'aek as a lackey of Korean bourgeois. No information is available as to how and when he ended his life. Pak was married to a Russian-born German girl. Despite the accusation of his activities among the Korean Communists abroad, Pak was the first and perhaps the best known and the most highly regarded of Koreans represented in the Comintern. Pak was a prolific writer when he wrote, and his articles appear in many early Communist journals and papers, such as *Narodnoe khoziaistvo, Krest'ianskii internatsional, Petrgradskaia Pravda, Kommunist internatsional, Zhizn'natsional'nostei,* and others.

D. The Alexeyevsk Incident, June 1921

The Shanghai group did much to advance the cause of communism among the Korean revolutionaries abroad and came into direct confrontation with the Irkutsk group in the Alexeyevsk Incident in June 1921. The factional struggles of the two groups burst out in an armed confrontation in the Russian Maritime Province, marking the beginning of the fall of the Shanghai group. This incident was an unfortunate confrontation for the development of the Korean Communist movement, not so much because of the fall of the Shanghai group as because the movement as a whole lost a principal force. The decline of the Shanghai group did not effect the subsequent and sustaining leadership of the Irkutsk group, nor did it result in a

*(Kommunisticheskii Universitet Trudiashchikhsia Vostoka)

coalition of the two groups.

Four documents presented here give a detailed account of the Incident, present the views of both sides, and contain two directives from the Comintern. The Shanghai group under Yi Tong-hwi received greater support from the Nationalists than did the Russianized Koreans of the Irkutsk group. The first document, item 11, was written by a Nationalist and recounts the sufferings of the national revolutionaries at the hand of the Irkutsk group. It combines a substantially detailed account of the Incident with a condemnation of the Irkutsk group. There is another document similar to this one, not as detailed but equally condemnatory, written by another Nationalist leader who suffered the adverse consequences of the Incident. His account of the incident did not appear until the following year, June 28, 1922, when the Nationalists renewed their vow to repay the injustice done by the Irkutsk group.[8]

The second document, item 12, is a short declaration of the victorious Irkutsk group, giving its version of the Incident, which is quite different from the story related by the Nationalists. Aside from the account of their successful undertakings, they pointed out the factional differences of the Nationalists with the Shanghai group and also deplored the militant attitude of Pak Chin-sun against the Irkutsk group.

One of the more immediate consequences of the Incident was the reaction of the Comintern as expressed in the third and fourth documents. The third, item 13, a decision made in November, 1921 by a three-man Committee of the Comintern, is a five-point statement generally in support of the Shanghai group. Partly condemning the Irkutsk group and cautioning the Shanghai group, it urged the Korean Communists to unite. The fourth, item 14, a decision made in April, 1922, is a short six-point directive which gave specific directions to the Korean Communists, such as ordering both factions to unite within three months, directing return of the funds that were given to

---

[8] This document is written by Yi Yong, and is entitled "Tearful Appeal to our Compatriots," see the full text in *JFMA*, reel SP 46 (sp. 150), pp. 98-105.

them earlier, designating the location of the headquarters in Chita, and urging them to direct political activities within Korea. This document is less condemnatory of the Irkutsk group and is relatively stringent in directing the Shanghai group to form a coalition with the Irkutsk group in the latter's territory in Siberia. This action can be attributed, in part, to the dominant role played by the Irkutsk group at the First Congress of the Toilers of the Far East, which was held some two months before the time of the second directive.

The two documents from the Comintern are available only in Japanese. Since the two Comintern documents in Japanese may be a translation of the Russian original or even the English original, some of the originality of the documents may have been lost in retranslation from Japanese into English. Although its general directives are unmistakably clear, some of the provisions and their meanings are difficult to decipher completely, such as point three of the November, 1921 directive. The Comintern's ignorance about the development of the Korean Communist movement is made clear by these documents, as is illustrated by their request for the return of funds by those comrades who had already died and their mistaken evaluation of the role their agent Shumiatsky played in the development of the Korean Communist movement. However, it was the failure of the Korean Communists, the Shanghai and the Irkutsk groups, to ultimately unite their efforts that gave an important meaning to this incident.

E. *The First Congress of the Toilers of the Far East, January 1922*

The First Congress of the Toilers of the Far East was held in Moscow and Petrograd from January 21 to February 2, 1922. It had a significant influence on the development of various Communist movements of the Far East. For the Korean movement the Congress had three important meanings:

First, the loud vocal support that the Congress gave to the revolutionaries of the East rejuvenated Korean revolutionaries despite the continuous rejection of their efforts by the West. The Koreans had developed high aspirations from the Versaille Peace Conference and the Washington Conference, particularly the implementation in Korea of the idea of self-determination that was so widely advocated after the World War I.

Second, the Congress was held shortly after the Alexeyevsk Incident, and the Korean delegation was dominated by the Irkutsk group. Of 124 delegates with decisive votes the Korean delegation of 54 was the largest from any one country, but members of the Shanghai group were not present. The Irkutsk group consequently gained much strength in their continued struggle with the Shanghai group.

Third, the Congress was attended by a large number of representatives from Korean nationalist groups, and many Nationalist revolutionaries pledged their support to the cause of communism in Korea after the conference. The Nationalists realized that the Communist International and the Russian Communists expressed far greater support for the cause of the Korean revolution against Japan than did those they had considered their unfailing supporters in the West. Thus, many supported the Communist cause after the Congress.

The three documents introduced here demonstrate the significance of the Congress to the Korean Communists. The manifesto of the Congress, item 15, is indicative of the militant attitude manifested by the Korean revolutionaries. These are eloquently stated in the manifesto. Perhaps too militant and bloody, for some of the words express well the emotions of the Korean revolutionaries against Japan. There is another slightly different version of the manifesto, a translation of the Russian into English.[9] The version presented here is an original English version of the Congress and includes all the organizations represented from China, Japan, Korea, Mongolia, and other countries, which are omitted in the other version.

[9] See another version by Eudin and North in *Soviet Russia and the East* (Stanford 1957), pp. 230-231. This version of the manifesto is a translation from the Russian original in *Pervyi sezd revoliutsionnykh organizatsii Dalnego Vostoka,* pp. 3-5, and it omits almost the last third of the manifesto.

The second document, item 16, is a speech delivered on the Korean revolutionary movement at the Congress. This thorough, well-written document traces the Korean revolution from the Tonghak rebellion of 1894, through the March First uprising of 1919, to the Communist revolution. For brevity, much of the irrelevant rhetoric and the account of the rebellion and the uprising are omitted here. Perhaps the most important aspect of this document is its discussions of the status of the Korean revolutionary movement of the time. It gives an account of the military in Irkutsk as the Korean base of the revolutionary army and the Korean Communist Party and reflects the position of the Irkutsk group after the Alexeyevsk Incident.

The third document, item 17, is a lengthy article written by one of the most well known Korean national revolutionaries, Kim Kyu-sik (see below for biographical information). This document is presented here not because the author is a Nationalist and non-Communist who professed the cause of communism in Korea but because he expressed well the general feelings of the Korean Nationalist revolutionaries after the Congress. The author is extremely well informed about the affairs of the time and exposes the untrustworthy West in favor of the East and communism. At the end of his discourse on the revolutionary movement in Asia against imperialism, he advanced a convincing argument stressing the importance of Korea in the Far East and stated that Korea was the key to the problems of the Far East, which required Korea to "get together" with the Soviet Union.

Kim Kyu-sik

Kim, a life-long revolutionary in the Korean independence movement, was a vice-President of the Korean Provisional Government in Chungking prior to the end of the World War II, and in 1946 became the chairman of the Legislative Council to prepare the laws of the liberated Korea. Kim was born on January 29, 1881 in Hongch'ŏn, Kangwŏn-do. Kim came to the United States to study and received degrees from Roanoke College (B.A.) in Salem, Va., and from Princeton University

(M.A.). Kim returned to Korea and became a principal of
Kyŏngsin High School, but soon fled Korea after the Japanese
annexation of Korea in 1910. Kim had participated in various
revolutionary organizations in China, and joined the Korean
Provisional Government when it was first established and served
as its Foreign Minister later. He also headed the Education
Ministry of the government. Kim represented Korean Youth
Party to the Versaille Peace Conference in 1919 and unsuccessfully pleaded the Korean case. When he found his efforts
fruitless, he and many Nationalist leaders lost much faith in the
West and looked to Russia for the assistance to their cause of
Korean independence. After their futile efforts at the Washington Conference which failed to discuss fully the Chinese and
other Far Eastern problems, many Korean Nationalists re-
sponded favorably to the call of the First Congress of the
Toilers of the Far East at Petrograd. Kim headed the Korean
delegation, and after the Congress the document cited here
appeared in the *Communist Review.*

Kim's expectation of realistic assistance from the Communists also did not materialize, and after much disappointment
from both the East and the West he resumed his independence
movement. Kim joined hands with Kim Wŏn-bong, a militant
Korean revolutionary in China, and found the National Revolutionary Party in 1935, and became its chairman. Later, when
the Korean Provisional Government was reorganized in October
1943 at Chungking, Kim became the vice-President of the
Government under Kim Ku who was then President. When
Korea was emancipated, he returned to Korea and actively
participated in politics of the liberated Korea. Together with
Kim Ku, he opposed a unilateral election and establishment of
the government in the South. In 1948, Kim travelled to the
North and discussed a unification problem with Kim Il-sŏng,
but his efforts failed again. He returned to the South but
abstained from any participation in the South Korean politics.
During the Korean war when the North Koreans came to Seoul,
Kim was kidnapped by the North Koreans, but he was already
in failing health at the time of the war. Kim did not participate
in the North Korean politics and died in the North. Kim was
sometimes known as Kim Chung-mun or Chin Chung-wen in
Chinese, and he was also known as Usa.

PART I

DOCUMENTS

Items 1–17

A. THE EARLY AGREEMENTS, 1920-22

Item 1: Agreement Between the Korean Communist Party and the Asian Bureau of the Russian Communist Party[1]

1. The Korean Communist Party shall receive orders from the Asian Bureau of the Russian Communist Party.

2. The Korean Communist Party shall have, as its primary task, the duty to propagate communism in the Far East. The headquarters of the Korean Communist Party will be in Shanghai, and the Korean Communist Party should build local committees; such as provincial, county, village, and other committees, to propagate communism.

3. The Asian Bureau shall recognize the Korean Communist Party's need to train its own military forces, and shall protect and provide arms and munitions to them.

4. The Asian Bureau shall give 300,000 yen[2] to the Korean Communist Party in Shanghai for the purpose of propagation of communism in the Far East.

---

[1] This agreement was concluded in late 1920 between the Korean Communist Party (the Shanghai group) represented by Pak Chin-sun and the Asian Bureau of the Russian Communist Party. The Russian original, or the Korean version, of the agreement is not available. This translation is from the Japanese version which is available in *JANA*, reel 128, (T1,193), 43,392-95.

[2] It is difficult to ascertain, if at all possible, how much this 300,000 yen is. Although it seems that the figure cited is in Japanese currency at the time of the Russian Revolution in Shanghai, it is not clear whether it is a comparable Japanese sum of original Chinese currency or Russian ruble.

Item 2:   The Russo-Korean Agreement[1]

1. The Russian government and people shall recognize the freedom of the Korean people to organize themselves under communism and give assistance to the Korean people.

2. The Korean people agree with the policies and ideology of the Russian government, and pledge to propagate communism in the Far East.

3. The Russian government shall allow the Korean people in the Far Eastern Siberia, who have organized themselves under communism, to recruit and station their armed groups, and shall protect the Korean residents who live in the region under communism.

4. The Korean groups shall receive instruction from the Chief of the Propaganda Section of the Far Eastern Bureau, appointed by the Russian government, until Korea becomes fully independent and until the propagation of communism in the Far East is completed.

5. The Russian government shall recognize the Chita Korean Communist Party Council as the representative of the Korean people in Russia until Korea attains full independence.

Officers:
  1. Headquarters:
     Chita Korean Communist Party Council.
     President   . . . . .Mun Ch'ang-bŏm
     Secretary   . . . . .Cho Hun
     Chief of Military Section   . . . .Yu Tong-yŏl
     Chief of Finance Section   . . . .Mikhail Chi

---

[1] This agreement was concluded in early 1921. The list of officers appended to and the article 5 of the agreement makes it clear that this agreement was made between the Russians and the Irkutsk group, the rival faction of the Shanghai group. The original language of the agreement might have been in Korean or in Russian, but neither is available. The Japanese version is available in *JANA*, reel 128, (T1,193), 43,359-60.

2. Branch Offices:

Chief of Khabarovsk	. . . . .Kim Ch'ŏl-hun
Chief of Nikolsk	. . . . . .Ch'oe Ko-ryŏ
Chief of Vladivostok	. . . .Cho Chang-hwan
Chief of Harbin	. . . . . .Yi Sŏng
Chief of Kirin	. . . . . . .Kim Ha-sŏk and An Pyŏng-ch'an
Chief of Shanghai	. . . . . .Sŏn-u Hyŏk and Ok Kwang-bin
Chief of Tokyo	. . . . . .Ch'oe P'al-yong
Chief of Korea	. . . . . . .Pang Wŏn-sŏng and Chang Kŏn

Item 3: Agreement between the New Korean Government and the Russian Government [1]

1. The New Korean Independence Army is to invite two military advisers from the Russian Government, and, when necessary, the Russian Government is to supply weapons, food, and supplies to the Independence Army.

2. The Russian government is to lease the First and the Second Mines south of Khabarovsk for the next ten years to the New Korean Independence Soviet Government.

3. The Russian Government is to allot a certain region to the Korean Independence Soviet Government and the Korean Independence Army is to station and operate in that region.

4. The New Korean Independence Soviet Government is to be relieved by the Russian Government of payment of railroad fares.

5. The Russian Government is to supply 6,000 rifles and ammunition to the New Korean Independence Soviet Government.

6. The certain region mentioned in 3 above is to be south of Khabarovsk toward Possiet near the Iman region.

---

[1] After the defeat of the Mensheviks in the Russian Maritime Province, the Red Army, in an effort to maintain order, disarmed most of the armed groups, including the Korean Revolutionary Army. Among the disarmed Koreans were Im Pyŏng-guk, Ch'oe Kyŏng-ch'ŏn, Kang Kuk-mo, and others, who led some 600 Korean revolutionaries. They were disarmed by the Russian Communists on November 14 and 15, 1922. Hearing this news, some of the other Korean revolutionary leaders, including the powerful leaders such as Yi Chung-jip and Kim Kyu-sik, fled with their soldiers from the Russian Maritime Province into Manchuria. This agreement was concluded in late 1922 between the Russians and the Korean Nationalists who remained in Russian Maritime Province. The Japanese version of the Korean original is available in *JFMA*, reel SP 46 (sp. 151), 14-16.

B. THE KOREAN COMMUNIST PARTY IN SHANGHAI, 1921-22

Item 4:   Manifesto of the Korean Communist Party[1]

This is the declaration and clarification of objectives of the Korean Communist Party Representative Congress, represented by the Communist Proletariat Revolutionary Congress, represented by the Communist Proletariat Revolutionary Organizations of the Korean Socialist Party, the Socialist Revolutionary Party and all other Communist and labor organizations. We pledge today to carry on the mission based upon the declaration and programs of two great proletariat revolutionary teachers, Karl Marx and Frederich Engels, which was declared some seventy-four years ago.

The history of all hitherto existing society is the history of class struggles. Freeman and slave, patrician and plebeian, lord and serf, guildmaster and journeyman, in a word, oppressor and oppressed, stood in constant opposition to one another, carried on an uninterrupted, now hidden, now open fight, a fight that each time ended, either in a revolutionary reconstitution of society at large, or in the common ruin of the contending classes.

In the earlier epochs of history, we find almost everywhere a complicated arrangement of society into various orders, a manifold gradation of social rank. In ancient Rome we have patricians, knights, plebeians, slaves; in the Middle Ages, feudal lords, vassals, guildmasters, journey-men, apprentices, serfs; in almost all of these classes, again, subordinate

[1] This is the first manifesto of the Korean Communist Party. The author of this manifesto is not known, but it is the manifesto of Yi Tong-hwi's party in Shanghai adopted at May, 1921 Congress. The head of the Publication Bureau of the Party was Cho Tong-u. The original Korean version is not available. The Japanese version is available in *JFMA*, reel SP 85 (sp. 205-4), 9,232-43 and also in *JANA*, reel 123 (T1,186).

gradations. The modern bourgeois society that has sprouted from the ruins of feudal society, has not done away with class antagonisms. It has but established new classes, new conditions of oppression, new forms of struggle in place of the old ones.

Our epoch, the epoch of the bourgeoisie, possesses, however, this distinctive feature: It has simplified the class antagonisms. Society as a whole is more and more splitting up into two great classes directly facing each other . . . bourgeoisie and proletariat.[2]

The enmity and struggle between the oppressor and the oppressed, the exploiter and the exploited, and the strong and the weak are intensifying daily and it has reached the people in the colonies as a national emancipation movement, and also as a proletariat's mass movement against the bourgeoisie.

The endless imperialistic and capitalistic expansion has reached the unprecedented form of a struggle for markets and the unjust modes of distribution, the mechanization of the industrial organization, and the capitalization of land, have produced more proletariats. The exploitation of the masses of the colonial countries by the ruling class and the thievery of the bourgeois against the proletariat has reached extremes of inhumanity. The struggle for the emancipation of those who have lost their freedom and those whose life and livelihood are not guaranteed is a necessary outcry to demand the right of their existence. The national emancipation movements in Ireland, India, Egypt, Annam, Persia, and of other countries, and the social revolutionary movement of the proletarian masses of the advanced countries are not accidental endeavors; it is only natural that their forces are fierce and rampant, and these movements will not cease until total victory is theirs.

The fact that the Japanese annexation of Korea is unnatural

[2] Karl Marx, *The Communist Manifesto,* Samuel H. Beer, ed. New York: Appleton Century Crofts, Inc., 1955, pp. 9-10. The original version of this portion of the document is a cursory translation in Korean of the Communist Manifesto. Instead of retranslating the bad translation into English, the original English version is presented here.

and unreasonable is very clear. Since the annexation, Japan has deprived us of all freedom of assembly and speech. Japanese interference reached an extreme when they intervened in our industrial enterprises and by irrational laws prevented the growth of these industrial enterprises. The social progress of the Korean people and the cultural development of the masses have been virtually halted by these inhumane acts, which have brought hunger to the material life and impoverishment to the spirit of the masses. We are striving to overthrow the Japanese yoke for the prosperity of our people. We have fought a hard fight during the past three years, since the declaration of war against Japan,[3] though our efforts have been weak, our sincerity and zeal have more than supplemented what we have lacked in forces and we believe that ultimate victory will be ours.

Our national emancipation movement is merely a step to the ultimate purpose of social revolution, and we are striving for the complete elimination of all of the classes of our present society. This is our belief and, at the same time, the common objective of all the toiling masses of the world. Thus, our enemy is all the exploiting classes of the world, as well as the Japanese militarists and financiers, and all the masses who share the common fate under the oppressions of the ruling class must unite their efforts. Thus, our efforts may be meager, but we express heartfelt congratulations to the Russian working masses and await with great expectation their success. We also expect the success of the activities of the Chinese mass revolutionary organizations and trust in the success of the birth of the recent Japanese socialist organization and Japanese Communist Party. Thus, we shall together destroy and drive out the roots of all the crimes of exploiting classes in East Asia, nay, in the entire world.

The World War of 1914, that resulted in great bloodshed for the world's masses, had its very roots in the purpose of satisfying the bottomless storehouses of the bourgeoisie of the

---

[3] Although there is no declaration of war against Japan, this refers to the March First Uprising of 1919.

capitalist countries, but it has been said that the war was a means to destroy imperialism and bring eternal peace, and also it has been said that the war was to emancipate the oppressed people of the whole world, thus deceiving the oppressed masses. Because of this deceiving propaganda, including such propaganda as Wilson's fourteen points, there were a few who placed great trust in the Peace Conference and the League of Nations. But even though cunning tactics and strenuous efforts were used to conceal the true face of their intentions, it became apparent that the primary objectives were in the war. The venerable Versaille Peace Conference is nothing but a meeting of hungry wolves to divide the territories of the defeated and collect reparations from the defeated. The difficulties of the English and the French in Europe and the antagonism between the United States and Japan over Pacific problems are all the same kind of problem.

The League of Nations is merely an organization to revive the already destroyed foundation of capitalism and its industrial organizations, and also it is the last stand of the organizational effort to suppress the toiling masses and their socialistic revolutionary movement, and thus it is a peculiar and worthless organization. The weak are always attempting to receive the help of others, just as one who is drowning attempts to hang on to the roots of anything nearby. We have until today always expected the true revival of the League of Nations by appealing to the leaders of the world emancipation movement and by pointing to justice and humanity, and it is not that we do not understand those who attempt to utilize the opportunities made available by the intense struggles of the United States and Japan in the Pacific, but look at the exploitations of the British in India, of the French in Annam, and of the United States in the Philippines. By observing these phenomena, it is not difficult to see who is truly our friend, and who is our foe. Our excitement over the Russian October Revolution is not without justification, because in carrying out the great task of world revolutionary movement we feel that we are on the same footing with them. Thus, we share the same fate with the working masses of the world and their organizations. We must unite to fight against our enemies in the League of Nations, the hounds of world capitalism and imperialism, and its supporter, the Second International.

The Third Communist International is truly the federation of the world's toiling masses and the only headquarters of the World Socialist Revolution, to which the Koreans have already been represented in the name of the Korean Socialist Party, and it is with the Comintern that we can share our fate in the struggle against the Capitalists. Our part is an independent Korean section of the Communist International.

We strive to establish the Korean Soviet government under the dictatorship of the proletariat, so that it can be possible to carry out the fight to destroy all the existing systems and establish the great society for ultimate happiness of all men. We trust that ultimate victory is ours, and that victory will be the victory of the working masses of Korea, which comprises seventy percent of the Korean population. All the proletariats unite under the Communist banner.

May, 1921
Korean Communist Party Congress

Item 5:   Platform of the Korean Communist Party[1]

The root of all the evil of present society is in the Capitalist system. Under the present Capitalistic production formula, the means of production and distribution are monopolized by a few capitalists. The so-called Industrial Revolution that began at the end of seventeenth century made all industries into gigantic enterprises, thus driving out all the small industries and handicrafts and concentrating control of all enterprises in a few hands; the development of the machine directly and indirectly reduced the need for supplies of labor power and resulted in an excess of labor supply. Unruly speculation produced a rapid transfer of lands to the large landowners and forced out the small landowners. As a result, a small number of Capitalists monopolized all the means of production and forced the toiling masses under their domain. The tragic result of their domination over the masses defies all description.

The great miseries of inequity in societies, the increase in the distance between the rich and the poor, the uneasiness of the livelihood of the great unemployed masses, and the difficulties of a great many people are all products of the Capitalist system. For these reasons, we are not excessive when we say that the root of all evil is in the Capitalist system. Internally, it is creating the tragedy of exploitation of the masses, but externally it is engaged in plundering the weak countries to expand markets, and ultimately the blood of the masses has been shed to fight for the acquisition of new colonies. It is not by accident that we advocate the destruction of all classes of modern capitalism by uniting the efforts of all the masses in the colonies and the masses of the advanced countries who share the same fate. The movement to emancipate the classes is now a world movement, an inevitable result of the awakening of the

[1] The Platform adopted at the first Congress and issued by the Central Executive Committee of the Korean Communist Party in May 1921. The Platform was written in Korean, but it is available only in Japanese in *JFMA*, reel SP 85 (sp. 205-4), 9,232-43.

proletarian masses and the movement will not cease until the solution of the class problem is arrived at.

The weaker your strength is, the more you must bring together your individual weak strengths to achieve difficult and great tasks; the union of our strengths is the prerequisite to our success. Our effort is to unite the workers under the banner of the Communist Party and to destroy all the classes of our present society, which is the root of all inequity and the lack of freedom, thus bringing about the harmonious development of everyone in the society. We must destroy the system of free economic competition and the private ownership of production machinery which are the backbones of the Capitalist system and the main force of anarchic condition in the industry, and we must change the system to state ownership and state distribution of products in order to attain the most equitable and harmonious world.

We believe that our workers' takeover of the government is the most efficient method to destroy the capitalistic system and thus bring about the autonomy of the Soviet government is the only political entity for the proletarian rule, is to mean that without the proletarian control of the political power it is not possible to stop the intrusion of the opposition and to bring about the first and most harmonious socialist workers' society. We recognize the necessity of an inevitable period of transition, and also it is evident that there must be some bloodshed in the struggle to attain our goals. We are not at all happy about the bloodshed, and will try to reduce it to a minimum; however, under the present conditions in Korea, we must realize that it is only class struggle, whatever the cost, that will bring about the ultimate emancipation of our people. All our ideals can be realized only after the complete emancipation of our people, and this emancipation can come only through the struggles of our working masses. Thus, the political platforms of our party must be centered on the ultimate victory of the working masses. The following is the outline of our political platforms in detail.

1. We abolish all private ownership of the means of production and all forms of free competition, and adopt the

centralized distribution of goods and establish nationalized systems to increase production and establish social justice for all. In other words, all production machinery, such as factories and mills, all modes of transportation such as railways and shipping, all daily indispensable services such as electricity, gas, and water, and all lands, mines, and forests should be nationalized.

2. For a compulsory and widespread educational system, elementary education should be free to all people.

3. Everyone who has reached the laboring age must perform labor as a duty to the country, without discrimination with regard to sex.

4. We must reorganize the family system to emancipate women, and set up public nurseries, public eating places, and public washing places.

5. To establish a firm foundation for a proletarian state, all privately owned property of the Capitalists should be confiscated.

The following are the immediate programs of our party. They follow closely the broad objectives of the Comintern, the world center of the revolutionary masses, which our party has joined under the name of the Korean Socialist Party.

A. Problems of National Emancipation

We must strive to destroy all Capitalist systems, internally the exploiting classes and externally the oppressors of our people, in order to bring absolute equality and a peaceful society. We realize fully that national emancipation is the prelude to the ultimate social revolution of our people. It is evident that we must help all the revolutionary organizations that agree with our principles, and there is no doubt that all of us need military organizations to carry out our revolution. We must act to establish military forces and to cooperate in this military endeavor. All those who are in the same situation as the class of oppressed people must unite and fight for the world revolution of the oppressed masses.

B. *Problem of National Education*

The future social relationship must be a cooperative one, and this must be accomplished by the self-awakening of each member of society. Thus, we believe that national education is the fundamental element in the emancipation of women and the oppressed. It is necessary to consider systematic and organized methods to educate the oppressed masses in the cities and villages which comprise seventy percent of our population. We must endeavor to accomplish this task in many ways, directly and indirectly, by utilizing schools, libraries, lectures, popular discussion sessions, and other means to foster the education of the people. We must, of course, in the process center our efforts towards the propagation and dissemination of communism.

C. *Problems of Religion*

The past events have amply proved that religious superstition is an obstacle to social emancipation. Therefore, we must carry on a scientific cultural movement and a religion-boycotting movement. The activity to degrade the faith of the believers should be avoided, because it may, on the contrary, strengthen their religious belief.

May, 1921
Central Executive Committee
of the Korean Communist Party

Item 6:   By-laws of the Korean Communist Party[1]

Chapter 1. Membership and Organization

Article 1. The membership of this Party shall consist of all those who propagate and subscribe to the ideals of communism, regardless of their nationalities (meaning Koreans who acquired other nationalities), within or outside of Korea.

Article 2. The membership of the Party shall consist of two kinds of members; the regular members and candidate members.

Article 3. All those who wish to join the party must have recommendations from two regular members of the Party, and the recommendations must then be referred to the proper local party organs for investigation. Those who are granted approval from the local party officials shall then become candidate members of the Party. After a considerable period of service those who have good records shall be recommended by the local party officials to become regular members of the party, and they shall become regular members of the party only after the recommendations of the local party officials are decided upon by the proper local party organs.[2]

Article 4. Those who want to withdraw their membership from the Party and those who are voted out of the Party by the party officials must receive reconfirmation from the proper local party organs, and must announce the decision of the local party organs together with the reasons for their withdrawal.

---

[1] This is the by-laws of Yi Tong-hwi's party in Shanghai, adopted at the first Congress of the party held in May, 1921. The original Korean document is not available. This translation is from Japanese which is in *JFMA*, reel SP 85 (sp. 205-4), and it is also available in *JANA*, reel 123 (T1,186).

[2] Throughout the by-laws, the wordings are not definitive and can often be interpreted in many ways. The Article 3 represents one of these in such phrases as "proper local party organs," and "considerable period of service," without specifying which organ or how long a period of time.

Article 5. The regular members have the right to elect and to be elected in the Party, and also enjoy the right to submit suggestions to the Party.

Article 6. A member of the Party is required to obey orders, keep party secrets, propagate communism, and observe all the laws of the Party.

Article 7. A member is required to report a change of address to his proper local party organization.

Article 8. No member of this party can join any organ of Capitalistic state organs or their political organizations or groups without the specific consent of or instructions from the Central Executive Committee of the Party.

Article 9. The structure of the Party is organized as follows:

    a. *Local Party Organization:* A Local Party Organiza tion is organized with more than 10 members of the Party and should be located in a proper sectional division of the locality. The organization of a Local Party Organization requires the consent of the County Party Organization upon the recommendation of the officers of the County Party Organization.

    b. *County Party Organization:* The County Party Organization is composed of representatives of the Local Party Organization.

    c. *Provincial Party Organization:* The Provincial Party Organization is composed of the representatives of the County Party Organizations.

    d. *Regional Party Organizations:*

       i. Regional Organization within Korea; the regional organization within Korea shall consist of representatives from all provincial Party Organizations within Korea.

       ii. Regional Organization within Russia; the regional organization within Russia shall consist of representatives of all Korean Communist local, county, and sectional organizations within Russia.

       iii. Regional Organization within China; the regional

organization within China shall consist of all Korean Communist local, county, and sectional organizations within China.

e. *Central Executive Committee:* The Central Executive Committee shall consist of representatives from the regional organizations of Korea, Russia, and China.

Article 10. The officers of the Regional Organizations within Russia and China shall decide upon the local, county, and other provincial party organizations in accordance with their need and proper division.

Article 11. The numbers of representatives from the local to the County, from the County to the Provincial, and from the Provincial to the Regional Party Organizations shall be determined by the officers of the County for the local, of the Provincial for the County, and of the Regional for the Provincial Party Organizations, in proportion to the membership of each Party.

Chapter 2. The Rights of Each Organization

Article 12. Each organization shall have autonomous control of its lower organizations.

Article 13. Each organization shall elect members to its Standing Committee and representatives to the higher Party Organization.

Article 14. Each organization shall have the power to make ultimate decisions on its Party organization.

Article 15. All decisions of lower organizations that counter the decision of a higher organization are null and void.

Chapter 3. The Standing Organs

Article 16. The Standing Organs of each organization shall consist of two kinds: the Standing Committee and the Inspection Committee.

Article 17. The number of members for the Standing Organs of each organization is as follows:

    a. Local Party Organization:
          Standing Committee . . . . three members
          Inspection Committee . . . two members
    b. County Party Organization:
          Standing Committee . . . . three members
          Inspection Committee . . . two members
    c. Provincial Party Organization:
          Standing Committee . . . . five members
          Inspection Committee . . . two members
    d. Regional Party Organization of Korea, Russia, and China:
          Standing Committee . . . . seven members
          Inspection Committee . . . three members
    e. Central Executive Committee . . seventeen members
          Inspection Committee . . . three members

Article 18. Duties of the Officers are as follows:

    a. *Central Executive Committee members:* The Central Executive Committee is the highest Executive Organ of the Party, and shall perform all business and planning duties of the Party. The Central Executive Committee shall also supervise all party organs, perform the financial duties of the Party and maintain the external relations of the Party.

    b. The officers of each Organization of the Party shall perform the duties of supervision, planning, financing, and other works of the Party organization.

Article 19. The officers of each lower organization must follow the directives of the upper party organ officers and must, at request, make a full report of their activities.

Article 20. Members of the Inspection Committees shall audit the accounts of the Party organization and inspect the general business of the Party organization and report at the general meetings.

Article 21. The election of members to the Inspection Committees and Standing Committees shall be by a two-thirds majority of the members present.

Article 22. The term of office for all officers of the Standing and Inspection Committees is one year, and they are eligible for reelection.

Article 23. All decisions of the Committees shall be made by a two-thirds majority.

Article 24. Officers of the Committees shall not have a vote in deciding matters in their Party organizations.

Chapter 4. Meetings

Article 25. The meetings of each party organization shall be of two kinds, regular and ad hoc, and the officers of the party shall call the meetings.

    a. *Regular Meeting*

        i. Central Congress . . . . . once each year.
        ii. Regional Congresses of Korea, Russia, and China . . . . . twice each year.
        iii. County and Provincial Organization Congresses . . . . . four times each year.
        iv. Local Meetings . . . . . once each month.

    b. *Ad hoc meetings.* Ad hoc meetings shall be called by the officers of the Committees with the consent of one-third of the members when they deem it necessary.

Article 26. Each regular meeting shall become official only with the presence of three-fourths of the expected members, and ad hoc meetings shall become official with two-thirds of the members present.

Article 27. Presidents of each meeting shall be elected temporarily for that meeting at the time of the meeting.

Chapter 5. Finances

Article 28. The revenues of the Party are derived from membership dues, contributions, and all other proceeds from other sources.

Article 29. The membership fee for a new member is one yen and must be submitted to the Party.

Article 30. The dues for a regular member is two percent of his annual salary; the lower party organs must submit twenty percent of their income to the immediately higher party organs.

Article 31. The obligation to pay dues will be waived for those who are unemployed or imprisoned.

Chapter 6. Punishments

Article 32. All members who violate the party by-laws shall be divided into the following categories for punishment.

- a.   Advice and warning within the Party.
- b.   Advice and warning publicly.
- c.   Cancellation of assigned duties.
- d.   Cancellation of privilege to submit suggestions.
- e.   Expulsion from the Party.

Article 33. Inspection of the violations and a decision concerning the member shall be conducted by the officers of each responsible Party organization.

Article 34. If the punished member does not follow the orders, a party officer must report to higher organs.

Chapter 7. Supplementary Rule

Article 35. The decision of a two-thirds majority of the Central Executive Committee is necessary to amend these by-laws.

Article 36. When it is impossible to call a meeting of the Central Executive Committee, the meeting can be substituted for by a joint meeting of the officers of the lower party organs.

**Item 7:   Income and Expenditure of the Korean Communist
            Party[1]**
            (Yi Tong-hwi at Shanghai in 1921-1922)

Income (presumably from the
      Comintern, total) . . . .   150,000 yen

Expenditure:

a.	For use at Headquarters	23,000 yen
b.	Transportation Expenditures	26,000 yen
c.	Salaries of Employees	8,000 yen
d.	Salary for the Printer	2,400 yen
e.	For Korean Operations	45,000 yen
f.	Northern (North China) Operations	1,900 yen
g.	Chientao Operation	9,000 yen
h.	For the Chinese and Formosan Communist Parties	11,000 yen
i.	For the Japanese Communist Party	11,500 yen
j.	To Kim Mu-myŏng	3,200 yen
k.	Utensils	1,500 yen
l.	Miscellaneous	4,500 yen
		148,600 yen

For the earlier Korean Socialist Party of Khabarovsk and
Vladivostok.
Income 400,000 yen   . . . . .   Expenditure 400,000 yen

---

[1] It is not clear exactly what period this expenditure record represents,
for example May 1921-May 1922, or just 1922. It is assumed that this
record represents one year.

   This document is available in Japanese in *JFMA*, reel SP 46 (sp. 150),
426-27. Here again the author of this document is not known except that
this document is the record of Yi Tong-hwi's party.

Item 8: [Korean] Provisional Government Proclamation No. 1[1]
(extract)

We have followed the teachings of our forefathers faithfully, respecting the righteous path of our ancestors, and have endured the unprecedented shame of our nearly five-thousand-year history.[2] We have suffered many hardships in order to accomplish the purest of all national endeavors, and except for a few who betrayed the cause of our country, we have been faithful to our cause.

However, the officers of the Independence Party[3] have committed a shameless act, and it is difficult to endure because it puts shame on our nation. The fact that the leaders of the Independence Party have committed such a shameful act is difficult to believe. We do not refer to the political rectification of any criminal act, but rather appeal to the general moral code of humanity and make known the immoral act that was committed.

As a holder of an important position, Yi Tong-hwi conspired with Kim Rip[4] and secretly sent Han Hyŏng-kwŏn to our

[1] This proclamation was issued on January 26, 1922 by Shin Kyu-sik, the acting Prime Minister of the Korean provisional government. The original Korean text is not available. The full text is not available in any language. Only the extract of the text is available in Japanese in *JANA*, reel 128 (T1,193), 43,415-17.

[2] Reference is to the Japanese annexation of Korea; this was the 4255th year of the Korean calendar.

[3] It is not clear why Yi's party was called as the Independence Party here. The correct title of the party is the Korean Socialist Party that Yi brought with him from Khabarovsk and Vladivostok.

[4] Little is known of Kim Rip. Kim was a Communist who followed closely the activities of Yi Tong-hwi. Due to the animosity that befell upon him from the alleged usurpation of the funds from the Comintern, the Nationalists do not regard him as a revolutionary of any importance. Kim Rip is from Myŏngch'ŏn, Hamkyŏng Pukto but spent most of his youth in the Russian Maritime Province. He was a charter member of the Korean Socialist Party at Khabarovsk and served Yi as his personal secretary. When he came to Shanghai to participate in the Korean

generous neighboring country [Russia] and acquired a great sum of money for the government. Yi and Kim, however, embezzled the money and put the blame on all the cabinet members and undermined the government, and this is the crime that should be condemned by gods and men alike. Kim Ŭi-sŏn,[5] who had been favorably treated by our government also betrayed us, forgetting the benefits that he had so constantly received, and his crime is difficult to forgive. Kim Rip and Yi Tong-hwi conspired together and embezzled the funds of our national treasury for their private use and carried on conspiratory acts under the pretence of communism. Their crime must be severely punished.

It is futile to list all the facts relating to the many young members of the Independence Party who betrayed the cause of our government. Some among them had accomplished little, but there were a few who diligently served the cause of our nation, and we waited their return, repenting their past mistakes and returning to the path of righteousness, but their deceit, self-assertive power, and those who followed them had profoundly bad effects on the good people.

The government is partially responsible for the deterioration of the matter to this extent, and it is difficult to announce this to the people on behalf of the Government, but it must be done.

The Fourth Year of the Korean Republic (1922)
January 26, 1922

Provisional Government, Kim was appointed as a Secretary-General of the Prime Minister's Office of the Korean Provisional Government, and there was some dissention among other revolutionaries of his "undue" eminence in occupying the office. He also participated in the creation of the Korean Communist Party in Shanghai, but after being accused of the usurpation of the government fund Kim was assassinated in the back alley of Shanghai with bullets to his back on February 8, 1922.

[5] The identity of Kim Ŭi-sŏn and the role he played in the affair are not clear. Kim however was neither an important Communist nor a known Nationalist leader.

Shin Kyu-sik, Acting Prime Minister, Vice-Minister of Foreign
            Affairs and Minister of Justice

Yi Tong-nyŏng, Minister of Internal Affairs
No Paek-nim, Minister of Military Affairs
Kim In-jŏn, Acting Minister of Education
Yi Shi-yŏng, Minister of Finance and Minister of Labor
Son Chŏng-do, Minister of Transportation

C. PAK CHIN-SUN IN THE COMINTERN, 1919-20

Item 9:   The Socialist Movement in Korea[1]

Note by the editor of the *Communist International:*

It is with particular pleasure that we publish this account of a Korean Communist.

In his oral report to the Executive committee, Comrade Pak said: the Korean workers want to belong to an International which does not support the colonial policies of the great imperialist powers; and this is why they join the Third International.

It was excellently put.

These simple words express the whole essence of the matter. The yellow Second International, screening itself behind the phases "civilization" and "progress," *supports* the imperialist states in their plundering campaigns against "colonial peoples." The Communist International proclaims the slogan, "get out of colonies," and supports the revolutionary liberation movement against the imperialist plunderers in all colonies. This is why millions of toilers of Korea, China, India, Persia, Afghanistan, etc., awakening for the struggle against their oppressors, look with hope to the Communist International.

To them all—ardent greetings from the international revolutionary proletariat, organized in the Communist International!

In Korea—one of the most backward countries of the East—it was quite recently that the mass Socialist movement began;

[1] This document was written by Pak Chin-sun in Russian and the text was delivered by Pak at the Executive Committee of the Communist International in late 1919. This document is available in its original Russian. See "Sotsialisticheskoe dvizhenie v Koree" [The Socialist Movement in Korea], *Kommunist Internatsional,* nos. 7-8 (1919), pp. 1,171-76.

therefore, its representatives are not able to give such a thorough account of their revolutionary struggle as the comrades-delegates of other countries.

From the autumn of 1910, that is after Korea lost its independence, there ensued a period of reaction and social stagnation in Korea. Japanese imperialism, having subordinated the Korean nation to its own authority—for the purpose of completely enslaving it—abolished any freedom of press and assembly in the country. The masses of the Korean people, suffering beyond expression under the cruel yoke of the conquerors, strived for liberation. These aspirations, however, could not easily develop in an atmosphere of barbaric repressions introduced by Japanese imperialists: any social initiative in the sphere of education, organization and activity of the masses met with a persistent opposition on the part of the Japanese authorities, who would not permit the legal existence not only of political but even cultural-educational organizations. It was in such terrible conditions that the entire Korean social movement found itself and it was in such conditions that our organization, *The Liberation Union,* emerged and developed. In 1910, the congress of organizers laid the basis for the first socialist cell in Korea by creating the Executive Bureau of the Union. But under the pressure of the ever-intensifying reaction the Executive Bureau emigrated first to Manchuria, and then to Siberia. From the very first days of its existence, the Union was subjected to a sharp criticism by the entire national-patriotic segment of society; the social conditions were also not favorable for the growth and strengthening of our organization: the ideas of the class struggle could not inspire the Korean toiling masses, in as much as the class struggle itself was a phenomenon known in Korea only by hearsay. The liberal-reform policy of the government during the period 1897-1907 for a time almost completely effaced all class distinctions, while the extremely slow development of capitalism failed to create the soil for the acute manifestation of class distinctions. The nobility and bourgeoisie, removed from power by the iron broom of Japanese imperialism, went hand-in-hand with the poor, bearing together the common heavy burden of the national liberation struggle. Among the masses of the people one could observe an extensive development of patriotic views aroused by daily struggle with the oppression of overseas conquerors. But each year the number of Union members increased; the better part of youth decisively took stand under our banner. The Union was the only organization holding that Korean independence could be attained only with a triumph of the revolution in Japan. The sincere protests of the Japanese socialists against the policy of the Mikado government, which had annexed Korea, and persecution of socialists on the part of the government provided the first stimulus toward a split in the midst of the Korean movement; the "United National Front" against Japan collapsed from that moment on. The ideologists of the new course, which had emerged out of this split, strove towards collaboration with leftist elements of Japan, but in this direction they failed to obtain any substantial results: mutual misunderstanding and mistrust made any collaboration impossible. The leaders of the Korean left course, saw in the entire Korean people as a whole a carrier of democratic ideas. They considered that under the yoke of Japanese bureaucracy the Korean nobility and bourgeoisie, which was being born in front of their eyes, would become true democrats. In this lay their chief mistake.

They did not believe that the laws of social development, discovered by the founders of economic materialism were correct. But the entire course of political and economic life of Korea in 1912-1917 crushed all the utopian views of the leftists, and the Great Russian Revolution compelled them to recognize their errors. It definitely dissipated the illusions of a "United Korean democracy," and the ever-increasing dissent within the Union ended in the inevitable split. The Khabarovsk conference of 1918 ascertained the split as a *fait accompli.* At this conference there was founded the Union of Korean Socialists, *Han'in sahoe-tang,* and with its foundation the Korean left movement joined the general current of the world Socialist movement. In Siberia, prior to the Czechoslovak uprising, the Union of Korean Socialists, which had obtained a possibility for legal existence, published its leaflets and laid the basis for a close rapprochement of all the Socialist parties of Eastern Asia for a joint struggle against Japanese imperialism; in addition, our union endeavored to do everything in its power to fulfill the duty of solidarity towards Russian comrades.

Whereas the Chinese revolution, which in its essence was a court *coup d'etat,* passed by completely unnoticed by the broad Korean masses, the Russian Revolution, which from its very first days dealt a fatal blow upon the decaying bourgeois system, on the contrary, woke up the Korean masses, who heard the appeals of the Russian proletariat and the great slogans of the revolution coming to them from the valleys of the Ussuri and inspired them with aspirations for a new life.

The "Rice riots" in Japan; the end of the world war with its results—the Versailles peace conference and the League of Nations, on which our national patriots and, in part, elements of the right wing of our union built their illusions; the defeats of the Socialists in the newly-created states and the March Uprising in Korea—all this gave a new meaning to our social life, whose wheel that was turning with dizzying speed gave birth to new events and new questions, which demanded of society conscious answers. Now, in April of this year,[2] in the vicinity of the city of Vladivostok, a united congress of their social organizations took place; that of the Union of Korean Socialists and the Union of New Peoples *(Shinmin-tang);* participating in the congress there were 49 delegates, representing 30,000 constituents, one third of this number was constituted by the members of the former organization and two thirds of the latter organization.

The left segment of the congress held fast to a purely class principle, tying its hopes to the movement of the entire world proletariat and to the Japanese workers movement in particular, whereas the right segment considered necessary a close contact with the native bourgeoisie and nobility, considering them as revolutionary groups at that moment. The right segment advised

[2] The year is 1919. The Korean Socialist Party which is referred to here as the Union of Korean Socialists, was found on June 25, 1918 at Khabarovsk.

the left wing to keep itself further away from the chauvenisti-
cally inclined Japanese proletariat. The victory at the congress
was obtained by the left segment, which considered it necessary
to carry on a struggle for the national liberation of Korea with
the support of the working class of Japan and other countries
and which looked upon this struggle not as a national
chauvenistic movement against Japan as a whole, but merely as
a movement against Japanese imperialism.

On the agenda of the congress there was a whole series of
questions. The questions of international politics were that
central point upon which all the attention of the delegates was
concentrated.

At the congress there took place the unification of both of
the Unions into a single party under the name of the Korean
Socialist Party *(Han'in sahoe-tang)*. In fact, the active members
of both groups even earlier had manifested a unanimous accord
on almost all questions and had acted with comradely solidarity. Now this unity was organizationally formalized.

The congress adopted a program containing the following
basic theses:

1. In order to secure the normal spiritual and physical
development of the Korean toiling masses it is necessary to free
Korea from the yoke of Japanese imperialism and capitalistic
exploitation.

2. Taking into account the fact that the interests of the
toiling masses of Japan and Korea are interrelated and that the
yoke of Japanese imperialism and capital is equally distressing
for them, it is essential to have close ties between the
revolutionary organizations of both countries.

3. In view of the fact that Korea is entering the Capitalist
stage, the party ought to organize the proletarian and far-
laborer elements, to educate them in the spirit of revolutionary
Marxism and to direct their daily struggle with capitalism.

4. The experience of the revolutionary movement of the
whole world, as well as the experience of our own revolution,
which took the form of agrarian disorders during the 1890's,
reveals that during the acute moments of the class conflicts

coercion by the exploited directed against their exploiters is indispensable for the triumph of equality and justice. Therefore, the party considers the Soviet form of government as the most expedient form of government.

The entire congress united around this program, with the exception of five delegates who disagreed with the above theses and who walked out of the congress.

Thereupon the congress turned to examining the question of the current situation. In spite of the fact that the Uprising which is led by national-patriots and directed by them towards a false path of national antagonism, would not be able, under such conditions, lead to desirable results, [however] the congress considered it inexpedient to oppose the revolutionary movement, whatever form it should take, and it resolved: by means of broad propaganda to endeavor to direct the movement into the channel of class struggle and to establish close ties with the Japanese Socialists for the purpose of joint struggle against the native and Japanese nobility and bankers.

Concerning the Versailles Peace Conference the congress adopted a resolution whose contents is as follows: since the representatives of the Allies assembled at the Versaille Peace Conference for the purpose of sharing the fruits of their victory and dividing the remainder of the world and since at this conference the small oppressed nationalities are represented by an insignificant minority, there could be no doubt that their just demands will not be satisfied and that the same fate also awaits the "Korean Question"; therefore the congress considers it necessary to fight, by means of propaganda among the masses, against the authority of the Peace Conference.

The League of Nations, in the opinion of the congress, is what the Holy Alliance was after the Napoleonic wars; by no means can it ensure the freedom of development to the small nationalities, who will constitute a minority also in this body. The congress therefore resolved to carry on intensified agitation and propaganda among the masses for the recall of the Korean delegates from the Peace Conference and from the League of Nations, should they turn out to be members of that latter body.

Further, the question of the Third International was discussed at the congress. The feverish activity in the field of
rearmament exhibited by Japan and by Germany who "bore a
grudge" against its conquerors, on the one hand, and the
rapacious appetites of the Anglo-French-American imperialists
on the other hand, may again, in connection with the
ever-intensifying racial antagonisms, lead to another clash of the
peoples of the whole world if the revolutionary Socialists of all
countries fail to rise up together against a new world war.
Recognizing all this the congress resolved: to begin negotiations
with the Socialist parties of Eastern Asia on how to unify their
common struggle against pan-Mongolism and to join the Third
International, which is to be organized in Europe for the
struggle against the evil of the world—the imperialism.

The resolution noted at the same time that, "on no account
can we, the Socialists of the East, work in contact with the
majority members of the Second International, who support the
colonial policy of their imperialist governments."

At the time when the congress was in session, we still knew
nothing about the Third Communist International that was
founded in Moscow. Considering Siberia as a base for its
political activity and observing with bitterness the ever-
increasing Japanese influence in the Far East, on the question of
Siberia and the Russian Soviet Republic the congress resolved:
since the triumph of the Russian Soviet Republic in the Far
East and the freedom of Korea are closely connected with the
fortunes of Japanese imperialism, and in view of the fact that,
for our party, which acknowledges the necessity of assuming as
a basis for the state-building in a future Korean republic the
principles of Soviet government system, it is particularly
important to be a near-by neighbor of Soviet Russia, rich in
revolutionary experience, which will render us invaluable
services not only in our common struggle with Japanese
imperialism but also in our struggle against the bourgeoisie and
nobility of our own countries, the Central Committee of the
Party is to be instructed that it immediately undertake the
proper steps.

The congress expressed its attitude towards the Korean

National Council in a resolution proposing to the members of the party that they give up their responsible positions within the organization of the Union if the Council, as in the past, will carry on the policy which is at variance with our party's tactics. The congress decided to relegate to the Central Committee of the party the decision of the question of a definitive recall of party members from the Union.

Finally, there were elucidated also at the congress questions concerning Japan, China and the entire Far East, and the elections to the Central Committee of the Party were also held.

Our native bourgeoisie told us over and over again that now was not the time for class squabbles, that it was necessary to mobilize all living forces of the nation for the common struggle against the Japanese yoke, oppressing us all to an equal extent; but the class conscious part of the toilers, represented by the party of Korean Socialists, resolved to resist the hypocritical and false protestations of the bourgeois politicians, for the toiling people will suffer just as much under the yoke of the Korean bourgeoisie as it now suffers from the arbitrary rule of the predatory Japanese imperialism.

From the moment of its last congress the Korean Socialist party definitely broke with the native bourgeoisie and nobility, adopted a platform of class struggle, and proclaimed the slogan of a "Free Korean Republic". Having thus entered on a new path of revolutionary struggle, our party energetically and boldly marches forward towards a bright future, confident in the fraternal cooperation between the Japanese and Chinese social-democracies who together with our party will carry on the fight against Eastern-Asiatic reaction for the final liberation of the toilers, for world revolution.

Such are the views of the Korean Socialist Party; wherever there are Korean proletariat and peasants who have not yet joined the party, we are attempting by agitation to attract them to our side.

Never before in the history of the world Socialist movement has the necessity for the close unity and firm solidarity of the working masses of all countries for the common struggle with world imperialism been so clearly sensed as at the present moment, after the European war. Conscious of this necessity, our party responds with joy to the call of the Third International, and I am convinced that in the nearest future we will fight shoulder to shoulder with the proletariat of Europe, America and all the rest of Asia for the world revolution and for the realization of the tasks of revolution in Korea.

Member of the Korean Delegation
Member of the Central Committee of the Korean Socialist Party
Dzhishun Pak [Pak Chin-sun]

Item 10: The Revolutionary East and the Next Task of the Communist International[1]

The First and Second Internationals were practically associations of the masses of Europe and America; they gave very little attention to "the Eastern question" and in general "to the question of the colonial nations". The majority of the officials of the Second International tried by all means in their power to keep the "colonial questions" in the background and to fence off the West European Labor movement from the revolutionary struggle of the enslaved colonial nationalities; they were afraid to put these questions openly and clearly.

Each time that they came face to face with the "Eastern problem" the official leaders of the Second International were no less timid and hesitant than the bourgeois politicians, with their constant hypocritical talk of homage to "democracy", civilization and culture. The complicated questions of the struggle of the subjugated populations of the colonies, constituting the majority of the whole of struggling humanity, were quite foreign to the ideologists of parliamentarism. Even when the Communist International was formed Asia was very poorly represented and this circumstance could not be reflected in the work in the East.

But the consciousness of the necessity of a joint revolutionary struggle of the working masses of the West and East was growing more and more; the great victorious October Revolution in Russia was the first bridge across the gulf between the proletarian West and the revolutionary East, and Soviet Russia became a link between two hitherto independent worlds. The necessity of a joint proletarian struggle in the West and East was never so strongly felt as at the present time when the ruling classes have transformed flourishing fields into a barren desert, and laid peaceful towns and villages in ruins; when the working

[1] This document was also written by Pak Chin-sun. It was written in early 1920 most likely in Russian. The document is available only in English in *Communist International*, nos. 11-12 (June-July, 1920), pp. 2,315-20.

class has decided to raise the banner of an implacable revolutionary struggle for the power of the workers' masses, for a new free life for all mankind.

At the present moment when the spirit of social revolution is roaring over the whole world, when the bourgeoisie is straining every nerve to delay the hour of its death for a brief space of time, the Second World Congress of the Communist International should direct its attention to the East, where the fate of the world revolution may be decided; for whoever is able to approach the subjugated nations of the East and make them his allies will come out as conqueror in this last struggle between labor and capitalism.

The acute economic crisis in Asia (an inevitable condition at the moment of transition from feudalism to capitalism) and the barbarous policy of the larger imperialist powers in the colonies have created favorable conditions for a revolution. This policy has developed strong Nationalist tendencies. Admitting that in the East the first stage of the battle will lead to the victory of the liberal bourgeoisie and the Nationalist educated intellectual groups, we must nevertheless now begin to prepare the forces for the following stage, by drawing from the depths of the agricultural masses, enslaved by the feudal regime, organized forces for an agrarian-socialistic revolution in Asia in the very near future. The industrial proletariat, if we exclude Japan, is too feeble in Asia to permit of our nourishing any serious hopes of an immediate Communist revolution, but the victory of an agrarian revolution is undoubted, if we are able to cope with the immediate problems of the great and bloody struggle.

The Russian proletariat, standing at the outposts of the world social revolution, was able to withstand the three years' onslaught of the world bourgeoisie only because it had the poorer and middle peasantry on its side. The advance guard of the European and American proletariat, uniting around the Communist International, must fight hand in hand with the many-millioned masses of the revolutionary East, if it desires a speedy and successful victory over the Capitalist class. The impossibility of such a victory without the collaboration of the "colonial" nations is so evident that argument is superfluous.

The history of the death without glory of the Second International shows clearly that, so long as the world bourgeoisie has a reserve power in the colonies in general, and in Asia in particular, so long will it be able to repulse the most desperate attacks of the rebellious proletariat.

The Communist International, while directing the awakening East on the right path of revolution, will strike at the very roots of opportunism and irresolution in the proletariat of the western countries; but action must be so coordinated and combined that the European proletariat shall sever the head of capitalism at the moment when the revolutionary base is dealing it a mortal wound in the stomach. The victorious rising of the "colonial" nations will sign the death warrant of all "Bernsteinism" and petty bourgeoisie trade-unionism. The prompt execution of this task will accelerate the triumph of the Communist International on a world scale.

The question now is, what forces are moving the revolution in the East? The majority of the former nobility, the liberal bourgeoisie, and the petty bourgeois educated circles, representing the intellectual forces of the revolution in Asia, taught by the experience of long years' of struggle against the foreign slave owners, and after an agonizing mental struggle, have understood at last that the revival of the East is not possible except through the rule of the wide circles of the working masses. The bankruptcy of the Second International coincided with the rapid development of revolutionary ideas in the East,—and it proved to the leaders that they are deprived of all hope of a free existence for their own people without the triumph of a social revolution in Europe, Asia and other countries. Before the Nationalists of Asia two opposite ways lie open: the one leading to personal prosperity, based on the certainty of suffering and gradual degeneration for the great masses of the people, the other leading to a social revolution, which will deprive them to a certain degree of material privileges but will bring liberation to their own people.

To our great joy the majority of the ideological Nationalists proved to be on the side of the revolution. Certainly, amid the revolutionaries there are elements which unite with us, internationalists, only with the object of attaining a national-political liberation, but we shall use their revolutionary zeal for the struggle against world capitalism, for the triumph of a social revolution in the whole world; and, should the revolution demand it in future, we shall know how to turn our arms against our quondam "ally" and the victory will undoubtedly be ours, as the masses of the East, but just liberated from foreign political and economic slavery, will hardly resign themselves to violence on the part of new rulers.

Such a policy—of supporting the Nationalist movements in the colonies—is impossible for those would-be Socialist governments, which fear to "arouse the feeling of patriotism" in the unlightened working masses of the countries whose ruling classes are carrying on a barbarous colonial policy.

But the Communist International has no grounds for fear of such "rousing", because the advance guard of the international revolutionary proletariat whose ranks are increasing every day will estimate its actions at their worth, and perfectly approve its far-seeing tactics. Thus although we are struggling jointly with the above-mentioned elements, we cannot look upon them as upon our comrades, with whom we may go on to the end without fear.

Uncompromisingly we must explain to the working masses of the East that national-political liberation alone will not give them what they are striving for, and that only social liberation will guarantee them complete freedom.

The victory of the first stage of the revolution in Asia will coincide with that of the Socialist revolution of the West. Proletarian Europe will not bear to remain an impassive spectator of the sufferings of the great working masses of the East, groaning under the yoke of bourgeois democracy. The European proletariat, full of a feeling of international solidarity, will come to their aid. We can predict with certainty that a dreadful yell will be raised in the bourgeois camp. But our western comrades (we may be sure) will meet with a hearty and brotherly reception on the part of the proletariat and working peasantry of Asia; the East was always opposed to foreign intervention only when it brought with it chains and slavery;

but the intervention of the Socialist proletarian West will be a
great and needed help to the working masses of Asia in their
struggle against every kind of exploitation. The proletariat of
the East is thirsting for such "intervention".

The Second Congress, which is called upon to give to the
revolutionary proletariat a definite plan to guide it towards a
successful struggle against world imperialism, will most certainly
not forget the great role of the revolutionary East in the
international labor movement.

And the working masses of the East, with the help of their
European and American comrades, after having vanquished the
foreign and native slave-holders, will transform Asia into a
Communist oasis of revolutionary achievements.

Theses on the tasks of the Communist International in the East.

1. At the moment of the greatest collision of two opposite
forces: Labor and Capital—the liberation movement of the
so-called "colonial nations", acquiring the form of gigantic
uprisings, is a great help to the struggling proletariat of the
advanced capitalist countries.

2. By degrees, as the chasm between Labor and Capital is
growing wider and deeper, the necessity of close and firm
solidarity between Communist West and Revolutionary East is
making itself felt more and more.

3. The long years' experience of the revolutionary struggle
of the European proletariat, which will end in the liberation of
the whole of suffering mankind, and the bloody examples of
the many years' liberation-war of the peoples of the colonies
impose the necessity of coordination in the revolutionary
movements in order to achieve a speedy victory over the
exploiters.

4. The supreme leading organ of this gigantic struggle
cannot be the pestilent "League of Nations" and its ally, the
Second "yellow" International, but only the International of
Labor, of revolutionary struggles and Communist proletariat—
the Third Communist International.

5. The Communist International is bound to denounce all the doubledealing of the agents of world capital, who appear under the guise of the "League of Nations" and who are preparing a campaign against those who are struggling for the happiness and free existence of the oppressed working masses of the whole world; and it is bound to denounce unfailingly the incapacity and revolutionary indigence and consequently absolute uselessness of the "yellow" Second International in the great struggle for liberation of the nations of the East.

6. In contradistinction to the Second International which, under the pretext of "civilization" and "culture", was upholding openly the plundering and barbarous policy of the bourgeois government, the Communist International is undertaking the direct guidance of the struggle of the subjugated colonial nations against their oppressors and imperialism.

7. The Communist International, carrying on an implacable struggle against petty bourgeois trade-unionism, opportunism and reformism, which are hampering the revolutionary impulse of the proletariat in the advanced countries, and raising the mighty East, just awakening to a new life, will strike at the very roots of irresolution, this poisonous cancer in the healthy body of the revolutionary movement of international socialism.

8. The peculiar features of the economic and cultural conditions of the West and the East set their special stamp on each of these two sections of working humanity, the proletariat of the advanced capitalist countries being undoubtedly the more developed, more conscious section of the international army of labor. But the task of the Communist International consists, naturally, not in separating into a special caste the industrial workers of the more industrially developed countries, which constitute the minority of laboring mankind, but, on the contrary, of the help of the most staunch and class-conscious western industrial workers in organizing the whole working mass of the awakening East that it may pour its great forces into the stream of the revolutionary struggle between labor and capital.

9. An implacable struggle against bourgeois pacifism, hampering the fighting energies of the revolutionary East, Pan-Mongolism and Pan-Islamism, enemies of the international

solidarity of the working masses and their collaboration in the struggle for freedom and the brotherhood of nations.

10. It is necessary to carry on an untiring propaganda for an agrarian revolution among the peoples of the colonies, especially in Asia, in order to give the liberation movement not only a political but an economic meaning; it is necessary to raise the class consciousness of the masses, to draw them into the public movement, to transform this movement from an intellectual movement to a movement of the masses explaining to them the historical mission of the proletariat and preparing them to seize power.

11. In expectation of this Socialist-agrarian revolution in the East the Communist International must immediately proceed to the elaboration of a revolutionary method of organization of a raw society—a Communist society, that is to say, to the creation of an economic plan for the most painless transition possible from the agrarian order to that of socialism, avoiding the cruel period of development of private capitalism in the East.

D. THE ALEXEYEVSK INCIDENT, JUNE 1921

Item 11: Declaration[1]

We consider it deeply regretable that it has become necessary to report in tears on a most tragic incident. This concerns the great tragedy involving Korean soldiers in the *Chayu-si*[2] in the Russian Maritime Province, during June of this year. This incident has been erroneously reported to various Korean newspapers, and considerable doubts have been stirred about the truth of the incident. In order to clarify our doubts we sent a few compatriots to the actual place of occurrence to investigate this incident, and have reconfirmed our doubts. The report of the investigation revealed that the incident, which occurred in the barren land of Alexeyevskaya, brought pathetic results, producing some 600 casualties among our compatriots. Some 200 or more died, 250 or more were missing, and 917 were captured as prisoners. It is important to recount the incident that brought about this disaster.

During March of this year, 1921, the headquarters for the Korean Volunteer Army was in Alexeyevsk. This army was organized by our compatriots who fled the hideous Japanese annexation of our fatherland and fought our enemies in northeast Chientao and the Russian Maritime Province, enduring unbearable difficulties and hardships only in order to bring success to our cause.

These armies had been pushed back by the oncoming great numbers of Japanese soldiers, although they fought tirelessly and retreated to the Russian territories only to reorganize and then strike back at our enemy. Their route of retreat was a

---

[1] This document was written by Ku Ch'un-sŏn and signed by the officers of six other Nationalist organizations. The declaration was issued on September 1921. The document was originally a portion of the document written in Korean and is available in Korean but not in its entirety. The English version is translated from the full text in Japanese available in *JFMA*, SP 46 (sp. 150) 46-58. This is also available in *JANA*, reel 123 (T1,186).

[2] The Korean name for Alexeyevsk, the railroad junction. It is now called Svobodny in the Russian Maritime Province.

difficult if not impossible one, encountering at times hills and mountains that no man had ever passed; they marched without food and water for scores of days, nibbling only grass roots and drinking polluted water, but their will to accomplish the grave task encouraged them and pushed them forward. They travelled extensively and their physical exhaustion was nourished spiritually and their will was rejuvenated to organize and fight against our enemy. The Korean Volunteer Army is the product of these gallant soldiers who gathered at Alexeyevsk. The participating soldiers of the Korean Volunteer Army were represented by the Saharin Company, Ch'ongryong Company, Iman Company of the Russian Maritime Province, and *Kwangbok* Corps, *Kunjŏng-sŏ, Ŭigun-bu, Todok-bu, Hyŏlsŏng-dae* of the Chinese (mainly Manchurian) territories. The officers elected after the formation of the Army were fifteen in all, including Hong Pŏm-do, An Mu, Sŏ Il, Cho Rip, Yi Ch'ŏng-ch'ŏn, Yi Yong, Ch'ae Yŏng, Ch'oe Chin-yŏng, O Ha-muk, and some others.[3]

There was a total of more than three thousand soldiers under these leaders, and it is not necessary to praise the preparations of these compatriots, for they were in part carrying out the wishes of all Koreans, but the confrontation of good and evil was inevitable.

There were some Koreans who had emigrated to Russia and formed an autonomous organization called the Korean Association *[Hanjok-hoe]*, but these people dreamed of transforming their organization into the controlling organization of the Korean revolutionary movement. They renamed their organization the Korean National Congress *[Taehan Kungmin ŭi-hoe]* and performed atrocities against our compatriots. Mun Ch'ang-bŏm, Kim Ha-sŏk, Wŏn Se-hun, and others conspired to finance the military forces with money that they acquired, and performed the detestable act of plundering a rich Korean,

---

[3] It is difficult to ascertain the relationship of these men with various armed groups mentioned here. Most of the leaders, however, can be identified, and although they are predominantly Nationalists, it is believed that they were in sympathy with or supported the cause of the Korean Communist leader Yi Tong-hwi who advocated the militant policy of fighting the Japanese with arms.

named Kim Wŏn-so, in order to send Wŏn Se-hun to Peking and Shanghai, thus earning the disrespect and anger of the members of the Korean Volunteer Army.[4]

In order to satisfy their personal desires they sold out the public cause and transferred a portion of the Korean soldiers into the Russian Army, and they also secretly organized the Korean Military Political Council *[Koryŏ Kunjŏng Ŭihoe]*, conspiring with the head of the Far Eastern Secretariat, Shumiatsky.[5] After appointing O Ha-muk, Kim Ha-sŏk, Ch'oe Ko-ryŏ, Yu Tong-yŏl, and one Russian as officers of the group, they conspired to place the soldiers of the Korean Volunteer Army under their control, but the righteous soldiers of the Korean Volunteer Army realized the cunning maneuvers of these men, who acted solely to satisfy their private wants and who disregarded duty to our fatherland, and they denounced the very existence of the Korean Military Political Council.

Realizing the attitude of the Korean Volunteer Corps, they secretly informed the Russians, accusing the Korean Volunteer Corps of being a spy organization of the Japanese, consisting of anti-revolutionary forces with narrow nationalistic inclinations. They pointed out the Japanese watches and insignias that the Korean Volunteer Army had taken in Chientao in combat with the Japanese as proof that they were anti-revolutionary forces. Because the Koreans dare to make such lies on their compatriots, the Russians reacted to the accusation of "anti-revolutionary," for they are allergic to such labelling. Thus, the Russian army, more than ten-thousand strong, with machine

---

[4] The organization mentioned here is the *Taehan Kungmin Ŭihoe,* the manifesto of the organization is available. The subsequent statement here indicates that Mun Ch'ang-bŏm did in fact cooperate with the Irkutsk group in opposition to Yi Tong-hwi.

[5] Boris Zakharievich Shumiatsky, also known as Andrei Chervonnyi, was a member of Bolshevik Party and was well-known to the Communists in Siberia. After the October Revolution, he became the chairman of Central Executive Committee of the Soviets of Siberia, and later became the head of the Comintern's Far Eastern Secretariat in Irkutsk. Later he held various posts including a membership at the Council of Ministers of Far Eastern Republic, ambassador and trade representative of the Soviet Union to Persia, 1922-25, rector of Communist University of the Toilers of the East in Moscow, 1926-28, and others.

guns, cannons, and other arms, surrounded the Korean Volunteer Corps and demanded their disarming within three hours. The Volunteer Army at first was puzzled and did not understand the true meaning of this demand; they hesitated, but soon received the great onslaught of the Russian attack. At the beginning of the attack, the Russian soldiers only threatened by shooting in the air, but the soldiers under O Ha-muk attacked with real bullets. A few rounds of fighting produced the casualty of a Russian company commander and full-fledged fighting broke out, with disastrous consequences to the Korean Volunteer Army.

Without realizing their inhumane action to the Korean Volunteer Army, the Russians divided their 917 prisoners into four classes; those listed under the first class were to be executed immediately, those listed under the second class were to be imprisoned until the whole world is Bolshevised, those listed under the third class were to be imprisoned for fifteen years, and those listed under the fourth class were to be exiled to European Russia for hard labor. The leaders of the Irkutsk groups, Kim Ch'ŏl-hun, Yi Sŏng, Sŏ Ch'o, Nam Man-ch'un, O Chin-haeng, Chang Kŏn-sang, An Pyŏng-ch'an, and a few others are busy attempting to conceal their inhumane action; the leaders of the Korean Volunteer Army, Ke Pong-u, Kim Chin, Chang To-jŏng, Pak Ae, Chang Ki-yŏng, Kim Tong-hwan, Kim Sŏng-u, Kim Kyu-min, Chu Yŏng-sŏp, Pak Wŏn-sŏp, Han Un-yong, An T'ae-guk, Pak Sang-ch'u, Ch'ae Inokenchi, and some thirty others are suffering in a prison on foreign soil. Oh, what a disastrous incident this was, and it is truly difficult to express our emotion. Some 600 of our compatriots, who left wives and children in the homeland to fight to save the fatherland, mercilessly fell in front of Russian guns. This tragedy is unprecedented, and this is a great shame to our people as well as a grave mistake in our history.

How must they have felt when the 600 gallant soldiers fell in the barren land of Alexeyevsk? It has been said that they were very gallant, and that the Russian soldiers who opened their guns against them later gave our soldiers a decent burial. It is difficult to stop a shiver of horror at that tragedy. What do the

souls of the 600 fallen soldiers tell us? What do the several
hundred of our compatriots who are in prison in Russia tell us?
We declare to the world that the crimes committed are
unforgivable, and that those immoral and virtueless people who
sold our people for their private benefit should be punished.
These are Mun Ch'ang-bŏm, Kim Ch'ŏl-hun, Kim Ha-sŏk, O
Ha-muk, Wŏn Se-hun, Yi Sŏng (Pyŏng-hui), Cho Hun, Nam
Man-ch'un, Ch'oe Ko-ryŏ, O Chin-haeng, Kim Ung-sŏp, Yu
Tong-yŏl, Sŏ Ch'o, An Pyŏng-ch'an, Chang Kŏn-sang, Ch'oe
Ŭi-su, Kim Ki-ryong, and others.[6] We intend to repay this
injustice fully and punish this crime.

Signed by
    Ku Ch'un-sŏn[7] representing *Kungmin-hoe*
    Yi Pong-u, Yun Tŏk-po
    Yi Hi-sam, representing *Kunbi-tan*
    Pak Tae-sŏng, representing *T'aeguk-tan*
    Kim Sŏng-wŏn
    Kim Sŏng-bae, representing *Shinmin-tan*
    Cho Ung-sun, representing *Nonong-hoe*

[6] Most of these leaders can be identified and they represent the
leadership of the Irkutsk group.

[7] Little biographical information is available of Ku Ch'un-sŏn. Ku is one
of the leaders of the Korean Nationalists in Manchuria and the Russian
Maritime Provinces, and since many Nationalist groups and leaders
suffered as a consequence of this incident, he and other leaders who were
not involved in the incident have issued the declaration.

Item 12: Declaration of the Korean Military Government Council[1]

1. *Concerning the Alexeyevsk Military Incident:* It is our purpose to correct the misinformed members and leaders of the Korean independence movement concerning the military incident in Alexeyevsk during the past June. There are considerable differences between the facts and rumors now circulating among the Koreans.

2. The military situation [the name of each company] near Alexeyevsk was as follows:

    a. In Alexeyevsk . . . . . O Ha-muk
    b. Saharin Company . . . . Pak Ilia [Pak Chin-sun]
    c. Iman Company . . . . . Pak Gregori
    d. Chientao Company . . . Ch'oe Chin-tong, Hong Pŏm-do, Yi Ch'ŏng-ch'ŏn, Hŏ Kun, An Mu
    e. Student Company . . . . Ch'ae Yŏng.

The above military companies were engaged in a severe factional struggle, and the struggle between the Saharin Company and the Alexeyevsk Company was the strongest.

3. *Organization and power of the Military Government Council:* The Military Government Council was organized to eliminate all factional struggle among the Korean groups. It has the power to include under its organization all Korean military organizations in the Russian Far East.

4. *The misconduct of the Saharin Company:* There were many leaders who agreed with the objectives of the Military Government Council and joined forces in Alexeyevsk, including Hong Pŏm-do, Yi Ch'ŏng-ch'ŏn, An Mu, Ch'oe Chin-tong, Ch'ae Yŏng, and Hŏ Kŭn, who led some 400 soldiers of the Chientao

---

[1] It is not clear who wrote this document, but it was issued on September 30, 1921 by the Korean Revolutionary Military Council which was headed by Mun Ch'ang-bŏm. It is possible that this document may have been originally written in Russian rather than Korean. The present translation is from Japanese available in *JFMA* SP 46 (sp. 150). This document is also available in *JANA* reel 123 (T1,186).

Company to join us in Alexeyevsk. However, Pak Ilia,[2] together with Kim Nŭng-hyo of the Saharin Company, opposed the move without any reason. We used a conciliatory method to come to terms with Pak Ilia, but Pak, who agreed with us openly, conspired secretly with others to oppose us, and even wrote a threatening note stating non-compliance unless we kill the seven men, Ch'oe Chin-tong, An Mu, Yi Ch'ŏng-ch'ŏn; Kim Ha-sŏk, Hong Pŏm-do, and O Ha-muk. We opened the Sixth Congress and attempted to come to an agreement with Pak Ilia, but Pak clamored to kill the seven leaders, waving his fists at them, and later threw a bomb at one of our commanders. The meeting thus adjourned without any success.

5. *Progress of the disarming incident:* Thus we decided to disarm the Saharin Company, and secretly instructed the Russian Company Commander to move to disarm the Saharin Company at Alexeyevsk, but the Saharin Company retaliated and this resulted in casualties: 37 dead, 4 injured, 50 escaped, 900 or more captured as prisoners. Pak Ilia escaped, and there were a few leaflets within the company that stated their opposition to the Military Government Council to the end.

6. *Concerning the prisoners:* After a close investigation, we have released all except some 75 leaders.

September 30, 1921
Korean Revolutionary Military Government Council

---

[2] Pak Ilia is a pseudonym of Pak Chin-sun. What is referred to here by the Irkutsk group is the leadership of the Shanghai group under Yi Tong-hwi.

Item 13: Decision of the Inspection Committee of the Communist International[1]
(November 15, 1921)

The Executive Committee of the Communist International and the Central Executive Committee of the Communist Party of the Soviet Union, after examining all the facts and documents, pass the following resolution on the Korean question, which was decided by the Inspection Committee appointed by the Executive Committee of the Communist International.

1. At present, the two organizations bearing the same name of "Korean Communist Party" and engaged in Communist activities are both an outgrowth of the Korean revolutionary movement; these are the Communist group represented by the Korean National Congress (Irkutsk group) and the Communist group of the Korean Provisional Government (Shanghai group). The origin of the disputes between these two groups is not clear, but it is evident that there are differences between the two groups and that the antagonism between the two is growing. The group in Shanghai was organized earlier than the group in Irkutsk, and the representatives of the Shanghai group, Pak Ae and Pak Ilia (Pak Chin-sun) had contacted the Comintern in 1919. The other Communist group, which had joined the Korean National Congress, was organized later, in June, 1920, and the Korean National Congress did not appear as a Communist organization until after April, 1921.

Although both groups criticize each other and claim that

[1] Although it is clear that this document was written by the Inspection Committee of the Comintern composed of Bela Kun, Kuusinen, and Safarov, issued on November 15, 1921 it is difficult if at all possible to verify the decision of this committee from the documents of the Comintern, because aside from the Japanese version from which this translation was made, the record of this decision can not be found. However, from the study of the early phase of the Korean Communist movement it is clear that this directive is authentic, although in the process of translation some meanings became obscure.

each is more patriotic or more internationally Communistic, these are mere disputes of words, and since the two groups are both representatives of Korean revolutionary elements, it is difficult to accomplish any concrete result without the merger of these two groups. The fact that the Far Eastern Secretariat of the Comintern had favored the Irkutsk group undoubtedly intensified the factional struggle, and each group claimed that it was truly the Communist Party representing the Korean revolutionary movement. However, these two groups had substantial reasons for their division, because most of the Irkutsk group was organized by uniting the emigrants abroad while the Shanghai group was organized with the elements of the Korean national revolutionary movement.

2. The reason for the intensification of the confrontation of the two groups is the Alexeyevsk Incident. This incident was caused by the attempt by the leaders of the Irkutsk group, which formed the Korean Revolutionary Military Council, to disarm the Korean Volunteer Corps. If, in fact, the incident was caused by the disturbances of the Korean Volunteer Corps or its leader (Pak Ilia), it was due to the intrigues of the Irkutsk group which chose to include a few disgraced leaders of the Korean Volunteer Army into the Korean Revolutionary Military Government Council, and is purely a factional struggle of the Irkutsk group.

On the other hand, the Korean Volunteer Army also committed an error by failing to respect the verbal agreement with the Commander of the Korean Revolutionary Military Government Council, Kalintanov Lee (Yi Sŏng), and a greater fault lies with a leader of the Shanghai group, Pak Ilia, who anticipated the bloody battle between the two groups and failed to prevent its occurrence. The fault of the other faction, the Irkutsk group, is that they extended the political struggle into a military one in the battlefield. (Despite the fact that the Irkutsk group had imprisoned a leader of the Shanghai group, Pak Ae, in May 1921, it is a detestable fact that a few former members of the revolutionary groups in Shanghai under the domain of the Shanghai group joined the Irkutsk group.)

Even at the time of the severe intensification of the factional strife there were no attempts to find a solution to the situation, but the strife was intensified further by a rude attempt to disarm the other group. This was unnecessary and unlawful. Furthermore, it was not necessary to fire cannons and machine guns for twelve hours for this kind of confrontation.

3. The Far Eastern Secretariat should have condemned the decision of the Special Korean Military Revolutionary Court, which was nothing more than an Inspection Committee of the Irkutsk group, to sentence Pak Ae to an eight-year imprisonment. The crimes cited against Pak Ae are as follows:

a. (Disobeying the order) to establish the Korean section in the Far Eastern Bureau.

(The authority to establish a section in the Far Eastern Bureau is in the Central Executive Committee of the Russian Communist Party and in the Far Eastern Bureau).

b. Interference with the activities of the representatives of the Irkutsk group in the Far East.

(This is a proven fact).

c. Disobeying the order of a representative of the Comintern, Shumiatsky, to move the Korean section to Irkutsk.

d. Appointing Pak Ilia and Kim Min-sŏn as the leaders of the Saharinski Company.

(This was the order of the commander of the Far Eastern Republic).

e. Appointing Pak Ch'ang-sik, who is not familiar with military affairs.

(This was the order of the Commander of the Far Eastern Republic).

f. Opening the conference of the representatives of the Korean Volunteer Army near Kufushinayask, contrary to the orders of Shumiatsky.

(This conference was called with the consent of the Commander of the Far Eastern Republic).

g. Interference with the opening of the conference of the All Korean Communist Party in Irkutsk.

h. Instigating the Korean Volunteer Army and opposing the Irkutsk group.

(The disarming of the Korean Volunteer Army took place on June 22, 1921, and Pak Ae was immediately imprisoned and had no time to instigate the Korean Volunteer Army).

i. Reporting the organization of the Korean Revolutionary Military Government Council in Irkutsk to the Commander of the Far Eastern Republic.

(This does not constitute a crime).

4. On the basis of these facts, the Inspection Committee recommends further investigation by another Inspection Committee composed of members who are familiar with the Incident, and orders the immediate release of comrade Pak Ae who is to appear in Moscow. Furthermore, any person among the some 80 prisoners, whom the members of the Inspection Committee consider it necessary to see in their investigation of the Alexeyevsk Incident, should be released.

5. The Inspection Committee considers it necessary that the two factions, the Shanghai group and the Irkutsk group, must have close relationships and has decided that the two groups must organize an Interim Central Executive Committee with an equal number of persons representing the two groups until a new Congress is convened including all revolutionary elements in Korea and abroad. The Far Eastern Secretariat has the responsibility to carry out this directive.

November 15, 1921
Bela Kun, Kuusinen, Safarov,
Members of the Inspection Committee

Irrushin
Representative of the All Russian Military Committee

Item 14: The Decision of the Executive Committee of the Third Communist International on the Korean Problem[1]

The members of the Committee elected by the Executive Committee of the Communist International to discuss the Korean problems, Kuusinen, Safarov, and Brantin, have reached the following decision on April 22, 1922 committee meeting after examining the documents and investigating various facts as well as questioning the leaders of both groups.

1. Those members who were expelled from the Korean Communist Party by the Executive Committee of the Korean Communist Party Congress in Irkutsk are hereby restored to their rights as full fledged members of the Party.

2. Henceforth, the four leaders of both groups, Pak Chin-sun, Pak Ae, Ch'oe Ko-ryŏ, Kim Kyu-gŭk, are not permitted to undertake any activity that bears a direct relationship to party affairs until the Korean Communist parties are united.

3. The Central Executive Committee of the Korean Communist Party must unite the two groups within three months.

4. During this period the Korean Communist Party shall not receive any funds from the Comintern, and the Committee directs a member of the Executive Committee of the Comintern, Comrade Yanson,[2] to resolve the financial situations of

[1] This decision of the ECCI was made by a 3-man committee composed of Otto Kuusinen, Safarov, and Brantin on April 22, 1922. Here again this decision is available only in Japanese and it is difficult to verify the decision with the documentary materials of the Comintern. However, subsequent activities of the Korean Communists in 1922 clearly attests to the directive of this decision, and there is little doubt that this document is authentic. The full text of this document is available in Japanese in *JFMA*, SP 46 (sp. 150), 428-30. It is also available in *JFMA*, reel S 721 (S.9.4.5.2-30).

[2] Yanson, Iakov Davidovich, is a Latvian by birth who was exiled to Siberia in 1914. He became active in Irkutsk after February revolution and became chairman of regional executive committee of Eastern Siberian branch. During 1918-20, he was the Irkutsk, and at the time of this incident he was the foreign minister of Far Eastern Republic, 1921-22. He

both groups. At the same time, all the money that is left to Comrade Kim Rip should be returned to the Comintern, and the accounting record of the fund, 200,000 yen, received from the Comintern should be returned to the Comintern by the man who received the money, comrade Han Hyŏng-kwŏn, in person in Moscow.[3]

5. The Central Executive Committee of the Korean Communist Party shall be located in Chita, and the Central Executive Committee shall have the responsibility of establishing a Korean Bureau within Korea.

6. The Central Executive Committee of the Korean Communist Party shall make correct political programs to direct the political activities in Korea, and, for the Korean emigrants residing in Russia and under the domain of the Far Eastern Republic, the Central Executive Committee shall make appropriate slogans to guide their activities.

---

later held various posts as trade representative of the Soviet Union including one in Japan, 1925-28, during which time he was reputedly Comintern's agent in Japan.

[3] Both comrades Kim Rip and Han Hyŏng-kwŏn were dead at the time of this directive. Kim on February 8, 1922 in Shanghai and Han was reported to have been murdered by Kim Rip earlier. It is difficult to ascertain how the Comintern came to the figure of 200,000 yen to be returned. Presumably this is the second installment of the 400,000 rubles that the Korean Communists received, but again the mixture of rubles and yen makes it difficult to estimate the fund.

E. THE FIRST CONGRESS OF THE TOILERS OF THE FAR EAST, JANUARY 1922

Item 15: Manifesto of the First Congress of the Communist and Revolutionary Organizations of the Far East to the Peoples of the Far East[1]

Toilers of the Far East!

Workers and peasants of China, Korea, Japan, Mongolia, of the Pacific Isles, Indo-China and the Dutch Indies! Ensalved nations of the Far East! You are suffering since dozens of years from the savage and arbitrary actions and the depredations of European, American and Japanese bandits. The Japanese oppressors have bespattered Korea with blood from end to end. The Japanese, American, French and English robbers are plundering and tearing to pieces China with her four hundred million population and building their own welfare on the blood and tears of the Chinese people. They do not look upon the representatives of the oppressed nations as human beings. They want gold that glitters, profits and riches, and in order to obtain the same, they are ready to sacrifice hundreds of millions of human lives. Chinamen and Koreans are not allowed to enter the gardens and other public places in the foreign quarters of Peking, Shanghai, Tientsin, Hongkong, Seoul and Chemulp'o—on a par with dogs. In these quarters foreign bourgeois, fattened on other men's sweat and blood, ride about in carriages drawn by men-horses, the rikshas, hastening them up with kicks and sticks. The most oppressed and brow-beaten slave of the rich of

[1] This is the manifesto of the FCTFE which was held from January 21 to February 1, 1922 in Moscow. The closing session was held in Petrograd on February 2, 1922. This document is available in English, Russian, German and Japanese. There are two English versions of this document. The version presented here which is from *The First Congress of the Toilers of the Far East* (Petrograd, 1922), and English translation of the Russian version which is available in E. J. Eudin and R. C. North *Soviet Russia and the East* (Stanford, 1957). The Russian version is available in *Pervyi sezd revoliutsionnykh organizatsii Dalnego Vostoka.* The German version is in *Der Erste Kongress der Kommunistischen und Revolutionaren Organizationen des Fermen Osten,* (Hamburg, 1922).

the world—the Chinese coolie—works for these parasites to a state of deadly extenuation. The Chinese peasant does unbearable labor, toiling 16 to 18 hours a day at a stretch, and nevertheless, the produce of his labor is null, for it goes only to enrich the foreign moneylenders and blood-suckers and filters into the pockets of their mercenary lackeys. The Korean pauper has no land wherewith to gain his daily bread. The land is in the hands of the Japanese planters, the landowners and capitalists, who with their bayonets and shooting force the refractory to do the work. Every word of protest, every cry of desperation is smothered by the rattle of mass shootings in the Philippines, the Isle of Formosa, Indo-China and the Islands of Dutch Indies, as well as in the neighboring British India, long since become a terrible prison for a people of 300 millions. Millions of laboring lives are bowed down to the earth on rice, coffee, cotton and other plantations and cruelly exploited. Only the other day has Mongolia freed herself from Japanese and white-guard clutches. The dominating classes of Japan have received the nick-name of "hangmen of the Far East"; the factory workers and the peasants, partly daily laborers on rented land, lead an existence good for lower animals. The heavy groans of hundreds of enslaved millions are heard everywhere. The oppressors will hear nothing of freedom and independence for the oppressed nations, nor of their human rights.

They have met lately in the hall of the American Exchange [capitol?] in Washington, in order to come to an understanding on the subject of the further plunder of the countries of the Far East. There they have signed their Alliance of the Four Blood-Suckers. Korea, the Russian Far East and Manchuria have been given over to be robbed and pillaged by Japan. The principle of equal rights of robbery in China was set up, leaving the leading role in this base affair to American capital. The universal blood-sucking machine—the Consortium of 1918— invented by America, intended to make all the Chinese peasants tributaries of American capital: they were to pay a considerable tax to the American bankers. Chinese industry was to become an American work-shop. Nothing came of this enterprise in 1918 owing to differences among the oppressors and the unanimous protest of the masses of the Chinese people. It is now desired to arrange a new consortium—an international firm for the military, financial and industrial robbery of China. Japan, America, England and France have, for the time being, put off a war, which was ready to break out, for dominion over the Pacific Ocean. They have put it off, but not definitely. They have put it off in order to be able to continue to rob in unison yet for some time.

The World War of 1914 has undermined their strength. The workers' revolution has taken them by the throat in Eruope on the very theatre of their bloody crime. They have struggled for four years against the Soviet Republic, the promised land of all oppressed and exploited, and must now openly acknowledge its strength and their own impotence to defeat the Soviets. They hope to reestablish their undermined power in the Far East through us and at the price of our lives, our blood and our labor. They bring new chains, new horrors and a still more terrible enslavement to the patient and resigned peoples of the Far East.

This must not, this shall not be! We desire to become the masters of our own fate and to leave off being the playthings of greedy appetites and imperialist vanity.

The cause of the freedom of mankind is our cause.

The Russian worker began the work, the European worker continued it, and we shall victoriously end the bitter strife going on between the parasites and the workers, to the good of hard-working hands and of backs bent in labor!

The Communist International has issued a great appeal: World proletarians and all oppressed nations of the world unite!

We will carry it to our destroyed villages to the slave plantations, the factories, schools and barracks.

We have met in the Red capitals of the Soviet Republic— Moscow and Petrograd—in order to raise our voices from this world tribune against the world executioners and against the Washington Union of Four Blood-Suckers.

We are the representatives of the four hundred million oppressed masses of China, the representatives of the national organizations of workers and peasants and the working intellectuals, as delegated by the Republican Party of southern China, of the revolutionary organizations of the provinces of Shantung, Hunan, Anhwei, Kwangtung, Szechwan, Chekiang; the towns of Hankow, Shanghai, Tientsin,[2] of the National Revolutionary Society of "Young China," of the Trade Union organizations; of the Union of Railroad Workers; of the Chinese Communist Party; of the Women's Patriotic League; of the National press, as represented by the *Republican Gazette* and the review: *the Pacific Conference and China.*

We are the representatives of the oppressed toiling masses of the imperialist Japan sent by: the Organization, *Rōdō-sha;* the Federation of the left wing of the Trade Unions of Japan; the Union of Printers of Tokyo, Osaka, and Kyūshū; the Miners' Federation of Kyūshū; the Labor press of Japan; and the Japanese Communist Party.

We are the representatives of oppressed Korea, groaning under the yoke of Japanese imperialism, as delegated by: the Big Workers' Union of Korea (Kyŏngsang-do); the Trade Union of Workers belonging to the Communist Party; the Union of Communist Youth of Korea; the revolutionary patriotic "League of Korean Christians"; the organization, "The Restoration of Korea"; the revolutionary Korean troops; the Amalgamated Union of the organizations of the Korean Youth; the Union of Youth, "New Korea"; the Union of Korean Students in China; the Club of Korean Students in Japan; the Central Union of Korean Students; and the editors of the paper, *The Independence of Korea.*

We are the representatives of Mongolia, as delegated by; the People's Revolutionary Party of Mongolia; the Revolutionary Union of Youth of Mongolia.

We are the representatives of the workers of the Dutch Indies, oppressed by the American, British and Dutch imperialism, as delegated by the left wing of the organization Sarikat-Islam; the Red Federation of Trade Unions of the Dutch Indies; the Communist Party of the Dutch Indies.

---

[2] There are names of other Chinese towns that are difficult to identify. They are Ha-Yuan, Han-Dzk, and Tian-Shan.

We demand equality, freedom and independence. We call to a just struggle on the just path all those who are no traitors to their people, to whom the paramount interests of the oppressed are near and dear, to those who are themselves slaves and desire to be slaves no more! We know that our executioners will grant us no liberty. We know that the struggle for freedom is a hard and strenuous one. But we wish to live and will take by force all that is ours by right, for we are the majority—there are hundreds of millions of us, and our strength is in our unity! We declare war to the death, to the Japanese, American, British, French and all other world rapacious plunderers. We declare war to the death to the mendacious Dudsiuns[?] and the lackeys of our oppressors in China. We declare war to the death to hypocritical and thievish American imperialism and the greedy British usurpers. Out with them from China and Korea, the Pacific Isles, Indo-China and the Dutch Indies! Out of the Far East!

The Japanese working class stretches out a brotherly hand to the workers of China and Korea. It takes its place in our general revolutionary union for the freedom of the peoples of the Far East. The sword of Japanese imperialism will snap in the hands of the Japanese proletariat. The world proletariat is with us. Our cause is its own cause. Its cause is the cause of our lives.

We conclude from now on an indissoluble union of the workers of the Far East under the flag of the Communist International. We will attain our freedom. We will overthrow the oppressors and establish a just workers' order, by seizing the land of the idle parasites and handing over the power to our own men from the ranks of the workers and peasants.

Organize!

Rally to our fighting ranks!

Form workers' and peasants' unions for the struggle with capitalism and imperialism!

Make ready for the struggle!

Down with the Washington plotters!

Down with the Union of the Four Blood-Suckers!

Long live the Alliance of the Workers' of the Far East!

Long live the Communist International!

Workers and Oppressed Peoples of the World, unite!

Item 16: The Korean Revolutionary Movement[1]
        (extract)

I.   Causes, Nature and Development of the Movement.

1. *The Aspect of the Korean Revolutionary Movement.*
The organized movement of the Korean revolution made its
first world wide echo by the independence outbreak of March
First, 1919. From then onwards, the Korean people have begun
to take an important place in the ranks of revolutionaries in the
present epoch of world reconstruction, and have been recognized as a real revolutionary people.

But the real beginning of the revolutionary movement in
Korea should not be looked for in the March event, but rather
one should go back to the fundamental causes, motives and
influences that gave rise thereto, in order to understand fully
the true nature of the movement. In other words, the historic
progress of the class struggle of the Korean people is simply a
landmark in the movement; and so, the event of the *Manse*
(Vive la Corée) demonstrations should only form an addition to
the record of historic popular experiences.

Although in order not to create confusion in our minds we
may take the March outbreak as the introduction to our
revolutionary movement, we must, nevertheless, study the
historical records which preceded and succeeded this landmark
and must get a clear conception of the causes, i.e., the beneficial
influence of the numerous activities and the effects therefrom
which gave the impetus to the sterner and more real undertaking. Therefore, the purpose of refreshing briefly the mem-
ories of the past, is to show that we are not narrating an entirely
new event.

---

[1] The author of this document is a man named Pak Kieng who is yet to
be identified fully. It seems clear from this document that Pak Kieng was a
member of the Irkutsk group. Pak read the document in English at one of
the sessions of the FCTFE. The Russian translation was made from the
English version and was read the following day. The full text is available in
English in *The First Congress of the Toilers of the Far East* (Petrograd,
1922), pp. 74-98.

2. *The Class Struggle.* [a paragraph omitted]. Thus, some of the remaining ruins and destruction of the past glory gave food for some pathetic sentimentality which worked on the imagination of the laboring and peasant masses. Korean society may be divided into two main classes—the *Yangban* (nobles and gentry) and *Ssangnom* (commoners), and although there is a middle class between the two, they are really either attached to the ruling class or are a specially privileged sect among the ruled. *Yangban* originally meant to comprise the civil and military officials but, later, it became a term designating the hereditary class, whether in or out of office, which ruled the common people and was endowed with special privileges, having in its own hands the decision over the life and death of the lower class. Thus, not only their dwellings, clothing and social system, but also the food and daily life, differed entirely from those of the common people. Although with the early abolition of the feudal appropriation of the land, the peasants could carry on their toil without great hinderance, yet, on account of the oppression by the *Yangban,* their life was turned into bitter serfdom, and, especially at the close of the Yi dynasty, the record of the reign of terror could fill many blood-stained pages.

Although the history of the class struggle of the Korean people is of slow growth, nevertheless, it was an uninterrupted, continued strife. However, it was mostly of a local nature and scope and therefore did not make itself very much felt. Any clashes between the classes were generally maneuvered to serve the interests of the political rivals of the workers. Thus, no remarkable results were obtained until the final issue in 1894, in the form of the so-called "Tonghak Rebellion," which has come to be the starting point for the pen of any historian of the Korean revolution, connecting past events with the subsequent happenings.

3. *The First Uprising of the Revolutionary Peasants— The Tonghak Rebellion.* The accumulated wrongs, especially towards the close of the 500 years rule of the Yi dynasty in the *Yangban* country of Korea, came to an unusual climax—the tide of the class struggle and the political revolution of the Korean

peasants. During the latter half of the 19th century, with the gradual eastward advance of the Western influences, the sudden and consecutive attacks on the part of the trade-cruisers of the several countries of Europe and America caused the awakening of a fraction of the ruling class, which made desolate cries for reforms and introduction of Western capitalistic ideals, which precipitated the coup d'etat of 1884. Afterwards, the intellectual class, taking upon themselves to represent the desire of the masses, took to revolutionary ideas and ideals of all creeds and colors, which gave birth to a period of nationalist movement. On the other hand, the Korean revolutionary peasant mass, realizing the unnatural state of the hereditary privileged class, and, finally, with the famine of 1893 as its direct cause, started a general uprising in the following year in a concrete and violent manner. So came the well-known Tonghak Rebellion. Although this movement of the masses took expression in the Tonghak (a religious sect) believers, and, outwardly, seemed a fanatic uprising, it was really a united upheaval of the oppressed millions against centuries of wrong and injury, and, going forward with deadly aim, it raised terror in the hearts of the superior classes in the whole East.

"Equalize the rich and the poor!" "Down with the privileged classes!"—these two were the real cries in the hearts of the Tonghaks, although some of the conservative masses were mistakenly led to an idea of "anti-West," "anti-Japan," and "clear the palaces of rascally elements" slogans, which expression was also misinterpreted as the slogan of this phenomenal upheaval. The reason for the latter lies in the fact that the political bandits, both within and outside the Government, tried to make this a weapon of propaganda in their strife for power. Also, the outside observers put the Korean Tonghak Rebellion in the same category as the Boxer Rising in China. This is because the results of those of the Boxer rebellion, which resulted in throwing open China's door to European and American capitalist exploitation.

However, this first uprising of the Korean revolutionary peasants and their united struggle created three historical phenomena in the annals of the Korean people:

a. It became the fuse that set fire to the Sino-Janesese war of 1895, which hastened the epoch of change in the whole Far East and, while, on the one hand, with the defeat and retreat of the Chinese armies to the North, it precipitated the destruction of the hereditary idea of pro-Sinoism on the part of some of the ruling class and thus undermined completely the basis of the old conservative political thought, on the other hand, it made a plea for reforms along modern lines of capitalistic statecraft, which found a few far-reaching echoes.

b. The millenium of the hereditary privileges of the ruling class of the *Yangban* suddenly lost its sublimity, and the whole system was shattered to pieces, while its foundation of support—the agricultural economic conditions—was shaken to give place to the organization of the new commercial and industrial means and occasioned the enrichment of the bourgeoisie.

c. The newly enriched bourgeoisie, having inherited the remnants of the old economic status and striving to expand themselves along capitalist lines, were finally led to welcome foreign capitalistic enterprises and to become absorbed by the accompanying exploitation.

4. *The Transition Period of the Revolutionary Movement.* [omitted]

II. *Intense Nationalistic Tendencies and Growth of Patriotism.*

5. *Rising Tide of Nationalism—the Ŭibyŏng (Righteous Army).* [omitted]
6. *Movement for Patriotic Social Culture.* [omitted]

III. *The Forcible Annexation and the Independence Movement*

7. *The Forcible Annexation.* [omitted]
8. *The Movement to Restore Independence.* The Korean people, having been forcibly annexed to Japan and finding themselves a nationally extinct people, felt more than anything

else the sudden tragic end of their history of over forty-two and a half centuries of national existence. Therefore, the revolutionary peasants and people of all classes and creeds united in a general struggle against imperial Japan and, with extreme nationalism in their hearts, became vigorous agitators for independence. In their minds they were the only really oppressed in the economic and political history of mankind, at the same time, they saw before them the Japanese, as their sole oppressors. Thus, from the day of annexation (August 29, 1910), the Korean people began to unite themselves morally and materially in a universal movement for the restoration of Korea's independence.

But the Mikado's Governor-General in Korea resorted to repressive means against the Korean movement, ten times more severe than during the "protectorate." The educational associations and other various organizations were dispersed, nearly all private schools were closed, and an attempt was made to obliterate the national history, language and culture. Of course, freedom of speech and of the press is not only prohibited but all newspapers are closed without exception, and anyone infringing this legislation was severely punished. Even the individual daily life of any one suspected as an agitator is closely "shadowed," and often he is thrown into prison and tortured without any substantial charge. Thus, one can imagine the fate which awaits any secret group or organization which is suspected of having any political aims. In following up the *Ŭibyŏng* the Japanese army made it their unfailing habit to massacre the people and to burn to the ground every village and town which was unfortunate enough to have been in the pathway of any passing *Ŭibyŏng*. Such villages and towns can be counted by the hundred. When any secret movement has been discovered, many a passer-by, although he or she may not have been in the least connected with it, and is entirely ignorant of the charge, is summarily killed with the others. There are tens of thousands of such victims, and those who are under suspicion are subjected to such economic limitations, that they are deprived of their means of livelihood. Thus, the report about "one kitchen knife to every ten houses" may not be a generally accepted fact, yet it illustrates the nature of Japan's oppression in Korea.

Under such circumstances, a large number of those connected with the movement, including those of the *Ŭibyŏng,* as well as of the different organizations, were obliged to go into exile abroad—to China, Manchuria, Siberia and America. This exile had not self-preservation for its object, but was the means of continuing and preparing for the struggle and, also, for abating somewhat the sufferings of their compatriots at home, and it was actuated by the sincerest and most self-sacrificing motives.

Yet, such organizations as the *Shinmin-hoe* [New People's Association] carried on their secret activities and kept alive the efforts of the Christian elements, together with the student leaders and energetic youths, mostly in the North; while the *Kwangpok-tan* (Restoration Society) composed of the fiery young men of the South, who had been further stimulated by the Chinese Revolution of 1911, set out to harass the enemy by destructive measures. However, the former groups received a severe blow by the wholesale arrests and imprisonment of a large number of the Christian leaders and leading educationalists of the land, under the pretext of the so-called "conspiracy case of 1911-13," while the latter's strength was greatly shattered by the premature disclosure of a plot in 1911, which caused the arrests and scattering of the majority of its most active members.

9. *Political Activities Abroad.* The Korean revolutionists who had exiled themselves abroad, in accordance with the geographical and other circumstances—whether in Siberia, Manchuria, China, or America—endeavored to keep alive the movement at home, while on the other hand, they secretly carried on the work of preparation for the inevitable day.

Nearly one million Koreans were scattered at first in Siberia, who had emigrated in the early days. By its geographical proximity to Korea, it had long been the haven of Korean political and other refugees, and, with the influx of the *Ŭibyŏng* and numerous political workers and agitators, especially since the annexation, this area was largely reinforced as one of the main bases of outside activities. Even before the annexation several organizations for the conduct of the Nationalist movement were formed in Vladivostok, such as the *Tong-in-hoe* (Cooperation Association) and others. In 1911, the *Kwŏn-ŏp-hoe* (Industrial Association) was formed, then appeared the *Chŏn-Ro Han-in-hoe* (All-Russian-Korean Association) which finally took the form of the *Taehan Kungmin Ŭi-hoe* (Korean National Council) whose organized activities were similar to those of a government. Though, on account of Russia's political changes and revolutionary events, as well as on account of the irregular coming and going of the Korean leaders themselves, the organization and its work have been readjusted to meet requirements and conditions, still it continued to be the central bulwark and one of the power stations of the Korean movement for independence.

Secondly, Manchuria, rather the northern and western Chientao also with an immigrant Korean population of nearly two million, became the nearest base of *Ŭibyŏng* and other activities outside of Korea. Although local conditions and economic means did not allow any large scaled and organized activities, yet it became the breeding ground for a number of organizations of all colors and creeds such as the *Pumin-dan* (Korean People's Association) and *Kanmin-hoe* (Chientao Korean Association) and others—and while becoming a connecting link of the home constituencies with Siberia, it naturally became the comparatively direct base for military undertakings and often managed to effect therefrom numerous armed attacks across the border in Korea, thus keeping the spark before the eyes of the people at home.

Thirdly, in America, Mexico and Hawaii the 7,000 Koreans were united into one general organization called the Korean National Association. Although few in numbers they were advantageously placed to conduct their respective work and organization in an effective way and became one of the directing forces connecting the churches and other constituencies at home with the outside activities. They have rendered considerable financial assistance since the March movement.

10. *Activities of the Religious Sects at Home.* [omitted]

11. *Seizing the Opportunity.* [omitted]

IV. The March Movement—Its Nature and Scope.

12. *The March Movement.* [omitted]
13. *Declaration of Independence.* [omitted]
14. *A Passive Movement.* The March demonstrations were a movement of non-resistance in the extremist sense of the word. Before the cold steel of the Japanese bayonet charges, suffering tens of thousands in dead and wounded, they still went forward with increased zeal and yet did not commit the least act of violence against the enemy. Vengeance had been laid aside. Although the Japanese Governor-General inaugurated a relentless slaughter and charged the crowds in a blind massacre under the pretext of retaliation for the death or minor injury of a few of their gendarmes and police from the promiscuous shooting by their own men during the general scuffle, the Koreans most rigidly carried out their first decision to do no violence at whatever cost and to demonstrate their demand with the cry of "manse" only. The Koreans' sole purpose was to show to the world the strength of their decision and their loyal adherence to the idea of "peace to all humanity." So, their passive courage was tested to the extreme, and they looked upon their own life as a mere speck to be sacrificed for the great cause. This unorganized movement of the motley crowd of peasants was orderly to the last point and devoid of any brutal violence.

The demonstrations, led by the *T'aegŭkki* (Korean national flag), went forward undaunted in the face of the firing and butchering of the Japanese soldiers and gendarmes, and often the flag-hand was shot or slashed down and replaced five to ten times in succession during the same advance until the enemy armed to his teeth dared not come further and receded of his own accord completely awestruck, when with loads of bleeding and dying bodies on their shoulders as their war trophies, the demonstrators returned homeward in a din of tragic songs and lamentations for the lost. Pogun in the Kyŏnggi province is only one of many such places, while in many localities the demonstrators met and cowed the Japanese bayonet charges with bared chests. And if one occasions any of the fiery young men, unable to withhold themselves further, attempted to show the least violence the whole throng sternly repremanded them for breaking their solemn decisions.

The motive of conducting the movement with such extreme non-resistance lies in the fact that the intellectuals and the religious leaders proposed to utilize the occasion of the Versailles Peace Conference in the vague hope of rousing the sympathy, and awakening the conscience of the *civilized* world and to obtain, if possible, their approval and interference. This was the prevailing idea with which they led the masses to their supreme sacrifices within the country and carried on their propaganda without.

15. *The Provisional Government.* [omitted]

16. *Diplomatic Efforts in Europe and America.* [omitted]

V.   *Japanese Repression and Korean Resistance.*

17. *Japanese Repression.* [omitted]
18. *Destructive Undertakings.* [omitted]
19. *Conflicts.* [omitted]
20. *The Base of the Revolutionary Army.* The Chientao affairs have undoubtedly caused a terrible setback to the expected advance on Korea and of the Korean independence army, but if one observes it from a historical point of view, it was really a turn for the better in enlarging the scope and intensifying the preparations for more effective and real undertakings in the inevitable struggle that is to come. The different units that had scattered themselves into Siberia came to realize the necessity of firmly laying the foundation for their future operations first and foremost by complete unification of the different groups and by thorough organization. Also the Chientao affairs have given occasion for the *Ŭibyŏng* in Siberia to join themselves with the incoming units under one united command, and at the same time to find ways and means of establishing a proper base for the training of men and for

efficient organization into a real fighting machinery.

In Siberia the Korean National Council was early organized and was the focus to which the northern Koreans gathered their efforts for military activities in connection with the Korean independence movement. Of course, in accordance with the change of the times and the local conditions this organization had many vicissitudes; yet for a while since 1919 it had chosen the Amur region as its center of military preparations, particularly in the way of building up an army. At the same time it came into touch directly and indirectly with the Russian revolutionary army. With the influx of the different detachments from Chientao, as mentioned above, all decided to combine the different units into one national military force and had convened themselves at Blagoveshchensk in order to accomplish this object, while linking themselves more closely with the Russian revolutionary army so that, with the latter's moral and material support, they commenced to constitute themselves into a properly organized, trained and armed force along modern lines.

Thus formerly scattered and heterogeneous Korean independence forces, after going through some unavoidable controversies,—the Blagoveshchensk conflict while in the process of unification,—finally united themselves under one command and also have become closely affiliated with Soviet Russia and the Communist International in opening up a new and definite path for the revolutionary Korean people. At present the nucleus of the Korean revolutionary army is the Korean brigade at Irkutsk, under the political supervision of the Korean Communist Party and attached to the Fifth Army of Soviet Russia which has the infantry and cavalry regiments and artillery regiment battalions etc., besides an officers' training school connected with the same.

VI. The Awakening of the Masses in Revolutionary Ideals.

21. *The Awakening of the Korean Proletariat.* The Korean people have gone through many stages of experiences and experiments in their revolutionary strife, viz., the March

movement, the Provisional Government, European and American diplomatic propaganda, minor destructive undertakings, premature armed combats, etc., and the real result they have obtained after many untold sacrifices, is their real awakening towards a genuine revolutionary movement and the entrance upon its only proper path.

This real awakening is all the more significant because it is an awakening of the Korean proletariat—that is the historic Korean revolutionary peasants and the newly conscious poor laboring masses—who had almost grown into passive indifference and are now again becoming self-conscious and are grasping the revolutionary ideals with eager and open minds. Having been themselves the real active hands in their revolutionary experiences, and having themselves made such huge sacrifices to its cause, they were naturally led in their present awakening and clear vision to class consciousness. So the people in Korea, without waiting for any Communistic propaganda from without have taken the call of class struggle of the poor peasants and workers trying to unite with all oppressed peoples of the world—and of the Far East in particular.

22. *The Uniformity of the Movement.* [omitted]

23. *Organizations of the Korean Communist Party.* While the proletarian awakening was taking place in the homeland, the revolutionary elements without took this opportunity to definitely raise the Red Flag. The Koreans residing within and about the territory of Soviet Russia having been in a position to come early into personal contact with revolutionary ideals and experiences, contributed no small share in connection with this first stage of real organized movement, thus giving birth to the constitution of the Korean Communist Party and its admittance to the Third Communist International, and joined the Korean movement with the world proletarian revolution.

Therefore, the different groups of the awakened Korean revolutionary elements are affiliating themselves with the Korean Communist Party and are trying to clasp hands with the Third Communist International, the directing power of the world revolution. And, to a certain extent, the various Korean revolutionary organizations that have convened here to attend the Congress of the Communist and Revolutionary Parties of the Far East at the invitation of the Communist International, have come with this end in view.

At present the Korean Communist Party is in fact becoming the real radiating power of the Korean revolutionary movement.

24. *Definite Revolutionary Program.* It is an open secret that the Korean revolutionary groups are rapidly turning red, but we must also not forget the fact that with the Provisional Government as their central organ the pro-American element and the religious sects— particularly the Christians—still remain to a certain extent, and their strength will not wane so very fast because of the Provisional Government with its short history, its establishments, and its personnel.

But it is a fact that the more intelligent elements among them are also awkening to the necessity of changing their methods in connection with the independence movement. The policy of the Korean Communist Party is to rally the Korean masses in a united stand against the exploitation of the imperialistic powers and to strive for the genuine emancipation of the Korean people, as the first and foremost steps to be taken. With these two main objects in view the Korean Communist Party decided to help as far as possible in the unification of the whole Korean revolutionary movement, and as a means towards such an accomplishment it is co-operating directly and indirectly with the present move on the part of the different groups to convene their respective representatives in a national constituent Congress in order to bring all the various elements into a harmonious, united and comprehensive central revolutionary directing organ. There is at present in Shanghai an Organizing Committee formed by the delegates from the different localities in order to undertake the preparation for the convoking of the said Congress.

Besides, at the occasion of the convening of the greatest Congress of the Communist and Revolutionary Parties of the Far East, the delegates from the various Korean revolutionary organizations will take it upon their shoulders to cooperate in effecting the above mentioned general unification, which fact will mark the opening of an important stage in the adoption of a definite general revolutionary program.

VII. Conclusion

25. *The Brightness of the Future.* If we summarize the above outlined facts, the Korean revolutionary movement finds its first concerted action in the early historic class struggle of the revolutionary peasants, passing through the stages of the national independence movement in reaction against the penetration of foreign exploitation. However, after numerous sacrifices, sufferings and setbacks it has finally entered upon the path of world social revolution.

The Korean revolutionary proletariat were first misguided by the different religious sects, then they relied upon the leadership of the intellectuals; but now they are really taking it into their own hands to lead the class that originally led them, to an exertion of effort towards the revolutionary accomplishment of the whole of humanity.

The future path of the Korean revolution is quite clear and certain, having joined itself to the world revolutionary movement. The future is bright.

Item 17: The Asiatic Revolutionary Movement and Imperialism[1]

We often speak of the necessity of a "united front" and "co-operative action" in connection with the revolutionary undertakings of the Far East. Recently we have come to realise this more than ever, since we have seen how the capitalistic powers of Western Europe and America have combined themselves to jointly exploit the whole of Eastern Asia. Even the great republic of America, which has made so much ado about its "altruistic" pretences and its world-wide "democratic" principles, threw off its mask at the Washington Conference when it formed the hideous quadruple agreement with the three notorious bloodsucker nations—England, France, and Japan. The First Congress of the Communist and Revolutionary Parties of the Far East, recently held at Moscow, judging from its proceedings as well as the resolutions and manifesto passed, gave expression in clear-cut language to the need of a "get-together" on the part of the peoples of Eastern Asia against the combined imperialistic aggression and continually intensifying capitalist oppression and exploitation.

However, the question is such that a "united front" must not only be discussed in theory, but should be made an *actual* fact, and that in the quickest possible way, and with the best available means. Therefore, it is now most urgent for us to take up concretely and definitely the different phases of our respective revolutionary movements in the Far East—whether it be in China, Japan, Korea, or Mongolia. Our fate is so closely interwoven, and as we have been thrown open alike to the combined attacks of capitalistic exploitation and imperialistic aggression, we can no longer stand at distances apart from each other and simply watch, with abstract negations, the complete enslavement, destruction, or final annihilation of our members.

[1] The author of this document is Kim Kyu-sik who seems to have written this article in English shortly after the FCTFE. This document is available only in English in *Communist Review,* Vol. III, no. 3 (July, 1922), pp. 137-47.

That insidious instrument called the League of Nations was formed by the association of the so-called free and independent states of this avaricious capitalist world, simply and solely to pledge one another's support in keeping the status quo at the time of the formation of this most heinous pact (see Articles X., XI., XV., XVII. of the League Covenant). It even clamped the lid down on any *prospect* of a "revolt" on the part of the oppressed peoples and weaker nations that had previously become victims of the Great Powers in their highway robbery and land-grabbing. But when the plunderers themselves could not come to a clear understanding regarding their own hideous programme regarding the permanent strangulation of their respective victims, when the senate of the very American nation that originated the scheme refused to ratify the agreement, and when they found themselves in dispute over so much of their spoils, they finally decided to "come together" and have definitely agreed among themselves even to discard, temporarily, all their differences in their combined intrigue for the complete enslavement of the exploited peoples for their own enrichment. Now we see the quadruple agreement—more vicious and decidedly of greater consequences than the Anglo-Japanese Alliance ever dreamt of being, and much more comprehensive and far-reachingly effective for their pillaging purposes than the League of Nations ever could be made to be.

In face of all this, what are *we* doing? What are we going to do? Are we really "getting together"? What are we doing to really effect this "getting together"? Let us just take a quick bird's eye-view of the present situation in the Far East and the revolutionary movement in the different countries.

The Far Eastern republic is still unable to get rid of the stranglehold that Japan has on her eastern frontiers, and there is also the combined and continued attacks of the white bandits that are being directed by the Japanese military command and aided by the cooperation of France and the other Powers. The other peoples of the Far East are, however, too weak and too much occupied with their own troubles to be able to take any active part in extending, even triflingly, a helping hand in the struggle against the combined imperialistic aggression on the

Asiatic mainland. Aside from a few hundreds of individual Koreans fighting in the ranks of the partisan units and as separate detachments, there is no cooperation of the peoples of Korea and China, even though they realise that their present slavery and oppression will be continued so long as Japan does not withdraw her military forces from Siberia. Japan still repeatedly promises to evacuate Siberia—as at the Washington and Genoa Conferences—because of a certain amount of pressure from the other Powers, and more so since the recent setbacks of the "whites," yet she still says that she will evacuate only when the life and property of her 8,000 subjects there are safe!

It is true that Mongolia, through the timely assistance of the Red Army of the Russian Far East, has been saved only recently from the clutches of Japan's imperialistic hegemony—by deliverance from the plunder and murder of Unghern and his paid maniacs and by repulsing the Chinese militarists. But the Chinese and the Korean people themselves were unable to render any assistance whatever, even in the way of necessary man-power and otherwise. Rather, the geographical remoteness and difficulty of communication made the whole question appear as a problem quite foreign to their regular line of thought, instead of a matter of vital importance to them all.

China is at present a seething cauldron of civil strifes, groaning under the iron heels of Japanese imperialistic aggression and European and American capitalistic exploitation. She is unable to manage her own affairs according to the will of her own people. Not only do the people of Korea and Mongolia simply watch with passive concern this struggle on the part of the Chinese people to establish a *real government of their own* in place of the hired and camouflaged machinery used by Japan and the other Powers, but even the Chinese people themselves are unable to act in unison of their own free will because of the nefarious intrigues and insidious underhand work of the Japanese, British, French, and American capitalists and financial groups and combines which prolong the internal factional fights and strife for the personal aims of the Chinese traitors, so that they, the foreign capitalists, may expedite and facilitate their plunder.

So we can readily understand why Korea has been struggling in a lone battle to regain her national freedom ever since she came under Japan's control. The other peoples of the Far East only took it as a matter of course when they heard that Korea had become a Japanese protectorate in 1905, and when she was finally annexed to Japan in 1910. In the same way they looked upon the March uprising of 1919 in Korea as a natural sequel in the case of a subject people trying to regain their freedom. Of course, before 1911 China herself was in the throes of suffering under the tyranny of her own Manchu despots, who were hastening the destruction of the entire nation and people; and yet the Chinese people, with the exception of a few far-sighted revolutionaries, hardly make an effort to even understand the real situation in Korea. How many of the other Far Eastern peoples realize that Korea, by her geographical position and political relations, is the Balkan Peninsula of the Far East? How many Chinese and other peoples of the Far East know that, from the strategical and historical standpoint, Korea is to China and Russia—as against Japan's imperialistic programme of absolute domination of the Asiatic mainland and mastery of the Pacific—what Belgium was to France and England's "safety" against a "Deutschland uber Alles." It is true that occasionally a few Chinese Liberal papers remark, "The teeth become cold when the lips are destroyed." But what have the Chinese people or nation really done in the way of any material or even moral support to keep the lips from being destroyed? The Mongolians understand so little about the international game of robbery that only a few—very few—of them realized that they should profit from the experiences of the Korean people.

It is needless to mention here that the non-revolutionary proletariat in Japan look upon the working masses in China and Korea not as fellow-laborers victimised by the capitalistic oppressors of their own country, but simply as creatures for them to exploit in turn as they themselves are being exploited. This is also the sad truth with regard to many Japanese artisans who are in Korea and Manchuria. The Japanese toilers (peasants and laborers) in Korea and Manchuria take advantage of the fact that they are given preferential rights in everything by the authorities and of the strong discrimination that exists in every way imaginable—work assigned, wages, hours, and treatment. This explains why the Korean people, no matter whether it be the intelligentsia or the laboring class, have an undying hatred for the reactionary Japanese elements, because of the treatment they get from the latter; and such hatred will grow more and more intensive so long as Korea is not freed from Japanese tyrannical imperialism and unrelentingly exploiting capitalism.

Will Japan Face War?

The questions that naturally follow are, What should be done? and What can be done? Much should be done, and all can be done. But before these queries are answered definitely, it will be well to meditate for a moment as to what will be the outcome of all this, or if one does not care to look too far ahead into the eventualities of this troubled world, what is going to happen in the *immediate* future. Then we shall be able to decide how we should go about it in the most effective and the quickest possible way. Of course, one can definitely foretell the future, but, judging from the past and watching the events that have led up to the present world situation, both in the West and the East, we can postulate:—*(1) From the standpoint of the European and American capitalistic Powers, the Far Eastern questions cannot be solved before Japan has had an armed clash; (2) and from the world proletariat view, when such a clash comes it will be necessary to take advantage of the situation at that time to effect the overthrow of the Japanese imperialistic capitalism in the Far East, and thus check the further advance of the Occidental exploitation of the Orient and emancipate the toiling masses of Asia and elsewhere.*

Much has been said about the probability of a war between America and Japan in the near future. During the Far Eastern Congress in Moscow, Comrade Zinoviev remarked that this clash may take place, at the latest, in about five years' time. Both the American and the Japanese public have entertained no little anxiety over such a possibility, and America's concentration of naval forces on the Pacific waters, as well as Japan's overt actions in Siberia and the Pacific islands, have only helped to confirm such fears. Many students of world politics now think that this conflict has been postponed by the "good results" attained at the Washington Conference, viz., the Quadruple Agreement. However, one only needs to consider the facts in the case, and not the spasmodic outburst of national indignation or international dissatisfaction over differences on minor issues, and one can clearly see, whether they have an agreement or not, conference or no conference, that there must be larger issues at stake before either America or Japan plunges into another war that will mean great consequences to the whole Far East and the entire world. One might briefly review the questions that rose during recent years, which seem likely to bring about such a conflict.

The questions that the United States of America wanted to settle with Japan were, and are still to a certain extent, the Yap Cable, the Siberia Evacuation, the Shantung Release, Equal Trade Opportunities and the Maintenance of the Open Door Policy in China (including Manchuria and Mongolia), and the Mexican Grudge. Japan's greatest complaint against America is the latter's immigration policy and the racial antagonism in California and the other States of the Pacific Coast. Then there is America's seemingly patronising attitude towards China and her Shantung loss. Japan also fears that America is gradually getting an immense economic hold on China by lavishly investing her surplus capital at every turn and opportunity in the development of that country's trade and industries, even to such an extent that Japan may have to fall back behind the line and make room for American capitalists when she herself was just about to eclipse England's long-standing lead in China's foreign trade. Moreover, Japan feels that America is quite capable of doing this because of her gigantic industrial development and the unlimited amount of cash at her command. However, are these real and sufficient causes to make it advisable for either America or Japan to launch into an armed struggle?

The question of the Yap Cable has been settled; but *how* has it been settled? America has control of an empty shadow of the cable line by controlling the connections between Yap, Guam, and the Philippines. Japan controls the line between Yap and Shanghai. In other words, the nominal control of the lines east and west of Yap, with no connection with the Asiatic mainland, can be of no earthly use to America whenever she has a war with Japan or when she wants to support Russia or China in case of an armed conflict between Japan and either of the two latter nations. Some Americans have boastingly said that it matters not because the United States will have so many radio stations in China to operate, besides having the cable connections between Manila and Hong Kong. But neither of these arguments will hold as far as America's interests are concerned in case of a war in the Far East, because radiograms can so easily be intercepted, as was done by the German Naval Command with the British Admiral Beatty's messages to Admiral Lord Jellicoe at the time of the Jutland battle. Besides, agreement seemed to have been reached to give up all foreign control of all radio stations in China, as a result of the Washington Conference. The cable messages can often be interrupted for weeks at a time, as for instance during the Paris Peace Conference in 1919, just when the Shantung question was being discussed and decided, the cable lines between Guam and Manila were interrupted three times, so that no communication could be made with the Far East by this channel for nearly five weeks. There were stories and rumors that a branch line had been found attached to the Guam-Manila leading straight to Nagasaki. Nevertheless, America does not care enough about entangling herself too much in the international problems of the Far East, and therefore, whether advantageous or not, or whether she has only the empty shell in the control of the Yap cable or not, she is not going to take up arms for the "trifling" affair of a cable connection with an island of only a few square miles in area, and just a mere speck somewhere in the far-away Pacific.

Of course, Korea was practically conceded to Japan by England and America in 1905, first by the revision of the Anglo-Japanese Alliance and the conclusion of the Russo-

Japanese Treaty of Peace in August and September, respectively, of the same year, and then by the purposely silent acquiescence to Japan's forcible protectorate on Korea in November. This question was not to be thought of even, much less to be mentioned or considered, no matter how many delegates and representatives the Korean people sent to Paris, Washington, or elsewhere. Therefore, there is no danger of the United States ever going to war with Japan on account of Korea, as China and Russia have done in the past.

Likewise, although a few of the United States senators, like Borah, Johnson, Reed, Norris, Thomas and others refused to ratify the Versailles Peace Treaty, because of the "Shantung Rape," even these very legislators would not dream of voting for any war budget for America to enter into a combat with Japan for any such matter. Besides, Japan has now found it necessary to save her face by agreeing to make a nominal withdrawal (from the Tsingtao-Iman Railway zone, though not from Kiaochow), while pulling the wires from behind the screen.

Siberia is a thorn in the eye for America to endure, but it is too much of a Bolshevik country for the American bourgeois democrats and reactionary republicans to fight Japan for it. America would like to "get in" on Siberian trade and natural resources by quietly asking Japan not to exercise a monopoly, but she would never go to war for this alone.

The only possible thing that might draw America into a war with Japan would be the blocking of equal trade opportunities and the closing of the "open door" of China and Japan. But even this is seemingly too materialistic and rather vague a question for the "altruistic" America to take up arms. Like France and the other experienced plunderer nations of the world, America would rather go to war to "defend justice, liberty, and human right," or to "make this earth safe for democracy," etc., and for illusioning her own as well as other peoples. In this way Japan grabbed Korea, occupied Manchuria and other parts of China, and is now staying on with a firm foothold in Eastern Siberia, *"only to maintain peace in the Far East,"* and *"to make these regions safe for life and property*

against 'bandit' attacks." The real fact is that America cannot
go to war with any nation, in any part of the world for any
cause, unless her Wall Street magnates think that it would be
profitable in the final reckoning of dollars and cents to pitch
into an armed struggle. Up till the time of the Washington
Conference and with the question of the renewal of the
Anglo-Japanese Alliance hanging overhead, it did look as if
America was chafing, because of the many difficulties her
financial groups found in connection with some of their
projects for investment of capital or for large financial and
industrial undertakings in China. After her mills and factories
had been increased and enlarged for production on such an
enormous scale, during and after the European war, and now
finding that her over-production cannot be dumped on Russia
because of the blockade policy, nor into Western Europe for the
reason that the latter wish to rehabilitate their own industrial
means, America must have control of the Chinese market and
raw material. But here she finds a snag in the fact that Japan,
with her cheap products and easy transportation, as well as by
her cunning methods of manipulating the Peking Government
authorities and Provincial Tuchuns, is able to keep out of China
nearly all foreign manufacture, and particularly American
goods. America would be willing, perhaps, to play a secondary
role in Far Eastern politics, as heretofore, if she were not
hampered in some of her financial undertakings and industrial
projects. But every time she tries to obtain a mining or railway
concession, or a permit to invest in and operate an industrial
plant, or even to establish a radio station or two, she finds that
Japan has a *priority* right or raises objection on some political
ground or otherwise. In other words, it seems as if it is not
possible for America or other Powers to have equal opportunities in trade and industry, and that the "open door" in
China is *only open to Japanese capitalists.* In these circumstances it would not take much additional provocation to draw
America to a fight with Japan, especially when we also consider
the "Mexican grudge" that America has against Japan. However,
since the Washington Conference, this conflict has been
postponed for the present. Besides, America would think twice

before actually going to war with any nation, and she would try much harder to avoid a conflict with Japan, because there is England still on the side of Japan—ever since the understanding reached by these two States about mutual assistance and reciprocal recognition of colonial and economic expansion in their respective spheres, Japan's undertakings in Korea, Manchuria, and other parts of the Far East, and England's interests on her Indian frontiers and in Central and Western Asia. Despite the hideous instrument called the Anglo-Japanese Alliance *(which has played such havoc by absolutely enslaving all the peoples of the entire Continent of Asia to Japan, England, and America)*, it would not be at all surprising to see the new Quadruple Agreement prolong its existence for ten years as stipulated by the Agreement itself (see Article III. of the said Four-Power Agreement).

In addition to the above-mentioned provocations, Japan is furious with America because of the "indignation" she claims to be suffering from the latter on the Californian or immigration question, and this is the only real issue for which she may take the initiative, as the other questions only concern her own provocative actions in the eyes of American and other nations. But, although Japan feels that she is even better prepared than America for a short and quick engagement (as was shown by statements made by Senator Reed of Missouri, on speaking of the new Naval Treaty agreed upon by the Powers as a result of the Washington Conference, from information furnished by the United States naval experts), she knows that if there should be prolonged warfare, the latter's financial resources and reserve strength far excel those of her own, and that once the conflict is started, it is likely to be a long struggle. Moreover, she realizes that just as soon as she enters into a combat with America or any other nation, Korea, China, and other nations and peoples of the Far East, and possibly some of her own working class, may keep her hands full. It will not be so easy, therefore, for Japan to precipitously plunge into a war with America, although she would like to have the first chance of giving America a slap in the face.

Japan may enter into a struggle with the Far Eastern republic of Siberia, and, through it, with Soviet Russia. However, this depends altogether on what attitude Japan takes from now on. If she continues to succeed in hoodwinking the world about her "eventual evacuation" of Siberia, and if she keeps on with her policy of abetting the white bandits and the black brigands in guerilla warfare against the Russian Far East, for the purpose of extending her imperialistic aggression on Russian territory, workers, and national resources, then naturally the Russian Far East will be compelled to enter into a real and intensive armed strife with Japan in self-defence to preserve its free existence. Of course, Japan already realizes that the Siberian expedition has been more costly than was expected, and has been, so far, a failure. Yet, so long as Japan has her present form of imperialistic government controlled by militarists, who are in turn controlled by the capitalist magnates like Mitsui, Okura, Mitsubishi and others, she will never relinquish her hold on Siberia—not any more than she will give up Korea, Manchuria, or any other of her present colonial acquisitions. If the Japanese statesmen were far-sighted enough, they would change their policy of immediate territorial expansion, and enter upon a programme of slow economic absorption. But Japan's public men and leaders are so greedy and short-sighted that they cannot see for themselves that, on account of their blind intoxication and passion for greater national grandeur and Pan-Asiatic harmony, day by day and year by year they are precipitating the nation and the people to an ultimate pitfall. Once Japan is engaged in warfare with Russia, the people of China and Korea will put all their strength and man-power to help to drive away the Japanese aggressors from the Asiatic mainland. This struggle may, after all come about before we expect it, and before the possible conflict between America and Japan. However, just at present, war-worn and famine-stricken Russia, with her lack of funds and need of economic rehabilitation, is not anxious for a life-and-death struggle with a power like Japan; while Japan herself, after having seen the resourcefulness of the Russian people during all these years of external and internal wars, in spite of all the blockades, Second International intrigues, attacks, and pressure on the part of the capitalistic powers, does not feel too sure of coming out unscathed from a real struggle with a government like the Russian Soviet Republic.

But the ultimate struggle will be between China and Japan, and this will be the *real struggle*. China, with her present unstable government, and weakened with internal strife, and foreign pressure—particularly Japanese—will not be able to declare war on Japan before she has a unified and powerful government properly constituted by the will of the Chinese people. Such a government may seem to be far off since the recent temporary defeat of the revolutionary Sun Yat-sen, but with the untiring efforts of other Chinese revolutionary leaders, together with the general tendency of the Chinese intelligentsia and students, it may not be long before the Peking Government totters down completely, as it has begun to do. The Peking Government has only been able to postpone its hour of expiration by the occasional injection of stimulants—usually of Japanese or some other capitalist source, intermingled with the manoeuvres and intrigues on the part of some powerful Tuchun or mammon politician like Hsu Shu-cheng (known as Little Hsu), Liang Shih-yih, Chang Tso-lin, and others. But, after all, the Chinese merchants and students have a powerful sway over China's economic and political situation, as has been shown time and time again by a sudden outburst of public sentiment expressing itself in a national campaign and general movement in the way of boycotts, strikes, etc., etc., as during the time of the Twenty-one Demands by Japan (1915), Yuan Shih-k'ai's (1916), the Paris Peace Conference and the Shantung Rape, and the recent Pacific Conference in Washington. So, in spite of all the underhand work and the power and influence wielded by Japan and the other capitalistic Powers of the world to keep China in a continually backward state and factional turmoil, she cannot be prevented from ultimately setting her house to order with a unified government of her own before very long. Besides, it is to the interest of Europe and America, in the long run, to deal with a stable and responsible Chinese government, in order to feel safe with regard to some of their investments, and while the imperialistic plunderers are trying to balance their power and come to an understanding in their respective exploitations. China can, in spite of them, make certain progress because of her undeveloped wealth resources, as well as by her intelligent student and working masses that are rapidly awakening to the needs of the present situation. Japan, however, will not relinquish the hold she already has on China, nor relax in her programme of aggression for some time to come, no matter what happens in China or in the outside world, unless a revolution takes place and her own imperialistic government is overthrown, and this is not likely to happen very soon. So Japan will continue to provoke China until the latter will be forced to take up arms. Moreover, when America finds that she must put a check to Japan's further advances into China and the Far East she may induce China to declare war on Japan. America would give China financial assistance and supply her with arms and ammunition and diplomatic propaganda.

In whichever case, it seems that China, sooner or later, will have to bear the brunt of a war with Japan, whether it be with America's assistance, Russia's co-operation, or by her own people with Korea's help. Japan is bound to face, before many years are past, a situation similar to that of the last days of Germany under the Kaisers and Russia under the Tsars. Although it may be only a question of time, yet the clash is inevitable one way or the other. Korea cannot expect to achieve her independence without outside aid and co-operation and without some such change in the international situation. For this reason the Koreans are endeavouring to prepare themselves for the eventual armed struggle and to seize the opportunity, whenever it comes, whether it be Japan's clash with America, Russia, or China, or when Japan is faced with a revolutionary uprising of her own working masses. In the same way, the Japanese revolutionary element, being so insignificant as yet, cannot attain its ultimate aim—whatever that be, either a political revolution and the establishment of a democratic republic or a real social revolution—before Japan herself is face to face with some outside combatant. Thus the success of the Korean revolutionary movement has a direct connection with any Japanese social upheaval and with the struggles of China and the Russian Far East against Japan. The political history of the world repeats itself wherever similar forces are at work. A political, much less a social, revolution in Japan cannot come about without affecting Korea. Without going back to the remote past, one only needs to be reminded of the far-reaching changes that have taken place in Europe—particularly mid-Europe—during recent years, and follow up the history and development of the Russian revolution.

Korea the Key to the Far East

Whether the possible changes mentioned above should come about one way or another, and whether the results be for the better or the worse, there is no getting over the fact that the *Korean question is the crucial point in the Far Eastern situation.* As already shown, Korea, with her geographical position, historical relations, and strategical advantages, has always been not only the pivot on which the Far Eastern problem revolves, but also the fuse that ignites the fire of international arms. We only need to recall to our memory the many wars that have been waged in the past between China and Japan on account of Korea—the Hideyoshi Invasions being the most notorious in the past, while the war of 1894-5 is the outstanding incident in the annals of recent decades, not to speak of the many intermediate and minor conflicts. As already mentioned, the Russo-Japanese war of 1904-5 was mainly caused by the Korean question. These facts go to show that *Korea is the key to the Far Eastern problems,* and therefore unless the question of Korea is properly settled, the whole Far Eastern situation will be in a turmoil regardless of whether it concerns Russia, China, or Japan.

This importance should not only be considered from the physical (that is, the geographical or strategical, besides the historical) and economic view-point, but also from the moral side. In the same way as the Chinese revolution had its moral influence on the Korean independence movement, so the March Movement of 1919 in Korea produced a marked effect not only on the agitation and the awakening of China and Japan, but it even had a bearing on the Indian movement to a certain extent. The Korean people have been forced to become revolutionary, *radically revolutionary,* because they have no other course. They are bound to revolt, because they know that they will be exterminated altogether if they continue to submit to Japanese oppression, while if they strike they will have nothing to lose—not any more than if they did not strike.

One need not argue at length to show that the revolutionary movement in the Far East cannot be quickly and properly achieved without making use of the very spark that causes the ignition—that is, the Korean revolutionary element.

The above brief review only goes to show that the fate of Korea is closely interwoven with the destiny of the other peoples of the Far East. The reciprocal bearing the one has on the other is of such a nature that the whole Far Eastern question cannot be dealt with, either separately or by considering the whole while ignoring any of the most vital parts. China's efforts must be assisted by Soviet Russia and co-operated in by the revolutionary masses of Korea and Japan. The Russian Far East must be defended against the encroachments of the Japanese imperialists and intrigues of the European capitalists, not by the Russians and Siberia alone, but also by the Koreans, Chinese, and Mongolians. The Korean Independence Movement must be achieved as the first step toward the final adjustment of the status of the whole Far East, not by Koreans alone, but with the assistance of Russia, China, and even with the co-operation of the Japanese working masses. The Japanese working masses must be assisted, now secretly, and later openly, by all the toiling masses of Russia, China, and Korea. We all have a common enemy, and are striving for the same goal. Therefore, it stands to reason that we should not only say that we *will* co-operate when the time and opportunity comes, but *we should co-operate NOW in preparing ourselves with plans for the future.*

PART II

THE COMMUNIST PARTIES IN KOREA

1925-35

COMMENTARY

The Communist Parties in Korea, 1925-35

AS THE fervor of revolutionary bolshevism subsided and the new Communist
order was established in Siberia and the Russian Maritime
Province, the Korean Communists who had joined and participated in the Communist activity during the period of chaos
came to realize that any meaningful Communist revolutionary
movement among the Koreans must begin with an awakening of
the toiling masses within Korea. Although the revolutionary
movement that began abroad had significant influence on the
origin of the Communist movement among Koreans, the
movement abroad had definite limitations, such as the propagation of communism only to revolutionary Koreans abroad and
immigrants; and difficulties, such as the severe factional strife
between the Irkutsk and Shanghai groups. The various groups,
though still divided, began to enter Korea in 1924 in order to
establish a party within Korea.

After the first party was secretly organized in Seoul in April,
1925, four parties rose and fell. In addition, two serious
attempts to reestablish the party in Korea after the demise of
the fourth party in 1928 were unsuccessful. Much of the
Communist activity within Korea during 1930 took the form of
regional Communist subversive action without a centrally
controlling organ. The Communists operated under extremely
adverse circumstances, including constant and efficient surveillance of the Japanese police. Although harsh Japanese suppression failed to extirpate the Communist movement in Korea,
even their regional movements dwindled to sporadic terroristic
undertakings. When the Japanese launched a "submission
operation" in addition to continued suppressive activities, many
Communists renounced communism and some even pledged
their loyalty to the Japanese emperor. The documents introduced in this section can generally be divided into three groups;
A) party actvities; B) regional activities, and C) the apostates.

A. *The Party Activities, 1925-28*

The rise and fall of the four parties within Korea was so rapid that a given party seldom had an opportunity to hold several party congresses in succession. Because all organized Communist parties were underground organizations, many records of their operation are not available. The lack of party documents and records of their undertakings is startling when contrasted with the activities and the persecutions resulting from their undertakings. This is partly due to the fact that the various parties did not write elaborate and lengthy manifestos which are customary in Communist party congress, and partly due to scarcity of documents known to have been written. For example, it seems clear from the Japanese prosecution records that the first party in April, 1925 expressed in writing a denunciation of the capitalist system and an avowal of their support for the Communist revolution in Korea, but the document in its entirety cannot be found, if indeed it did exist. The second party, in contrast, seems not to have written or issued any declaration. Generally few documents are available on either the first and the second parties or their youth organizations. Although there are no existent documents of any importance on the third party, the leaders of the third party, prior to its formation, issued a formal declaration known as the *Chŏng-u-hoe* declaration. It called for a general "change of direction" and became the foundation of the third party. The complete document in its entirety is yet to be located. The fourth party, which held an elaborate founding congress, apparently issued several to them but somewhat shorter in length (10 chapters and 57 articles) are the by-laws of the fourth party, which are also available but are omitted here.[1]

A short and very cursory seventeen-point slogan of the first party is presented here, item 20. Although its precise wordings are difficult to verify, it reflects some of the goals and programs of the first party. This slogan was uncovered during an

---

[1] See the complete text of the by-laws of the fourth party in *JFMA* reel SP 46.

interrogation of Kim Ch'an, one of the founders of the first party.

The most valuable documents of the second party are a collection known as the "Hwang-san reports," item 21. These short but important reports were written by Kang Tal-yŏng (alias Hwang-san), chairman of the second party. Most were sent to the Comintern and to his agents abroad. Eight of the fourteen reports known to have been written are available and involve factional struggle, accounts of party expenditures, establishment of bureaus abroad, and other activities of the second party. A list of the reports' titles is available and is included below. However, some important documents, such as the Report no. 1 on the "Present Condition of the KCP," (March 26, 1926), are not available. The precise meaning and implications of some of the documents are not clear, although documents such as report no. 10 on the condition of all sections of the Korean Communist Party clearly reflects the factionalism which prevailed among the Tuesday Association and the North Wind Association.[2] Aside from these documents, there are a few organizational principles on the formation of cells and fractions that the second party adopted for their operational guidelines.[3]

During the third party epoch various factional groups maneuvered for power and numerous Communists headed the party in rapid succession in a very short period of time. Only a few documents of any significance were produced and most of them are not available. In addition to the records of the Central Executive Committee meetings and the texts of the by-laws of the fourth party, there are other documents of the fourth party available, including its theses on the national emancipation movement. The latter are omitted here because they deal

[2] The Tuesday Association is a group that returned to Korea from China and Siberia to establish the first party. The North Wind Association is a rival group of returned students from Japan. See the detailed activities of these and other groups in D. S. Suh, *The Korean Communist Movement, 1918-1948* (Princeton, 1967).

[3] Full texts of these are available in Japanese, see Tsuboe Senji, *Chōsen minzoku dokuritsu undō hishi* [Secret History of the Korean People's Independence Movement], (Tokyo, 1959) pp. 619-21.

primarily with the party's unsuccessful efforts in a united front organization, *Shin'gan-hoe.*[4] The document presented here on the fourth party is a resume of the directive of the Comintern, the full text of which is unavailable. A short seven-point directive from the Comintern, it was discussed at the founding Congress of the fourth party.

Otto Kuusinen, writing in 1931, indicated that the Comintern dispatched a directive to the Korean Communist Party after the formation of the first party in 1925 in Korea. There is no record that the Korean Communists received this document, but it is perhaps the first of a few documents that the Koreans received from the Comintern. It is difficult to relate these two documents, for neither the full text of this document nor the Comintern's directive of 1925 that Kuusinen referred to are available. Furthermore this resume of the directive is available only in Japanese along with other supporting documents designed for use in prosecuting Korean Communists in a Japanese court. The fourth party is reported to have prepared a theses in reply to this directive, but it is not available. If the document can be authenticated, it is important because it follows closely the intent of the better known directive from the Comintern, the December theses of 1928, and because it is perhaps the only directive that came to the Korean Communists when the fourth party was in operation. Later Comintern directives all came after the end of the four parties within Korea.

After the fall of the fourth party, several attempts on the part of various factions, at times united but often not, were made to reestablish the party. The manifesto, item 23, of one of these organizations, the Korean Communist Party Reestablishment Association, was written on June 25, 1929, and reflects a reaction of the Korean Communists to the December Theses which came to them earlier in 1929. It closely evaluates the past party movement, and vows to reestablish the party in Korea.

---

[4] *Shin'gan-hoe* was a united front organization created jointly by the Communists and the Nationalists in January 1927. It was dissolved in 1931 when the Communists no longer found the organization useful to their purpose.

The effort failed. The political programs, item 24, which followed on December 20, 1929, appear to be the work of Han Wi-kŏn, who retreated to Shanghai following the demise of the fourth party. He and his comrades unsuccessfully attempted to reestablish the party in Korea. The platform evidently a preliminary study of some much more detailed theses appeared under the name of the Initiatory Group in the 1930's.

B. The Regional Activities, 1932-35

In contrast to the general absence of documents on the four parties and their activities during the 1920's, the regional activities of the 1930's produced a substantial number of documents. This output can be partly explained by two characteristics of the regional activities. The first is the relatively small and localized undertakings of the regional activities, which gave the Communists a chance to reevaluate their limited purpose and to concentrate on their objective of organizing and indoctrinating the local Communists. This is in contrast to the national officials of the parties who expended much time and effort in preventing the police from uncovering whatever little they had written. The second is the general growth in number of the regional activities during the early 1930's that eventually penetrated into labor and peasant movements. The fall of the four parties and the subsequent efforts to reestablish the party along with the economic chaos of the late 1920's which coincided with the rise of the regional activities, gave impetus to the Communists who capitalized on malcontent among peasants and laborers.

In addition, the lesson that the Communists learned from the early party activities led to a more mature and closer attention to smaller and important problems of an immediate and practical nature. Most of the documents concerning regional activities focus less on condemnation of the capitalist system and glorification of the Communist order, and the proclamation of the grandious idea of establishing a party to drive out the imperialists and create the Communist system, than on the

problem of particular regional operation and the tactics of
particular labor or peasant unions. Their concern was concentrated primarily on the courses of action that should be taken in
lower level organs, student cells, factories, and streetcorner
cells. This section includes material relating to regional activities
in Cholla provinces, a typical slogan of red peasant union, and a
selection from the writings of various leaders who were active in
the regional activities.

Item 25 is from a journal, *Chŏkki* [Red Flag], an organ of
the Chŏnnam League of the Korean Communist Party Reestablishment Preparation Association, and defines the role of the
regional organization. It succinctly points out the difficulties of
the Communist movement and recognized such problems as the
illegality of the movement's organization, the diversity of its
fronts, and difficulties in finance. This document and the
platform of the Chŏnnam League, item 26, are the work of Yi
Ki-t'aek,[5] a leader in the southern regional movement. The
Chŏnnam platform is merely a listing of immediate objectives
and duties of the region, but these were later developed into
detailed and comprehensive programs for the Communists. This
fact is especially noticeable in the theses of Chŏlla Pukto
regional movement, item 27.

The Chŏnpuk theses was the most comprehensive document
produced by any regional organization. The significance of this
document lies in its thorough analysis of all the problems
connected with the movement—problems concerning their
leadership and the detailed demands of laborers, peasants,
women, minors, youths, and students. Perhaps most important
is the extent of their concern with such minor but still vital
aspects of their movement as the methods of writing handbills

---

[5] Yi Ki-t'aek, alias Yi Tŭk-ryong, was born on February 15, 1904 in
Chŏlla Pukto. He was very active in the Japanese Bureau of the Korean
Communist Party, and served three-year sentence in Japan as a result of his
participation in the 8-29 incident, one of the major Koren Communist
incidents in Tokyo in 1928. Yi returned to his native province in Korea,
and worked to reestablish the Korean Communist Party. His regional
operation consisted primarily of three southern provinces of Chŏlla
Nam-Puk-to, and Kyŏngsang Namdo.

and employing barricades and the other tactics of operations in front organizations of the movement, such as the Red Labor Union, Red Peasant Union, anti-Imperialist League, and the MOPR [Mezhdunarodnoe Obshchestvo Pomoshchi Revoliuchii]. The author of the theses has not been positively identified, but the document was uncovered at the time of the arrest of Kim Ch'ŏl-ju and some 42 of his associates in Chŏlla Pukto.

Numerous materials for propaganda purposes were written by these local organizations, particularly at the time of the Japanese invasion of Manchuria. These were variously directed to the Japanese soldiers and peasants in Manchuria, sometimes in the form of condemnations and sometimes in the form of appeals. There are also numerous materials, though of little significance, that were written for various Communist memorial days, such as May Day.

Only one of the many action programs and slogans of the various regional peasant and labor unions is presented here both because these items are short and cursory and because in many cases they are similar in nature. The particular item presented here, item 28, is the slogan of the Pukch'ŏng Red Peasant Union of Hamgyŏng Namdo. It is the work of a prominent North Korean leader, Han Sang-du.[6] Much of Han's earlier Communist activities is still unknown, but in conjunction with the Red Peasant Union movement in Pukch'ŏng he was arrested along with two other leaders (Pang Pŏm-su and Chu Chin-kyŏng) and some 93 fellow workers. He served a 3-year jail sentence from 1933. There are other documents of similar nature readily available, such as the Action Programs of the Myŏngch'ŏn

---

[6] Han Sang-du is one of the very few old Korean Communists who still maintains a powerful position in the North. He began as a chairman of the Party's Hamgyŏng Pukto provincial committee in 1954. He was elected to the membership of the Central Committee of the WPK (Workers' Party of Korea) at its third congress in April 1956. He was elected to the Political Committee as one of four candidate members of the Committee. He was also elected to the Presidium of the SPA (Supreme People's Assembly) in September 1957. He held numerous cabinet posts including the Ministeries of Metal Industry in 1958, Finance in 1961. He is currently a chairman of the Commission for the Supply of Materials.

Leftist Labor Unions and the slogans of the Munch'ŏn Peasant Union.

Many important leaders emerged in the regional organizations during the 1930's, among them Yi Chae-yu, Chu Yŏng-ha, Hyŏn Chun-hyŏk, Kim Il-su, and Kang Chin. This leadership group includes some who survived the war and later became prominent political leaders in the North. There was no coordinated effort among these and other leaders on a national scale, although each did much to advance the cause of communism within Korea. Item 29, written by Chu Yŏng-ha,[7] who was very active in regional activities in both Hamgyŏng and P'yŏngan provinces during the 1930's, concerns the training of comrades. Since most of the past failures had resulted from the lack of training in underground activities, this document was written to combat the increasing rate of police arrests by teaching comrades how to keep the secrets of the party, to keep the cells intact, to act properly when captured by the police, to fight the national reformists, and to perpetuate the Communist activities within Korea.

Of like nature and written by another important Communist, Yi Chae-yu, who was martyred before the liberation of Korea, are the Communist guidelines for schools. This document is

[7] Chu is a graduate of the KUTV who returned to Korea in November 1930 to engage in Communist subversive activities in the factories of the Hŭngnam fertilizer company. Later joined by his fellow KUTV graduate, Kim Yong-bŏm, he worked in Red Labor Union in P'yŏngyang. Immediately after the liberation of Korea, Chu was one of the first leaders to emerge in the North, and became the chairman of the Wŏnsan City People's Committee in September 1945. Chu was subsequently elected to the Central Committee of the North Korean Workers' Party in 1946 and became one of the two vice-chairmen, sharing the position with Kim Il-sŏng, under the chairmanship of Kim Tu-bong. Chu was later also elected to the First Congress of the Supreme People's Assembly, and was Minister of Transportation of the first North Korean Cabinet in 1948. In October 1948, less than a month after his appointment to the Cabinet, Chu was appointed as the first ambassador from the Democratic People's Republic of Korea to the Soviet Union. He held that post for approximately three and a half years until February 1952 through the Korean War. At the Sixth Plenum of the Central Committee of the Workers' Party of Korea in August 1953, Chu was purged for his alleged participation in the power struggle to oust Kim Il-sŏng in North Korea.

omitted here as it is simply a lengthy listing of items without any concrete analysis. Yi has written another document analyzing the special characteristics of the Korean Communist movement. In it he gave a lengthy explanation of the difficulties peculiar to the Korean movement, but notwithstanding its suggestive title, "Special Characteristics of the Korean Communist Movement and Pro and Con of its Development," he said little about the possible development of the Communist movement in Korea. Most ironic and tragic for the Korean Communists, perhaps, is the fact that many of these leaders who attempted to map tactics and strategies for regional movements were later arrested and interned.

C. The Apostates

Statements made by the Korean revolutionaries, both Nationalist and Communist apostates, are available in abundance because the Japanese authorities circulated these statements in an effort to encourage others to renounce their revolution. In contrast to the simple statements made by the Nationalists which revealed aspirations for a soft and peaceful life, the Communist apostates generally made long, elaborate, and carping criticism of their movement. Regardless of the format these statements, reports "random thoughts", or whatever took, the Communist apostates usually followed a set pattern in their writing.

In general, there are three parts to these statements: first, an arduous and emotion-filled denunciation, often inadequate if not incorrect reasoning, of communism in Korea together with a fatal prophecy for the Communist movement; second, an elaborate analysis of the shortcomings of the Korean Communist movement which occasionally provided some views of their inner struggles but mostly involved the condemnation of fellow Communists in an attempt to rationalize their abandonment of the movement; and third, a sudden realization and recounting of their errors in participating in the Communist movement and a subsequent pledge of loyal support for Japan.

Only one of many of the available documents of this sort is included here, item 30. Written by Kang Mun-su,[8] a leader in regional activities in the northern provinces of Korea and an active participant in the Manchurian General Bureau of the Korean Communist Party, this selection typifies most of the writings by the apostates. Among similar writings by the Koreans actually within Korea are statements by such contemporaries of Kang Mun-su as Ch'oe P'an-ok in the southern provinces and Cho Sŏng-ho in the northern provinces. In the bureaus abroad, there were many who wrote such statements, including Kim Tu-jŏng and In Chŏng-sik of the Japanese Bureau in Tokyo, and Yi Tong-baek in Manchuria. In addition, a few prominent Japanese and Chinese Communists who had close relationships with the Korean Communists also renounced communism and encouraged the Korean Communists to abandon their revolutionary movement. Included are Sano Manabu of Japan, Li Yao-k'uei, chairman of the Manchurian Provincial Committee, and Hu Pin, chairman of the youth corps of the Manchurian Provincial Committee.[9]

[8] Kang was born in 1904 in Chientao, Manchuria, where his parents had emigrated from Hamgyŏng Pukto. He finished his grammar school in Chientao, and went to Nikolsk in the Russian Maritime Province for his high school education. He attended a normal school there, hoping to become a teacher. It was at Nikolsk where Kang came to know and admire Yi Tong-hwi. Shortly after his acquaintance with Yi, Kang received advice and a recommendation from Yi to go to Moscow to pursue his education. After the completion of three years at the normal school, Kang was enrolled at the KUTV in 1924. Kang seems to have had trouble with other Korean students at the KUTV, and it is reported that Kang was expelled from the school before his graduation. After his return to Manchuria he actively participated in the First Chientao Communist Party Incident of October 1927, but escaped the arrest. He also actively participated in the Communist Youth movement in Manchuria in the region of Kirin and T'unhua. He later came to Korea in early June 1929, and participated in the Korean Communist Party Reestablishment Preparation Association in Hamgyŏng province as a head of political section under the chairmanship of Kim Il-su. Kang was arrested in July 1931 at the time of the fifth incident in Korea, and was sentenced to a six-year imprisonment. The report was written during his imprisonment. Kang is also known as Kim Il-song.

[9] See Ch'oe P'an-ok's statement in *Kōtō keisatsu-hō* Vol. III (n.d.), pp. 1-30. For the statements by Cho Sŏng-ho and Kim Yun-kyŏng, see *Shisō*

The Communist apostates had a substantial weakening effect on the movement within Korea and on revolutionaries abroad during the 1930's, not only by divulging information concerning the underground activities of the Communists but also by encouraging other Communists to renounce their revolutionary movement. This was particularly effective when it was done by leaders of the Korean movement and by Japanese and the Chinese leaders having close relationships with the Koreans. One of the most dramatic incidents in regional activities in the 1930's involved the actions of a Japanese Professor, Miyake Shikanosuke, at the Keijō Imperial University, who sympathized and assisted a few of his students and some Communists. Among the more important Communists assisted by Professor Miyake were the late Yi Chae-yu and Pak Mun-kyu.[10] Professor Miyake was later arrested, and, during his years in prison, he wrote three of the more elaborate documents denouncing communism and severed his relationship with the Korean Communists.[11]

geppō, Vol. III, no. 4 (July 1933), pp. 31-35. For Yi Tong-baek's statement, see *Shisō geppō* published by the Ministry of Justice, no. 78 (December 1940), pp. 317-19. For the statements of submission by both Li Yao-k'uei and Hu Pin, see *Hankyō sōsho,* No. 2 (April, 1939), pp. 115-27.

[10] Pak is currently a Secretary-General of the Presidium of the North. He was elected to the post in the fourth Congress of the SPA in December 1967. He held the same position earlier from October 1959 to October 1962. Pak is an intellectual, one of the old Korean Communists who miraculously maintains high political positions in the North. He was elected to the membership of the SPA in all four Congresses from 1948 to 1967. He also held numerous cabinet ministerial positions including such Ministaries as Agriculture in the first Cabinet of 1948, State Inspection in the second Cabinet of 1957, Interior in the third Cabinet in 1962. He was originally a member of the Central Committee of the South Korean Workers' Party in 1946. He was elected to the membership of the Central Committee at the third Party Congress in 1956 and was reelected in 1961 at the fourth Party Congress. Pak was born in November 1906 in Kyŏngsang Pukto. He is one of very few Koreans who graduated from the Keijō Imperial University during the Japanese occupation of Korea.

[11] For Professor Miyake's statements, see the complete texts in *Shiso iho,* No. 1 (December 1934), pp. 109-25, and also *Shisō ihō,* No. 4 (September 1935), pp. 203-06.

A. THE PARTY ACTIVITIES, 1925-29

Item 18: Agreement between the Chinese and Japanese Police Authorities Embodying the Principles to Regulate the Residence of Koreans in Chinese Territory[1]

Article 1. For Koreans residing in Chinese territory, the Chinese authorities shall regulate their residence in accordance with the Regulations for Bandit Suppression, by which a strict census of the Koreans shall be taken; Koreans shall, after a register has been kept for each family, give a mutual guarantee for good conduct, and they shall be held responsible for each other's misconduct.

Article 2. The Chinese authorities shall issue a circular order to the various counties (hsien) within their jurisdiction, strictly forbidding the Koreans residing therein to enter the territory of Korea with arms. Any Korean who violates the provisions of this Article shall be arrested immediately and handed over to the authorities in Korea to deal with.

Article 3. The Chinese authorities shall immediately dissolve the Korean societies, cause their arms to be handed over, and conduct a search and confiscate all arms and munitions found in their possession.

Article 4. The various local authorities shall from time to time conduct a thorough search for, and cause to be confiscated, such arms and munitions as are found in the possession of Koreans, with the exception of shotguns used on farms for scaring away birds.

Article 5. The Chinese authorities shall immediately arrest and extradite those leaders of the Korean societies whose names had been designated by the authorities in Korea.

[1] This agreement was concluded on June 11, 1925 between Yu Cheng, Police Commissioner of Fengtien Province, and Miyamatsu Mitsuya, Police Commissioner of the Government-General of Korea. This document is available in Chinese, Japanese and English. The English version is available in V. K. Wellington Koo, *Memoranda Presented to the Lytton Commission,* Vol. 1 (New York, 1932), pp. 173-76. For the Chinese and Japanese version, see *JANA,* reel no. 102, (T592), 08,176-82.

Article 6. The Chinese and Japanese authorities shall notify each other of the actual facts about the suppression of the Korean societies.

Article 7. The Chinese police shall not trespass into the other's territory. In case of emergency one party may request the other to take any necessary action and vice versa.

Article 8. With reference to all cases hitherto unsettled, the two parties shall sincerely come to a settlement within a definite time.

> *June 11, 1925, at the Office of the Commissioner for Foreign Affairs of Fengtien Province.*
> *Yu Cheng, Police Commissioner of Fengtien Province*
> *Mitsuya Miyamatsu, Police Commissioner of Korea, Vice-Royalty.*

Detailed regulations governing the supervision of Koreans, as agreed upon between the Chinese and the Japanese Police authorities.

Article 1. For those Koreans residing within the jurisdiction of Tungpientao in the Province of Fengtien, the Chinese authorities shall, in accordance with the Regulations for Bandit Suppression, issue to each of them a Residence Certificate after being satisfied that he or she is a person of good character. In addition, a record is to be kept for each family, and a mutual guarantee is to be given by each Korean, with a view to facilitate supervision. The form of the Residence Certificate is to be decided upon separately.

Article 2. For those Koreans residing within the jurisdiction of Tungpientao in the province of Fengtien, after the first census has been completed, a general investigation is to be conducted once in Spring and again in Autumn (not exceeding twice a year), except in the case of monthly investigation which are necessary when changes are made in the records and guarantees.

Article 3. A Korean residing within the jurisdiction of Tungpientao in the Province of Fengtien shall, in the case of removal out of the said jurisdiction, return his or her Residence Certificate to, and apply for a Removal Certificate from the local police station five days prior to his or her removal, so as to facilitate future investigations. The form of the Removal Certificate is to be decided upon separately.

Article 4. All matters relating to an application for the arrest and extradition of Koreans as well as their arrest and extradition as provided in the Agreement of June 11, 1925 shall be carried out by the police authorities under the direction of the higher local authorities in a manner as speedy and as simple as possible.

Article 5. If a Korean of bad character is found in a county along the river on the eastern border of the Province of Fengtien, carrying arms and with intent to invade the territory of Korea across the river, he or she shall, after his or her guilt is established upon arrest and hearing by the Chinese local authorities, be extradited according to the Agreement of June 11, 1925, and handed over to the Japanese authorities in Korea across the river. For this purpose the Koreans may be handed over to the nearest Japanese police station across the river. A Korean of bad character found in the interior of the province of Fengtien shall, after his or her guilt is established upon arrest and hearing by the Chinese local authorities be handed over to the nearest Commissioner of Foreign Affairs for extradition to the Japanese consul.

Article 6. In order to prevent disastrous consequences and for the purpose of facilitating supervision, all meetings or societies held or organized or to be held or organized by Koreans residing in the Province of Fengtien, in whatever name or under whatever pretext, shall be strictly suppressed or dissolved if the existence of such meetings or societies is prejudicial to the local peace and order of China or Japan, or if their purpose is otherwise improper. Those who openly organize themselves and parade with arms shall be strongly suppressed and, upon their arrest extradited in accordance with the provisions of Article 5.

Article 7. If a group of Koreans of bad character whose arrest was applied for by the authorities in Korea are arrested by Chinese authorities, they shall, upon hearing, be extradited in accordance with the provision of Article 5. But in case there be no such person or persons as designated, the authorities in Korea shall, in order to avoid misunderstanding, be informed with a written notification.

Article 8. After receiving a request from one party, as provided in Article 7 of the Agreement of June 11, 1925, the other party shall at once take all necessary measures to meet the situation and inform the former of the results of the action the latter has taken.

Article 9. If, in case of emergency, an oral request is to be made by one party for the purpose of the preceding article, it shall be communicated to the other by sending at most two armed persons across the river with an "advice note" (the form of the "advice note" is to be decided upon separately). A written request shall be communicated between the Chief of a Chinese Police Station and the Chief of a Japanese Police Station as officers of the lowest rank.

Article 10. With a view to the realization of the Agreement of June 11, 1925, and the strict enforcement of the same, the two parties direct their respective officers and their subordinate police authorities to mutually supply information and to co-operate with frankness, so that each party may be constantly kept acquainted with the views of the other party.

Article 11. All outstanding cases between the two parties which occurred in the eastern districts of the Province of Fengtien shall be settled in a mutual spirit of sincerity and fairness by the local authorities of both parties within five months from the date of signature of the present regulations. In case any dispute arises in the future, it shall likewise be settled by the local authorities of both parties in a fair manner.

Article 12. The present Regulation shall be promulgated and enforced by the two parties respectively on and from the day when the exchange of the same takes place.

July 8, 1925 at the Office of the Police Commissioner of Fengtien Province.
Yu Cheng
N. Kunimoto for Mitsuya Miyamatsu

Item 19:   By-Laws of the Korean Communist Party[1]

CHAPTER I. GENERAL RULES

Article 1. This party is named the Korean Communist Party.

Article 2. This party has its headquarters in Korea.

Article 3. This party considers the fulfillment of the political programs of the party as its primary objective.

CHAPTER II. MEMBERSHIP

Article 4. Membership in the party shall be of two kinds: regular membership and probationary membership.

Article 5. The party receives its regular members from those who served terms of the probationary period as probationary members or from the members of the Korean Communist Youth Association.

Article 6. The probationary members shall serve in the subsidiary revolutionary organs and uphold the objectives of the party.

Article 7. The probationary period for probationary members is as follows:

1. Laborers . . . two months or more.

2. Peasants and small industrialists who do not exploit other laborers . . . six months or more.

3. Office workers and others . . . one year or more.

Article 8. All those who seek admission to the Party who are in categories 1 and 2 of Article 7 shall have three recommendations: one from a regular member of the Party, one from a basic leader, and one from an officer of the particular local Executive

---

[1] This is the by-laws of the first party, April 1925. It is not clear who actually wrote the by-laws. The first chairman of the party was Kim Chae-bong. Many provisions are similar to the Yi Tong-hwi's by-laws of May 1921. This document is available, so far, only in Japanese in *JANA,* reel 102 (T625), 08,790-806.

Committee of the Party (when there is no Executive Committee of that particular region, an officer of the Central Executive Committee can recommend in place of the local officer). All those who seek admission to the Party who are in the third category of Article 7 shall have four recommendations: one from a regular member of the Party, one from a basic leader, one from an officer of the particular regional Executive Committee (when there is no regional Executive Committee, a recommendation must be obtained from the Central Executive Committee), and one from a member of the Central Executive Committee. An application for admission is decided upon by the Central Executive Committee. An application to become a probationary member of the Party requires two recommendations, one from a regular party member and one from a basic leader, and the application is decided upon by the Central Executive Committee.

Article 9. Any person who is a member of other revolutionary organizations and has served the party with special contribution or merit can become a member of the Party with a recommendation from a basic leader, two recommendations from two members of the Provincial Executive Committee (the Provincial Executive Committee can be substituted for by the Central Executive Committee), and two recommendations from two members of the Central Executive Committee.

Article 10. All young men who are twenty-five years of age or younger must first become members of the Korean Communist Youth Association, and can become members of the Party only after the approval of the Central Executive Committee of the Youth Association.

Article 11. Any member of the Party who is moving from one district organization to another must receive permission from the Executive Committee of the district, and must register his move in the new district where he has moved.

Article 12. Party members shall enjoy the following rights and privileges: 1) participation in discussions, 2) participation in decision-making, 3) the right to elect and, 4) to be elected (only those members who were admitted before the end of 1925). These rights and privileges do not apply to probationary members.

Article 13. Party members shall perform the following duties:

1. Strict observance of party rules and platforms.
2. Obedience to the decisions of the party organ and party factions.
3. Presence at the meetings of the party organs and its factions.
4. Payment of dues.
5. Report of old and new incidents and conditions of the party and other relevant activities.
6. Strict observance of party secrets.

The probationary members are to be responsible only to duties 5 and 6 of those stated above.

CHAPTER III. PARTY ORGANIZATION

Article 14. The organizations of the Party are as follows:

1. Basic organs; the basic association with a basic leader in a factory, farm village, army, government, or school.
2. County organs; the county organization consists of the county convention and a county executive committee.
3. Provincial organs; the provincial convention and a provincial executive committee.
4. Central organs; the Party Congress and a Central Executive Committee. There shall be liaison offices in Manchuria, Vladivostok, Japan, Shanghai, and in other places under the direction of the Central Executive Committee.

Article 15. The levels of authority and responsibility, as well as the line of obedience to decisions shall be as follows: the basic leader, basic association, county executive committee, provincial executive committee, central executive committee, the national Congress.

Article 16. The organizational structures from the central organs to the county level organs must obey decisions of the

Central Executive Committee, and organs at the county level
and below must obey decisions of the Provincial Executive
Committee.

CHAPTER IV. BASIC ORGANIZATION

Article 17. The basic association of the party is composed of
three or more members in a certain industrial center; it can be
established by the county Executive Committee and must be
approved by the Provincial Executive Committee. However,
when there are less than three members of the Party in a certain
industrial center, one member must establish the basis for a
basic organization and must receive directives from the Executive Committee of that region, or he must join an existing basic
organization.

Article 18. Basic association meetings are called by the basic
leader as follows: 1) regular meeting, once per week; 2) ad hoc
meeting, at any time when there is an emergency or a directive
from the higher organization.

Article 19. Duties of the basic association are as follows:

1. Meetings of the members.
2. Discussion of the reports of the members.
3. Propagation of the slogans and the decisions of the Party
to the masses.
4. Training of the Party members.
5. Various duties of organization and propaganda.
6. Participation in the political and economic life of the
community.

Article 20. The basic association shall elect its basic leader of
the organization. On special occasions, the Executive Committee of the region can appoint the basic leader.

Article 21. The basic leader shall represent and direct the
basic organization.

Article 22. A basic inspector shall be elected by the basic
organization. In special circumstances, the basic inspector can
be appointed by the Executive Committee of the region.

Article 23. The basic inspector shall examine the general conditions and finances of the basic organization.

CHAPTER V. COUNTY ORGANIZATION

Article 24. The highest organization in a county is the County Congress.

Article 25. The County Congress shall be organized with representatives of the party members in the county.

Article 26. The number of representatives to attend the County Congress shall be determined by the Provincial Executive Committee.

Article 27. The County Congress shall not come into session unless a majority of the representatives are present.

Article 28. The County Congress shall be called by the County Executive Committee as follows:

1. Regular Meeting, once a year.
2. Ad hoc meeting, called by the County Executive Committee in case of an emergency situation.

Article 29. The County Congress shall discuss the following:

1. Discussion of the reports of the County Executive Committee and Inspection Committee.
2. Election of members of the County Executive Committee and Inspection Committee. Under special circumstances, the Central Executive Committee can appoint these.
3. Election of candidate members of the County Executive Committee and Inspection Committee. Under special circumstances, the Central Executive Committee can appoint these.

Article 30. The number of members of the County Executive and Inspection Committees shall be determined by the County Congress.

Article 31. The term of office of the members of the County Executive and Inspection Committees shall be one year. Members whose terms have expired can be reelected.

Article 32. The County Executive Committee shall consist of members elected by the County Congress. A vacancy in the County Executive Committee shall be filled by a candidate member, elected by the County Congress, who is elected by the County Executive Committee and approved by the Central Executive Committee. Under special circumstances a new member can be elected in a special election.

Article 33. The County Executive organ is the highest organ during the period from one County Congress to the next County Congress.

Article 34. The County Executive Committee shall have the following duties:

1. Direction of the work of the basic organizations in the County.

2. Organization and propaganda.

3. Calling meetings of the basic leaders in the county.

4. Making a monthly report of the activities within the county to the Provincial Executive Committee. Giving notices to the basic organizations in the county.

5. Organizing and leading factions in the front organizations of the county.

Article 35. The County Executive Committee shall have the following bureaus, and assign to them members of the Executive Committee: 1) Secretariat, 2) Organization Bureau, 3) Propaganda Bureau.

Article 36. The County Executive Committee shall elect a secretary of the Committee from among the members of the Committee. Under special circumstances, the Central Executive Committee can appoint the secretary.

Article 37. The secretary shall represent and lead the County Executive Committee.

Article 38. The County Inspection Committee shall consist of members elected by the County Congress. A vacancy in the County Inspection Committee shall be filled by a candidate member, elected by the County Congress, who is elected by the County Executive Committee and approved by the Central

Executive Committee. Under special circumstances a new member can be elected in a special election.

Article 39. The County Inspection Committee shall inspect the conditions of the County Executive Committee and the financial accounts of the County.

Article 40. The County Inspection Committee shall elect one person to be chairman of the Committee. Under special conditions, the Central Executive Committee can appoint the chairman.

Article 41. The chairman of the County Inspection Committee shall lead and supervise the activities of the Committee.

CHAPTER VI. PROVINCIAL ORGANIZATION

Article 42. The highest organization of a province is the Provincial Congress.

Article 43. The Provincial Congress shall be organized with representatives of the party members in the province.

Article 44. The number of representatives to attend the Provincial Congress shall be determined by the Central Executive Committee.

Article 45. The Provincial Congress shall be in session with the majority of the members present.

Article 46. The Provincial Congress shall be called by the Provincial Executive Committee as follows:

1. Regular Meeting, once a year.

2. Ad hoc meeting, at a time of emergency, by the decision of the Provincial Executive Committee or by a directive from the Central Executive Committee.

Article 47. The Provincial Congress shall discuss the following matters:

1. Discussion of reports from the Provincial Executive Committee and the Inspection Committee.

2. Election of members to the Provincial Executive Committee and the Inspection Committee.

3. Election of Candidate members to the Provincial Executive Committee and the Inspection Committee. Under special circumstances, the Central Executive Committee can appoint these.

Article 48. The number of members of the Provincial Executive Committee and the Inspection Committee shall be determined by the Provincial Congress.

Article 49. The term of office of the members of the Provincial Executive and Inspection Committees shall be one year. Members whose terms have expired can be reelected.

Article 50. The Provincial Executive Committee shall be organized by the members elected at the Provincial Congress. A vacancy in the Provincial Executive Committee shall be filled by a candidate member, elected by the Provincial Congress, who is elected by the Provincial Executive Committee and approved by the Central Executive Committee. Under special circumstances a new member can be elected in a special election.

Article 51. The Provincial Executive Committee shall be the highest executive organ between the Provincial Congresses.

Article 52. The Provincial Executive Committee shall have the following duties:

1. Direction of the work of the County organizations in the Province.

2. Organization and Propaganda.

3. Calling meetings of the representatives of the County Executive Committees for consultation.

4. Reporting monthly to the Central Executive Committee concerning the activities within the Province, and giving notice to the organs within the province.

5. Organizing and leading factions in the front organizations of the province.

Article 53. The Provincial Executive Committee shall have the following bureaus, and assign to them members of the Executive Committee: 1) Secretariat, 2) Organization Bureau, 3) Propaganda Bureau.

Article 54. The Provincial Executive Committee shall elect a Secretary of the Committee from among the members of the Committee. Under special circumstances, the Central Executive Committee can appoint the secretary.

Article 55. The secretary of the Provincial Executive Committee shall represent as well as direct the Provincial Executive Committee.

Article 56. The Provincial Inspection Committee shall consist of members elected by the Provincial Congress. A vacancy in the Provincial Inspection Committee shall be filled by a candidate member, elected by the Provincial Congress, who is elected by the Provincial Executive Committee and approved by the Central Executive Committee. Under special circumstances a new member can be elected in a special election.

Article 57. The Provincial Inspection Committee shall inspect the work and the accounts of the Provincial Executive Committee.

Article 58. The Provincial Inspection Committee shall elect one person to be chairman of the Committee. Under special circumstances, this person can be appointed by the Central Executive Committee.

Article 59. The chairman of the Provincial Inspection Committee shall lead and supervise the activities of the Committee.

CHAPTER VII. CENTRAL ORGANIZATION

Article 60. The highest organization of the Party is the Party Congress.

Article 61. The Party Congress shall be organized with the representatives of the Party members.

Article 62. The number of representatives to attend the Party Congress shall be determined by the Central Executive Committee.

Article 63. The Party Congress shall be in session with the majority of the members present.

Article 64. The Party Congress shall be called by the Central Executive Committee as follows:

1. Regular meeting, once a year.
2. Ad hoc meeting, at a time of emergency, by the decision of the Central Executive Committee.

Article 65. The Party Congress shall discuss the following matters:

1. Discussion of the reports of the Central Executive Committee and the Central Inspection Committee.
2. Discussion of current problems and making decisions on party policies.
3. Amending the party platforms, by-laws and regulations.
4. Election of the members of the Central Executive Committee and the Central Inspection Committee.
5. Election of Candidate members to the Central Executive Committee and the Central Inspection Committee.*

Article 67. The term of office of the members of the Central Executive Committee and the Central Inspection Committee is one year, and members can be reelected.

Article 68. The Central Executive Committee shall be organized with the members elected at the Party Congress. A vacancy in the Central Executive Committee can be filled by a candidate member, elected by the Party Congress, who is elected by the Central Executive Committee. Under special circumstances a new member can be elected in a special election.

Article 69. The Central Executive Committee shall execute the following matters:

1. Making the party record.
2. Directing the work of the Provincial organizations.
3. Planning and executing all party activities.
4. Control of party finances.
5. Organization and propaganda.
6. Opening enlarged committee meetings.

*Article 66 does not appear in the original document.

7. Sending reports describing the condition of party activities every two months to various provincial organs.

8. Election of the representatives to the Communist International and to the Enlarged Committees.

9. Directing the activities of various factions in the front organizations throughout the country.

Article 70. The Central Executive Committee shall have the following bureaus and assign to them members of the Central Executive Committee: 1) Secretariat, 2) Organization Bureau, 3) Propaganda Bureau, Special bureaus, such as a Women's Bureau and others, can be established by the decision of the Central Executive Committee.

Article 71. The Central Executive Committee shall elect one member of the Committee as the Secretary of the Party.

Article 72. The Secretary of the Party shall direct and represent the Central Executive Committee.

Article 73. The Central Inspection Committee shall consist of members elected by the Party Congress. A vacancy in the Committee shall be filled by a candidate member, elected by the Party Congress, and decided upon by the Central Executive Committee.

Article 74. The Central Inspection Committee shall inspect the work of the Central Executive Committee and the financial accounts of the Party.

Article 75. The Central Inspection Committee shall elect a person to be chairman of the Committee. Under special circumstances, this person can be appointed by the Central Executive Committee.

Article 76. The chairman of the Central Inspection Committee shall represent and supervise the Committee.

CHAPTER VIII. FINANCES

Article 77. The revenues of the Party are derived from membership dues and other income.

Article 78. The membership fees are as follows:

1. Those without income . . . ten cents and up.
2. Those with income . . . . . three per cent of total income.

This does not apply to the probationary members.

Article 79. The fiscal year for the Party begins with the closing day of the Party Congress and ends the day before the opening day of the next Congress.

Article 80. The budget of the party organs shall be decided by the respective Executive Committees (all those below Provincial Executive Committees shall require approval of the Central Executive Committee), and must be reported to and approved by the regular Party meetings.

CHAPTER IX. FRACTION ORGANIZATIONS

Article 81. When there are three or more regular party members present in a front organization, a fraction shall be organized. Each Executive Committee can direct its members to participate or withdraw from the fraction activities.

Article 82. Each fraction shall propagate the policies of the party and influence the masses, and direct the front organization activities.

Article 83. There are two kinds of fractions in the Party.

1. Ad hoc fraction . . . . each front organization's Congress
2. Standing fraction . . . . Executive Committee of each front organization.

Article 84. Each fraction must follow the direction of its regional superior organization.

Article 85. A member of the regional executive Committee must be present at each fraction meeting.

Article 86. A fraction meeting must decide the following in advance: 1) candidate officers of the front organizations, 2) discussion items of the front organization movement.

Article 87. Each fraction shall elect a leader of the fraction. Under special circumstances, the regional Executive Committee can appoint the leader.

Article 88. The fraction leader has the duty of leading and supervising fraction activities.

Article 89. If the front organization has a fraction of the Korean Communist Youth Association, all can join the fraction in a joint effort.

CHAPTER X. PUNISHMENTS

Article 90. Any party member who fits into any one of the following categories shall be expelled from the Party upon verification by the Central Executive Committee

1. A member who did not perform his duty.
2. A member who is absent from three consecutive meetings of the basic organization.
3. A member who does not pay dues three times.

Article 91. Any organ of the party that does not follow the directives of the superior organ shall be dissolved by the decision of the Central Executive Committee.

CHAPTER XI. RELATIONSHIP WITH THE KOREAN COMMUNIST YOUTH ASSOCIATION

Article 92. This Party directs the activities of the Korean Communist Youth Association.

Article 93. One member of each level of Executive Committee of the Party shall be a member of the Executive Committee of that respective level of the Korean Communist Youth Association.

CHAPTER XII. SUPPLEMENTARY RULES

Article 94. These by-laws become effective from the day of adoption.

Article 95. These by-laws can be amended only in the Party Congress.

Item 20: Slogans of the Korean Communist Party[1]

1. Complete overthrow of the Japanese imperialist rule and complete independence of Korea.

2. Establishment of an eight-hour labor law (six-hour law for minors), establishment of a minimum wage, unemployment compensation and relief, and establishment of social security.

3. Political, economical, and social equality for women. Payment of maternity benefits and granting of a set period of rest with pay prior to and after birth.

4. Compulsory education and professional education for all at government expense.

5. Abolition of all miscellaneous taxes, and establishment of one progressive income tax.

6. Freedom of speech, assembly, and association. Abolition of the slave education of the colonial authority.

7. Exposure of the deceptions of the social opportunists and national reformists.

8. Change the imperialistic war of exploitation to an anti-imperialistic war of revolution.

9. Support the Chinese Soviet revolution. Support the Soviet Union.

10. Down with Japanese imperialism. Destroy all feudalistic forces. Long live Korean national emancipation. Long live the Communist International.

11. Korea is Korea for the Koreans.

12. Overthrow the yoke of the Governor-General's tyranny.

13. Make elementary education a compulsory education. Use the Korean language in schools. Replace the principals of elementary schools with Koreans. Give freedom of student

---

[1] This document lists 17 slogans of the Korean Communist Party (the first party of April 1925). The slogans first appeared at the interrogation of Kim Ch'an, a ranking member of the Central Executive Committee of the KCP. It is not clear whether Kim Ch'an recounted these slogans by memory or a copy of a document listing these slogans was uncovered at his trial. This document is available in many places but only in Japanese. Each slogan of the document is the same in every source. See among others: *Shisö iho*, no. 4 (July 1931), and also *JFMA*, reel 355 (S.9.4.5.1-2).

association to the students of the High Schools. Universities must center their attention on Koreans.

14. Abolish the Asia Development Company. Abolish the Japanese Immigration Systems. Abolish the County Farmers Association.

15. Boycott Japanese goods. All Korean bureaucrats in the Government must resign. All Japanese factory workers should have general strikes.

16. Do not pay tenant fees to the Japanese landowners. Do not learn from Japanese education. Sever all commercial relations with Japanese merchants.

17. Free the imprisoned revolutionaries. Withdraw the armies and gendarms.

Item 21: Hwang-san Reports[1]

No. 1   Report on the Present Conditions of the Korean Communist Party (March 26, 1926). [not available]

No. 2   Report on theSendingof [Korean] Representatives [to the Comintern]. [not available]

No. 3   Report on the Sending of Additional Delegates from the Central Executive Committee. [not available]

No. 4   Reports on the Election of the Central Inspection Committee Members and Revolutionary Committee members. [not available]

No. 5   Letter to Comrade Kim Ch'an.

No. 6   Report on the Aliases of a Member of the Central Executive Committee. [not available]

No. 7   Letter explaining the Budget of the Party.

No. 8   a. Opinions on the Problems of the Russian Maritime Province. [not available]
b. Directive based on the Investigation Reports on the Conditions in Shanghai and Manchuria.

No. 9   To Comrade Cho Tong-u.
Letter Explaining the Problems of the Russian Maritime Province. [not available]

No. 10   Report on the Conditions of all Sections of the Korean Communist Party.

No. 11   Report on the Establishment of the Interim Shanghai Liaison Office.

No. 12   Report on the Establishment of the Interim Japanese Bureau. [not available]

[1] This document consists of 14 separate reports written by Kang Tal-yŏng, alias Hwang-san, the Chairman of the second party of the KCP in 1926. Only 6 reports (nos. 5, 7, 8b, 10, 11, 14) out of 14 are available and presented here. Report no. 9, a letter to Cho Tong-u, explaining the problems of the Russian Maritime Province is not available, but a note on Cho Tong-u is inserted. These reports were written during March and April of 1926. These reports are available in Japanese in *Shisō geppō*, Vol. II, no. 8 (November 15, 1932), and also in Vol. II, no. 9 (December 15, 1932).

No. 13   Report on the Establishment of the Manchurian General Bureau, [not available]
No. 14   Letter to Kim Ch'an, Chairman of the Manchurian General Bureau, April 6, 1926.

Report No. 5.   Letter to Kim Ch'an[2] in the Shanghai Liaison Office

1. Cho Pong-am[3] is not a member of the Central Executive Committee.

2. The Manchurian General Bureau is yet to be established.

3. Kim Chŏng-kyu and Yi Pong-su have been sent to Japan to contact the Japanese Communist Party.

4. Since it became dangerous [to be here] as a result of

---

[2] Kim Ch'an: Kim is one of the seventeen charter members of the Korean Communist Party. Kim was very active in the early stages of party operation and became chief of the party's propaganda section. He was born in 1893 in Myŏngch'ŏn, Hamgyŏng Pukto, studied at Meiji University of Japan for a short period of time, but left school to organize *Ch'ŏlhyŏl-tan* [The Blood and Iron Corps] in Japan to attack pro-Japanese Koreans in Japan. Kim escaped the arrest of the First Party Incident and fled to Shanghai, and was directed to succeed Cho Pong-am in organizing the Manchurian General Bureau. He did organize the Manchurian General Bureau for the Tuesday Association group, but he soon fell into the camp of the liquidationists who advocated complete liquidation of Communist activities in favor of the Nationalist movement. He was later expelled from the Party for this. Kim was arrested on April 10, 1931 at Harbin, but even after his release he abstained from the Communist activities and joined hands with the Nationalists in Manchuria and worked for *Chŏng'ŭi-bu,* a Nationalist organization. After the liberation of Korea in 1945, Kim appeared briefly in North Korea. He was elected to the Central Inspection Committee of the North Korean Workers' Party in August 1946, and was elected to the membership of the Central Committee of the Workers' Party in its second congress in March, 1948. Kim was known by many names; such as Kim Nak-jun, Hwang Ki-ryong, Kim Su-am, Kim Pyŏng-gu, and others.

[3] Cho Pong-am was one of the founding members of the KCP in 1925. He was the first official delegate to the Komsomol, the Communist Youth International. He left Korea for Moscow in 1925, thus avoiding the arrest during the first incident. He apparently was not elected to the Central Executive Committee of the Second Party.

the First Party Incident [Shinŭiju Incident],[4] Kang is going down to Chinju to work in *Chosŏn ilbo* [Korean Daily, newspaper] for a month.

5. There is a general lack of funds in the Party, and it is essential that the Party receive some financial contribution.

April 6, 1926
Hwang-san

Report No. 7   Letter Explaining the Budget of the Party

Fiscal Year, 1926

Expenditures:
A.	For Party Congress	3,600 yen
B.	For Party Organizations	134,840 yen*
C.	For Party Activities	215,360 yen
D.	For Reserve	10,000 yen

Details of the Expenses:
A. For Party Congress—details not given.
B. For Party Organizations:

1.	National Organs	41,600 yen
2.	Provincial Organizations	62,900 yen
3.	Manchurian General Bureau	10,400 yen
4.	Interim Japanese Bureau	11,020 yen
5.	Interim Shanghai Liaison Office	6,760 yen
6.	Interim Vladivostok Office	2,160 yen
		134,840 yen*

C. For Party Activities—details not given.
D. For Reserve—details not given.

---

[4] The first Party Incident is often referred to as the Shinŭiju Incident because the first arrest that resulted in the mass arrest fatal to the first party occurred in a town called Shinŭiju.

Report No. 8.

    a. not available

    b. Directive Based on the Investigation Reports on the Conditions of Shanghai and Manchuria [extracts, meaning is not clear, dated March 10, 1926]

    The reports of Chin To-sŏng, who recently returned to Korea from Shanghai to comrade Kim Ch'ŏl-su: there are six or seven men led by Yi Tong-hwi and Ke Pong-u in Vladivostok who consulted with Pak Ŭng-ch'il who was sent by Yun Cha-yŏng and Yi Yŏng [to establish a Bureau in Manchuria]. They have also consulted with Cho Pong-am and this was reported to Yŏ Un-hyŏng by Chŏng Paek.

Report No. 9.   To Comrade Cho Tong-u[5]

    Letter Explaining the Problems of the Russian Maritime Province. [not available]

---

[5] Cho Tong-u: Cho was the first official representative of the Korean Communist Party of 1925 to the Comintern. He was born in 1892 in Ch'ŏngsan, Okch'ŏn County, Ch'ungch'ŏng Pukto. He studied in Shanghai and participated in the formation of the Korean Provisional Government in 1919. He was arrested in 1920 in his role in the organization of the New Thought Research Association, and was imprisoned for four years. When he was released, he helped found the first party of 1925, and left Korea for the Comintern as its official delegate. After reporting to the Comintern and receiving recognition from the Comintern of the Korean Communist Party as a section of the Comintern, Cho returned to Shanghai only to be arrested on January 27, 1928 with Chŏng T'ae-hi. After his release he again attempted to reestablish the party in Korea under the direction of the Comintern's Far Eastern Bureau, but was again arrested in 1933 and was imprisoned for two years. After the liberation of Korea in 1945, he was briefly mentioned in the defunct Korean People's Republic as an acting Minister of the Internal Affairs. Cho did not participate in North or South Korean politics. He is also known as Chang Tae-jin.

Report No. 10. Report on the Conditions of All Sections of the Korean Communist Party

TO THE CENTRAL EXECUTIVE COMMITTEE OF THE COMINTERN:

Concerning the measures taken to expel party members:

The following members of the Party have been expelled from the Party: Kim Yak-su, Sŏ Chŏng-hi, Chŏng Un-hae, Kim Ma-myŏng, Shin Ch'ŏl, Yi Ho, Pae Tŏk-su, Song Pong-u, Yi Kyu-sŏng, Yi Ch'ung-bok, Yi Hŏn, Cho Tong-hyŏk.

The reasons for their expulsion are as follows:

1. Kim Yak-su, Sŏ Chŏng-hi and Chŏng Un-hae had neglected the by-laws of the Party and had committed reactionary activities against the Party. They also committed the crime of revealing the party secrets during the First Party Incident [Shinŭiju Incident].

2. The above named persons hero-worshipped Kim Yak-su, and they mismanaged the relief fund, in the amount of 20,000 yen, by depositing the fund under the name of Kim Yak-su for the purpose of utilizing it as expenses for propaganda activities of the North Wind Association. Furthermore, when vacancies occurred in the Central Executive Committee after the First Party Incident, these men ignored the by-laws of the Party and freely appointed persons from their own faction.

3. When the newspaper, *Chosŏn Ilbo* [Korean Daily], was closed, Kim Yak-su crushed the effort to revive the paper by the Party.

4. The Party was very lenient in not expelling him at that time. The Party made a special effort to make Kim Yak-su realize his mistakes and repent, but he neither showed any sign of repentance nor corrected his past mistakes. Furthermore, one of his followers, Song Pong-u, had an affair with Hŏ Chŏng-suk, fianceé of our comrade Im Wŏn-kün, who is suffering in jail, for the purpose of acquiring the secrets of the Tuesday Association.

5. After the First Incident [Shinŭiju Incident], Kim had

erroneously supported the expulsion of the Shinhŭng Youth League from the Hanyang Youth League.

6. These men of the North Wind Association sent two men of their group, Yi Hŏn and Shin Ch'ŏl to Vladivostok to contact the remaining Irkutsk Group leaders, Ch'oe Ko-ryŏ and Kim Ha-sŏk, and conspired to destroy the party. (The Seoul faction sent two of their men, Kim Yong-man and Ch'oe Ch'ang-ik, to counter the efforts of the North Wind Association).

7. On March 30 [1926], these men had summoned the delegates of the Korean Labor-Farmer League, who came to Seoul to attend their national Executive Committee meeting in a restaurant, Yŏlpin-lu, and had announced the fall of our Party and attempted to create a new Party. The expenses for this occasion were met by the relief fund.

8. These men of the North Wind Association had conspired with the Seoul Faction to destroy the party and establish one of their own faction.

April 6, 1926.

Hwang-san
Chairman
Central Executive Committee
Korean Communist Party

Report No. 11.   Report to the Comintern concerning the Establishment of the Interim Shanghai Liaison Office.

Because of the difficulties involved in direct correspondence with the Party in Korea, all correspondence from the Comintern to the Party is to be handled by the Interim Shanghai Liaison Office. The following are the officers in charge of the office:

Chairman, Kim Tan-ya
Members, Cho Tong-u and Kim Ch'an

Report No. 14. Letter to Kim Ch'an, Chairman of the Man-
churian General Bureau. (April 6, 1926)

The following are appointed to posts in the Manchurian
General Bureau:

> Chairman, Kim Ch'an.
> Members of the Executive Committee:
> > Cho Pong-am (alias Pak Ch'ŏl-hwan), Pak Ung-ch'il, Ke
> > Pong-u, and one Chinese assistant.

The range of the activities of the Bureau is as follows:

1. Control of all lower organizations and their activities.
2. Organization of basic organs and cells in Manchuria.
3. All other activities and planning for the bureau are based
strictly on the by-laws of this party.

Item 22: Directives of the Communist International[1]

1. The first and foremost task of the Party is to liquidate all factional differences and to unify the remnants of previous party members to establish a strong and sound party. The Comintern supports the decision of the Party in their fight against the Seoul Youth Association in an effort to liquidate factional differences and to organize a new revolutionary Communist youth group during the period from August 18 to November 14, 1926.

2. The social composition of the membership of the Korean Communist Party does not meet the need to solve the problems confronting the Party. The intelligentsia should be replaced by more laborers and peasants.

3. The Party must penetrate deep into the factories and villages.

4. The mere organization of a proletarian vanguard is not sufficient; the Party must strive to organize labor unions and peasant unions.

5. ,The Party must lead not only the proletariat but also the peasants.

6. The Korean Communist Party must win over the national revolutionary mass parties.

7. The Party must lead and direct the national mass parties, and indoctrinate the elites with Marxist and Leninist doctrine.

[1] This short seven-point directive of the Comintern was discussed at the founding Congress of the fourth Party on February 27, 1928. This document seems more like a resume of a full text. The fourth Congress is reported to have written a reply to this directive but neither the reply nor the full text is available. This document which may have been written in English or Russian is available only in Japanese in *JFMA,* reel S 722 (S.9.4.5.2-30), report of November 28, 1928.

Item 23: Manifesto of the Korean Communist Party Reestablishment Preparation Association[1]

To all Korean Communist Comrades:

Advancing definitively from the period of historical inevitability the class struggle of the Korean proletariat is now confronted with the important step of making fundamental and qualitative changes. There is no doubt that the Korean proletariat movement has made a rapid development due to subjective ideological conditions and objective circumstances during the past ten years, making progress step by step towards the ultimate realization of communism in Korea. However, in view of the special conditions prevailing in Korea, it has been necessary as a preparatory process in the formation of a class party and a vanguard party, to confront a period of confusion and other miscellaneous difficulties. Thus, cunning history has once again forced us to undergo unimaginably difficult experiences, had taught us invaluable lessons, and has shown us the path of our true victory.

It is a fact that the internal difficulties of world capitalism have reached a limit and that their center of operations has moved to Asia, thus bringing the danger of an imperialist's war to the Pacific. It is a characteristic of the recent world condition that the Capitalist's imperialistic army is concentrated in the Pacific against the international proletariat.

These conditions determine the Japanese imperialistic position, its role, and their extremely reactionary politics. Their expanding financial monetary capital forces the government to prepare for a new war and to launch aggression, making inevitable their confrontation with the Soviet Union and the Chinese revolutionaries. Their fear of the rising proletariat

[1] This Manifesto was issued on June 25, 1929. The chairman of the KCP Reestablishment Preparation Association was Kim Ch'ŏl-su, but it is not clear who wrote this manifesto, because Kim was soon arrested. This manifesto which was written in Korean is available in Japanese in *Shisō geppo*, No. 6 (September 1931), and it is also available in *JFMA*, reel S 355 (S.9.4.5.1-2).

movement in their own country, as well as the revolutionary movements of their colonial countries of Korea and Taiwan, forces them to increase harshness daily in their reactionary oppressive policy. Their foremost target is the destruction of the Communist party, which is the best representative of and the leading element of the proletariat class.

Particularly in Korea, the great arrests of past two to three years have reached the limit of torture, murder, imprisonment and other ruthless and brutal measures, resulting in our loss of more than five hundred of our best revolutionaries, and these oppressive measures are continuing against the rise of the socialist and other revolutionary movements. The fearful black cloud of white terror is pressing heavily upon Korea, and Japanese oppression reached its limit and became sheer violence when they began to punish those who had expressed mere complaints.

How did we answer this unreasonable, barbarous oppression? The rank and file of the Korean Communists were mercilessly defeated under enemy pressure. We must realize, with great pain, the defeat of our past efforts. Among the various circumstantial conditions, the more obvious tendencies of our struggle are the appearance of cowardly rightist thoughts and dangerous ultra-leftist thoughts. It is a reality of the Korean revolutionary movement that the Korean Communists failed to supply the vanguard leadership for the naturally rising revolutionary fervor of the oppressed masses, who daily suffer loss of their livelihood under the Japanese. Under these circumstances, the Korean Communists must thoroughly reexamine the basic difficulties and study the shortcomings of the movement, and make constructive criticisms for the self-examination of each member.

From the very beginning, the Korean proletariat movement was plagued with factional struggles, and its development was accompanied by factional development. Many factions were born in this process, such as the Shanghai faction, the Irkutsk faction, the Seoul faction, the Tuesday Association faction, the M.L. faction, and others. These factions attributed the development of the movement to the birth and growth of their own faction. It is true that there was a difference in their policies, reasonings, and practices, but in truth they were all merely movements of thought groups that were filled with and led by petit bourgeoisie and intelligentsia. Thus, they were separated from the masses and engaged purely in factional struggles. The factions produced more factions and their struggles brought more factional struggles, and there were no strict and disciplined secret organizations. They showed their special characteristics as petit-bourgeoisie and intelligentsia by cowardly engaging in small problems of daily concern instead of attacking the fundamental problems, and by attempting to solve noble and great problems instead of undertaking the practical problems of the masses. Greatly impressed by proletarian ideology, they dealt with problems unscientifically, with slander rather than with principles, and engaged themselves solely with the benefit of their faction rather than of the toiling class. These are the greatest shortcomings of the Korean Communist movement; however, confronted with a most important transitional period, the Korean Communists must rectify the fundamental contradictions and destroy the fetters that keep them from progress. What are the attitudes that they must take? There are difficulties that accompany as in all the fronts of our movement, but it is our duty to face these difficulties and problems, and to concentrate all our efforts to reestablish a party that will correctly represent all the benefits of the proletariat.

First of all, we must go to the laborers and their factories, particularly to the industrial laborers and the poor peasants; we must engage in the proletarian mass movement and establish a firm leadership of the proletariat by changing the foundation of the party to the laboring class. We must thus establish a firm and disciplined organization, and, at the same time, we must be firm in our ideological, disciplinary and theoretical foundation for establishing a Leninist party through a united and common struggle. Only through this process can the Korean Communists face the historically necessary mission of our time. The past factional struggles are all erroneous, and all Korean Communists must abandon their factional affiliations, as well as courageously dissolve their factions. In all Korean Communist fronts the most arduous and faithful elements are gathered under the banner of the Korean Communist Party Reestablishment Preparation Association to carry out our historical mission in Korea.

The kind of criticism of our past and reappraisal of our task in reestablishing a united bolshevik party are both the demands of our proletariat and the course directed by the Comintern. However, we must point out the various views and activities of the remnants of the petit bourgeoisie, who do not have ability to criticise themselves and carry out the movement. It is futile to compare our efforts to unify the movement, based upon a firm theoretical origin, with the efforts, based upon infantile theories, of a new faction of those who deny all their past leaders. However, the following are a few points of caution to which we must pay attention.

1. Contrary to our position, there are those who advocate independent individual activities in the factories and thus a natural growth of the party, but we know that they deny a unified leadership and disperse our efforts in order to create their own new faction to recreate the past.

2. There are others who blindly advocate the organization of "elite" elements. These elite elements are those who hide from the masses and engage solely in conceptual discourses in the rear, and thus once they appear on the open stage, their true picture can be easily discerned, because they fail to analyze the fundamental historical process, except mechanically as a phase of social progress. Their dialectics are replaced by eclecticism, and it is inevitable that they have special characteristics of subjective, self-centered judgement. Thus, their efforts in attempting to hide in old or new factions, to enlarge the factional domains, or to use the new factions to enhance their control are nothing more than unprincipled attempts under eclecticism.

3. There are those gamblers among the leaders who attempt to pursue factional struggles and to decide the fate of the party by the outcome of the factional struggles. They are petit

bourgeoisie who are most afraid of self-criticism; they failed to understand the directive from the Comintern and by deceiving the workers, tried to utilize proletarian ideology to strengthen their faction, falsely calling it the Korean Communist Party. It is of no use to point out that these are blind people who do not comprehend their own contradictions and mistakes, and it is easy to reveal that these are the ones who advocate the extension of factional strife in the movement. The Korean Communists must rid themselves of all remnants of such past demands and errors and must attempt to reestablish a party under a fundamentally new approach.

Comrades:

The heroic Korean proletariat has fought the poisonous, unprecedented thieves of Japanese imperialism under the most adverse of conditions, and we are now standing on the threshhold of writing the first page of the establishment of a class party from this past struggle. Our truly enduring party has developed through many revolutions, which created a scene of carnage littered with the bodies of our comrades, and we are trained with the bloodshed of our comrades. This important task must be performed through criticism of the past, self-criticism, and the most courageous and profound self-denial.

Comrades of the Korean Communist Movement:

Let's go into the laboring masses.

Fundamentally liquidate all unprincipled factional struggle. Strengthen discipline and a strict and well organized party. Reestablish a Leninist, Bolshevik and Unified Communist Party.

Reestablish through struggle.

Dear Comrades of the Korean Communist Movement:

Unite under the banner of the Korean Communist Party Reestablishment Preparation Association

POLITICAL PLATFORM:

1. The Korean Communist movement in the past struggled for the revolutionary development of the proletariat, but in truth this was a movement of a few intelligentsia and their thought organizations. Although they were a section of the Comintern, they engaged in unprincipled factional struggle, disengaged themselves from the masses and shamelessly revealed the nature of petit bourgeoisie, but this was, for us, the preparatory process in the establishment of truly Leninist Bolshevik Party.

2. The present stage of the Korean Communist Movement: The most important and decisive duties of the Korean Communist Party establishment movement are to end the factional struggle and to realize the mass movement. The party membership must be changed from the intelligentsia to the laborers, and the party leadership from intelligentsia leadership to labor leadership, thus transforming the party into a truly Leninist and Bolshevist movement. This is the demand of the present Korean proletariat movement and the directive from the Comintern.

3. The Korean Communist Party Reestablishment Preparation Association is making fundamental criticisms of the past, realizing fully the present situation of the Party, and is striving to organize the party under Leninist principles. Everyone must abandon his past and join the Korean Communist Party Reestablishment Preparation Association, the only organization to reestablish a theoretically, ideologically and practically unified organization.

4. The Korean Communist Party Reestablishment Preparation Association is the successor to all the past Communist revolutionary activities and considers it a duty to lead all political organizations and their struggle to reestablish the Party.

5. The Korean Communist Party Reestablishment Preparation Association must carry out the above duties.

Item 24: Political Programs[1]

I.   The Korean Revolution and the World Situation

A.   Recognize the decision of the Sixth Congress of the Comintern (December theses).

B.   The Korean revolution is a bourgeois democratic revolution, but it is a part of the world revolution because its vanguard is directed against Japanese imperialism.

II.   Characteristics of the Present Stage of the Korean Revolution and Our Strategem

A.   Special characteristics of the Korean revolution are as follows:

1.   Japanese imperialism is pressing all segments of our society.

2.   Existence of private ownership of land by landlords.

3.   The bourgeois class is extremely weak and most of the bourgeoisie are in the landlord class.

4.   The proletariat class is yet in its infantile stage.

5.   Existence of large number of peasants who demand land reform.

6.   The Korean revolution is in part dependent upon the process of the world proletariat revolution.

B.   The present stage of the Korean revolution is that of the bourgeois democratic revolution, from its social characteristics. There is no scientific truth in the statement that the present stage of the Korean revolution is already that of the proletarian revolution.

[1] This program was issued on December 20, 1929. It is most likely that the program was written by Han Wi-kŏn, the leader of the Sixth Incident. This document is available in Korean, its original language, in *Lenin chuŭi,* Vol. II, no. 1 (January 15, 1930), pp. 1-30.

C.   The central objectives of the present stage of the revolution are emancipation from Japanese imperialism and land reform. However, these two great duties are unseparable, and, therefore, unless complete emancipation is accomplished the land reforms cannot be realized, and unless a great peasant revolution accompanies the national emancipation struggle it is difficult to accomplish the revolution of emancipation.

D.   Although at its present stage the Korean revolution is a bourgeois democratic revolution, the vanguard of the bourgeoisie must be the proletariat. The proletarian class must become the leading force, and their unions must be the center for the city's petty bourgeoisie, intelligentsia and bourgeoisie; they must unify the resistance of the Korean revolutionaries against Japanese imperialism.

E.   It is necessary that the Korean proletarian revolutionaries dissociate themselves from those forces that endanger and interfere with our revolution and they must withdraw from the purely national bourgeois revolution. Consequently, it is necessary for the Korean proletarian revolution to isolate the bourgeois elements in order to bring victory to the revolution.

F.   The political power that results from the bourgeois democratic revolution must be in the hands of the proletariat and the peasants. Large numbers of the working masses must participate in national affairs, and a government of proletarian soviet must be established in order to bring the workers' democratic dictatorship.

G.   Although the first step of the Korean revolution is the bourgeois democratic revolution, this is merely a predecessor to the socialist revolution. It is a mistaken idea that the realization of the socialist revolution can be accomplished without completion of the bourgeois democratic revolutionary stage, and, at the same time, it is also a mistaken idea that there exists a wall of ten thousand miles between the bourgeois democratic revolution and the socialist revolution. The very existence of countries with a proletarian dictatorship and the world proletarian revolutionary movement are assurances of and assistances to the victory of the socialist revolution in Korea.

III. Political Programs of the Present Stage of the Korean Revolution

A.   Overthrow of Japanese imperialism.

B.   Complete national independence.

C.   Establishment of a proletarian soviet government.

D.   Nationalization of large industries and confiscation of all Japanese capital and banks.

E.   Confiscation of land from the large landowners and distribution of the land to the tillers.

F.   Eight-hour labor laws, protection of wage increases, establishment of relief and security systems.

G.   Abolition of miscellaneous taxes, establishment of uniform progressive tax systems.

H.   Association with the world proletarian masses.

IV. Criticism of the Past Korean Revolutionary Movement

A.   The history of the Korean revolutionary movement and the Communist movement.

1.   The Korean revolutionary movement can be divided into three periods. The first period began shortly after the March First Movement by the national revolutionaries; during this period there was no proletarian revolution.

2.   The beginning of the proletarian revolution was the second period. During this period, the activities of the Communist intelligentsia replaced those of the national revolutionaries. This process eventually brought about a confrontation of the proletarian movement and the independence movement of the national revolutionaries. Korean emancipation was not the ultimate purpose of the Korean Communists.

3.   The third period was the period of the "change of direction". This is the period of united efforts by all national revolutionary fronts. It was during this period that the Korean Communists first realized that the present

stage of the Korean revolution is that of the bourgeois democratic revolution and they attempted to understand the characteristics of the Korean national revolutionaries, the necessity of Korean independence, and the need for cooperation with revolutionaries other than the proletarian revolutionaries. Thus began the cooperation of the Communists and the nationalist revolutionaries.

B.   The more important shortcomings of the past revolutionary activities by the Korean Communists are as follows:

1.   Communist party establishment movement and factionalism.

a.   It was the history of factional struggles that led the Korean Communists to their failure to create favorable conditions for an effective Communist movement.

b.   The more important reasons for the failure of the Korean Communists to establish a party are:

i.   the rank and file all consisted of intelligentsia and there was a general lack of a proletarian base.

ii.   the lack of understanding of Communist revolutionary theory; their unions among themselves were not based upon theoretical understanding, but rather on their factions.

iii.   the low level of leadership of the masses.

c.   The factionalism enervated the Communist movement and this has its social origin in feudalistic diversion.

d.   The Communists failed completely because they failed to revamp the basis of the class composition of the party and failed to rid themselves of factional struggles, but rather engaged in prolongation of their past endeavors.

2.   Indifference concerning the theory of communism.

a.   Because of the lack of understanding of and general indifference to Communist theories, the Communists failed to devise good tactics and strategy for the movement.

b.   Although a few Communist leaders today attempt to study the theories of communism, most of their attempts are confined to a formal, duplicative, and abstract study, for the most part on dead issues of communism.

3.   Lack of understanding of the relationship between the Communists and the laboring class.

a.   The Communists thought of themselves as something other than the laboring class and considered themselves as benefactors of the laboring masses. The Communist party was not understood to be the party of the laborers, but rather it was a party of the intelligentsia who worked for the laboring class.

b.   The slogan, "Let's go to the factories," sounded as though the Communists had progressed, but this also was the outcry of one member of the intelligentsia to another.

4.   Policy concerning the economy of Korea.

a.   The Communists first thought that economic struggles, such as strikes, tenant disputes, and other struggles of the laborers, were the highest forms of struggle.

b.   The Communists thus downgraded the Nationalists, who were engaged in a political struggle and refused to cooperate with them.

c.   This was somewhat corrected by the

"change of direction," but it is not completely
rectified.

5.   Important mistakes in the change of direction
and the united front.

a.   Tendency to downgrade the economic
struggle and the natural growth of the movement.
The supporters of the change of direction of the
Korean Communists put forth such slogans as
"Change from economic struggle to political
struggle," and "Change from the natural growth
movement to objective and conscious movement,"
and they advocated the rectification of past economic
and non-political activities, but they committed a
serious error in downgrading the economic struggle of
the masses and the natural growth movement. Their
lack of understanding concerning the united effort of
political and economic struggle forced them to
neglect the affairs of the labor unions and the
economic struggles of the peasants.
b.   A change of direction without the laboring
masses was only a change of direction of the
intelligentsia, and the masses remained as they were.
c.   Negligence of class positions because of the
united front. It was a step forward from the time of
the anti-united front period to form a united front
with other anti-imperialist revolutionary groups, but
it was two steps backward when the Communists
neglected class consciousness and advocated the
abolition of the class movement in the united front. It
was the action of opportunists to advocate the abolition of independent Communist activities and the labor
class movement for the sake of the united front, to
refrain from criticism of the anti-proletarian elements
in the united front, and to reject and refuse the
hegemony of the proletariat in the national emancipation movement. These are the reasons for the creation

of the present united front organizations, *Shin'gan-hoe.* It is now impossible for the Communists to lead this organization, and it is led mostly by the national reformists.

6.   On lawful and secret movements.

a.   The common consensus now is to reject lawful revolutionary activities and to return to secret revolutionary activities.

b.   It is now disadvantageous to utilize lawful organizations to operate various activities.

c.   There is little future in the secret movement.

7.   Important shortcomings of the labor union movement.

a.   Weakening of the organization of industrial laborers.

b.   Unions are not centered on factories, occupations, and industries.

c.   General lack of Communist leadership in factory organizations.

d.   General lack of contact between the political and economic struggles.

e.   General lack of Communist leadership in various strikes.

f.   Failure to recruit young laborers and women laborers into the unions.

8.   Important shortcomings of the peasant movement.

a.   General lack of adequate understanding of the peasant movement.

b.   Lack of organization.

c.   General lack of activities in farming villages.

       d.   Peasant movement did not have the land reform movement as its ultimate objective.

V. *The Present Situation of the Korean Revolutionary Movement*

       1.   Intensification of the poisonous Japanese imperialistic colonial policies.

       2.   Uncertain future of the capitalist states.

       3.   The Japanese have intensified their pressure to prevent the development of the Korean revolutionary movement, and have also attempted to transform the national revolutionaries into national reformists.

       4.   The great slump of the Korean revolutionary movement.

       5.   The most significant characteristic of the present stage of the Korean revolution is the unevenness in the subjective condition and objective situation of the Korean revolution. The natural growth movement of the masses, laborers and peasants, and students is progressing rapidly. The objective situations of today arouse the masses despite oppression and the unpreparedness of the subjective conditions. The Pul-i tenant disputes, the Wonsan labor disputes, and general student demonstrations throughout the country are the most representative examples of this fact. Among these, the most basic laboring struggle is the most profound class struggle of them all.

VI. *Our Present Duties*

       1. Duty to devise new tactics and strategy.

       2. Reestablishment of a Communist Party and liquidation of all factions. In order to attain this:

       a.   Start activities among the laborers.

       b.   Change the foundation of the party from the intelligentsia to the laboring masses.

       c.   Create cells in every factory.

    d.   Strive to learn revolutionary theories.

    e.   Win over the laboring masses of the proletariat and the peasants.

    f.   Develop the skills for secret activities.

    g.   Correct all past mistakes.

3. Duty to win over the laboring masses:

    a.   The present strategy of the Korean Communists lies in the acquisition of the laboring masses.

    b.   The Korean Communists must spearhead the leadership of the laborers in their struggle against the capitalists and of the farmers in their struggle against the landlords.

    c.   In their leadership the Korean Communists must be such as to lead these struggles and not be authoritative or mechanical in their leadership.

4. Duty in the struggle against the national reformists:

    a.   National reformism is a national danger.

    b.   The Communists must isolate and expose the national reformists and those who advocate autonomy under the Japanese.

    c.   The Communists must expose all shades of reformists and intelligentsia and their dealings with the Japanese.

    d.   The provincial, county, and city councils are the best examples for exposing the deceitfulness of the Japanese imperialists and the true picture of the Korean national reformists.

    e.   The Korean autonomy movement is nothing but a movement to interfere with the Korean emancipation movement. There is no support of the people for the Korean autonomy movement, but if the intelligentsia and the bourgeoisie join the movement, it can become dangerous. Raise your voices louder in repeating the slogan "Down with the autonomy movement."

5. Duty in the national united front.

a.   It is absolutely necessary to form a united front of certain elements of the national bourgeoisie and intelligentsia with the Korean proletariat and peasants in their struggle against Japanese imperialism. We must struggle against these ultra-leftist infantile elements who refuse to join the united front. At the same time it is also important to struggle against those elements that are willing to abandon the Communist class struggle in the formation of the united front.

b.   The following are points needing special caution in the formation of the united front.

i.   The basis of the united front must be the proletariat and the peasants.

ii.   The Communists must have assurance of their right to independent activities as well as the right to criticize the non-proletarian elements in the united front. These conditions must be fully understood in the united front.

iii.   The united front must have a connection with the peasant struggle for land reforms.

iv.   The proletariat must strive to take the hegemony of the united front.

c.   The various organizations in the united front, such as *Shin'gan-hoe, Kŭn'u-hoe,* and the *Youth Federations,* cannot show any force in the struggle. It is important to win over these organizations, but it is the duty of the Communists to engage in an independent struggle to win over the masses of laborers and peasants.

6. Duty in the secret movement.

a.   Under the adverse conditions of our movement, we must change our form of struggle, reduce open struggles and master underground and secret activities.

b.   The secret movement is not confined to Communist activities, but also must be applied to the political and economic movements of the masses, the laborer's struggle against the owners, the farmer's struggle against the landlords, and the students' struggle against the schools, and other organizations must also master secret movement organizations and other skills.

7.   Duty in the labor movement.

a.   The most important is the workers' movement.

b.   The important points in the workers' movement are:

(1) acquisition of the large labor unions that include all factory, mine and railroad workers, and other transportation workers.

(2) the past movement that was not centered on the factories was a mistake.

(3) communism is the only ideology that should be taught.

(4) lead effectively the daily struggles of the workers.

(5) a flexible leadership should be applied, so that past mistakes are not repeated.

(6) intensify the youth and women's movements.

8.   Duty in the peasant movement.

a.   The central slogan is confiscation of the land from the landowners and distribution to the tillers.

b.   Tactical policy in the peasant movement should center on the landlords. We must form a proletarian army with the poor peasants in the villages, acquire the middle class farmers as allies, and neutralize the rich farmers.

c.   *Formation of the peasant organization.* A peasant Guild, Peasant Committee, Peasant Consumer

Association, and others must be organized.

d.   Reduction of taxes on farmers, reduction of tenant fees, a fight against the usurers, assurance of tenancy, increase of wages in the villages, abolition of forced prices, abolition of forced labor, and other demands of these types should be the center of the peasant struggle.

9.   Problems of other groups.

a.   The Communist must unite all groups. The joint struggle should enhance the liquidation of factional struggles and the establishment of the party.

b.   Constructive criticism of each group and among the comrades in an effort to rid all shortcomings of an anti-bolshevik nature.

10.   International duty.

a.   Support the Soviet Union and the Chinese revolution against Japanese imperialism.

b.   Strive for unification of the world's revolutionary movement, together with the Japanese and Chinese Communists.

December 20, 1929

B. THE REGIONAL ACTIVITIES, 1932-35

Item 25: Our League as a Regional Organization[1]

We have audaciously expressed in a previous declaration the fact that our league is a regional organization of the Korean Communist Party engaged in an effort to reestablish the Party, but we think it is necessary to expatiate on our purpose and to give a proper understanding of our league to the general working masses.

The fact that Korean Communists have a regional organization, despite the united front, may have some of the dangerous characteristics of a factional strife and may, indeed, sound peculiar to those small number of people who are not familiar with the reality of Korea. However, a detailed analysis of our struggle proves this to be the truth. Mere sentimental hope is not enough to produce correct tactics and strategy. In fact, the task confronting the Korean Communists today is the task of unification of all fronts; however, the method that should be employed to bring about this united front successfully can become apparent only as a result of comprehensive analytical research on the detailed subjective and objective conditions.

Our front is extremely dispersed. Not only is it dispersed, but there is no mass organization of peasants and laborers to speak of. On the other hand, our enemy's cunning spy policy and mad terror policy resulting from their aggressive wars show their extreme barbarity. We must know that the internal and external conditions confronting us today are quite different from those faced by the Russian Party during early 1900 in its unification problems, and from the reestablishment problems faced by the Japanese party in 1924. Therefore, if a few of our comrades hastily organize a national organization and dispatch organizers

---

[1] This declaration was made by the Chŏlla Namdo branch of the KCP Reestablishment Preparation Association under the leadership of Yi Ki-t'aek. The declaration was issued in Korean and first appeared in a journal *Chŏkki* [Red Flag], no. 1 (July 15, 1933). Neither the journal nor the declaration is, so far, available. This translation was made from Japanese available in *Shisō geppō,* Vol. IV, no. 1 (April 1934), pp. 39-41.

to various regions and call it a national party, this is not a party, because, as Lenin said, such a party is of no use, even if a few leaders, who have a close relationship with the masses but are incapable of leading them, call their organization a party. This cannot even become a preparatory organization for the reestablishment of the Party, because an organization that does not have the masses as its base facilitates the intrusion of spies, who can easily expose the organization to our enemies even before the formation of the party. Of course, it is nothing but reactionary reasoning to say that we must be satisfied with a regional organization only.

From the above analogy we assert that in order to accomplish the organization of a national body we must first organize regional organizations. These Communist revolutionary organizations must always lead the struggle of the masses, and by training the masses politically and establishing a firm discipline in the organization, the party must root deep into the masses. These sound developments in the regional organizations necessarily bring unity of all fronts. Only the united front that results from these processes can truly be the basis of a disciplined bolshevik party. However, this does not mean that we must have regional organizations in all thirteen provinces of Korea before we can attempt to establish a national party. The organization of a national party must come when at least several regional organizations have their roots deep into the important organizations. Thus, the development of the regional organizations should not be carried out independently, and different regional organizations, although they may undertake their tasks independently with strictly independent organizations, must have a close cooperation of the revolutionaries and an exchange of their party organs and news. Thus, these mutual direct and indirect relationships of the various regional organizations can become an important lever in eliminating all dangers of factionalism.

Some of our comrades criticise this reasoning as anarchistic, but, comrades, the difficulties of our revolutionary movement, such as the illegality of our organization, the diversity of our fronts, the lack of revolutionary comrades and the difficulties of our finances, do not fall away like floating clouds in a blue sky. These difficulties can only be eliminated one by one through a persistent struggle that reflects the reality and persistence of various difficult and unbearable revolutionary conditions. Therefore, it is incorrect to criticise us in this difficult stage of our endeavor, pointing out the small regional diversities in the present stage of the movement.

Comrades: forget the dream of creating a national organization in one sweep, without any obstacle in front of our path.

Let us struggle courageously without rest for theoretically sound objectives.

Unify the vanguard fronts with struggle.

Enlarge and enforce the Communist regional organizations.

Destroy sectarianism and opportunism.

Long live the Chŏnnam League of the Korean Communist Party reestablishment movement.

Long live the reestablishment of the Korean Communist Party.

Fight with a demonstration on August 1, International Red Day.

Item 26: Platform of the Chŏlla Namdo League[1]

DUTY AND PLATFORM OF OUR LEAGUE

The Japanese imperialists are ruling with an absolute dictatorial rule and are oppressing the toiling masses of Korea.
Politically they fetter all political freedoms by depriving the
people of their basic rights, and economically they exploit the
people by monopolizing all the basic means of production, such
as the land, factories, mines, transportation, and other large
economic organs. Because Korea is a colony, serving only the
interests of Japanese imperialism as a supplier of natural
resources, its modern industrial development is extremely
meager, its feudalistic agrarian system has not been changed,
most of the land is owned by the Japanese imperialists and a
few local landowners, and the majority of the Korean peasants
suffer famine caused by these imperialists. Furthermore, the
peasants who do own a small patch of land are suffering from
excessive taxes and are fast becoming the subjects of the
Japanese imperialistic usurers.

The peasants who lost their land and even the privilege of
taking the roots of herbs and the bark of trees have had to leave
their villages. In the towns and villages there are great masses of
unemployed. The peasants who lost their lands and the
hundreds and thousands of laborers who were thrown out of
the factories are forming a great unemployed mass suffering
famine and poverty.

The Japanese imperialistic war policy, which attempts to
destroy the Soviet Union and the Chinese revolution and tries
to make a monopolistic colony of all of Asia, is creating a tragic
situation of famine and poverty by lowering the wages of the

[1] This platform was written by Yi Ki-t'aek, alias Yi Tŭk-ryong, who
returned to Korea from Japan to head the regional organization of Chŏlla
Namdo. Yi earlier served a jail term in Japan as a result of his participation
in the 8-29 incident. This platform was issued in May 1933, and it is
available only in Japanese in *Shisō geppō,* Vol. IV, no. 1 (April 1934), pp.
36-39.

laborers in inverse proportion to the murderous inflationary rise in prices. The laborers and peasants realize that their future is either death or a struggle against these imperialists. However, in their struggles the masses and their organizations are suffering from the merciless military and police terror of the imperialists, and their renewed efforts in the struggle, by changing from daily economic struggles to a more comprehensive political struggle, have met crushing blows. But the incessant increase in daily economic struggles in the villages and factories is a sign of the advance of revolutionary efforts, and, at the same time, this is the moment for a great socialistic, national and political struggle to fight for rice, land, and the freedom of our people.

The current Korean revolution is an anti-imperialist revolution. It is part of the coming world revolution, and it is a bourgeois democratic revolution that is fast becoming a socialist revolution with the material and spiritual aid of the advanced countries. With these tactical views, the following general action platforms are properly listed for the present revolutionary stage.

1. Complete overthrow of the Japanese imperialistic military police and bureaucratic dictatorial political systems, and complete independence of Korea.

2. Creation of a soviet republic of the Korean laborers and peasants.

3. Confiscation of all the Japanese imperialists' financial and industrial enterprises in Korea: banks, railways, sea transportation, mines, factories, and all other establishments. Nationalization of these confiscated enterprises by the Korean soviet state.

4. Confiscation of all the Japanese imperialists' companies, religious shrines and churches, and those of all the other parasitic landowners. Distribution of these confiscated goods to the working masses and peasants. Nullification of all the credits of landlords, banks, usurers, and financial guilds.

5. Enactment of eight-hour labor laws and fundamental reform of the living condition of the laborers.

6. Opposition to imperialistic wars.

7. Support of the Soviet Union and the Chinese soviet revolution.

Now is the preparatory stage of the revolution. In order successfully to accomplish this revolution, which demands the absolute hegemony of the proletariat, the leadership of the proletarian vanguard party must include peasants and laborers, small artisans, and the petty bourgeoisie. In order to win the masses of toilers, and revolutionary camps must first separate these masses from the fascist national reformists who, instead of carrying on a revolutionary struggle for complete national emancipation, have conspired with the Japanese imperialists and entertain the illusion that the Japanese imperialistic military advance to Manchuria may bring some advantages to the Koreans. It is also necessary to separate the as yet unawakened masses of the people from these social reformists and their legal organizations and from the officers of these organizations.

In order to carry out these broad political objectives, the immediate needs are to reestablish the party and to consolidate our heroic revolutionary organization.

1. Reinforcement of the party reestablishment struggle.
2. Consolidation of the revolutionary anti-factions in all reformists guilds, and establishment of industrial, peasant and revolutionary labor organizations.
3. Enlistment of nationalist revolutionaries into the anti-imperialist camp by creating an anti-imperialist league for a united effort in creating a united front against the imperialists.

The above-stated political and organizational duties can only be carried out by broad daily agitation and propaganda activities. We must link these agitation and propaganda activities with slogans that support the partial and detailed demands for the benefit of the masses. We must not be idle in leading the daily struggle, because during the preparation period for the revolution the masses are interested in these partial and detailed demands. It is important to point out the platform of partial and detailed demands in order to link it to the general and tactical platform of the masses.

1. Opposition against military and police oppression of

peasant activities and strikes. Unlimited freedom for the organizational activities of the laborers and the strikes of the labor unions, as well as for peasant activities and the peasant unions. Opposition to the interference of the authorities (police, administrative organs, and courts) in the struggle of the laborers and peasants against the landlords and capitalists.

2. Immediate release of all political prisoners and all victims of police brutality—leaders of the peasants and laborers, participants in tenancy disputes and strikes, Communists, and national revolutionaries—and death to all police officers who tortured the revolutionaries to death.

3. Unlimited freedom of assembly, speech, and publication for the laborers. Complete freedom of political assembly and demonstration for the masses. Establishment of Peasant Committees for the peasants and Management Committees for all enterprises; elimination of all duty to report to the authorities. Establishment of red self-defense corps in villages, mines and factories. Establishment of the right of collective bargaining.

4. Abolition of all oppressive laws against Koreans, as well as those against laborers and peasants—the Security maintenance law, police law, assembly investigation ordinance, security law, Ordinance no. 7, publication law, newspaper law, tenancy dispute ordinance, and others. Abolition of all laws that hamper the independent industrial development of Korea— rice control laws for the peasant industrial guilds, the common selling system for fabrics, silk, and other materials, taxes on liquors, forest ordinances, and other bad laws.

5. Abolition of all feudalistic restrictions. Opposition to the oppression of our natural culture. Opposition to the enforcement of the Japanese national culture.

6. Reduction of or immunity from tenant fees. Abolition of all high interest bonds of landlords, banks and other financial organizations against the peasants. Refusal of payment of this interest. Free distribution of farm fertilizer, seeds, and other necessities, and free rental of all farm equipment. National subsidies for the losses of farmers due to unexpected price slumps.

7. Absolute opposition to semi-slave labor conditions.

Opposition to the dormitory system that does not allow freedom. Opposition to the slavery labor contract system. Opposition to the discrimination between Korean and Japanese laborers. Opposition to the double exploitation of women, youth, and the Chinese. Insistence on the same wages for the same labor. Lawful punishment of public or private deals concerning women and children.

8. Opposition to the rationalization of Capitalists. Eight-hour labor laws for adults. A six-hour labor law for youths eighteen years old or younger. A four-hour labor law for youths sixteen or younger. Abolition of the child labor system. A forty-six hour work week. Paid holidays of one day per week and two weeks per year. Other benefits such as maternity benefits.

9. A general rise in wages. A system of minimum wages to assure the basic subsistence level of living for married laborers. Opposition to all exploitation of wages. Lawful punishment for nonpayment of wages.

10. Immediate establishment of unemployment, sickness, and old-age insurance at the expense of the Capitalists. Opposition to the control by the factory heads of social insurance funds. Control of the funds by the laborers. Reduction of the rent and fees for water and electricity, and immunity from these fees for the unemployed. Establishment of a league of the unemployed and a league of renters. A realistic unemployment relief operation.

11. Opposition to the industrial undertakings, such as the rubber, marine, salt, and other undertakings of the imperialist financial combines of Mitsui and Mitsubishi, that exploit the working masses of Korea. Opposition to the rise in prices by inflation. Opposition to state subsidies to the Japanese Capitalists with the blood tax of the thousands and millions of Koreans, such as national assistance to private railroads and other enterprises. Stoppage of wasteful spending of the national treasure for police and prisons and the expenses of high Japanese bureaucrats. High taxation rates for all bankers and Capitalists. Abolition of taxes on the poor and the unemployed. Confiscation of all funds from speculation, and use of these

funds for the poor of the cities and villages.

12. Immediate cessation of invasion of China. Immediate withdrawal of the Japanese Army from Manchuria and Korea. Support of the Soviet Union and the Chinese revolution.

May 1933

Korean Communist Party Reestablishment Cholla Namdo League, Central Executive Committee

Item 27: Theses of the Chŏlla Pukto Movement[1]

I.   *Introduction*

Spearheaded by a possible attack on the proletarian fatherland, the Soviet Union, the climate of the world's political and economic conditions is worsening daily. The suppression of revolution by the mass murder of Korean and Chinese laborers in Manchuria and Mongolia marked the beginning of the oppression of the Far Eastern revolutionaries and the invasion of the Soviet Union.

In the Far East, Japanese imperialism, the pillar of reaction, is stirred to its foundations by the mixed currents of world history and objective conditions. In order to strengthen their disturbed foundations; the Japanese imperialists have extended oppression of the masses and economic exploitation to a point beyond expression. The condition of a Korean village is the same as the chaos of a typical colonial village, and middle and small peasant classes are disappearing very rapidly, and the proletarian masses are left wandering about on a starvation level. All of these facts are in accord with the process of world revolution.

With the General Strike at Wŏnsan in 1929, the Korean proletarian masses demonstrated their counter assault, and this can be seen especially in the recent demonstration at Hamhung.

In view of these objective developments, it is the duty of the Chonpuk [Chŏlla Pukto] movement to establish a new organization and to institute policies to carry out a part of the national revolutionary movement.

---

[1] This document was written by Kim Ch'ŏl-ju who headed the Chonpuk regional organization in 1933. This document was originally written in Korean which is, so far, not available. The document is available only in Japanese in *Shisō geppō,* Vol. IV, no. 1 (April 1934), pp. 41-54.

II. *Criticism of the Past Movement*

1. Concerning the activities of the independent lower organizations in the mass struggle: The result of the lower organization activities was an enervation of the mass movement; they hardly escaped from theoretical discussions to actual daily struggle.

2. The lack of effort to train proletarian leaders: As a result, only a small number of active elements were secured, and even these elements were not provided with proper conditions for struggle, so that they could not extend their efforts beyond the limits of opportunism. However, the past Chŏlla Pukto movement was subjected to constant arrests, and thus criticism must be confined to the above two items.

III. *Reorganization of the Core Leadership of the Chŏnpuk Movement*

1. Chŏlla Pukto will be divided into six regions with a representative in each region, and these representatives will organize a Chonpuk Leadership Committee.

2. This Committee shall meet once each month, to discuss and decide the more important issues.

3. A Committee Secretariat shall be organized and shall be responsible for all the other sections of the Committee.

4. The Committee shall establish a Political section, Organizational section, Agitation and Propaganda section, and Financial Affairs section.

5. The Political section shall discuss and decide all political problems: Its decisions can be amended only by the Secretariat.

6. The Organizational section shall divide the tasks of the organizational effort and shall take the lead in solving organizational problems. Its decisions are subject to approval by the Political section.

7. The Agitation and Propaganda section shall perform agitation and propaganda functions directed towards the organized and unorganized masses. Its decisions are subject to

approval by the Political section.

8. The Financial section shall undertake solution of financial problems and shall supply the necessary funds to each section. Its decisions are subject to approval by the Political section.

9. Since all of these sections are under the direct supervision of the Secretariat, all decisions of the various sections require the signature of the Secretariat.

10. The Secretariat has the duty of supplying materials to all sections, and shall receive and examine the reports of all sections.

11. Each regional representative, with the consent of the Committee, can organize a regional committee.

12. The Regional Committee shall follow all directives from the Leadership Committee.

13. The Regional Committee shall organize a Regional Secretariat, supply materials and lead the regional movement.

14. The Regional Secretariat shall discuss political problems, lead the organizational efforts, dispatch agents to as yet unorganized places, and widen the organizational efforts in the region.

15. The Regional Committee shall organize local committees and lead the activities of the local committees. A Local Committee shall have one secretary.

16. The Local Committee shall be subject to the control of the Regional Committee; it shall take care of all political problems and attempt to expand its membership.

17. The Local Committee shall have local meetings to discuss and decide on plans for local activities.

18. The local meeting is the decision making meeting and all the decisions of the local members shall be reviewed in the meeting.

19. The local meeting shall be called by the local secretary, and all decisions and directives require his signature.

20. The Local Committee has the duty and responsibility of reporting all plans and activities of the Local Committee. All problems of a political and national character shall be solved in a proper Communistic manner.

21. The Local Committee shall concentrate its efforts on the great industrial organizations, particularly the government-owned factories and industrial plants.

22. The Local Committee shall not act as a centralized organ; each member shall act independently and instinctively to bring about maximum effectiveness.

IV. Duties and Characteristics of the Reorganization of the Core of the Chŏnpuk Leadership

1. From February to August 24, 1928, the national party disintegrated and the national class movement became a regional movement outside the bounds of organic and unifed effort. Thus, Communist activities were not able to carry out their historical missions. In this national political situation, the Chŏnpuk movement also developed slowly as a regional form.

2. The class duty of this group is to develop a lower-class struggle for the daily benefit of the working masses, to provide Communist training of the organized masses and to expand organizational efforts with the non-organized masses. Thus it will follow the process of the national organizational struggle.

3. However, a successful struggle has been impossible because of the rampage both of national reformist elements, the inevitable product of the third period in national political conditions, and of social opportunists taking advantage of the national political and economic situation.

4. At the same time, despite the harsh experiences with the intelligentsia in the past, the Leninist strategy of fundamental liquidation of the intelligentsia has not been completely established.

5. Our future plan is to establish a profound strategy, and to perform the duties required of a group born with a class mission. We must struggle to establish cells and to give Communist discipline to the laborers and peasants.

6. The process of achieving the unity of the national and regional organizations is as follows: an organizer who received a directive is to organize a regional committee in the region assigned, and then carry out all necessary political and

economic struggles. The organizer shall strive to establish a Communist cell in each major industry of the region. When local cells are established, these cells will in turn select their leaders to organize a regional leadership and this regional leadership, with other regions, will establish a national organization.

7. A group reorganized under this process is not a complete group and reorganization is not an end in itself, but rather the group must strive to expand its organization to as yet unorganized regions and must attempt to enlist the masses. In gaining the masses the organization is in a transitional stage. Therefore, the regional groups are temporary organizations that facilitate the work of the lower mass organizations, and when these mass organizations are firmly established the dissolution of the regional group is inevitable.

V.   Action Platform of the Chŏnpuk Leadership Committee

1. Opposition to the second imperialist war.
2. Down with Japanese imperialism and establish a proletarian government.
3. Support the Soviet Union and the Chinese revolution.
4. Unconditional withdrawal of the imperialist army from Manchuria and Mongolia.
5. Free distribution of land to the peasants.
6. Unconditional and immediate release of all political prisoners.
7. Establishment of an eight-hour working day.
8. Absolute opposition to discrimination against Koreans by the Japanese, and absolute political equality of the two before the law.
9. Unconditional repeal of all oppressive laws against the peasants and laborers and the security laws.
10. Establishment of state social and life insurance.
11. Absolute freedom of speech, association, publication, and organization.
12. Opposition to closed courts and demand for open hearings and open courts.

VI.   *Special Demands of the Laborers*

In order to accomplish the historical mission to establish firmly the determination and class spirit of the physically and spiritually enervated laborers, and at the same time to insure the safety and livelihood of the laborers, the following special demands are listed as a part of our struggle:

1. Assurance of an eight-hour working day and establishment of a minimum wage.

2. Establishment of a labor system by laborers elected by the laborers.

3. Establishment of a rest period and complete sanitation facilities in all factories.

4. Opposition to wage discrimination against youth laborers, and insistence on the same pay for the same work.

5. A special wage system for night work, and prohibition of night labor for youths.

6. Absolute opposition to discrimination between Japanese and Korean laborers and equal treatment of both Japanese and Korean laborers at equal pay.

7. Complete freedom of Korean laborers to go to Japan.

8. A thirty-two hour work week and abolition of working on Sundays.

9. Establishment of a paid holiday system for all legal public holidays and labor memorial days.

10. Establishment of a six-hour day and a twenty-four-hour week for young laborers.

11. No labor for youths of sixteen or younger and abolition of dangerous work for laborers eighteen or younger.

12. Abolition of discrimination between laborers on the basis of sex. Insistence on equal treatment at equal pay.

13. A ten-month working year and payment of wages throughout the year.

14. Abolition of labor above the age of forty-five, and establishment of state old age homes and assurance of livelihood.

VII. *Demands of the Peasants*

The world financial chaos has reached the factories and farms. The chaos in the colonial countries, particularly in Korea, and the economic chaos has had a special meaning for the villages and farms. Therefore, the living conditions of the Korean farmers have reached a record low. In order to develop the class movement and to upgrade the class consciousness of the Korean laboring farmers, the following demands are listed as a part of our struggle.

1. Establishment of a maximum tenant fee. Abolition of the grain submission system.
2. Abolition of the system of land owner's agents, and opposition to double exploitation.
3. Abolition of tax on irrigation water, and establishment of state irrigation works to be utilized without cost.
4. Land reform on the basis of a farmer-centered system.
5. Abolition of private ownership of the land and free distribution of lands confiscated by the state.
6. Absolute opposition to Japanese immigration and reservation of the right to use the land to Koreans only.
7. Immediate dissolution and abolition of such exploiting organizations as the forest guilds and the county farmers associations, and abolition of their policies.
8. Absolute freedom of the farmers to reclaim wasteland and absolute opposition to state confiscation of these lands.
9. Firm establishment of tenancy contract laws and regulations and absolute opposition to their constant change.

VIII. *Demands of Women*

In order to give class consciousness to working women and to bring more women to active roles among the working masses, the following demands are made as a part of our struggle:

1. Establishment of an eight-hour working day, and opposition to discrimination between laborers on the basis of sex.

2. Equal treatment of both sexes with equal pay.

3. Establishment of a maternity system allowing eight weeks paid leave before and after the birth.

4. Establishment of nurseries and rest places and complete facilities for sanitation and medical aid.

5. Abolition of night work for women, and abolition of dangerous work for women.

6. Reform of inhuman and unsanitary treatment in the factories.

7. Abolition of youth labor below eighteen years of age.

8. Establishment of equal treatment of the sexes and the social equality of the sexes.

9. Abolition of the forced marriage system for girls eighteen years or younger and establishment of a free marriage system.

10. Abolition of feudal laws and regulations, and absolute guarantee of social rights.

IX.   Demands of Minors

1. Establishment of a six-hour labor system and a twenty-four-hour work week.

2. Abolition of night work and dangerous work.

3. Establishment of a compulsory education system and free distribution of necessary supplies.

4. Enactment of a protection law for minors.

5. Abolition of labor for minors sixteen years or younger.

6. Abolition of discriminatory wage systems for minors and establishment of equal wages for equal labor.

X.   Demands of Youth

In order to arouse the class consciousness of Korean youth, who have a special place in the class struggle, the following demands are listed.

1. Abolition of dangerous and night work for youth.

2. Establishment of equal wages as adults for equal labor.

3. Establishment of an eight-hour work day and thirty-two-hour work week.

4. Establishment of facilities to engage the youth in cultural sports and other recreational activities within the factory.

5. Assurance of the social position of youths eighteen years or older.

6. Assurance of the right to vote for youths eighteen years of age.

XI. Demands of Students

In accordance with their lively historical development, the general trend among the students has changed from educational slavery to radicalism, and, particularly after the Kwangju student incident, which gave the air of being the eve of the great revolution, the all-Korean student movements have progressed rapidly. These conditions are all part of our class struggle and, furthermore, the student movement is part of our youth movement; in order to upgrade the class struggle we have listed the following demands.

1. Abolition of slavery conditions in the educational system.

2. Establishment of student autonomy within the schools.

3. Opposition to military training in the schools.

4. Assurance of the right of the students to strike and absolute opposition to the interference of the judicial police in the schools.

5. Absolute freedom to study the social sciences.

6. Expansion of the use of the Korean language and in Korean history lessons.

7. Abolition of Japanese language lessons in the elementary schools and institution of Korean teachers.

8. Absolute opposition to the hiring of Japanese teachers in the elementary schools, and institution of Korean teachers.

9. Compulsory elementary education and free distribution

of necessary supplies.

10. Abolition of the use of the Japanese language by elementary school children and institution of the use of the Korean language.

11. Reduction in the teaching of Japanese history and geography and an increase in the teaching of Korean history and geography in the elementary schools.

12. An educational system based on Korean students in Korea.

XII. Social Policy

The breakdown of Capitalism, now in its third stage, together with the rapid fall of the petty bourgeoisie in the cities and the chaos among the middle class farmers, show clearly the path of the future. It is our immediate duty to arouse class consciousness for the benefit of the city and village laborers and peasants. The following are the demands in support of our struggle.

1. Establishment of state-supported homes for the aged and orphanages.

2. Establishment of compulsory education in the elementary schools and abolition of tuition.

3. Establishment of a jury system based on election by public nomination and state support of court fees for the poor.

4. Establishment of common dwelling places and immunity of the unemployed and the poor from rent payments.

5. Establishment of social aid facilities for the poor and exemption from all taxations.

6. Absolute opposition to forced confiscation, and the enforcement and abuse of the official authority of tax officials.

7. Absolute opposition to violence and private execution and the other abuses of the official authority of tax officials.

8. Abolition of the prostitution system.

9. Establishment of a state compensation system for released prisoners and assurance of their immediate livelihood.

10. Reduction of the unified income tax.

11. Reduction of all trading taxes, housing taxes, and land taxes.

12. Abolition of the system of state withdrawal of land, and abolition of state orders for forced selling.

13. Establishment of compulsory national labor and compensation for this labor.

14. Abolition of the various systems that burden the private citizens without compensation for national industries.

15. Disarming of all proletarian citizens and dispersal of all military organizations.

16. Establishment of free hospitals for laborers and peasants.

XIII. Action Policies

1. The immediate task of Communists with scientific Marxist and Leninist views of life and materialistic dialectic world views is to instigate a political struggle of agitation and propaganda activity against the unsatisfactory economic conditions that prevail. The objective conditions prevalent in the world at present endanger the livelihood of the proletarian masses and necessitate economic and political struggles.

2. Particularly in Korea, since the Wonsan general strike in 1929, economic strikes and political demonstrations are prevalent in the cities and villages, and there are countless episodes of heroism, together with a rapid development of communist activities. The Communist class movements are progressing in parallel to the development of world economic chaos and internal political disturbances.

3. The chaos in the farm areas resulted in a rapid decline of the middle-class, and there is a rapid flow of poor peasants to the cities. Therefore, the activities of the peasants have important characteristics.

    a.   National organizers or Leninist strategists must penetrate into the factories, schools, farms, stores and streetcorners, and conduct agitation and propaganda activities and transform all of the economic and political dissatisfaction into daily Communist struggles.

b.   The activities of the farmers are extremely important. Our activities should be directed to the organization of basic independent Communist units and also leftist factions in the peasant organizations. Revolutionary organizations must be formed to oppose the bourgeois peasant organizations and to carry out the revolutionary destruction of these organizations. They must have as their objective the establishment of a Red Peasant Union to direct the daily struggle of the peasants.

c.   Whatever their methods, at times openly, when conditions for secret penetration into the factories are not suitable, and at times secretly, the Communists must expand the daily struggle of agitation and propaganda activities in the factories and must spread Communist discipline and organizational structures. Thus we must gain the masses of the production front and organize Red labor unions to oppose the Committees established by the capitalists within the factories. At the same time, we must organize factions in the already established labor unions and also organize leftist factions in the rightist labor unions. We must carry out all these programs most courageously and heroically.

d.   The activities of class struggle in the various shops, schools, street-corners and other places have a special importance in Korea as a colony. The political and economic double exploitation have reached the limits of oppressive measures and the political dissatisfaction of the people is at its height. We must emphasize the ideas of anti-Japanese imperialism and create MOPR, which is one of the basic organs of anti-imperialistic struggle. Through these processes of daily struggle, we must mercilessly expose the national reformists, who comfort the Japanese imperialists, and the socialists, who commit anti-class activities, and there must be revolutionary and progressive activity to transform the various organizations that worked to abolish slave education, to dissolve the *Shin'gan-hoe,* and to transform the bourgeois youth league into a vanguard labor-peasant league.

e.   In order to accomplish the transformation of the class movement into a successful Communist movement, a tour of the sectional agitation and propaganda groups should be organized to instill in each sectional movement a feeling of common responsibility to strengthen the entire movement, and to expand the membership of the movement as well as to educate its leaders. The programs of the agitation and propaganda tour should be, in detail, as follows:

(1)   Expose the political and economic dangers confronting the world powers.

(2)   Expose the craze for preparation for the second world imperialistic war.

(3)   Expose the truth of the Sino-Japanese incidents and the innumerable murders of Chinese and Korean workers.

(4)   Extol the rapid progress of the Soviet Union and its social development.

(5)   Extol the rapid growth of the Chinese revolution.

(6)   Extol the great wave of internal revolutionary heroic fervor and teach its practical applications to the masses.

f.   At present there are no unlawful publication activities throughout the country, although the current political situation necessitates and demands such publication. In these circumstances, we must initiate a fund-raising group to raise 300 yen for the movement's basic funds and 200 yen for a publication fund. This must be accomplished within three months.

g.   At present, leadership training of the laborers and their appointment are the immediate tasks confronting the masses. Therefore, each region must have a leadership training center to train the leaders in Communist documents and theories, and in practical strategy and tactics;

the materials to be used for training these leaders require practical and strategic facts, in order to raise the Communist viewpoint of these leaders. For example, the training centers can have readers' discussion sessions, special research lectures, and similar programs. Its training materials must include the following:

(1) Methods of writing handbills.

(2) Methods of organizing demonstrations.

(3) The tactics of strike leadership.

(4) Methods of employing barricades.

(5) Criticism of the past movement, and devising of future bolshevik tactics and strategy.

(6) The true picture of the Japanese annexation of Korea and the history of the Korean Communist Party.

(7) The significance of the Russian revolution and the future of the world revolution, the history of the Communist International, and the history of the Communist labor movement.

h.   For the unified control of the entire movement and for the establishment of a national organization, heroic activities must be accomplished, such as enlisting 100 members by recruitment and training five officers, all within three months.

XIV.   Organizational Policy

1. The duties of national organization and the unification of the class movement and organizational efforts are the historical mission of the Communists and one of tasks of class struggle. Therefore, it is an immediate and important task to clear out the confusion created by socialist and other opportunists from our fronts.

2. The duties of organizers assigned to factories and other industrial plants are to establish a mass organization to facilitate the daily struggle under bolshevik tactics and strategy and to

gain the workers by taking up their inequities and dissatisfaction in the plants and factories through agitation and propaganda. The Korean Communists had found in the past that their efforts in organizing and expanding economic and political struggles not only ended at the halfway mark, but also that their efforts were interfered with by the infiltration of the socialists and opportunists.

3. These objective facts are one of the eloquent proofs of the need for organization through struggle and struggle through organization. Therefore, we must carry out the reestablishment of our central vanguard organization from the focus of the tactical revolutionary organization of one locality and one region.

4. An organizer dispatched to a region must organize a factory officers' corps in each factory, in order to centralize the daily activities and to discuss fully the political and economic facts within the factory, and must initiate further independent lower organizational cells in the factories. The officers' corps is the organ for mass struggle and the cells are the basic units of all organizations in the factory. Therefore, the first organizational task within a factory is the organization of the cells.

5. When there are more than three cells in a factory, a factory divisional association must be organized, and when there are more than three Factory Divisional Associations in one region, a regional council should be organized. When there are more than three different Regional Councils in a region, a preparation committee should be organized for the organization of Labor Unions. When there is only one industry in the region, a Labor Union Organizational Preparation Committee should be created to undertake independent activities. With this process the ultimate objective of organizing a Red Labor Union should be successfully carried out. The political characteristics of the Regional Council are acting as a reservoir of the mass organizations, its active power in establishing the Red Labor Union, and its education of conscious elements. The Labor Organization Preparation Committee is a transitional organization to the ultimately created Red Labor Union.

6. Organizational activities within the peasant movement

are important tasks, and the organizer of this decisive task must be cautious and fair in all of his activities. The circumstances and conditions of the peasant class adversely affect the chances for organization, necessitating an effort to arouse organizational consciousness. All organizations and their activities must be those similar to those of the modern proletariat.

7. In the farms, a village corps should be organized as a liaison unit between the elementary organizations. When there are more than three village corps, a village leaders' corps should be organized, and when there are two village leadership corps in a village, a village peasant committee should be organized to further a sound peasant movement.

8. An organization to penetrate into schools, streetcorners and shops, and to fight for the dissolution of the *Shin'gan-hoe* and the youth association must be established. Within the schools, organizations such as readers' associations and special research associations must be organized to lead the student movement and to train organizers for future activities. When there are more than three readers' associations within a school, an all-school leadership group must be established to lead the activities and to organize a regional organization for school teachers.

XV. Organization and Activities for the Establishment of Red Labor Unions

1. The task of establishing a Red Labor Union is one of the most immediate and important duties, and it is impossible to carry out the plan of vanguard organizations and their policies without a Red Labor Union.

2. The Regional Leadership groups must organize a Red Labor Union Organization Preparation Committee and actively undertake a struggle for the benefit of the masses of the region.

3. A Red Labor Union Organization Preparation Committee that has received a directive from the Red Labor Groups must establish a political section, organizational section, publication section and financial section of the organization.

4. Each section should have a secretarial bureau, which

has a duty to supply materials and decide on activities.

5. The secretarial bureau is directly under the secretariat of the Red Labor Group and must report on political activities as well as on future plans.

6. The Secretariat, upon receiving the reports and plans from each section, must evaluate them and give serious consideration to future Communist activities and Bolshevik organization.

Central slogans of the Red Labor Union:

a.   Establish a nationwide organization from the various industrial organizations.

b.   Reestablish the Korean Communist Party.

c.   Support the Soviet Union and the Chinese Revolution.

XVI. *Organizational Activities of the Red Peasant Union*

The organization of the Red Peasant Union is the same as that of the Red Labor Union, but it must be a unified national peasant organization.

Central slogans of the Red Peasant Union:

a.   Establish a unified national organization.

b.   Confiscate all land and make a free distribution of land.

c.   Support the Soviet Union and the Chinese Revolution.

A.   *The Factory Cell.*

1.   The daily activities of a factory cell must be to strengthen the central organization of the Red Labor Union. Thus, the members of a cell must discuss all political and economic factors unsatisfactory to the workers and arouse class consciousness. The overall

mission should be to take over the factory committee and to establish divisional associations.

2.   It is the responsibility and the duty of the cell to report the activities and future plans of each individual at cell meetings to be discussed in the light of correct Marxist doctrines. The activities of a cell are not centrally controlled, but rather are daily and independent activities.

3.   The cell is one of the basic organizations of the Party, as well as a basic organ of the factory. Therefore, cell activities are very important and must have a significant role in the organizational activities of the Factory Divisional Association and the Regional Council. The primary effort of the cell must be in the realization of the class struggle, and its revolutionary activities must be directed towards support of the struggles of the Factory Divisional Association and the Regional Council.

B.   The Peasant Cell

1.   All of the basic activities of the peasant cell are similar to those of the factory cell and its activities have great importance. The organizational struggle and activities of the peasant cell are extremely difficult.

2.   The daily activities of the peasant cell or the village cell are not in the increase of political and economic benefits to the cell members, but rather are in organizing and enlisting many as yet unorganized peasants into the Communist organization. Furthermore, they must publicly or privately point out the reasons why the peasants should rely upon the Communists.

C.   The Streetcorner Cell

1.   In a typical colonial country like Korea, it is the mission of the streetcorner youth movement to organize an anti-imperialist united front of all fighting labor and peasant unions. Particularly, the struggle to dissolve the national youth federation, in theory and practice, must be

the most important task of the streetcorner youth movement.

2.   Dissolution cells must be established to dissolve the existing National Youth Federation, in practice as well as in theory.

3.   The streetcorner cell must follow the leadership of and have an organic union with the youth section of the labor-peasant unions. The members of the cell must be organized along the transportation lines in order to have speedy liaison with the labor and peasant unions.

4.   Special research groups must be organized in the streetcorner cells under firm revolutionary objectives to educate the organizers, to study true Marxist principles, and to strengthen the internal as well as the external forces. The cell must actively struggle for the ultimate organization of the united efforts of all fronts.

D.   The Student Cell

1.   The Korean student movement, which has characteristics typical of the colonies, has the most class consciousness of city, village or other revolutionary movements. The students are equipped with advantages of literary activity and keen sensitivities in their desire for learning that can arouse class consciousness most effectively.

2.   Therefore, the active elements in the schools must organize a Readers' Association in each school to carry on organizational activities and to educate the elements in the groups.

3.   If the whole school is organized, then a school leadership section must be established, to help organize the sectional, regional and national organizations. In the process of this organization the Communist elements must train themselves by staging a strike and a struggle against slave education.

E.   The Fraction Cell

1.   The important mission of the fraction cell is the establishment of fraction activities within a rightist or official organization.

2.   The fraction cell, rather than expanding itself, must penetrate into all levels of another organization to gain members and to expose corrupt labor leaders and other officials to the masses, and thus to help eliminate and separate these corrupt leaders from the masses.

3.   The fraction cell must penetrate into all national reformist organizations as well as religious organizations, such as Ch'ŏndo-kyo and the All Korean Peasant Unions, and expose their plans publicly and thus gain the trust of the masses. A special caution to the fractional cell is that its activities should not be drastically illegal. These activities transcend the bounds of the activities of the rightist movements. The more intensive the white terror of the non-Communists, the more important is the mission of the fraction cell, and the more necessary is speedy exposure of corrupt labor leaders.

4.   The fraction cell must have a constant and organic relationship with the revolutionary groups within each region. In the peasant unions, the fraction cell must work toward the destruction of the existing peasant unions. They must also work toward the destruction of the existing unions, in order to create independent, heroic Red Labor Unions.

XVII.   The Anti-Imperialist League

1. The anti-imperialist league is one of the basic organizations of the national united front, and thus it is not a factional but rather a supra-factional organization. The basic organ is the cell and individuals who join the anti-imperialist league must first belong to a cell.

2. The third period of decisive chaos of the international capitalists brought a definite worsening of the level of the world

masses, and the preparation for the mad second imperialistic world war has caused a further deterioration in the daily life of the working masses. Amidst the whirlwind of these deteriorating Capitalist powers, the Soviet Union has heroically and successfully established a socialist state and has completed a five-year plan. The International Communist anti-Imperialist League, which supports the proletarian fatherland of the Soviet Union and the Chinese revolution and which opposes the mad imperialists' second world war, was born amidst favorable conditions and its development has been rapid.

3. Under these international conditions, the birth of an anti-imperialist league in Korea was natural and history proves this solemn fact. The duty of the anti-imperialist league in Korea is the formation of an anti-imperialist united front and a struggle for the benefit of the working masses.

Action platform

1. Absolute opposition to the second imperialists' world war.

2. Support of the Soviet Union and the Chinese revolution.

3. Organization of the Anti-Imperialist League and its revolutionary struggle.

XVIII. MOPR

1. It is the immediate task of the MOPR to support the families of those tens and thousands of revolutionary vanguard elements who were arrested under the constant white terror.

2. The birth of the MOPR in Korea was natural, in view of the internal and external situations. The duty of the MOPR must be to carry out benevolent and philanthropical activities for our comrades. It should be a spiritual, lawful, and materialistic aid, but from the point of view of the class struggle and not from a feudalistic moral conception. Thus, it must have a significance as a class movement and not as relief work of a moral and humanistic nature.

3. The MOPR shall organize a Red Committee as a part of the class struggle and this Committee shall have political, financial, publication and comfort sections.

4. The Political section must be directly under the supervision of the Red Committee for all political activities and must supply materials to the various sections.

5. The Financial section deals with financial problems under the direction of the political section and must get the consent of the political section for all its decisions.

6. The Publication section must undertake all agitation and propaganda activities and its decisions must also receive the approval of the political section.

7. The Comfort section must be engaged in the tasks of comforting and giving material aid to the families of imprisoned or arrested revolutionaries. The decisions of this section must also get the approval of the political section.

Central slogans:

      a.   Struggle for the success of the Chinese revolution and support the Soviet Union.

      b.   Struggle for the establishment of a nationwide MOPR organization.

      c.   Opposition to the second imperialistic world war and struggle for the unification of the Japanese and Korean proletariats.

In the realization of the various policies and tactics described above, publication activity is one of the most important and immediate tasks. This publication activity must be a well organized and planned activity that includes articles of theoretical discussions as well as of revolutionary activities. Therefore, publication work is one of the most important parts of the movement.

Item 28: Slogans of the Pukch'ŏng Red Peasants' League[1]

1. Let us go to the peasant masses with the most easily understandable slogans for the benefit of the peasant masses.

2. Let us initiate struggles by linking the oppression and the colonial exploitation of Japanese imperialism, as well as the contradictions of Capitalist society, regardless of size, to the discontent and interests of the peasant masses.

3. Let us assist the mass organizations, such as the consumers' union and sports organizations, that include the general peasant masses.

4. Let us explain in detail the factors that link the peasants' interests to the general characteristics and influences of the imperialistic war. Let us oppose the imperialistic war. Let us transform the imperialistic war into a revolution.

5. Let us develop detailed activities in order to train active elements in each village.

6. Let us initiate an edification campaign.

7. Let us strive to gain the trust of the peasant masses.

8. Let us struggle for the interests of the peasants in any organization or association of the peasant masses.

9. Let us initiate an opposition faction movement in any reactionary peasant organization.

10. Let us reestablish the Pukch'ŏng Red Peasant League, explaining that this organization is the weapon to fight for the interests of the peasants.

Nahat'ae-ri . . . . Han Sang-du and Cho Pyŏng-dae
Nimangchŏn-ri . . . . Chu Chin-kyŏng
Chukjŏn-ri . . . . Pang Pŏm-su

---

[1] This document is presumably written by Han Sang-du who headed the Pukch'ŏng Red Peasants' League, the Tŏksŏng branch of the KCP Reestablishment Council. This type of slogan appeared in abundance in 1933-34. This particular one was written in December 1932, and is available in Japanese in *Shisó ihò*, no. 2 (March 1935), pp. 50-51.

Item 29: On the Training of our Comrades[1]

Why do the Japanese imperialists actively oppress the revolutionary workers?

Today, in Korea, the workers struggle through strikes and boycotts to gain economic benefits by opposing the factory owners, but the Japanese police suppress the struggle and imprison most courageous and active elements of our working comrades.

Why do the Japanese imperialists, joined even by the Korean capitalists and landlords, hate and oppress the Communist and revolutionary labor movements? It is because they know that when the revolutionary labor movement and the Communist movement succeed in ejecting the Japanese imperialists from Korea and attain emancipation and complete independence, their lands will be confiscated and distributed to the peasants, and the working class will be assured of complete emancipation. They learned this from international experience. What is it that they understand? They understand the fact that the sacrificial deeds of the imperial Russian labor movement and of the Communists courageously destroyed the atrocious rule of imperialist Russia and established a workers' state; and they know that a socialist state, where the conditions of the laborers improve daily and there are no unemployed laborers has been established and that the capitalist and landlord classes have been liquidated. Today they are in the last stage of raving madness to save their corrupting system, shivering at the sight of the great revolution successfully progressing in China.

They also know (although they keep it in strict confidence) that the Japanese Communist and revolutionary workers' movements are growing rapidly and that incidents opposing the Capitalist landlords and the Japanese emperor are frequent within their army, which is the basis of Japanese imperialism. Our enemy, the Japanese Capitalists, landowners and imperial-

[1] The author of this document is Chu Yŏng-ha, a noted Korean Communist. It is assumed that this document was prepared in 1935. It is available only in Japanese in *Shisō ihō*, no. 6 (March 1936), pp. 13-18.

ists, know the failure experienced by the other Capitalist states and are raving to save themselves from the same failure.

Our Korean laboring class must also learn from the experiences of the international labor movement how to bring victory by courageously opposing the Japanese imperialists, Capitalists and landlords with strong and firm organizations. The struggle of the laborers and peasants against the Japanese imperialists is not an isolated struggle. We have as our allies the laborers and peasants under the leadership of the Japanese Communist Party, which demands the complete emancipation of Korea, the laborers and peasants who occupy one-sixth of the territory of China, the Chinese Communist Party, which has 400,000 members and a Red Army of 350,000 soldiers, and several thousands of voluntary army soldiers in Manchuria. See, our strength is great. The struggle of the Korean laborers and peasants is part of the world revolution, and that is why the barbarous, inhuman spies are torturing and threatening the revolutionary workers.

Organization and Secret Preservation

Comrades: What is the path that we must go at a time when the wages of labor are declining daily and the prices for rice, rent, fuel, and clothes are soaring? For us, the workers, there are no rights or freedom.

Comrades: There are two paths ahead of us: one is to die as slaves, suffering the exploitation and oppressions of the Japanese imperialists, the other is to lead a revolutionary life fighting the capitalists and landlords as the laborers and peasants of Soviet Russia and China have taught us.

Revolutionary workers, comrades, there is only one path that leads to our survival, the path of revolution. The experiences of Soviet Russia and the Chinese Soviets teach us the deeds that must be done by the Korean workers. Our Korean workers are yet to have any profound organizations and unions. We must organize labor unions in the factories, offices and other working places, to lead the masses to general strikes and to aid the masses to realize that they themselves must struggle against the factory owners.

However, the most important struggle is the struggle against spies. The spies are working with watchful eyes opened day and night, by sending agents (dogs) of the police, threatening innocent workers with torture, and making more spies. But our struggle must not fall before these tactics and we must unite strongly to fight for the working class.

1. First, we must improve the organization in the factories. Unless we improve our organization, it is difficult to keep secrets, and the entire organization can be destroyed when there is an arrest by the police. Therefore, each working cell must be organized with only a three- to five-man group, and there must be no talk with anyone outside of the group about the organization of the cell, regardless of how trustful they are. When an organizer is engaged in propaganda activities among the masses, he must not reveal what sort of organization is in back of him. When contacting other organizations, one must not contact the head of the cell and one must be cautious in his activities and words.

2. In order to influence great numbers of the masses, it is important to organize lawful mass organizations, such as friendly gatherings, mutual assistance groups and picnic groups. At the time of general strikes, a strike committee must be organized, but only one or two members of a cell should lead the strike committee.

3. When acquiring new comrades, two recommendations must be presented and an intensive investigation must be conducted.

4. Because of the fact that many agents of the police penetrate among the laborers, it is important to watch newly recruited members in their daily activities, their family conditions, and even in the places they go with friends for recreational purposes. This is an extremely important task in strengthening our work. Look at the process of arrests in the past P'yŏngyang Red Labor incident. There were many police agents and spies in P'yŏngyang city engaged solely in finding a lead for the arrest. Therefore, we must expose the police agents among the workers, separate them from the masses, and watch

and investigate every move they make.

5. The organizers must avoid meeting each other as much as possible, and when a meeting is necessary, a place should be well selected and one person must stand guard at all times.

6. All secret documents, newspapers, and magazines must be burned after each comrade finishes reading and discussing them.

7. During a strike, a strike committee must be organized, and in order to prevent the infiltration of police agents and spies and to combat informers, a political searching corps should also be organized.

Duties of The Comrades When Arrested by the Police

Comrades: We must strive to avoid arrests by the police, but we can not think that there will not be an arrest of even one comrade in the process of our struggle. Therefore, it is an important duty to prepare ourselves to act as revolutionary workers in order to keep the secrets of our organization. Look at the past failures of our comrades. There are numerous incidents of the total destruction of our organization because one comrade confessed the structure of our organization and the names of our comrades within four or five hours of their arrest by the police. The reason is that there was no prior organizational training for this. First of all, an organizer knew more than he needed to know. Secondly, there were no strict disciplines within the organization, and because of the existence of a few impure elements, the organization could not properly support the mass movement. Thirdly, our comrades ordinarily thought that there is no other way than to give a full confession when arrested, but this is because they did not prepare themselves for arrest. These past mistakes and shortcomings must not be repeated in our future organizational undertakings. When arrested by the police one must remember that there is a close relationship between the preservation of secrets and of the organization itself. Therefore, one must be cautious and give considerable thought to this problem.

What kind of attitudes must the revolutionary workers and the Communists take when arrested by the police? There are only two ways to fight the Japanese imperialists in this case.

The first requires, regardless of the individual will, a heroic struggle to eliminate the danger of falling into the trap of police persuasion or of confessing under police threats. Let us discuss this in detail, in order to see how to carry out this task. There are generally three occasions when comrades get arrested.

1. Arrested in a preliminary investigation without any lead on the part of the police.
2. Arrested because of police informants or a slip of the tongue of our comrades.
3. Arrested because of the uncovering of party documents or other evidence.

First of all, when arrested, one must know the reason for the arrest. The police investigation method is similar regardless of the supporting evidence for the arrest.

1. They threaten with torture.
2. They persuade with sweet promises of release if a confession is made, and investigate by deceiving the weak and undetermined comrades.
3. They use the method of threatening the families.

Therefore, it teaches us what attitude we must take both when arrested and at the time of the investigation. We must examine the situation at the time of arrest as well as the conditions of the investigation, and when it is clear that the police do not know or have any evidence, we must insist on our innocence. When the police do have evidence, we must admit guilt and say only that our participation in a strike and a leftist labor union was solely because of the difficulty of a worker making a livelihood, and nothing more. If we were to expose our organization the police would not reduce the punishment but rather would have trapped us more completely. The attitudes of our comrades should be clear, in order to escape arrest. It is permissible to lie and make excuses and even to talk a little of oneself, but on all other occasions we must seal our mouths and be silent during all their inquisition. Our comrades: even when we are arrested we must be calm and not be afraid and we must struggle against the barbarous torture of the dogs with strong endurance and proletarian courage. Comrades: We are the fighters of the working class; we are the heroes of Korean emancipation. Only with this spirit and with courageousness in our various activities can we emancipate our workers and attain our objectives in this world.

Tasks of the Struggle Against the Korean National Reformists

The Korean National Reformists are appearing in various forms in the historical development of the literary struggle of the workers and peasants, deceiving the masses with flattery and at times with insults, and, furthermore, attempting to exterminate and sell out the revolutionary masses as direct advocates of the Japanese imperialists. They are trying to deceive and destroy the Korean proletariat movement by moralistic and self-protective words, hiding their true attitude as hounds of the Japanese imperialists, and are trying to corrupt and instigate the masses with propaganda and various organizations, such as Christian organizations, Ch'ŏndo-kyo, Tong-a ilbo, Chosŏn ilbo, Chung-ang ilbo, Shin Tong-a, Samch'ŏlli, Shijo, Nongmin-sa, and others. The Japanese imperialists are treading down the masses under the control of Japanese imperialism, despite the fact that there is a significant contradiction in the political and economic development in Korea as a colony of Japanese imperialism.

Thus, the Korean industrial bourgeoisie became their hounds and failed to participate in the anti-Japanese struggle. Let us examine the economic foundation and fundamental role of the Korean National Reformists.

1. Objective and activities of the Korean National Reformists. What is a National Reformist? The Korean National Reformists oppose the revolutionary class struggle against the Capitalists and factory owners, and oppose the class struggle of the workers and peasants against Japanese imperialism in Korea. While the proletarian class is struggling against the Japanese imperialists, the National Reformists are supporting the Capital-

ist system. They attempt to reform the life of the peasants and laborers within the lawful limits of the capitalist system or to reform the society by a partial elimination of the Japanese imperialists' policy; for example; they insist on the improvement of peasant culture in order to upgrade peasant life in Korea.

2. The shortage of food in the farm villages is due to the shortage of money; the peasants must sell their harvests when it is cheap in the autumn and must buy when goods are more expensive, resulting in a gradual deterioration. Furthermore, the peasants are poor because they know little of other farm work, such as raising chickens, pigs, and fish.

3. Because there is no labor insurance law, this measure should be considered by the authorities.

4. In compliance with the farmland law passed last year, the tenant conditioning committee has decided to prevent tenancy disputes and peasant struggles.

5. A few social and economic reforms under the aegis of the Japanese imperialists are advocated to allow self-restoration and the power of self-assertion. These are all measures to oppress and extinguish the revolutionary struggles of the peasants and laborers. Therefore the Korean National Reformists are the great enemy of our proletarian class.

The basis of the social and economic growth of the Korean National Reformists is the Korean bourgeoisie and the landowning class, and they are merely the messenger of the small group of the bourgeoisie and intellectual class. What kind of contradictions lie between the Japanese imperialists and the Korean National bourgeoisie?

1. Since Korea is a colony of the Japanese imperialists, political sovereignty is with the Japanese imperialists and not in the Korean bourgeoisie. In other words, administrative and political state sovereignty cannot be possessed by the Korean bourgeoisie.

2. Thus, there is no free Korean agrarian development, and this development is controlled by the Japanese imperialists. There is no heavy industry in Korea, and even the development

of light industry is suppressed or these light industries are allowed to develop only as raw material processing industries for the heavy industry in Japan.

3. Since there is no financial strength in the Korean bourgeoisie, all industrial investment must be controlled by the Japanese imperialists.

4. Even the markets for products are monopolized by the Japanese imperialists and the Korean bourgeoisie are losing their markets and gradually deteriorating.

5. The more the Japanese imperialists control the economy, the more they exploit the laborers and peasants in Korea and the less benefit can be gained by the Korean bourgeoisie.

6. In spite of these contradictions and the confrontation of political and economic facts between the Japanese imperialists and the Korean bourgeoisie, the Korean bourgeoisie attempt to obey the Japanese imperialists.

Historical Reactionary Activities of the Korean Bourgeois Reformists

Since the Japanese annexation of Korea, the Korean bourgeois and the National Reformists have tried to influence the masses under the pretense of advocacy of Korean independence within Korea as well as abroad, and because of this anti-Japanese struggle the revolutionary mass within Korea has supported their struggle in the cities and villages in Korea. Already at this time, the Korean bourgeoisie was afraid of rapid progress and the revolutionary zeal of the masses and pushed the masses behind (by saying, "Shout independence, but do not take up arms.") Therefore, the March First movement ended in defeat, and the Korean Nationalists sold out the revolutionary masses by making them their agents. Since then the Korean working class has changed its movement to a different direction. They have developed a proletarian class movement by first establishing the Korean Communist Party in 1925, and after the arrest of the first party there were expanded strikes in the cities and villages. These developments were under more favorable conditions for rapid progress than the Chinese revolution in 1925 and the growth of the Soviet Russia. Realizing these developments, the Korean bourgeois Nationalists feared more, and joined and cooperated with the Japanese imperialists instead of opposing them, becoming their agents to oppress our proletarian class struggle. Comrades: Let us cautiously but strongly fight the Korean National Reformists, who deceive the revolutionary masses, by exposing their deceptive and criminal policies to all the masses, and let us win over the masses who still suffer under the National Reformists. They are our great enemies.

C. THE APOSTATES

Item 30: Report[1]

I have abandoned Marxism, in which I long believed with an earnestness that surpassed religious zeal, and now suffer under the name of so-called "apostate" and "party-selling rebel". In front of my fellow prisoners as well as before the prosecutor and judge, with a determination that will endure the persecution of the cross, I declare my withdrawl from the Korean Communist Party, which I served with blood and tears and devoted my youth for the past seven years. I am writing with a clear mind to give the detailed reasons and causes of my withdrawal from the Korean Communist Party.

I. The first contradiction that I felt in the materialism and materialistic interpretation of history which are the basic theory of communism was the reasoning that a human being is merely a thing just as any other thing and that the spirit of a human being is nothing more than the reflection of a thing. Therefore, in the historical process it is not human consciousness that determines social existence, but social existence that determines human consciousness. All of the history of mankind is the result of economic demands and economic relations and any spiritual products—art, morality, philosophy, religion, and others—are nothing more than by-products resulting from economic processes.

However, if the human consciousness or spirit is determined by materialistic conditions, what is the difference between a human being and an animal? How can religion, which is created by human spirit, philosophy and other metaphysical cultures, be explained? Is it possible to create a human spirit with a science that cannot even make a physical human body? Marxist materialistic answers explaining these questions are too unreasonable and prejudicial, and the only way to answer these

[1] This report was made by Kang Mun-su in 1934, after his arrest. It is most likely that the report was written originally in Japanese, for Kang was proficient in Japanese and was in a Japanese jail at the time of the writing. This document is available only in Japanese in *Shisō geppō*, IV, no. 3 (June 1934), pp. 40-50.

questions is with idealistic explanations.

A human being is in part a sensual existence and in part a supersensual existence. In physical life it is happiness, and in spiritual life it is morality that represent the highest theory of life, and these two theories attain their highest and absolute existence in God.

However, happiness is not the gift of material things, but is attainable only by the spirit, and all history and culture are created from the unending work of the spirit. The work of the spirit is centered around the absolute existence of God, but human beings experience unhappiness because of their uneasiness in facing the unending struggle against the process of life, disease, old age, and death, because of their incapacity to comprehend the workings of nature, and other causes, and thus they seek comfort and peace from omnipotent God. In this way develops religion which controls human emotional life, and the domain of religion can not be invaded even today, when the advance of science is significant.

The workings of the human spirit appear in many shapes other than the desire for food and sex, such as the desire for knowledge and fame, and in order to fulfil its endless desires, economic and political relations become more complicated. The human struggle for existence intensified with the progress of mankind and appeared as social and political problems for the satisfaction of human desires or the tendency to control with power. The most intensive control is in the socialist state, and the general economic relations in a socialist state are controlled by one big power. It is the extreme social phenomenon in contrast to free competition, the illness of Capitalism.

The first steps of the Russian revolution were as follows: the Russian Communist Party in the military Communistic period destroyed the Capitalist market, abolished the currency, nationalized all means of production as well as land and means of transportation, distributed industrial products to the peasants and agrarian products to the industrial workers, and created a virtual barter system, and attempted to build an idealistic Communist society, but this ended with tragic failures. The most important reason for their defeat was the destruction of the market and, secondly, was the creating of conditions destroying the free choice of the laborers. The destruction of the market eliminated competition in the production process, and the unworkable economic management made economic planning more difficult; these factors produced a deterioration of industrial and agricultural production and virtually stopped foreign trade. Despite the fact that the free choice of labor is part of the Communist ideology, the forced labor system was widely practiced and there is widespread confiscation of foods and a great lack of materials resulting from the boycott by the other countries. Although they attempted to protect their authority with unlimited power, the social uneasiness of the peasants reached such extreme levels and with such danger to the proletarian political authority, that even Lenin had to institute a so-called state capitalism which proclaimed a new economic policy in 1921 to revive the market and recognized the private onwership of commercial and industrial as well as agrarian production. This system continued until 1928, and the new economic policy restored foreign trade and led to a slow recovery of the Russian industries to the pre-war level. However, even during this period under the new economic policy, large production machinery was nationalized and foreign trade was conducted entirely by the state, and, because there was no competition in production processes, the problem of inferior products was not easily solved. The seriousness of this problem can be seen by the heated discussion within the Russian Communist Party at the time. The conclusion reached by the Central Executive Committee of the Russian Communist Party, which appeared in *Pravda* in Moscow, in analyzing the causes of the difficulties was that there was a general lack of self-consciousness on the part of the laborers and a lack of modern skills in comparison to other countries, but that the fundamental and true causes were the nationalization of all great industrial production machinery and the national mono-poly of foreign trade. It is natural to have an adverse influence on the level of production if a laborer is to be engaged in the same work all the time. I think the present Russian slogan of transformation of labor is nothing more than an ideal. It is true that there will not be such period when one can freely decide between mental endeavor and physical labor. Just as in the workings of the human brain and spirit, as well as in their differences in appearance, the complete solution of the social problems of good and evil people, intelligent and non-intelligent people, happiness and unhappiness, is impossible. Even at a time when little human labor brought riches, there occurred an exploitation of others' labor; I think that all the discriminations and inequities in human society are perhaps continuous, as are the natural phenomena of day and night.

At present in Russia they have finished a fifteen-year national economic plan and have entered into a twenty-five-year plan. Although they call the fifteen-year plan with national mobilization a victory and a success of the socialist economy, it is not a success, in view of the very fact that they had to launch a twenty-five-year plan, and the quality of their industrial products deteriorated and the agricultural products and harvests never met their anticipated growth. A survey of Russian foreign trade shows that their imports are in excess of their exports. Since 1930, when the Russian Government trade bureau realized that Russian products were not able to compete in the international market because of their inferior quality, they have instituted a dumping policy which became one of the main causes of international disputes.

The twenty-five-year plan reported by Stalin and Molotov in the joint meeting of the Control Committee and the Central Executive Committee of the Russian Communist Party at the close of the fifteen-year plan is thus a sign of the failure of their previous plan. The task of the twenty-five-year plan is thus the improvement of the quality of industrial products, the improvement of agricultural products, and the denial of the capitalistic attitudes and conceptions of the toiling masses.

However, what underwrites the failure of the twenty-five-year plan is the policy under the fifteen-year plan that proclaimed forced labor and the extermination of private capital, destruction of the market and the dumping policy as a new foreign trade policy. As a result of the five-year plan, Russian industries are said to have developed in a way surpassing those of every other country, and industrial production is said to have reached three times the pre-war level. Pre-war Russian leather shoe production was 400,000 pairs, but this doubled in 1932, producing 800,000 pairs. From a statistical point of view it is an impressive development, but it is an interesting fact that the average life of a pair of leather shoes manufactured prior to the war was one year, but the average life of a present shoe is only four months, and from this one example we can easily see the deterioration of quality in the Russian products and the deception of their statistics. The most impressive Russian industry today is production of coal, steel, crude oil, and sheet metals, which is second only to the United States production, but the reasons for this development are their total inheritance from old imperial Russia, their occupancy of one-sixth of the land mass of the earth, their so-called limitless Ural Mountain mines and Baku oil fields, and the cheap labor forcibly imposed upon Russian laborers by the Communist dictatorship. It is known that a great many forced laborers were utilized in putting through the Trans-Siberian railway in 1932.

A society that forcibly supresses human desires loses the power and drive for social and cultural development and results in a system in which a human being becomes nothing more than a machine under forced labor. There is no reason to build a kind of society which requires such high sacrifices, and also the facts of the Russian experience prove that communism is nothing more than a fantasy.

I saw the absurdities of this society while I was in Russia for many years, but I always interpreted it with good will, expecting a better future. Now if I think back, a thousand emotions crowd into my mind.

II. From my many years of tearful experiences the objective and subjective shortcomings of the Korean Communist Party can be summarized as follows:

A. Factionalism can be regarded as a cancer to the Korean revolutionary movement. The incurable factions, such as the

Shanghai, Seoul, North Wind, M.L. and other factions, constantly fought each other. There are many Korean Communists
who fought against factionalism, but all of their efforts came to
naught because the walls of factionalism were unbreakable. The
factionalism and conservative politics existing during the 300
years of the Yi Dynasty were so intense that even the
conception of state and national consciousness were lost. We are
the descendants of these traditions, and under this unhappy
inheritance our Communist movement was destroyed, buried
under an unprincipled factionalism.

Absolute secrecy is the life of a Communist party, but
because of this factionalism a tragic mistake is repeated again
and again, becoming a near tragedy. The most vividly remem-
bered factional struggle is that between the Shanghai faction
and the Irkutsk faction in Russia's Alexeyevsk in 1920, which
produced some 700 casualties. There are numerous incidents
other than this famous incident near Amur river, such as the
200,000 yen Incident of the 1922 national conference in
Shanghai, the 1925 Korean Mass Movement Leaders Conference
between the Tuesday Association and the Seoul faction, and
others.[2] The recent race to join the Chinese Communist Party
in Manchuria, like the mistakes of the Li Li-san line, is beyond
expression, and the factional struggles there exposed a tragedy.
Even in our case, the lead for the arrest was again due to
factionalism.

B. The next reason is the ignorance of the historical and
social characteristics special to Korea. The greatest mistake of
the Comintern lies in basing the direction of the Communist
revolution upon their own experiences in other countries of the
world, culturally and racially different. Each country has its
own special historical background and conceptions based upon
social conditions and cultural environments, so the formalized

---

[2] These incidents are grossly exaggerated to support his argument for
factionalism. For the Alexeyevsk Incident, see items 11-14; the 200,000
yen Incident seems to refer to the disputes between Yi Tong-hwi and the
Korean Provisional Government, item 8. The 1925 Leaders Conference
refers to the time of the creation of the first party in Korea in April 1925.

and formularized world revolution directives of the Comintern, when put into practice, expose its own mistakes. At the time of the European War (WWI) the German Communist Party under such brilliant leaders as Karl Liebknecht and Rosa Luxemburg seemed to be far stronger than the Russian Communist Party, but during the 1918 revolution they were defeated and they lost their political power to the National Socialist Party. This is because the pure German laboring class has returned to the banner of the National Socialist Party. Recently the German Communist Party has claimed a membership of 200,000 and is said to have nearly 100 members in the legislative assembly, but they are torn to pieces by the Nazi dictatorship, which is proof of German patriotism in a difficult and disadvantageous German position in international relations. In 1919 Italian Communists occupied every production machine in Italy, but they were defeated by Mussolini and his party. The same year in Hungary, Bela Kun even organized a Soviet government for four months but was defeated by the opposition of the peasants. In the same year in Northern Europe, the proletarian dictatorship in Finland also fell. All these incidents clearly indicate that their failures were due to the fact that their historical backgrounds and special national characteristics are different, and that nationalistic and socialistic concepts did not mesh with Communist ideology. If we were to look for a similar example in Japan, the recent isolated position of Japan following the Manchurian incident can be cited, but it is natural that the Japanese Communist movement is also raising the banner of Japanism. To receive the leadership of Russia is to import the Russian culture; thus rejection of its leadership by culturally more advanced countries such as Japan and others is only natural. A similar argument can be used in the case of Korea, and thus the success of the Communist revolution in Korea is impossible.

C. One of the other reasons is the shortcomings in the policy and tactics of the Communist Party. In contrast to the limitless power and various policies of the Government-General of Korea, the Korean Communist Party not only has the disadvantages of being a secret movement, but also their organizational methods and policies for the movement follow a formalized and fixed formula which always ends in defeat. The organizational framework of the Communist party is fixed in instructing its members in how to organize a mass organization, how to utilize the faction and how to lead the movement, and therefore no matter what sort of underground activities were conducted there was no other road than the road to failure.

The policy of the organizations and the methods of Communist activities are the same both in states where the existence and all the activities of a Communist party are lawful, such as England, France and Germany, and in states where even a mass organization with a leftist leaning is unlawful, in such states as Korea and Japan. It is truly a laughable matter that the Comintern is satisfied with its formalized leadership stationed in Russia, which has the only Communist Party in the world with incomplete economic statistics. Herein lies the greatest mistake of the leadership of the Comintern.

D. The policies of the Communist Party are mutually incompatible struggles and therefore, as a practical process, the formation of the national front that the Communists advocate is impossible. According to Lenin's discussion of Nationalist problems, the colonial national emancipation movement is a part of the world proletariat revolutionary movement and true national emancipation can be attained only through the proletarian movement. But if this is true, it must be concluded that the Koreans must be united without class distinction in the anti-Japanese imperialist movement. Here then appears the absolute demand for a national united front.

However, according to the policy of the Communist Party, the Korean bourgeois and landlord classes must be absolutely opposed, because they share common interests with the Japanese imperialists. They also say that religion is the opium of the people and thus must be exterminated. Therefore, no matter how they struggle for a united front, in practice they are separated from or hated by the masses.

The Communist Party also says that the laborers must assure themselves of the leadership in the Korean National united front, but in Korea eighty-four percent of the Korean people are peasants and there are less than ninety-nine thousand proletariat in all of Korea; the Communists, by insisting on proletarian leadership, ignore the peasant masses and excessively overvalue the laborers. Because they insist on the proletarian dictatorship in the national united front, the Communist Party is separated from the masses of all classes. We have experienced through *Shin'gan-hoe* and *Kŭn'u-hoe* how the general public hated the Communist Party and its policy. In view of the experience of Chiang Kai-shek's coup over the Communists in the Kuomintang in 1927, the hatred of the Korean nationalist leaders toward the Korean Communist Party was intensified.

E. Another reason is the lack of political concern on the part of the Korean people. The isolation policies of the Yi Dynasty for 500 years and the politics of power struggle by the nobles within Korea resulted in a complete indifference towards political training and education by the people. Because the authorities were satisfied with toadyism and were deeply involved in the struggle for power, the general public had little concern for the state.

F. Because there is no conscription law in Korea, there is no military training in Korea. Military training has a great influence on national consciousness and on national spiritual union, and in practice has a great influence on the ultimate revolutionary movement. The ancient spartan spirit was a gift of military training. The present Japanese national patriotism is the gift of the ancient way of the warriors and modern national conscription. It is said that the Russian Communist Party before the revolution was not idle in giving military training to its members in a large building. A revolution is the struggle between power and power, and the Korean Communists, who do not even have an opportunity to learn how to shoot a rifle, are bound to end their movement in tragedy.

G. Even the way the houses were built is a shortcoming. A secret movement that must guard its secrets needs a solid building. It is said that the revolutionary Russian Communist Party utilized a large building for the military training of its members. Concerning the first Communist party incident, Sakae Toshihiko remarked that Japanese buildings are not suitable for a secret movement, and he abandoned all illegal activities. The poor Korean buildings cannot hide a single secret document nor a single duplicating machine; they have no value for a secret movement.

H. The Japanese Communist Party was weak and was not able to help the Korean Communist Party. Until now the basic theoretical belief of the Korean Communist movement was the theory that the Japanese Communist Party was in a position to lead the Korean Communist Party, and that cooperation between the two was necessary. However, the present Japanese Communist Party leaders, such as Sano Manabu and Nabeyama Teishin, have already submitted to the Japanese authorities, thus leaving the Japanese Communist Party in a poor situation, and as a result the Korean Communist Party faced the most difficult problems.

I. Other shortcomings were the errors of the Comintern directives and the tyranny of the Russian Communist Party. From 1920 to 1921, and again from 1925 to 1928, the directives of the Comintern were in a fog because they directed the ridding of factionalism on the one hand and promoted it on the other. In 1920, although the Comintern recognized the Korean Communist Party of Yi Tong-hwi, Pak Chin-sun, and Kim Rip, the head of the Comintern's Far Eastern Bureau, Shumiatsky, a Jew, in an attempt to establish his own forces in the Asian countires, established a new Irkutsk faction with those Koreans, such as An Pyŏng-ch'an and Nam Man-ch'un who were dissatisfied with the Korean Communist Party, thus igniting the first flame of factionalism. After that, in 1924, the Comintern on the one hand directed Yi Tong-hwi and Nam Man-ch'un to organize a Party in Korea and directed them to reorganize an Organization Bureau to do the task, but, on the other hand, Voitinsky, also Jewish, who is head of the Far

Eastern Bureau stationed in Shanghai and a subordinate of Shumiatsky was dissatisfied with the Organization Bureau made up of the Shanghai and Irkutsk factions and organized a new thought group called the Tuesday Association, centered around Kim Ch'an and Cho Pong-am of the Irkutsk group. In the Spring of 1925, a party centered on the Tuesday Association was organized and was recognized as a section of the Comintern. Thus, this was the cause of factionalism among the three factions, the Shanghai faction, the Tuesday Association, and the Seoul faction in Korea.

And in 1929, when the danger of Sino-Russian conflict was imminent, centering on the Chinese Eastern Railway problems, the Comintern dispatched a directive to Asian Communists to protect the basic proletarian wall in the Far East and fight the Imperialist advance toward Russia, thus demanding the sacrifice of the proletariat of other countries. As a result of the Manchurian incident, however, the Russians feared a direct confrontation with Japan in northern Manchuria and declared that the Chinese Eastern Railway was a relic of the Russian imperialist period, and that they would sell it on purely economic grounds. It is said that talks are currently being opened between the Russian and Japanese delegates. This is a betrayal of the expectations of the proletariat of all countries and is a policy that exposes the Russian defeat in the Far East.

One more example: in 1920 the forces that helped defeat Semenov in the Russian Maritime Province were the work of Korean partisans, but the Russian treatment of the Koreans was tyrannous. The forcible disarming of the Korean partisans, maltreatment of the Korean veterans, and neglect in giving assurance to the veterans were, together with the problems of Korean autonomy in Russia, the seeds of the discontent of the Koreans in Russia. In the question of autonomy, despite the fact that there is a regulation calling for autonomy for populations of 300,000, the 350,000 Koreans are yet to receive permission for autonomy. From time to time, a Korean delegation went to Moscow to plead their case, but with no success. But an interesting fact is that autonomy was granted to the Buryat people of less than 250,000, near Outer Mongolia in

Baikal. The reason for denying autonomy to the more than 350,000 Koreans in the Russian Maritime Provinces is that the Russian Maritime Provinces are militarily important and strategic in Russo-Japanese relations. In contrast to this, the reason for granting autonomy to the Buryat people was that the Russians wanted to put Inner and Outer Mongolia under their sphere of influence; also, it was a policy to befriend the Mongolians in order to exterminate a stronghold of Russian white guards still holding out in Mongolia.

One last example occurred at the end of 1928, when all Communist countries fell into financial difficulties because the Comintern suddenly adopted a policy of economic independence and curtailed its aid. And there was even the so-called "Red Gang" incident, but Russia had already lost the zeal for world revolution. The revolutionary zeal of Lenin's time, providing financial support for the revolution, has all but disappeared.

I have always considered all these adverse facts more favorably and supported communism with tears and toil, but in retrospect I am truly filled with emotion. When I realized all these shortcomings of the Korean Communist movement, I lost all my faith in the belief that the only way to save Korea is through communism.

III. I have withdrawn from the Communist Party and denounced communism for the above-stated reasons. And now I would like to state my future, as a conclusion to this report.

My future path must be in a lawful movement suitable for the reality of Korea. It is of no significance whether it is a rightist national movement or an autonomy movement, so long as it is a lawful movement to bring economic and political benefits to the Korean people. I have in the past engaged in a constant denunciation of the Nationalist movement and of Christians and Ch'ŏndo-kyo people engaged in the autonomy movement, but in comparing their movement with the merits of the Communist movement, our Communist movement was nothing more than an empty non-practical endeavor for which we paid high sacrifices.

Therefore our movement must be a sound autonomy movement within legal bounds. A sound autonomy movement is in reality a lawful movement.

I am not impressed with the Japanese ruling policy of Japanese-Korean harmony. To assimilate 20 million people with four thousand years of history would be a near miracle. Behind the policy of Japanese-Korean harmony there is a strong Korean demand, which is essential for the success of the policy, to give Koreans a voice in the rule of Korea. Although there is a great progress in Korea, since the Japanese annexation Japanese capital has devoured the Korean industrial and production machinery and has even reached to the farmers in Korea. This drove out many Koreans of economic and political significance to Siberia and Manchuria. I have been deeply impressed by reading Komai Tokuzō's book, entitled *Record of Building Manchuria,* for his progressive thinking. In his conclusion he criticized the Korean ruling policy by saying that there is no doubt that Itō Hirobumi is one of the greatest politicians that Japan has ever produced, but his ruling policy did not succeed in Korea. The opposition to that policy continued and resulted in the uprising of 1919 and the Shanghai bombing incident. He has hinted that it is not any easy task to assimilate the 20 million Koreans with the Japanese, both nations having long separate histories. I was happy to know that there are such able political leaders as Komai, and how beneficial it would be for the Koreans if such a person was to rule Korea. It is not easy to really comprehend the importance of 20 million Koreans to Japan at this time when Japan is isolated. Even though Ireland did not have a history much different from that of England, their struggle lasted a hundred years, and finally they gained independence. We can see many such examples in history, and therefore it is important to have an autonomous system that respects the Koreans and that has organs in which the Koreans can be represented.

Next I will discuss the Manchurian problem, which has a close relationship to the Korean problems. I was deeply impressed with the political ability of Mr. Komai. Why did Japan make Manchuria independent by sacrificing 10,000 soldiers and sustaining military expenses of millions and even risking a world war? Considering the fact that Japan had to bring together a scattered people to organize a token government, it was a significant achievement on the part of the Japanese people.

Japan's policy was to satisfy the discontented thirty million Manchurians internally, and to insist externally that Manchuria is for the Manchurians.

However, today, the Communists are insisting that Manchuria is a product of Japanese imperialism and that they must oppose and fight against this aggression, but their insistence is nothing more than an unconscious supporting of the old warlords and an ignoring of the inevitable facts. It was inevitable that Japan had to expand in order to accommodate seventy million people crowded in small islands. We must also realize that the Japanese are maltreated in Manchuria by the indigenous bandits.

Recently the Korean Government-General launched a ten-year plan to emigrate 20,000 Korean households per year, and if this is a fact, Manchuria can become an ideal place for 30,000 Koreans within two or three years. Some eight hundred years ago Manchuria was a stage where our ancestors lived during the Palhae and Koguryŏ periods, and thus Koreans also have grounds for participation in the Manchurian problems.

For these reasons, even if I am presently not in a position to know about the outside world, the Manchurian problems are of great interest to me. I was born and raised in Manchuria and wandered about the land from corner to corner; thus, the Manchurian problems and the Korean problems in Manchuria are great subjects of my research and curiosity. Therefore, when I become a free man, I want to go to Manchuria and, as a faithful citizen, build a foundation for Koreans in Manchuria.

However, the problem that needs to be reexamined is the removal of threats to the security of the Koreans. Manchuria is bordered by both Russia and China, and is known to be the center of the Independence and Communist parties. It is also a place where drifters and politically recalcitrant as well as economically malcontented people assemble, and where Chinese oppression of the Koreans is severe, becoming an important

issue between the Chinese and Japanese. But the most important task in assuring the safety of the Koreans in Manchuria
is to protect the Koreans from the activities of the Russian
Communists, and to train the Koreans in the spirit of the
founding of Manchukuo together with the sound development
of Manchukuo.

A few days ago, when I heard from the judges that my friend
Shin Il-yong has abandoned his former ideology and is actively
working on the Korean problems in Manchuria, it was heart-
warming news to me that such a sound mind has grappled with
the difficult problems of the Koreans in Manchuria. I too
someday want to join him and walk the plains of Manchuria.

PART   III

THE COMMUNIST INTERNATIONAL

1928-35

COMMENTARY

The Communist International, 1928-35

WHATEVER the justification, the Comintern is more often condemned than praised for their role in the development of the Communist revolutionary movement in the East. If it is misguidance that marks the role of the Comintern in the Chinese and Japanese movements, it is relative indifference and often no guidance that characterizes the role of the Comintern in the Korean movement. This is indicated by the relatively few directives that came from the Comintern to Korea and the few theses in reply that were written by the Koreans to the Comintern. Seldom did Koreans play a role of importance or deliver a significant speech in the Comintern. Thus, documents pertaining to the Comintern's role in the Korean movement are few in number.

Some materials that deal with the Comintern have already been presented: Pak Chin-sun's participation in the Comintern, items 7 and 8, the Comintern directives at the time of the Alexeyevsk Incident, items 13 and 14, and a short cursory resume of the directive to the fourth party, item 22. Although active participation by the Korean delegates started shortly after the first congress of the Comintern, official relationships between the Korean Communist Party and the Comintern did not begin until after the fifth congress in 1924. They became more extensive between the fifth and sixth congresses (1924-28) when the Korean Communist Party was officially admitted as a section of the Comintern. As the seventh congress in 1935 was the last congress before the Comintern's dissolution in 1943, the documents presented here are mostly from the period between the sixth and seventh congresses. These can be divided into three groups: A) Comintern materials concerning Korea, including directives and theses from the Comintern; B) documents from the Comintern's front organizations; and C) communications from the Korean Communists to the Comintern.

A. Of the Comintern, 1928-31

The loud vocal support for the First Congress of the Toilers of the Far East was not followed by a concrete Comintern program for the Korean revolutionary movement. The Korean Communists in turn failed to unite their factions as the Comintern ordered them. Most questions concerning the Korean Communists were taken up by the Far Eastern Secretariat located in Irkutsk, and later Shanghai, but there were no significant developments. The Comintern's bureau in Vladivostok sent agents and money to help the Korean Communists within Korea, but the bureau's precise organization, leadership, and relationship with the Comintern and the Korean emigrants there are not clear. Only after the formation of the party within Korea in April 1925 did the Korean Communists journey to the Comintern to revive direct relationships. The first document, item 31, presented here is a resolution adopted by the 46th session of the sixth congress of the Comintern, endorsing the decision of the Executive Committee of the Communist International (ECCI) to admit the Korean Communist Party as a section of the Comintern. Although it was on September 1, 1928 at the sixth congress when the formal Comintern approval was made, the Korean Communist Party was approved for admission in April, 1926 between the sixth and seventh plenums of the ECCI. The sixth plenum was held during February and March, 1926, and the seventh plenum was held in December of that year. It may be correct to assume that the Korean delegate from the first party, Cho Tong-u, succeeded in having the party admitted to the Comintern in April, 1926.

No specific resolution was given to the Korean Communists at the sixth congress in July-August 1928. The theses for the revolutionary movement in the colonies and semi-colonies adopted by the sixth congress deal partly with the Korean Communist revolutionary movement, and only the part which deals with Korea is here presented, item 32. The original theses are divided into four parts; an introduction, the characteristic features of colonial economic and of imperialist colonial policy,

Communist strategies and tactics in China and similar colonial countries, and the immediate tasks of the Communists. The extract included here deals with the immediate tasks of the Communists in Korea. Although the theses covered the major Asian states and northern Africa as well as Latin America, the movements in China and India were emphasized.

Shortly after the sixth congress, on October 8, 1928, a short directive reportedly written by the Korean section of the Asian Bureau of the Comintern was given to a Korean Communist named Kim T'ae-kŭn (?), who is alleged to have been the secretary of the Central Committee of the Korean Communist Party in Vladivostok. Little information exists concerning the Korean named Kim and the activities of this Korean section of the Asian Bureau in Vladivostok, but it is clear that the directive had little or no influence on the Korean movement.

If any single directive can be considered as a major document, it would be the Resolution of the ECCI on the Korean Question, commonly known as the December Theses, item 33. The theses were written shortly after the sixth congress of the Comintern and were adopted by the Political Secretariat of the ECCI on December 10, 1928. Although the theses arrived in Korea soon after the fall of the fourth party, when there was no official party in operation, the theses did guide many subsequent efforts of the Korean Communists to reestablish the party. The document is important because it analyzed the Korean movement and gave encouragement to the Korean Communists. It pointed out some of the important short-comings of the Korean Communists while recognizing some of the obstacles the Koreans encountered in their operation.

Perhaps the more serious consequence of the theses was the way they were received by the Korean Communists. The Korean Communists interpreted the preface of the document as a statement expelling the Korean Communist Party from the Comintern. It is clear from the full text of this document, however, that expulsion was not mentioned. Many speculations exist concerning the expulsion and readmission of the Korean Communist Party to the Comintern. If the Korean Communist Party was in fact expelled and readmitted to the Comintern, neither the expulsion nor the readmission is recorded, and no documents recording such actions are available. The Korean Communists, writing in 1934 to the Comintern, said that the "Korean Communist Party states with pride that it considers itself as a part of the organized international Communist movement, a section of the Comintern." If in fact such expulsion did occur, it must have been a drastic action because only three months prior to the alleged expulsion in September 1928 at the Sixth congress the Comintern endorsed the admission of the Korean Communist Party as a section of the Comintern. As there were no significant events either in Korea or the party to justify such drastic action, the alleged expulsion would have been most unusual.

Aside from the December theses there were no important directives from the Comintern after the sixth congress, and it was not until 1931 that another theses came to the Korean Communists. This document, commonly known as the Kuusinen's Theses, item 34, was written by the late Otto Kuusinen, a Finnish Communist who long served the Comintern in various positions. Kuusinen wrote a number of articles concerning other Asian Communist movements. His article on the Korean movement is a very comprehensive and thorough evaluation compared with most writings on other Communist movements. Aside from a few factual mistakes, he seems to have studied the Korean movement well and he pointed out some of its important mistakes. His criticism centered around the condemnation of the chronic ills of the Korean movement, especially its factionalism. Although factionalism did hinder the movement of the 1920's, Kuusinen ignored some more important issues of the Korean Communists at the time he wrote. The major problems of the Korean Communists at the time of the theses were not necessarily those relating to the factional struggle but rather those involving their strategies of underground activities and tactics of union strikes and tenancy disputes. Kuusinen did little to map the future course of the Korean movement and failed to incite the Korean Communists to renew their efforts and reestablish the party in Korea.

In the theses Kuusinen refers to two other documents that the Comintern issued to the Koreans, one in 1924 and another in 1925, and even quotes from one of them. Neither of these documents is available. It is doubtful that these documents reached the Korean Communists, for nowhere, except in Kuusinen's Theses, are these two documents mentioned or cited.

B. The Front Organizations, 1930-32

The majority of the Comintern's front organizations were in operation in Korea, but like the role the Comintern played in the party, the front organizations had little effect on the advancement of the Communist cause in Korea. The Profintern (the Red International of Labor Unions) and the Krestintern (the Peasant International) attempted to influence the Korean labor and peasant movements, but had little success. Following the first and the second party incidents, the MOPR (the International Red Aid) was organized in Korea and mobilized women comrades to help the imprisoned revolutionaries. Funds were occasionally made available by the Koreans abroad and by the Comintern to give relief to the families of the imprisoned. The KIM (the Young Communist International) actively supported the Korean youth movement as well as the Korean Communist Youth Association (KCYA), but the Korean youth movement generally was dominated by the Nationalist groups during the late 1920's and 1930's, and the occasional directives and theses which were pertinent had little effect in Korea.

Most of the available documents from the front organizations to Korean Communists originated in the early 1930's. None are available for the 1920's. For example, there are no records of the operation of the MOPR, which was active during the late 1920's at the time of the party activities. Nor are any of the Krestintern documents available. The documents introduced here are those of the Profintern and its subsidiary, the Pan Pacific Trade Union, and the KIM, all of the early 1930's.

The first document, item 35, is a directive from the Profintern to the Korean Trade Union movement, which is commonly known as the September Theses. The Theses, which appeared in Korea in September 1930, was a product of the fifth congress of the Profintern, held August 15-30, 1930. The Theses contains a 17-point directive to the Korean Trade Unions. The first four articles generally described the conditions of the labor movement in Korea, while the remaining articles pointed out the duties of the Korean labor unions. In keeping with the other directives that came to the Koreans from the Comintern and its front organizations, the theses attempted to direct the Korean labor movement on the basis of a cursory knowledge of the conditions of the labor movement within Korea. In many respects the theses are similar to articles in *Revoliutsionnyi vostok* written by the Korean revolutionaries living in Russia. Perhaps the most important feature of the document is its outright condemnation of the united front organization, the *Shin'gan-hoe,* which was subsequently dissolved by the Communists. This is perhaps the first official statement from non-Korean organizations condemning the *Shin'gan-hoe;* the Nationalists, in an effort to save the organization, accused the Communists of blindly following this directive in undermining the organization.

Item 36 is an article which appeared in the Bulletin of the Red International of Labor Unions, *Eastern and Colonial,* and which describes the condition of the labor movement after the fifth congress of the Profintern. Although not directly referred, this article attempted to evaluate the labor movement within Korea after the Profintern's September theses were issued. There was, in fact, a rapid increase in the numbers of the strikes and labor disputes. However, many of these were sporadic and unorganized incidents and were generally caused by the economic chaos that accompanied the Japanese militant policy before and after the Manchurian incident rather than the directive, which had been in existence for only a short time.

The first Pan Pacific Trade Union conference was held in Hankow, May 20-26, 1927, to consolidate the trade unions in the colonial countries. Cho Pong-am, a member of the executive committee of the KCYA, is reported to have represented the Korean trade unions at this conference. Subsequent conferences were held in Vladivostok and Shanghai. Item 37 is the directive issued by the secretariat of the Pan Pacific Trade Union to the supporters of the Union in Korea. This was the follow-up to the September theses and was issued in October 1931. It is often referred to as the October Theses. The directive discussed the past mistakes of the Korean labor union movement, pointing out the failures to capitalize the discontent of the masses for the strikes. It also pointed out that the Korean trade union leaders had failed to follow the intent of the Profintern Theses, which directed them to wrest control of the labor unions from the national reformists by winning over the workers. The directive pointed out the duties of the labor unions under some twelve specific headings and even provided slogans under which the workers should fight.

The next directive introduced, item 38, is from the KIM, the Young Communist International, to the KCYA. The directive is perhaps the only one ever written by the KIM for the Korean movement. Although the KCYA was very active within Korea their participation in the KIM was less vigorous. An eight-point directive stating the duties of the Communist youth movement, it pointed out a few important tasks, and some past mistakes and included a condemnation of the *Shin'gan-hoe*. The directive was issued in January, 1932 under the name of the Executive Committee of the KIM. However, it is not clear what caused the theses to be written, particularly at a time when there was almost no active youth movement within Korea. Cho Pong-am represented the first party within Korea and was responsible for the admission of the Korean Communist Youth Association to the KIM in 1925. Yang Myǒng and Han Hae represented the fourth party to the fifth congress of the KIM which was held in Moscow August 20–September 18, 1928. It is not known who, if anyone represented the Korean Communists at the sixth congress of the KIM, held September 25–October 10, 1935. The directive came in between the two congresses, while in point of time the nearest executive committee meetings held were those of the enlarged plenum of the executive committee in December, 1929 and a plenum of the executive committee in December, 1932. However, the circumstances surrounding the issuance of the directive are not really known.

C. *The Korean Participation, 1933-35*

Many Korean representatives participated in the various Comintern Congresses after the first representative, Pak Chinsun, so ably spoke for the Korean Socialist Party, but none represented the Korean Communist Party more effectively than did Pak. Cho Tong-u represented the first party of 1925 and was instrumental in having the Korean Communist Party admitted to the Comintern as a section. Kim Tan-ya, Kim Kang, Yang Myong and others represented the Korean Communist Party to the Comintern during the 1920's but they were not very active and left no record of any importance.

It was not until the early 1930's, when the Communists attempted to reestablish a party within Korea, that a group known as the Initiatory Group actively represented the Korean Communists in the Comintern. Two documents, items 39 and 40, were written by this group and were widely circulated during February and March, 1934, some time before the opening of the seventh congress of the Comintern in 1935. It is difficult to identify the precise composition of the group and extent of their organization and activities are not known. But, judging primarily from the nature of the action platform and the analysis of the factionalism in the second document, this group seems to have been led by the M.L. group and Han Wi-kŏn, who was active in the fourth party. He later fled to Shanghai and engineered the Sixth Incident in Korea, which was a futile effort to reestablish a party in Korea from Shanghai.

Perhaps the most striking feature of item 39 is the claim that the Korean Communist Party was a section of the Comintern, p. 34. This statement clarifies much speculation on the expulsion and readmission of the Korean Communist Party. It should be noted that the Comintern in its December Theses recognized the fact that the Korean Communist Party was not actually in existence at the time. This fact is noted in the next document, item 40, p. 2, but it is far from an outright expulsion of the party from the Comintern.

The second document is addressed to the factory, mill, and village Communist groups in Korea, although it deals primarily with the problems of factionalism. Given the context of the document, it apparently was a reply to Kuusinen's theses condemning Korean factionalism. The translation presented here is from the *Inprecorr;* a slightly different translation in the *Communist International,* (Vol. XII, no. 9, May 5, 1935) from the Russian original is also available.

These documents, their evaluation of the Korean movement, were largely exercises in polemics, because it was not factionalism that marked the movement in the 1930's, but rather a struggle by the Korean Communists for its very perpetuation, by whatever faction. They were in need of fresh strategies and tactics for underground operations against the Japanese police.

The third document, item 41, is a speech by Kim Ha-il, the Korean delegate to the Comintern in its seventh congress. Little information exists on Kim and his relationship with the Initiatory Group except for the fact that Kim, like the members of the Initiatory Group, was a member of the M.L. group. Kim apparently operated in Vladivostok and worked for an influential leader of the M.L. group in Manchuria named Pak Yun-sŏ. Kim was also a friend and fellow comrade of Han Pin, the leader of Communist activities in the Russian Maritime Province who later joined the Communists in Yenan. Kim delivered the speech in a session presided over by the Italian Communist Togliati, alias Ercoli.

The document is fiercely anti-Japanese in nature and provides little discussion of the united front theme of the Congress. The total absence of mention of the failure of the Communists' united front in Korea during the early 1930's in his speech is noteworthy. It would have been difficult to have advocated a united front with the Nationalists in the mid-1930's in Korea because the Communists severed the united front, despite the insistance of the Nationalists. There were a few Korean Communists present at the seventh congress, but they seem to have been from the Russian Maritime Province, particularly from Vladivostok, and most of the details are not known. However, regardless of the representation or Kim's speech, the impact of the united front and the seventh congress was not felt by the Koreans at home.

PART III

DOCUMENTS

Items 31—41

A. OF THE COMINTERN, 1928-31

Item 31: Resolution on the Admittance of the Communist Parties of Cuba, Korea, New Zealand and Paraguay, of the Irish Workers League, the Socialist Party of Ecuador and the Revolutionary Socialist Party of Colombia into the Communist International[1]
[extract]

The growth of influence of the Communist International in the colonies and semi-colonies has found organizational expression in the rise of new Communist parties and in the affiliation of revolutionary workers' parties to the International.

The Sixth World Congress welcomes the formation and affiliation of these new sections to the Communist International as further proof of the confidence the workers and peasant masses and the oppressed peoples have in the Communist International and in its leadership in the struggle against colonial oppression, and as a confirmation of the truly world character of its work.

The Sixth World Congress therefore endorses the decisions taken by the Executive Committee in the period between the Fifth and the Sixth World Congress concerning the admission as sections of the Communist International,

> of the Communist Party of Korea,
> of the Communist Party of Cuba,
> of the Irish Workers League,

and furthermore resolves to admit to affiliation to the Communist International the Communist Party of New Zealand and the Communist Party of Paraguay. [two paragraphs omitted]

By admitting these seven new sections the Communist International is able to establish closer contact with additional millions of workers and peasants in countries exploited and

[1] This resolution was passed on September 1, 1928 at the Sixth Congress of the Comintern. Two paragraphs concerning the parties of Ecuador and Colombia are omitted here. This document might have been written in both Russian and English. This document is available in English in *Inprecorr*, Vol. VIII, no. 83 (November 23, 1928), p. 1579.

oppressed by the brigands of imperialism.

By coordinating the struggle of these workers and peasants with that of the proletariat in the imperialist home countries with that of the workers and peasants and the emancipated nations in the USSR and of the millions of colonial slaves, the Communist International develops and organizes on an ever increasing scale the revolutionary solidarity of all the oppressed, which is the necessary pre-condition for their victory over the bourgeoisie and imperialists the world over.

Item 32:   Theses on the Revolutionary Movement in the Colonies and Semi-Colonies[1]
[extract]

In Korea the Communists must strengthen their work in the ranks of the proletariat and in their efforts for a general increase of activity and strengthening of the workers' organizations and peasant federations. They must attempt to secure the reorganization of the trade unions so that they include the most important strata of the working class and combine economic struggles with political demands. At the same time they must associate in the closest possible fashion the demands for the national emancipation of the country with the slogan of the agrarian revolution, which is acquiring ever-more pressing importance in consequence of the growing pauperization of the peasantry under the plundering colonial regime.

In the ranks of the toiling masses, from which are derived the big religious-national unions (*Ch'ŏndo-kyo,* etc.), it is necessary to carry on a patient, revolutionary educational work in order to liberate them from the influence of the national reformist leaders. The Communist movement must be strengthened in all existing revolutionary mass organizations, instead of attempting to create a general national revolutionary party. On the basis of individual membership, endeavors must be made to coordinate and unite the activities of the different national revolutionary organizations with the aid of local committees of action so as to create, in fact, a bloc of revolutionary elements criticizing in so doing the half-heartedness and vacillations of the petty bourgeois nationalists and continually unmasking them before the masses. New forces must be drawn into the Communist Party,

[1] This is an extract of the widely circulated theses of the Sixth Congress on the revolutionary movement in the colonies and semi-colonies. Only the part that deals with the immediate task of the Korean Communists (Part IV) is presented here. This document is available in Russian, English, Japanese and Korean. The document might have been written in both Russian and English. The English version presented here is from the *Inprecorr,* Vol. VIII, no. 88 (December 12, 1928), pp. 1,659-76.

above all from among the industrial workers; this will be the best guarantee for the Bolshevik development of the Party, and especially it will facilitate the absolutely necessary liquidation of the harmful spirit of fractionalism in its ranks.

Item 33: Resolution of the E.C.C.I. on the Korean Question[1]

To the Revolutionary Workers and Peasants of Korea.

Dear Comrades!

The revolutionary movement in Korea is passing through a severe crisis. The blows of persecution by the Japanese imperialists are raining down upon it. The advance-guard of the working class, the COMMUNIST PARTY is being born to the accompaniment of severe birth-pangs. The severe birth-pangs are caused not only by the objective conditions (weak development of industry and a resultingly weak development of the working class and the working youth, fluctuation of its membership and weak organizations of the working class), not only by persecution on the part of Japanese imperialism, but also by those regrettable inner quarrels and conflicts which for several years have rent the Communist movement in your country. The birth of the Communist advance-guard of the Korean proletariat is accompanied by severe birth-pangs, and the class enemy is endeavoring to disintegrate the movement not only by means of the most furious white terror but also from within.

Japanese imperialism is intensifying its assault upon your country. The working class and the peasantry are beginning to stir, as the events of the last months have proved. But the Communist movement, torn by inner disputes, cannot be the initiator, the organizer and the leader of the revolutionary

---

[1] This document is more commonly known as the December Theses because it was adopted by the ECCI on December 10, 1928 and was issued to the Koreans in December 1928. A noted Japanese Communist, Sano Manabu, reported that the decision was prepared by a committee of four men: Sano Manabu, Chü Ch'iu-pai, Mif, and Wiltanen. It is assumed that the decision was originally written in English or Russian or both. Most of the translations into Japanese and Korean were made from the English version. The document is available in Russian, English, Japanese and Korean. The English version presented here is available in *Inprecorr,* Vol. IX, no. 8 (February 15, 1929) pp. 130-33. The Japanese version is available in abundance. See, for example, *Nippon kyōsantō tēze,* (Tokyo, 1951). See the Korean version in *Kegŭp t'ujaeng,* no. 1 (May 1929).

struggle, so long as the closest connection is not established between the individual revolutionaries and the working masses, so long as the Party does not exert its organizational influence upon the national revolutionary movement.

The Executive Committee of the Communist International, after having thoroughly discussed the situation in the country and the position of the revolutionary movement, has adopted the following resolution, which is to assist the revolutionary workers and peasants to form their revolutionary advance-guard:

RESOLUTION

The key positions in Korean economics are all in the hands of Japanese finance capital. American and British capital has but an absolutely negligible share in the mining industry. With this exception which barely merits any attention, Japanese capital has taken possession of all major economic positions. Transportation (railways, steamships), the mining industry, foreign trade, the banks and the entire credit and monetary system and the few industrial enterprises which deserve that name (textile, cement, leather, matches, sugar), the manufacturing concerns of any size (distilleries, paper factories, fat producers) are in the hands of Japanese. But Japanese imperialism has very strong positions also in the sphere of agriculture. The irrigation system, the colonization fund of the country, the forests, fishing, the tobacco fields, etc., are controlled by Japanese imperialism, which was able to grab vast tracts of land for the Japanese colonists and plantation owners. The role of Korea in the system of Japanese imperialism is to be an agrarian hinterland supplying raw material for Japan and serving as a market for Japanese goods; the principal mission of Korea is to supply the Japanese market with rice. The Korean population is fed on inferior food while rice is exported to Japan. The mining resources of the country were used during the world war more intensively, but the industry has barely emerged from its post-war crisis. Even the light and manufacturing industries are developing very slowly and modern large-scale factories can be counted on one's fingers. Meanwhile the export of farm products and the import of manufactured goods is rapidly increasing. The increase in arable land, the construction of irrigation systems, the extension of irrigated areas, the improvement in forestry and the petty-agrarian reforms, have not improved the position of the people as it was accompanied by intense exploitation on the part of Japanese imperialism. Korea is a typical colonial country in the sense outlined in the Theses of the VI Congress of the Comintern. It is merely an agrarian and raw material base of Japanese imperialism. But from this point of view the importance of Korea is becoming more significant.

Japanese imperialism exploits Korea not only economically, but also by other than economic means, squeezing vast sums of money out of the country in the form of taxes, customs tariffs, excise duties, State monopoly profits, etc.

Japanese imperialism grabbed not only the key and central positions in the government, but almost all more or less important positions in general. Korea is of enormous importance for Japanese imperialism also from a strategical point of view. Korea, together with the Kwantung Peninsula, is the main hinterland of Japanese imperialism on the Asiatic continent from where Japanese militarism can direct its blows both against the USSR and against China. To the extent that the coming war of the Pacific becomes more imminent the economic and strategical importance of Korea is increasing. Korea will have to maintain a big Japanese army, the police and the armed forces intended for the suppression of the revolutionary movement, and for military purposes in general. Japanese imperialism has its own military, police and bureaucratic machine for the administration of Korea, deprives the country of the opportunity to develop its own culture, deprives it of the opportunity independently to develop its productive forces, and retards its industrial development. Owing to the poor industrial development of the country the overwhelming majority of the population, over 80%, is occupied in, or depends on agriculture. The number of industrial enterprises of a modern type in 1922 was 664, employing 50,000 workers;

there are only 30 enterprises of all sorts with a fixed capital of over one million yen.

The agricultural relations, notwithstanding the rapid development of commodity and money relations, are chiefly of a pre-capitalist type. The peasants having less than one uno[2] of land comprise 83.7% of all land-owning peasants. The peasants possessing from one to two uno constitute 9% of the total. At the same time, 64.4% of all irrigated rice fields and 57.4% of all dry fields are cultivated by tenants. Most of the tenants hire land because of want. Rent in kind, crop sharing, semi-feudal relations between landlord and tenant, slave-forms and methods of exploitation, is what characterizes the positions of the tenants. A relatively small group of landlords exploit the vast majority of starving peasants. Independent peasants are exploited in the form of taxes, usury, cheating, false weights and measures, etc. Terrific exploitation makes for the majority of the peasants even simple reproduction of values and labor power impossible. Even official statistics admit that about 1,300,000 farms are run at a loss. No doubt that the poor peasant is the main figure in Korean agriculture both among the independent peasants and the tenants. There is no doubt a process is going on in Korea of transition of land to the landlords, merchants, usurers and speculators, including Japanese, a process of concentration of land in the hands of landlords of various types and origin, and a process of breaking up agriculture among the peasants. Emigration to Japan, Manchuria, the Far East, etc., does not solve the problem of pauperization of the great mass of peasants. The yoke of landed exploitation, the yoke of exploitation on the part of the Japanese financial and administrative apparatus, is distinguished also by the pre-capitalist slave methods of exploitation of the peasantry employed by merchant and usurers capital. These economic factors—the domination of capital towards the development of large scale agriculture, etc.—determine the position and role of the classes in the class struggle of Korea.

---

[2] "Uno" is undoubtedly a land unit, but it is not known as to the size of the land. In fact, it is not clear in what language the word "uno" is.

Thanks to the poor development and juvenile character of industry the Korean proletariat is still very weak. Not only is it numerically small, but is to a large extent still connected with the villages and is not sufficiently class-conscious. On the other pole, in view of the dominating, subjugating and determining role of Japanese capitalism, the big landowners are closely attached to it and the urban bourgeoisie—the manufacturers, merchants and usurers—connected with large-scale agriculture or directly subordinated to Japanese capital, is coming ever-closer towards it. The vast majority of the Korean population consists of economically enslaved peasants who are suppressed and downtrodden by the terroristic police regime and who have no prospects of an improvement of their position without a revolution.

That is why the revolution in Korea will, by its social and economic content, be directed not only against Japanese imperialism, but also against Korean feudalism. It will be directed towards the abolition of all pre-capitalist remnants and survivals, towards a cardinal change in the agrarian relations, towards a cleansing of the land from pre-capitalist forms of slavery. The revolution in Korea must be an agrarian revolution.

Thus the overthrow of imperialism and the revolutionary solution of the agrarian problem is the main objective historical meaning of the revolution in Korea in the first phases of its development. In this sense the Korean Revolution will be a bourgeois-democratic revolution.

Of all classes in Korea, as well as in any other colonial country, the proletariat is the most consistent anti-imperialist class. To the extent that the working class will grow and organize, especially the industrial workers, its leading role in the revolutionary movement will increase and the basis for the development of a Communist movement will be created. Apart from the proletariat, the toiling peasantry and the mass of the urban petty-bourgeoisie constitute a motive force in the revolution. The basic mass of the bourgeoisie constitutes, especially since the experiences of the Chinese Revolution, at best only a national-reformist opposition to Japanese imperialism, whilst the big landowners are completely on the side of the Japanese imperialists.

Under these conditions the national liberation movement in the majority of modern colonies, including Korea, is not only an anti-imperialist and an anti-feudal movement, but is closely linked up with the class struggle of the proletariat against the imperialists, the feudal lords and the national bourgeoisie. The proletariat of the colonial countries, in alliance with the broad masses of peasants, enters the political arena as an independent political factor which must have the hegemony in the revolution.

The Korean proletariat will not be able to take over the leadership in the national-revolutionary movement if the Korean Communists will not link up organically the agrarian problem with the national revolution. Inasmuch as the Korean bourgeoisie is bound up with big land ownership, in view of its dependence upon landed property, it is not interested in a radical agrarian program and will find it very difficult to gain leadership over the peasants. (A big danger in this respect is its agency—the national-reformist petty-bourgeoisie.) The agrarian problem of Korea can be solved only by revolutionary and plebeian methods (by means of seizure of land from all big landowners).

There can be no victorious national liberation struggle without an unfoldment of the agrarian revolution. It is precisely the almost complete absence of control between the national-liberation struggle and the struggle for land that is responsible for the weakness and the defeat of the revolutionary movement of the recent years (1919-1920). A victory over the imperialist yoke presupposes a revolutionary solution of the agrarian problem and the establishment of a democratic dictatorship of the proletariat and the peasants (in the form of Soviets) through which the bourgeois-democratic revolution under the hegemony of the proletariat is transformed into a Socialist Revolution.

Under these conditions, the peasant problem, the problem of the agrarian revolution, is of greatest importance for Communist activity in Korea. Only by bringing the peasants under their influence, only by appealing to them by means of intelligible and popular slogans and demands, will the working class and its vanguard be able to accomplish a victorious revolution in Korea.

The method by which Japanese imperialism has hitherto administered the country consisted in direct and open domination of the bureaucratic apparatus of operation. Japanese imperialism does not even formally share its power with any of the native classes of Korea. The governor-general's consultative body consists of picked and pro-Japanese representatives of the Korean feudal aristocracy and has no backing of any considerable sections of the Korean bourgeoisie and liberal intellectuals. Opposed by a wide front of workers and peasants, which is still weak, but carries with it the possibility of great complications in the future, Japanese imperialism is according to some indications ready, especially since the experiences of the Chinese Revolution, to resort to certain safety measures so as to secure its position in Korea by the winning over and attraction of a certain section of the bourgeoisie and the bourgeois intellectuals to its apparatus of occupation.

The more far-sighted representatives of imperialist Japan are beginning openly to speak of the necessity of partial reforms in Korea, understanding that the present conflict between the colonial regime and the growing revolutionary forces in the country cannot be overcome with the help of police measures alone.

Meanwhile, terror against the Communists and radical nationalists is being multiplied. The class labor and peasant movement has actually been outlawed. The suppression of the press has become more brutal. There is thus the possibility that Japanese imperialism will within the next few years try to crush the development of the revolutionary movement not only with the knout, but also by granting small concessions to the exploiters. The latter, however, will not be able to satisfy the proletariat nor the peasants and the broad sections of the urban petty-bourgeoisie. The national revolutionary movement in Korea which has a firm social basis to stand on will develop also in the future.

The rapprochement of Japanese imperialism and the big

native landowners has not failed to influence the position of a considerable section of the intelligentsia which plays a big role in the organization and leadership of the nationalist movement. These changes in the class relations in favor of conciliation with Japanese imperialism, just as the growing repressive measures and persecutions of the national-revolutionary organizations, cannot fail to influence the position of the latter. We may expect growing national reformist tendencies in their ranks, a diminishing of their revolutionary character and their transformation into a loyal "opposition". With the elimination of the Communists (through imprisonments, etc.) from the national revolutionary movement, the tendency of growing national reformism is becoming ever more pronounced.

The main line to be followed by the Communist movement of Korea in the present phase of development is, on the one hand, to strengthen the proletarian revolutionary movement, to guarantee its complete independence with regard to the petty-bourgeois national revolutionary movement, and, on the other hand, to strengthen the national revolutionary movement by lending it a class character and dissociating it from compromising national-reformism (i.e. from the bourgeois-democratic movement, the vacillations of which must be untiringly and mercilessly exposed).

The present situation and the existing class relations in Korea determine the political and organizational tasks of the Korean Communists. The years of factional struggle could not fail to retard their development and to confront them now with tasks, the accomplishment of which will be no child's play. The first of these tasks is a conscious and constant formation of Communist cadres with sound Communist views, the working out of a genuine Communist conception and a true scientific Marxian-Leninist mode of thinking; it is about time to discard the superficial pseudo-scientific phrases which have so frequently been our stock in trade till now; a profound discussion of all problems arising from the tactics of the movement is necessary.

The ranks of the Communist Party of Korea have in the past consisted almost exclusively of intellectuals and students. A

Communist Party built on such foundations cannot be a consistently Bolshevik and organizationally sound Party. The first task of the Communist movement of Korea is therefore to strengthen its own ranks. The problem of improving the social petty-bourgeois intellectual composition of the Party, and the lack of contact with the workers constituted until now one of the main causes of the permanent crisis in the Communist movement in Korea.

The Korean Communists must do their utmost to attract first of all industrial workers and also poor peasants, who have not given up their farming, into the Party. The Communists will be able to accomplish this great task only if they effect a sharp break with the old methods of organization of intellectual circles and undertake mass Bolshevik work, particularly in the factories and trade unions. More intensive work must be carried on in the labor and peasant organizations, in the old and new national revolutionary mass organizations, some of which, like the *Shin'gan-hoe, Hyŏngp'yŏng-sa, ch'ŏndo-kyo,* etc. are semi-religious associations. Fighting for the toilers in those organizations the Communists must expose the half-heartedness and the indecision of the national-reformist and other opportunist leaders. In their organizational work the Communists must avoid mechanical methods such as, for instance, the mechanical organization of nuclei, etc.

Oral and written agitation among the toiling sections of the population must be developed much more extensively than hitherto. The Communists must respond to every social event in the country. Such events should be interpreted from the proletarian point of view and from the point of view representing the interests of all toilers of Korea. The response to Communist leaflets and oral agitation coming from the sympathising and hostile sections of the population and their press will be the best measures of the quality of Communist work.

The methods of work in the national revolutionary organizations must also be changed. The illegality of the Communists obliges them to work in the mass organizations more under cover, to carry their propositions, suggestions and resolutions through non-Communist members of those organizations. This of course does not mean that the Communist must be so clandestine that their work should be entirely invisible or unfelt. On the contrary, the work of the Communists must be felt on every step. The Communists must always and every-where, if occasion demands, come out clearly and stop at no sacrifices, openly advancing the Communist point of view and methods of solution of problems. But they must work for the desired results also by means of deeper contact with the masses of these organizations and by means of deeper influence and greater popularity. This will protect the masses against the influence of the anti-Communist forces even when the Com-munists will be arrested or will suffer losses and defeats.

The frequent failures of the Korean Communists show that the Party was unable to organize its conspirative work properly. The employment of correct conspirative methods is therefore one of the most urgent tasks. Great pain must be taken to prevent the presence of agents-provocateurs in the Communist ranks. It must be particularly borne in mind that with the present factional struggle the Japanese spies and agents-provoca-teurs can penetrate the Communist organizations without any difficulty and that the creation of an ideologically compact and truly Bolshevik basis for the Communist Party is one of the first prerequisites for the struggle against provocations.

The ECCI considers the task of ideological consolidation of great importance and advises the Korean Communists to concentrate their attention to it; on its part, the ECCI will take every step towards a most speedy restoration and consolidation of the Communist Party of Korea.

The Communists must be able to overcome the political indifference of the working masses in the Japanese govern-mental enterprises in Korea. The higher wages in those factories and the rapid dismissal of "undesirable workers" by the administration render Communist work among those workers very difficult, but, nevertheless, the Party must find a way of reaching those workers.

The Communists must devote special attention to the trade unions. The latter are still far from being militant class organizations. They are rather workers' associations which constitute no danger for the employers. The trade unions must be imbued with the class spirit, and must be reorganized and strengthened. This is an immediate task of the Communists. The percentage of industrial workers in the unions must be increased.

In the sphere of work among the peasants, the Party must become more active among the tenants and half-tenants. The activity of the masses can be raised and the workers and peasants can be drawn into their mass organizations only if the Communists will learn to do mass work and to link up organically the final aim of the movement with the daily needs, requirements, and demands of the masses.

Much more system is necessary in the daily activity of the Party. It will not do to limit those activities to discussing from time to time "big" problems which, as experience has shown, do not always arise from the requirements of the class struggle. A most important element of work is the concentration of attention on questions of the practical requirements of the movement, which gives rise also to great and general problems.

Only by means of practical work and the following up of all questions of the Communist, labor and national bourgeois movements, can the guiding abilities of the Communists be tested and evaluated, can the value of their statements and the force of their arguments be measured. In their practical work the Communists must not labor without a plan and haphazardly; they must be guided by a definite program of action arising from the peculiarities of the situation and the given circumstances. In all their work and action the Communists of Korea must strictly preserve the full independence of the revolutionary labor movement, which must be definitely dissociated from all of the petty-bourgeois groups and parties. But "whenever the revolutionary struggle demands, a temporary collaboration is permissible, and under some conditions even a temporary alliance of the Communist Party and national-revolutionary movement inasmuch as that movement is revolutionary, is permissible." (Colonial Theses of the VI Congress of the C.I.). This collaboration, however, must by no means "find expression in a fusion of the Communist movement with the bourgeois-revolutionary movement" (ibid). With regard to the bourgeois opposition the Communists may conclude agreements with them "if the action of the bourgeois opposition can be utilized for the development of a mass movement and if such agreement will in no way restrict the freedom of the Communist Party in its agitation among the masses and in their organizations. In this connection, Communists must not only fully preserve their political independence and reveal their own position, but on the basis of action they must open the eyes of the toiling masses under the influence of the bourgeois opposition so that they may see the unreliability of that opposition and the danger of that opposition and the danger of the bourgeois-democratic illusions disseminated by it." (ibid).

The Korean Communists will have to advance in the future, and popularise more energetically, the slogan of the agrarian revolution as an organic part of the national revolutionary movement. They will have to fight more energetically against the bourgeois-nationalists, expose their half-heartedness and inconsistency in the struggle against Japanese imperialism as well as against the big landowners, and they will have to take steps to prevent their falling under the influence of the nationalists who use radical phrases and are the most dangerous opponents of the Communists. The Communists must remember that the conquest of the national apparatus without the necessary preparatory work among the masses is no guarantee that they will have any contact with the masses.

By constantly advocating the Communist program, the Korean Communists must coordinate the slogans of the daily struggle with the main slogans of irreconcilable struggle against Japanese imperialism, for complete national independence, for a democratic dictatorship of the proletariat and the peasants (a Soviet Government of workers and peasants), for the agrarian revolution, i.e. the distribution of the estates and the State lands to the peasants without compensation, for the nationalization of the mills and factories, etc., etc. It is at the same time necessary insistently to advance in the day to day activity the partial demands of the working class, fighting for the recognition and extension of the rights of the unions and the labor organizations, demands in the sphere of social legislation (the eight-hour day, six-hour day for juveniles, equal pay and equal working conditions for men and women, equality of conditions of Korean and Japanese workers, labor protection, etc.).

Special partial demands and slogans should be advanced by the Communists in the course of the struggle in the interests of the peasants, including the demands for limiting the rates of rent to a certain percentage of the crop, fixation of definite tax rates, abolition of compulsory prices on certain agricultural products, passing of laws against feudal tyranny, etc. Finally, the Communists in their daily work must advance demands for political rights and liberties (against all forms of arbitrary power of State officials, against political persecution, for freedom of speech, the press, assembly, association, strikes, etc.).

The Korean Communists must invariably and in all cases come out sharply against the imperialist policy and military action of Japan. Slogans of struggle against imperialist war and for the Soviet Union must be advanced and the work organized—considering this task, propaganda and agitation, of special importance in the daily activity of the Korean Communists.

Fighting against the Japanese terrorist regime, defending the legality of the labor and peasant movement, the Korean Communists must find ways and means of entering the arena of an open political struggle on the part of the mass movement. Thus the question of utilization of all legal possibilities is rising before the Communist Party of Korea in its full scope.

This utilization of the legal possibilities must, however, be to a certain extent kept also within certain limits. Thus, for instance, the utilization of the liberal bourgeois press for the discussion of Party questions and for polemics which tend to discredit the ranks of the Party is intolerable. The Korean Communists must see to it that the discussion of such questions and problems of the Communist movement be possible in their own publications.

The enumerated measures of a political and organizational character cannot of course embrace all tasks of the Korean Communists. However, they can serve as a pre-requisite for the development of extensive and profound work of a truly Communist nature.

The ECCI is convinced that a conscientious and serious attitude of the Korean Communists to the tasks arising from the present situation in the country will help them to overcome the maladies of the past and to restore and strengthen the Communist Party of Korea on the basis of the decisions of the ECCI.

Comrades, Workers and Peasants!

Such is the estimation of the situation given by the Comintern and the tasks resulting therefrom for the revolutionary workers and peasants.

The ECCI earnestly hopes that the Korean Communists will carry out the instructions of the above resolution, and will—in a severe struggle, demanding great sacrifices—establish the iron cohorts, the Communist Party. The ECCI will support you in this struggle. Without the restoration and consolidation of the Communist Party a consistent and determined struggle for the emancipation of the country from the yoke of Japanese imperialism and for carrying out the agrarian revolution is impossible.

Item 34: On the Korean Communist Movement[1]

Comrades, I wish to elucidate some basic questions of tactics and strategy in the Korean Communist movement. I wish to explain them from the point of view of the decisions taken by the Sixth Congress of the Comintern.

In an appraisal of the significance of the theoretical controversies in Korea, two points of view have come to light. Some comrades, in order to justify the factional struggle, have attempted to portray this struggle as a matter of principles. They said that, as a matter of fact, in Korea there were cases of theoretical disputes as well as the disputes between diverse camps, and that this, said they, was a very useful thing, and that important theoretical disagreements should not be concealed. They concluded that such disputes were necessary. On the other hand, there was revealed the opinion that theory would lead to nothing in Korea since practical work upon which all attention should be concentrated was neglected there, that all these theories was something colorless and dull, whereas the tree in bright blossom—is the tree of life, the golden tree, as it is said in the *Faust*.

The circumstances in Korea are such that one has a great temptation to adopt the point of view that practice must be everything whereas theory is of a very slight significance. In my opinion, this is a completely erroneous view. And when we maintain here that there are no substantial differences on point of principle among the different factions in the Korean Communist movement, this should not be interpreted in the sense that the questions which up to now were touched upon in disputes among these factions are unimportant and that it more or less makes no difference which position one would

[1] This document was written by the late Otto Kuusinen in 1931 in Russian. It is obvious from the content of the document that it was first delivered as a speech by Kuusinen in a meeting. The exact date and the nature of the meeting are not known. The document was later translated into Japanese, but there is as yet no Korean translation. See the original Russian version in *Revolyutsionnyi vostok,* no. 11-12 (1931), pp. 99-116.

take on these questions. We should be understood in the sense that neither of the factions is able to prove that it is this faction that holds to a correct policy line whereas the remaining factions take the anti-party stand. Not only neither of the factions had a correct line but on many questions there were even cases when one could not tell that this or that faction had a false policy line since frequently there was no consistent line whatsoever.

This does not mean at all that there were no deviations. There were many deviations in case of both factions and various comrades—the deviations that appeared in their speeches and statements. So numerous were they that it was often difficult to determine which of deviations had a preponderance and which was in the foreground. Such cases were not infrequent when deviations of all colors of the rainbow could be seen in one and the same comrade. Comrade Mad'yar has already cited some quotations from Korean journals.[2] They contain terrible things from a theoretical viewpoint—things that make your hair stand on end.

This mish-mash found in the Communist literature and in declarations of the Korean Communists reflects the under-developed state of the process of education and self-determination of classes in Korea. This is a fact. But it also means that we must exert every effort toward finding a correct solution for the basic theoretical problems that confront the Korean movement: It would be completely wrong to think in terms of letting the comrades from the All-Union Communist party (of Bolsheviks), from the German Communist Party, or from the Communist parties of other more developed countries engage in discussions of theoretical problems, whereas in our Korea the problems are simpler and we can give up the idea of their theoretical analysis. This is entirely wrong and, in a certain sense, it is just the other way around. At the least, the basic strategic problems of the Korean Communist movement are not less but much more

[2] Mad'yar who wrote numerous articles on China and the Far East in the 1920's may have been a member of the Communist Party of the Soviet Union or an agent of the Comintern, but specific reference here of his writing and the journals he had cited can not be identified.

complicated than those in some developed Capitalist countries. Why is it so important to formulate these questions in terms of as great theoretical clarity as possible?

Firstly, it is because the Korean proletariat is very young, is still very backward, and is insufficiently class conscious (we must not idealize the proletariat). The experience the Korean proletariat has, as a class, is comparatively insignificant; there has been very little participation of the proletariat in the Communist movement. The revolutionary intelligentsia still plays a predominant role in the movement.

Secondly, there is relatively poor development of Marxist-Leninist education, especially among Korean workers; and, thirdly, there is the complexity of the fundamental problems of the revolutionary workers movement in Korea.

What is the essence of this complexity? I shall attempt a brief elucidation of this question.

It is known that when we speak of our tasks within the international Communist movement, we emphasize the struggle on two fronts as one of our fundamental tasks. In all Capitalist countries, on the one hand, the struggle against right opportunist policy *Khvostism*[3] is necessary, and, on the other hand,—that against "left" sectarianism, against policies leading to isolation from the working masses. Here the question is that of correct combination of mass nature of politics with revolutionary character of politics; only through their correct combination can correct Bolshevik leadership over the revolutionary mass movement be obtained. That is how matters stand in both Korea and other countries. But in Korea and in similar colonies, this is not the end of the problem. There one has to consider this fundamental problem of revolution and of revolutionary strategy also from the point of view of correct combination of proletarian class politics with the national liberation struggle. It is necessary to disassociate oneself, on the one hand, from overestimating the nationalist element and, on the other hand, disassociate oneself from underestimating it and

---

[3]*Khvostism* means following behind or following in the tail of something or someone, "tailism".

from one-sidedness, from excess and leaps in class politics. This means that the way the question is formulated is more complex than it seems. But that is not the whole thing, by far not the whole thing.

We observe significant complexities in the revolutionary movement in its various stages. In capitalist countries, the question is mainly that of the correct combination of our slogans of action, the everyday slogans with ultimate slogans, i.e. the slogans of proletarian socialist revolution. The most immediate basic strategic goal in the imperialist countries, the developed capitalist countries, is the achievement of a proletarian dictatorship. In Korea and other similar colonies, it is also necessary to keep this goal in mind—a socialist revolution, but the most immediate basic strategic goal is different there—namely, a revolutionary-democratic dictatorship of the proletariat and the peasantry, which will, as a matter of course, develop later into a socialist proletarian dictatorship. This means that in Korea and in colonies similar to it, it is first of all necessary to keep in mind a bourgeois-democratic revolution, but such a bourgeois-democratic revolution which later on can develop and will develop into a socialist revolution. Of course, one should also keep in mind the varying degrees of maturity of the movement.

The question about danger of lagging behind events or of attempting to leap over inevitable stages are also much more complex in Korea than, for example, in imperialist countries. This situation is further complicated by the fact that the process of self-determination of the classes is proceeding rather slowly there. All this peculiarity of development complicates greatly the formulation of our problems. With such multiple complexities in the formulation of basic problems of our strategy and tactics in colonies similar to Korea, it is not at all surprising that we encounter there so many deviations from Leninism, the deviations which more or less have taken shape, to say nothing of individual errors.

It is necessary to bring some order to this kaleidoscope, to this proliferation of various deviations from Leninism. It is necessary to classify basic categories of these deviations.

Basically, all these deviations in the Korean revolutionary movement are only the reflections on the workers' movement of main tendencies in the bourgeois and petty-bourgeois environment surrounding this movement. What are these main tendencies in bourgeois and petty-bourgeois environment? Four main currents may be discerned: (1) national reformism, the main trend of the national bourgeoisie; (2) national radicalism, which is also known as the national revolutionary tendency; (3) social reformism; and (4) social radicalism. Here we have two bourgeois-nationalist tendencies—right and left, and two social-democratic tendencies—social reformism and social radicalism and the characteristic feature they possess is their underestimation of the national liberation struggle. This was discussed in the theses of the Sixth Congress of the Comintern, although it is hardly reflected in the discussions of the Korean Communist factions. I wish to call attention to some of the most important points in the theses of the Sixth Congress, especially to paragraphs 19 and 22.

In paragraph 19 it is said: "Where an incorrect estimate is made of the basic national reformist trend of the national bourgeoisie, in these colonial countries there arises the possibility for grave mistakes in the strategy and tactics of the Communist parties concerned. In particular, two kinds of errors are possible:

(a) Failure to understand the difference between national reformist and national revolutionary tendencies may lead to a policy of *Khvostism* vis-a-vis the bourgeoisie, to an insufficiently clear-cut disassociation of the proletariat from the bourgeoisie, to the stifling of the most important revolutionary slogans (especially the slogan of agrarian reform), etc. This was the basic error into which the Chinese Communist Party fell during 1925-27.

(b) The underestimation of the special significance of bourgeois national reformism, as distinguished from the camp of feudalism and imperialism, due to its mass influence in the ranks of the petty bourgeoisie, peasantry, and even the working class in part—at least in the initial stages of the movement—can lead to sectarian politics, to the isolation of the Communists from the working masses, etc. In either event, insufficient attention is given to the realization of precisely those tasks which were defined already by the Second Congress of the Comintern as special tasks of the Communist Parties of colonial countries, i.e., the tasks of struggle against the bourgeois democratic movement within one's own nation. Without this struggle, without freeing the working masses from the influence of bourgeoisie and national reformism, the main strategic goal of the Communist movement in a bourgeois democratic revolution—the hegemony of the proletariat—cannot be attained. Without the hegemony of the proletariat, an organic part of which is the leading position of the Communist party, the bourgeois democratic revolution cannot be completed, to say nothing of a socialist revolution."

There are a few more points in the theses of the Communist International that describe this difference. Here, the question is not whether the Korean bourgeoisie can play a revolutionary role or not, or whether Kemalism or something of the sort impossible there. This, of course, is completely out of the question. But in Korea, in the process of the development of class struggle, there should emerge its own national revolutionary and national radical tendencies. This is perfectly clear. I do not know whether anyone has ever seen such Korean revolutionaries, but I would not at all be surprised to find national revolutionaries even in the Communist factions. On the contrary, this would be, to a certain extent, a natural phenomenon if many of the Korean national revolutionaries acted as Communists and if they themselves were convinced that they were Communists in true sense of the term. This will persist until such time when the process of final self-determination is completed within themselves. You are aware of the fact, for example, that in Tsarist Russia at one time Marxism was in fashion; many bourgeois, who later emerged as the ideologists of the bourgeoisie, had once been "Marxists".

Especially now, with the existence of the U.S.S.R., with Marxism and Leninism being widely disseminated, and with the existence of the Comintern, many bourgeois national revolutionaries in the colonial countries at the very beginning of the movement will act as Communists. This must not be forgotten.

In paragraph 24, it is stated: "If the main trends of the parties of big national bourgeoisie are incorrectly assessed, then there appears a danger of a wrong assessment of the character and role of the petty bourgeois parties. As a general rule, these parties in their development progress from national revolutionary to national reformist positions." This pertains to Sun Yat-senism and Kuomintanism in China, to Gandhiism in India, and so forth.

Further on in the theses it is stated: "In a country such as India, it is possible for some new and analogous radical petty bourgeois groups and parties to appeal also, but one should keep in mind that these parties, essentially speaking, are linked with the national bourgeoisie. The petty bourgeois intelligentsia, who leads these parties, puts forth national revolutionary demands but at the same time—more or less consciously—it represents the capitalist development of its country."

One should not conclude whatsoever that where the nationalist parties of this sort have not yet taken shape these tendencies are altogether lacking. For us it is understandable that in all capitalist countries, there is social reformism, or social fascism. As a rule it is emphasized that there is no ground for social reformism in the colonies. In my opinion, one ought not indulge in this illusion. In colonies where the ruin of the peasantry and the urban handicraftsmen is considerable, the ranks of the proletariat are joined by ever-increasing strata from the peasantry and other petty bourgeois strata, bringing along a peasant and petty-bourgeois ideology.

Furthermore, in a country like Korea there is a privileged stratum of workers in the skilled Japanese workers, and it would be surprising if social reformist or social fascist current did not find support among them. Social radicalism is also a natural phenomenon. This current, similarly to social reformism, is characterized by its underassessment of nationalist aspect, but, on the other hand, it is the antithesis of social reformism in the sense that this deviation leans closer to the side of anarchism or left syndicalism—one can even say Trotskyism, and so on.

It often happens that the followers of this tendency [of social radicalism] are represented only by small groups and factions, organizationally isolated from the masses. At the same time, the existence of these groups is not an accidental phenomenon.

As I have already said, in reality all these tendencies very often are not so sharply defined and are not so sharply fenced off from each other because they have not yet completely taken shape, and they do not exist as parties yet. But when it comes to these tendencies' reflection on the workers' movement in the form of deviations within the latter, I think we will do well if during our criticism and self-criticism of deviations in the Communist movement, we seek their fundamental roots. I am warning you that a certain degree of prudence is required here; we should not indiscriminatingly reveal people's addresses, as is often done by Korean comrades in their factional struggle.

For the Korean party self-criticism is essential, but it seems to me that it is also essential for us. I feel somewhat surprised that the comrades who used to undergo our criticism, on their part, have not criticized us at all. Yet in some questions we are not without errors, and this is especially true to the Korean question. In my opinion, our cause demands not the concealment of such errors, but it rather demands that we discuss them openly. In the course of many years we have not had sufficient opportunity to become thoroughly acquainted with the truly complete problems of the Korean Communist movement and therefore gravest mistakes have been committed. I have in mind a couple of resolutions on the Korean question. Perhaps the comrades are still not familiar with these resolutions. If so, then it is understandable why they have not criticized them. One is the resolution of 1925.[4] It is the first resolution written on the

[4] This resolution of the Comintern on the Korean Communists is nowhere available. The time referred here as the formation of the Korean Communist Party and the formation of the Central Committee of the party is April 17, 1925. Two official delegates, Cho Tong-u to the

Korean question. It was written at the moment when news was received from Korea that a congress of the largest Korean Communist organizations had been held, at which the unification of these groups and elections to the central committee took place.

The resolution declared:

> The main political and organizational task of the Korean Communist organizations in the area of mass work in the near future must consist in giving priority to the national liberation struggle uniting, with the workers and peasants, all other strata of toilers: artisans, the intelligentsia, and the petty and middle bourgeoisie.

Thus the party slogans should be stressed from this point of view. In another paragraph it is stated that "the question of forming in Korea a national revolutionary party of the Kuomintang type" is being worked out, jointly with the Korean Communist Party.

In another resolution it is stated:

> In confirmation and further elaboration of the foregoing decision, to consider that the most important task facing the revolutionary movement in Korea at the present moment is the task of a broad national

---

Comintern and Cho Pong-am to the Communist Youth International, did go to Moscow to inform the formation. Cho Pong-am reported that he did inform the Comintern of the formation of the Party and sought an admission of the Korean Communist Party to the Comintern but reported to have been rebuffed because of the lack of evidence and also because he was a delegate to the Communist Youth International, and it was not until the following year that Cho Tong-u, the official delegate to the Comintern, reported to the Comintern. The Korean question was taken up between the Sixth Plenum which was held during November and December of 1926. It is doubtful that the Comintern issued a directive in 1925 which Kuusinen mentioned here, and even if they have issued a directive in 1925, it is unlikely that this is the result of the newly formed Korean Communist Party.

revolutionary front that would include along with the working class and the peasantry, artisans, the intelligentsia, and the petty and partially middle bourgeoisie.

Considering that at the present moment the creation of a new national revolutionary organization is inexpedient, in the future it will be necessary to raise the question of more thorough unification of the existing national organizations and the creation out of them of a single party of the Chinese Kuomintang type. The work of mutual co-ordination among different national organizations subsequent to their unification into a Korean Kuomintang, under the present conditions in Korea, could be considerably facilitated by the presence in the country of a united Korean Communist Party, which by penetrating all these organizations, will promote their unification and reconstruction according to a definite plan, provided that there is a high principled leadership on the part of the Central Committee of the Korean Communist Party. As to the tasks and perspectives raised before the Korean Communist movement, the resolution speaks for itself. Here [i.e., in the resolution] there is raised the task of unifying with the assistance of and under the leadership of the Communist Party, all the mass national organizations. Here in the final account, the Communist Party is lumped together with all these parties.

"All this work must be conducted not in the name of the Communist Party but under the slogan of a consistent struggle for independence of Korea."

The resolution goes on: "certainly the Korean Communist Party must strive also to have its members in leading positions in the national organizations." But this is immediately followed by a warning that they should not concentrate attention on it. "But its basic task is, with a reliance upon revolutionary worker and peasant elements, to push the national organizations to the left, to draw them (i.e. all national organizations without distinction) *in toto,* together with their leaders, into the national revolutionary struggle based on the tactics of a united national revolutionary front organized around a definite program of action. From this point of view the Korean Communist Party in particular under existing conditions must struggle most decisively against any attempts at splitting up the mass national organizations." At the end there is a mood of determination, but not in favor of the Communist movement, and not in favor of its independent existence and the struggle with national reformism. There is a determination, [however], when it is spoken of working masses, withdrawal from these national organizations; and on the contrary, when it is spoken of the posts in these organizations and the expulsion of the national reformists, then there is no determination whatsoever, and there is only a warning.

"These organizations must be drawn *in toto,* together with their leaders, into the national revolutionary struggle." But we know that together with their leaders it is difficult to draw them into the national revolutionary struggle since these leaders would sooner wish to betray the revolution than engage in revolutionary struggle.

Comrades, if these errors were not so grave and if there was no outright deviation, I would not mention them.

Now it is entirely clear to me that at one time a correct line was not given to the Korean movement, and herein is one of the reasons—only one of the reasons, yet a rather important one—which has complicated and hampered the development of the Korean Communist movement. We ought to correct these mistakes. There are also other resolutions. There is, for example, a resolution of 1924.[5] With regard to the national revolutionary and national reformist mass organizations, the spirit of this resolution corresponds to the directives of the Sixth Congress.

Just what did the Sixth Congress of the Comintern point to? What are the concrete tasks of the Korean Communist Party? Four or five basic points must be distinguished. At first, the Communists in Korea must intensify their work in the ranks of the proletariat; and, in their attempt at a thorough intensification of activity and strengthening of the organizations of

[5] So far, this document also is not known.

worker-peasant federation, they must struggle for the reorganization of trade unions, the latter's embracement of the working class, and the coordination of economic struggle with political demands. At the end, it said: "New forces ought to be drawn into the Communist Party, first of all from among the industrial workers. This will be the best guarantee of the Bolshevist development of the Party and is absolutely essential for the liquidation of the evil factional spirit within its ranks."

First of all it is necessary to concentrate attention upon recruiting party members from among the proletariat and upon organizing the industrial proletariat. Secondly, at the same time Communists must connect as closely as possible the demand for national liberation of the country with the slogan of agrarian revolution, which acquires ever greater significance because of the growing pauperization of the peasantry under a rapacious colonial regime. The fundamental thing here is the slogan of agrarian revolution. As we see, in the above-mentioned two resolutions, all attention was centered upon national liberation, upon the slogan of the independence of Korea. This means that from the three basic tasks of a bourgeois nationalist revolution only one task was taken into account. The question of an agrarian revolution was set aside, as was the third and not an insignificant task—that of the achievement of the hegemony of the proletariat. In this way what came out were the national revolutionary, or, more accurately, bourgeois national revolutionary tasks.

I will cite another excerpt from the thesis of the Sixth Congress. "In the ranks of the working masses who are enveloped by the large religious nationalist leagues, *Ch'ŏndokyo* and others, it is necessary to undertake patient, revolutionary educational work in order to free them from the influence of national reformist leaders." This is something completely different from the directives that I have cited, in which it was stated that [it was necessary] to push the national organizations to the left, together with their leaders. The mistake that had been committed earlier was corrected by a decision of the congress.

Paragraph 36 [states]: "Communist influence must be

strengthened in all existing revolutionary mass organizations. Instead of trying to create a general national revolutionary party (à la Kuomintang) on the basis of individual membership, it is necessary to aim at coordinating and unifying the activities of various national revolutionary organizations with the aid of joint action committees, creating a *de facto* block that would be under proletarian Communist leadership, and at the same time criticizing the half-heartedness and vascillations of the petty bourgeois nationalists and ceaselessly exposing them before the masses." Of course, if we speak of a *de facto* block, not of a formal one, then this is very important. It depends on the kinds of mass revolutionary organizations that exist in the country. At one time we were told that the *Shin'gan-hoe* had more than ten thousand members but we put little faith in this. Now it turns out that this point was greatly exaggerated and that this organization is mainly a superficial and not a real mass organization. But here [in the resolution] it is spoken of mass revolutionary organizations. Even a *de facto* block with superficial organizations is not recommended by the resolution.

In Korean practice, as in the practice of many other countries, one can note instances of groups switching from one deviation to the other, the opposite deviation. One cannot exclude a possibility of individual comrades' rolling downhill from the position of social radicalism towards social reformistic deviation and even *vice versa.*

The basic mistake of "left" deviation was the mechanical transfer of slogans from an environment for which they are appropriate into Korean situation where they are still completely out of place. This is a very frequent phenomenon. You are aware that an incorrect application of slogans—such as the slogan of armed rebellion, of dictatorship of the proletariat, etc. When in the process of practice they are being confused with one another regardless of the fact that in one period of time they constitute slogans in perspective whereas in another period of time they are slogans of action—can have a disastrous effect on the party. "Left" slogans which are saturated with leftist phrases and which are advanced irrespective of concrete circumstances are essentially opportunistic. In this connection there is a notorious example. The German opportunistic renegades, Brandler and others, wanted to become more leftist than the Comintern and raised the slogan of worker control over production since, in their opinion, this was a basic revolutionary slogan, etc. But in fact it turned out that this and other slogans similar to it served to hide their opportunistic deviation. It must be kept in mind that the Comintern advances this slogan for those countries in which a revolutionary situation still does not exist and that it uses this slogan as the slogan in perspective. In this way the masses are mobilized and prepared for decisive battles. In contrast to this, they, the "leftists," demand the realization of the immediate control of the workers over enterprises. This has another name—economic democracy.

It is thus also with the question of the hegemony of the proletariat. When we advance such a slogan, as a slogan which is indispensable under present circumstances, what do we then commit ourselves to? It commits us first of all to the practical struggle for the attainment of the hegemony of the proletariat, and this means organizing the proletariat, creating professional organizations, organizing a strong party to struggle for the eight-hour working day and for the development of cultural and political educational work, and so forth. All this arms the proletariat and prepares it for the realization of its hegemony.

Lenin's words that a Marxist is he who drives socialism to a state of the dictatorship of the proletariat have been rightly emphasized. Without the appropriate conditions the slogan of proletarian hegemony cannot have any significance, and the slogan of proletarian hegemony without struggle for this hegemony is a non-Marxist slogan.

***

Comrades, we have no intention of proposing some kind of rotten compromise either of slurring over important political questions of principle or of former factions' uniting together or of members belonging to various factions' uniting together on the basis of stifling important questions of principle. Absolutely not. Our policy line is clear. This line was defined by the Sixth Congress of the Comintern, and we can state with a complete confidence that on the basis of this line the unification, a real unification of the truly Bolshevik Communist forces of Korea, is possible. The duty of all Korean Communists after the Sixth Congress was, in my opinion, to give concrete expression to the basic principles in the theses of the Sixth Congress as applied to the concrete reality in Korea, to Korean conditions. But it seems to me that the Korean comrades have poorly performed this duty. At least we have benefited little from the factional discussion that followed the Sixth Congress. It turned out [to be] as in Gogol's "The Inspector General"—a heated argument breaks out around him who was the first to say "Mm"—Dobchinsky or Bobchinsky. All the arguments were centered around trivial matters.

***

As you know, in many parties factional skirmishes were taking place for years. There are parties that have become [universally] notorious in this respect such as the Polish and American parties, but the record belongs to the Korean factions.

There are cases when factional struggle is permissible and necessary. Some Korean comrades evidently thought that in Korea this was just the case. When is factional struggle permissible and necessary? When the struggle is conducted against agents of the bourgeoisie in the workers' movement and also those within the same party with Mensheviks, or the case of German comrades, when they were [formed] an independent party. Not so long ago, [that is] last year, the Comintern openly called upon the Swedish comrades to engage in a factional struggle against the rightists. This was the second time that it happened in the Swedish party. The first time the Comintern called upon them to engage in a factional struggle was in 1924-25. The Comintern gave full freedom [of action] for the factional struggle. Thus we are not always against factionalism, but it is necessary to understand when it is permissible and necessary and when it is harmful. It is permissible only in those cases when we can set for ourselves an aim of splitting the party, and we set this aim for ourselves when the question is that of struggling against the agents of the bourgeoisie.

The third condition is approval by, or permission from, the Comintern. Many Korean comrades have forgotten about this. They thought that since the Bolsheviks at one time carried out a factional struggle against the Mensheviks this was also permissible in Korea. But, comrades, when the Bolsheviks were carrying out their factional struggle there was no Comintern. Since 1919, however, no factional struggle is permissible without the authorization of the Comintern. Of course, no such authorization had ever been granted to you. The factions did not take into consideration the fact that factional struggle is permissible only under definite circumstances and that otherwise it is harmful, harmful from a Communist point of view.

Last year Comrade Stalin spoke a lot and in detail about the harm of factionalism for the Communist movement. His speech was recently published in the first issue of the *Bolshevik*. I would recommend even the memorization of those passages in Comrade Stalin's speech where he speaks about the harm of factionalism. He is speaking about the American party but from the passages which I shall cite you will see that it looks as if he knew very well the factional situation in the Korean Communist movement. There are four points in which comrade Stalin enumerates that what constitutes the harm of factionalism. "First of all," says he, "it consists in the fact that factionalism weakens the feeling of party loyalty, dulls revolutionary flair, and it blinds the party workers to the extent that in their passion for factionalism, they are forced to place the interests of the faction higher than those of the party, of the Comintern, and of the working class. Factionalism not infrequently brings the matter to a point when the party workers, blinded by the factional struggle, are inclined to assess all facts and all events in the life of the party not from the point of view of the interests of the Party and of the working class, but from the point of view of the interests of their own factional parochialism and those of their own factional intrigues." This is the first point, [namely], weakening of feelings of party loyalty and the loosening of party discipline. This is very closely related to that quality which in the process of the class struggle constitutes the main weakness of the party bourgeoisie that is, inability for disciplined action, inability for organization, and inability for subordinating the will of the majority to the organization— subordinating the organization to its leadership. This weakness is the weakness of the petty bourgeoisie, and it is reflected in the Korean Communist movement.

It is known that in the "Conditions for Admission into the Comintern" the necessity for iron discipline is strongly emphasized. This emphasis is made with full confidence because without such discipline, without the strictest discipline, the Communist party cannot fulfill its leading role in the revolutionary movement. Otherwise one will have a party which does not lead but only follows at the tail of the masses. One gets not a leading Communist party but the destruction of party unity.

There were many factions in the Korean Communist movement but even if there had been only two factions this would have been completely enough to paralyze the party, to paralyze the party's capacity for revolutionary war. Under Korean conditions it would have been even more necessary to maintain iron discipline since there are on the whole very few workers in the party. In the factional groups one has to look for workers with binoculars in one's hands and even then they are not to be found. When in 1902 the Bolsheviks argued with the Mensheviks about the first paragraph of the party statute, they, [the Bolsheviks], concentrated their attention on the nature of conditions that had to be laid down in order to strengthen the party and prevent an excessive influx into the party of petty bourgeois elements. But in the Korean Communist movement it often happened that the conditions for admission of workers into the party were made difficult so that there would not turn out an "excessive" influx of workers into the factions, so that the ranks would be "purified" of worker influence, and spared from predominant worker composition. With a staff such as this, which lacks discipline, which is split into factions fighting among themselves, no army in the world could be victorious. In factional struggle, as Comrade Stalin points out, there is a principle of: "Everything for the interests of the party."

By way of illustration, Comrade Stalin cites the example of the American Party. There certain individuals were simply swindlers, but nevertheless their friends in factions, even though they knew what sort of people these swindlers were, did not set themselves apart from them and defended them, simply because they were partisans of their factions. Comrade Stalin says that in factional struggle every sliver, every piece of cord, every soldier even a poor one, and every officer even a poor one,—all count. The participants in factional struggle do not care what sort of a person one is as long as he is a partisan of their own faction. This attitude is adopted with regard to factional partisans and factional friends, but, on the other hand, with regard to the opponents of factionalism, the strictest measures are recommended for dealing with them. Here such a purge is necessary which would result in the situation when 100 percent Bolsheviks alone, in the opinion of another faction, will be able to remain within the party, i.e., such Bolsheviks who in countries such as Korea do not exist at all.

Comrade Stalin's second point is very distinctive: "Secondly, the harm which comes from factionalism consists in the fact that factionalism interferes with educating the party in the spirit of principled politics, interferes with nurturing of the cadres in the spirit of honest, proletarian, uncorruptible revolutionism, which is free from rotten diplomacy and from unprincipled scheming. Leninism holds that principled politics are the only correct politics. Factionalism, on the contrary, thinks that factional diplomacy and unprincipled factional scheming are the only correct politics. This, as a matter of fact, explains why the atmosphere of factional struggle cultivates not the principled politicians but rather clever factional speculators, experienced swindlers, and Mensheviks who know how to swindle their opponent and none will be the wiser. Although such "educational" work by the factionalists runs contrary to the fundamental interests of the party and the working class, still the factionalists feel no concern about it. They recognize only their own factional diplomatic intrigues and their scheming interests. It is thus not surprising that principled politicians and honest proletarian revolutionaries meet with no sympathy among the factionalists. However, the factional dodgers and speculators, the unprincipled schemers, and back-stage-deal experts in organizing unprincipled blocks—all stand high in their [factionalists'] esteem."

Was it like this in the Korean movement? I think that it was and, moreover, very often. The people referred to by Comrade Stalin are numerous. But some people may object to what I say on the ground that the factionalists after all had their platforms, their programs, and so forth, and that because of this how can it be possible to describe all the leading comrades by means of a single brand?

On that score Comrade Stalin has also made a point: "What are these factions and their leaders mainly engaged in? What have the factional leaders of the majority and minority mainly been engaged in recently (he is speaking about the American party)? They have been engaged in factional squabbles and in all kinds of factional trifles; they have been engaged in formulating good-for-nothing and miserable platforms, in drawing up tens and hundreds of corrections and petty amendments to these platforms. Weeks and months are wasted on trapping the factional enemy, catching him, digging something up from his personal life and, if there is no way of digging it up, then fabricating some sort of fable."

The characteristic point here is the fact that even if the questions of principle are raised or even if a platform which outwardly seems principled is worked out,—all this is subordinated to the goals of the factional struggle. Everything, even the best platforms, become factional weapons in order to fight the opponent with greater effect. Even the authority of the Comintern is sometimes used for these purposes.

I will introduce a couple more citations from Comrade Stalin's speech:

"Thirdly, the harm that comes from factionalism consists in the fact that factionalism, by weakening the party's will for unity and by undermining the iron discipline of the party, creates within the party such a specific factional regime under which all the internal life of the party becomes exposed before the class enemies and the party itself confronts the danger of becoming a plaything in the hands of the bourgeoisie, i.e., the police." This was what happened many times in the Korean Communist movement. The way Comrade Stalin illustrates this point is very distinctive: "It usually happens in the following manner. Let us say that some question is being decided upon by the Politburo of the Central Committee. In the Politburo there are the minority and majority, each of whom views every decision from its own factional point of view. If the party is dominated by a factional regime, then the dealers of both factions instantly notify their followers about a certain decision by the Politburo, tyring to prepare them for favoring their faction and to indoctrinate them accordingly. Usually, this mode of notification is systematically repeated; and the reason why it is systematically repeated is that each faction considers it its duty to inform, in a manner profitable to itself, its own followers and to keep them mobilized and prepared for fight with factional opponents. As a result, the important and confidential decisions of the party become the property of the street. And since the street merges with a surrounding environment, the agents of the bourgeoisie are given access to secret party decisions which makes it easier for them to make use of the data about the internal life of the party turning them against party interests. Although such a regime threatens the party with complete demoralization of its ranks, still the factionalists do not care about that because they place the interests of their own group above everything else."

This, more than once, was also the state of affairs in the Korean party. The situation in Korea after the Sixth Congress was such that even if the Comintern had wanted, though it did not want, to transfer the leadership of Korean Communist Party into the hands of one faction or another it could not have done so even for the simple reason that the police knew the whole factional intrigues and the membership and leadership of each group. How could the Comintern then recommend one or another of these factions to a position of party leadership? It would have been entirely wrong.

The last and very important point in Comrade Stalin's speech is as follows: "Finally the harm that comes from factionalism consists in the fact that factionalism undermines at the root any positive work in the party, robs the party workers of the desire to occupy themselves with the questions of the daily needs of the working class (wages, the working day, improvement of material conditions of the working class, and so forth), slows down the party's work on the preparation of the working class for class battles with the bourgeoisie, and thus creates such situation in which the prestige of the party is inevitably bound to fall in the eyes of the workers, whereas the workers will have to abandon the ranks of the party instead of joining it in whole groups."

This was precisely what happened in the Korean Communist movement. It is no wonder at all, therefore, that the attractive power of the party fell year by year. One thus got a situation which could only be called the bankruptcy of the Korean Communist Party.

For many years the Comintern was pursuing a course of unifying the Communist groups that existed in Korea or [unifying] the better elements of these groups. Some people think that this was an erroneous course. But in my opinion the mistake did not consist in this. The mistake firstly consisted in the fact that a correct, completely correct, political line for the party was not worked out; secondly, it consisted in the fact that the leading nucleus of the party was not composed of the best anti-factional elements but instead the party leadership was handed over to the factionalists which is the same thing as entrusting a dog with guarding a butcher shop; thirdly for a long time it was not known whether the party leadership was fighting against the factional or anti-factional course, and only later did it become clear that it systematically pursued a factional course.

Thus after the Sixth Congress of the Comintern there was a question of what to do further. What could have been done? One could have once more undertaken the experiment which had been done many times in the past, with a new group or

with a new faction at the head. But the Comintern retorted that
this was impossible and that nothing good could come of it. A
serious anti-factional course was adopted, not a course designed
to unite the existing factions but a firm course designed to
destroy them, to liquidate these factions, and to create a new
party, a new leading nucleus.

Someone advanced the proposition that the Japanese police
also stand for the liquidation of all the Communist factions in
Korea. This comparison is at least unfortunate. In factional
struggle there is not only deviations but also nonsense. This is
simply nonsense. It simply makes no sense to compare the
Comintern's policy aimed at liquidating the factions and at
creating a new and truly Communist party with the goals of the
Japanese police.

Thus far there have been few positive results coming from the
anti-factional course which was adopted [by the Korean
Communist Party]. Yet, one can say that to a great extent the
success has already been achieved in paralyzing the factional
work of the former groups and factions and placing them in a
situation of certain disorientation. In my opinion, this is also a
step forward. For the time being the factions have not yet been
fully liquidated, but these factions to a certain degree already
resemble the wandering shadows of those who are in purgatory,
as it is said in Finnish national poetry. These are the spectres of
communism, but not the spectres of communism about which
Marx and Engels speak in the "Communist Manifesto" and
which are the scarecrow for the bourgeoisie but the spectres
which scare nobody.

The leaders of the factions, the factional headmen, who
warm themselves by their factional fire, seem very cunning. It
would be preferable if they carried out an open struggle against
the Comintern, but they do not wish to do it. They say that
they are partially in favor of the Comintern line and are also
against factions. We, they say, have disbanded ourselves on our
own and we wish nothing; you will have to prove that we are
still factionalists. In short, as Comrade Stalin says, they know
how to leave none the wiser and think that no one will notice,
wherein lies their diplomacy. They set up their united factional

committees to create a new party, publish their journals, etc., but at the same time they say: you will have to prove that we are factionalists. There is no need to prove it. Others even go farther, saying that they are in favor of the Comintern line and even struggle for the liquidation of factionalists and factions; i.e., the Seoul faction members are for the liquidation of the M.L. faction members. In the latest issue of the Korean *Bolshevik* they even speak of fighting on two fronts—for the liquidation of both the M.L. faction members and the Tuesday Association faction members.

In short, they seem to be struggling for the liquidation of factionalism. But this is a very cheap way of doing it. The kind of cheap liquidation of factionalism has existed in Korea at the time but it is not called the liquidation of factionalism but rather factional struggle. While the factionalists say that they do not engage in any factional activities in their opinion, they seem to think that they are kings in exile, pretenders to the throne of the future Communist party in Korea.

Our answer to them is this: They are of no need for the future Communist Party of Korea; they would only be harmful elements in the revolutionary movement. But they are not even capable of doing any great harm because we hope to be able to carry out a successful struggle against them.

Imagine that the factionalists were right about one issue or another. Even if they had been right, we could have still replied, even in that case, that they were pursuing the correct line on a particular question so poorly, in such a faction-like manner, and so harmfully that, as a result, they ended up in a complete isolation from other revolutionaries, the environment of the workers, and the working class. And this is even worse; it shows what failures they are as leaders of the Communist party. They do not see that all these quarrels over whose viewpoint is better are but a gnat compared to the elephantine harm which they brought about by their factional struggle. The factionalists have to be completely resmelted if any use is to be expected of them. The history of the revolutionary movement in Korea will either be resmelting the factionalists, if they are still not absolutely spoiled material, even as utility waste, or it will be turning them into political corpses. In this we must assist history in order to speed up this process, and it is not something difficult to do because the factionalists in Korea have always been trees without roots.

The foundations of a genuine Bolshevik party are other than those upon which up to the present time the Communist groups in Korea have been created. The first foundation is a healthy proletarian membership together with the best, truly Communist, forces from among the revolutionary intelligentsia—the forces which have deep roots in the depth of the laboring masses. The second foundation is iron discipline and unshakable unity of a revolutionary party. This is also the indispensable foundation for a truly Bolshevik party. At the same time, there must be an able application of secrecy completely different from that which you have had up to now. The third foundation is a politics of principle based on Leninism as well as its correct concretization. And the fourth foundation is a merciless and systematic struggle against any remnants of factionalism.

It is completely insufficient for the factionalists, the comrades from the former factions, to simply cease their activities as factions. It is essential that they conduct an active struggle against factionalism, and first of all the struggle against the groups to which the comrades formerly belonged. This is precisely the first duty in the task of elimination of factionalism. This is the case when whoever is not for us, he is against us. But how is it with the Korean Communist journals, or rather journals of the Communist groups in Korea—that is, the *Kegŭp t'ujaeng* [Class Struggle], the *Bolshevik*, and others—are they for us or against us? It is very difficult to say. In any case, it is not clear whether they are for us, and this means that they are against us and that we must carry out struggle against them.

I shall point out one more thing. It is necessary to cast aside factional suspiciousness with regard to those comrades who in this struggle will be the adherents of the Comintern line provided that those comrades themselves wish to be supporters of that struggle. It seems to me that the principal, open and secret, weapon of the factionalists in the nearest future will consist in their disseminating factional suspiciousness with regard to the adherents of the Comintern in this struggle. For the reason that comrades formerly belonged to one or the other of the factions, the factionalists will disseminate, with regard to them, the suspicions that in a clandestine manner they are still continuing to carry out the factional struggle of the former faction. But since there are almost no comrades who did not formerly belong to some faction or another, any further work would be completely impossible if it is impermissible to draw in active struggle those comrades who formerly belonged to factional groups but who have now strongly renounced these groups. We are convinced that some comrades have sincerely renounced the positions taken by their former factional groups and that they will openly struggle against the factionalism of their former groups. Such comrades are needed for the cause of the Korean Communist movement.

But it is necessary for everyone to give up factional suspiciousness with regard to them, the suspiciousness which has no basis as far as those comrades who will now openly carry out the struggle for the Comintern's anti-faction line are concerned. This is essential if we wish to accomplish anything. If it happens that one of the comrades who has promised us to struggle against factionalism will still be a hidden factionalist, then he must be driven out from the movement. But to be suspicious and sow suspiciousness without basis is offensive.

Comrades, I am coming to the close of my speech. I recall how Lenin, in 1921, after the internal struggle in the German Communist Party, the harm of which is completely impossible to compare to the harmfulness of your internal factional fights, told the German comrades that there had been enough of factional struggle. As far as the Korean movement is concerned, we have many more grounds not only to demand it but to struggle for it. At that time Lenin said that there was a bit of exaggeration made by those comrades who struggled against rightists, hunted rightists, and querulously persecuted their rightist opponents in the German Communist Party. Lenin on this basis concluded that this [little] "bit" was sufficient to destroy the party.

We have significantly greater grounds, comrades, to say what is necessary in order to create a serious party and so that all seriously and actively help us to liquidate factionalism in their countries. The cause of the Korean revolution demands it. Even if we succeed in rapidly liquidating factionalism and creating a new and genuine Communist Party, even in that case we will be faced with many and great difficulties.

In order to bring the struggle to victory, it is necessary to exert all effort of Korean revolutionaries and of the Korean proletariat. In any event, many sacrifices will be necessary. But a situation when factionalism no longer exists but there is only a strong revolutionary party—[this] is also a guarantee for victory.

B. THE FRONT ORGANIZATIONS, 1930-32

Item 35: The Tasks of the Revolutionary Trade Union Movement in Korea[1]

1. The world economic crisis has acutely affected Japanese economy. Korea is the largest colony of Japanese imperialism, which is also experiencing the effects of the crisis in the sharpest forms. Japanese capitalism is endeavoring to shift the burden of the crisis to Korea. The chronic agrarian crisis in Korea, resultant upon the imperialist landlord's usurious exploitation of the countryside, has become greatly sharpened as the result of the bad harvest, the taxation burdens and the fall in prices. Japanese imperialism, caught in the clutch of the crisis, is intensifying its offensive against Korea, exploiting it as a market and as a raw material source.

The crisis is worsening the position of the Korean working class, dirving ever larger numbers of peasants off the land and hastening their pauperization, while the urban petty bourgeoisie are being rapidly ruined. Wages are being reduced, working hours lengthened, rationalization is being carried through chiefly by the intensification of the working process, and particularly at the expense of the women and young workers.

Unemployment in industry is being aggravated by the growth of unemployment in agriculture and the return of Korean workers from Japan. The police regime, the espionage system at the factories, beatings-up, fines, relentless persecution of the labor movement, lack of any elementary rights—these are what characterize the position of the proletariat in Korea.

2. Against this background of crisis we see that the national

[1] This document is the resolution adopted by the Executive Bureau of the Red International of Labor Union (R.I.L.U.) on September 18, 1930. This document is often referred to as the September Theses, and it was a product of the fifth congress of the R.I.L.U. held in August 1930. The document was originally written in English, and it is available in *Resolution of the Fifth World Congress of the R.I.L.U.*, (London, 1931), pp. 152-58. A Japanese translation was made from this English version, and it is available in *Taiheiyó ródo-sha*, vol. I, nos. 9-10 (October-November, 1932), pp. 53-61.

emancipation struggle against Japanese imperialism, in general, and the class struggle of the proletariat, in particular, is growing and becoming sharper. The Wŏnsan strike, the mass support to this strike, the wave of student strikes and mass demonstrations, particularly the May Day demonstrations of the workers and peasants, the increased number of rentiers' conflicts, the new outbreaks of partisan movements in Chientao, the large number of workers' strikes—all these have only been advance struggles, signalizing the approach of new, larger mass movements of the proletariat.

Japanese imperialism bribes the national-reformist bourgeoisie with promises of local self-management in order, by utilizing them, to stem the new revolutionary wave. The national reformist bourgeoisie and its organs, *Chosŏn ilbo, Tong-a ilbo,* part of *Ch'ŏndo-kyo,* who fear the growth of the revolutionary wave in Korea, the revolutions in China and in India, and the successes of socialist construction in the USSR, see in Chiang Kai-shek and in the Chinese counter-revolution an example worthy of imitation, and seek collaboration with Japanese imperialism, vilifying the USSR.

Shin'gan-hoe is likewise a national-reformist organization, as has been proved by its policy of sabotage during the student and workers' movements. The workers' strikes, the increased activity of the urban petty bourgeoisie, and the increasing number of peasant movements, go to prove that the maneuvers of Japanese imperialism and Korean national reformist bourgeoisie, their reapproachment and joint struggle against the revolutionary movement, have been unable to stem the growth of the mass struggle.

3. The young Korean proletariat is beginning to play an increasingly important part in the national emancipation movement in Korea. The turning-point in the development of the revolutionary labor movement of Korea was the Wonsan strike and the support it received from the entire proletariat of Korea.

That the class struggle of the proletariat is becoming the chief factor in the national emancipation struggle in Korea is proven by the disunited spontaneous outbreaks in the transport, textile, mining and other industries, by the miners' strike in

Shinhŭng, which went as far as armed clashes with the police, the fifty more or less large strikes in 1930, the furious terror instituted by Japanese imperialism against the labor movement, and the increasing efforts of the national reformist bourgeoisie to strengthen their position in the labor movement.

The support given to the workers' strike struggle by the peasant masses, the inclination of the workers and peasants towards joint movements, go to show that the prerequisites are maturing for an alliance between the proletariat and the peasantry under the leadership of the working class.

4. The class struggles of the proletariat which have occurred recently have displayed the militant qualities of the young working class of Korea: stubbornness in defending their class interests (the Wŏnsan strike which lasted three months, the textile workers' struggle, women in Pusan, etc.), the self-sacrifices and class solidarity (practically the whole of the working class, like one man, supported the Wŏnsan strikers), the desires for revolutionary methods of struggle, and the lack of confidence in the reformist labor leaders. The widespread participation and big part played by the women and young workers in the recent strikes are especially characteristic.

The struggles also showed up the great weaknesses and defects of the trade union movement in Korea. The chief weakness of the trade union movement is that the Korean proletariat does not possess its own revolutionary trade union organizations.

The General Confederation of Labor of Korea has about 47,000 members. However, it is headed by petty bourgeois and nationalist elements. It is only in a few local organizations that the workers have succeeded in driving the petty bourgeois and national reformist leaders out of the leadership. The Federation does not fight against rationalization, does not defend the interests of the unemployed and does not even organize the economic struggles, not to speak of the political struggles, of the proletariat. It does not educate its members in the spirit of the proletarian class struggle, does not direct the strike struggle. It is not built on the principle of election; its rank and file organizations at the factories, railways, etc., are either not crystallized or are completely absent. No general membership meetings are called, partly as the result of the bans by the Japanese police and defeatist legalism. (This shows complete submission to other Japanese police regime).

The Federation not only does not fight the police regime, but in cases of disputes arising persuades the workers to accept arbitration, sending petitions and requests to the employers, the Chamber of Commerce, the police, and the Governor-General. In a word, it refuses to apply the revolutionary methods of the class struggle.

All these circumstances, taken together, determine the character of the Federation as a reformist body. This does not in the least mean, however, that all the Federation organizations are reformist, and it would be absolutely ridiculous to consider the entire membership to be reformist. On the contrary, the reformist leadership is steadily losing influence over the membership; the workers spontaneously strive to turn the Federation organizations into revolutionary unions. These desires of the workers have to contend against colossal difficulties which consist not only in the ruthless persecution by the Japanese authorities, and the resistance of the fascists, but chiefly, in the lack of a strong, revolutionary party of the proletariat, in the unprincipled group struggle and the lack of organization of the left wing.

5. This determines the immediate tasks of the R.I.L.U. supporters in the Korean trade union movement. The foremost task of the R.I.L.U. supporters is to consolidate and organize a left wing inside the Federation. At first our forces and attention must be centered on the largest points of concentration of the working class (railways, mines, ports, textile and tobacco factories, power stations, chemical factories, etc.).

The left wing must draw up a concrete program of demands for the workers, taking into consideration the specific interests of each industry, the conditions of each district, consolidating the workers around this program, raising the masses to the struggle for its realization. The left wing, after corresponding preparation, must set up factory committees, elected, as a general rule, by all the workers of the given enterprise. The factory committees must be set up without consulting the legal authorities, consolidating the masses around them. Every movement of the working masses must be utilized for the formation of factory committees. Factory committees are permanent organizations representing the interests of all workers, organized or unorganized, of the given enterprise. Where conditions do not permit this or at small factories, mills, handicraft shops, factory delegates should be organized. Simultaneously a most consistent struggle must be conducted for the recognition of the factory committees and factory delegates, for the recognition of the unions as such, against all restrictions in their activities, against police control.

In the process of the struggle the left wing should systematically expose the opportunist and treacherous policy of the reformist leaders and win over the membership of the trade union organizations. The left wing leaning upon its rank and file organizations, and actively participating in the class struggle, must put as its task not only the conquest of the organized, but also the conquest of the unorganized workers.

6. Here it should be borne in mind that the consolidation of the working masses around the left wing, the exposure of the reformist leaders, is only possible in the process of the struggle for the most vital demands of the workers. Questions of wages, working hours, social legislation, treatment of workers, fines, housing, unemployment insurance, social insurance, must occupy the center of attention of the propaganda, agitation, and struggle of the left wing.

In Korean conditions, where practically the whole industry is in the hands of Japanese capital, where the Japanese military police colonial regime openly comes out against the workers to defend colonial super-profits, practically every economic struggle becomes a struggle against Japanese imperialism, a political struggle. The working masses, through the struggle for their immediate economic interests, must be led to the struggle for political rights (right of unions, meetings, speech and press), to the struggle against police violence and for the liberation of the political prisoners, and to the struggle against Japanese imperialism and for the agrarian revolution. It is only in the course of this economic and political struggle that the proletariat will be freed from the influence of the petty-bourgeois and national-reformist elements.

At the same time the left wing must conduct a relentless struggle against the police unions (Hamgyŏng Namdo Nodonghoe, etc.), against arbitration by the Chambers of Commerce, the police and Governor-General, against the intereference of the national reformist organizations in the economic struggles.

7. The task of the R.I.L.U. supporters should not be limited to working in the Federation organizations. The same activities should also be conducted in all the trade unions which do not belong to the Federations. Where there are no trade union organizations, or where they are not mass organizations, the tasks of the R.I.L.U. supporters consist of establishing revolutionary unions. The revolutionary unions must be built on the industrial principle, and must have strong rank and file organizations, in the form of revolutionary factory delegates and factory committees elected by all the workers. The revolutionary unions may affiliate to the Federation while retaining their independent leadership and revolutionary character. The work and struggle of the left wing organizations inside the Federation and in the independent unions must be closely connected with the newly formed trade unions.

8. Special attention should be paid to the organization of the agricultural laborers. Insofar as the agricultural laborers belong to the Peasant Federation, they should be organized in special groups, these groups subsequently being turned into an independent revolutionary agricultural workers' union.

9. A very big part in Korean industry is played by the women and young workers. The task of the left wing is to draw the women and young workers into the trade unions. This task can only be accomplished by defending their specific interests. The left wing must put forward and fight for special demands for the women workers (abolition of night work, leave before and after confinement, creĉhes for children, equal pay for equal work, etc.), and for young workers (six-hour day, wages during apprenticeship, free training schools, etc.). It is necessary to fight for the formation of special youth and women sections in

the trade unions, putting forward the women and young workers themselves for their leadership.

10. As the consequence of the crisis, the restriction of production, closing down of factories, ruination of the peasantry and the return of the Korean workers from Japan, unemployment is becoming steadily more acute. The task of the left wing is to organize the unemployed to head their struggle, linking up the unemployed with the movement of the workers in jobs.

In this sphere the demand for state unemployment benefits must become the central question around which the unemployed and employed workers should be mobilized. At the same time the left wing must fight for the non-payment of rent by the unemployed, benefits to buy rice and fuel, the abolition of payment for gas, electricity, etc. Joint meetings and demonstrations and other mass movements of the unemployed and employed workers must become one of the methods of fighting unemployment.

11. The left wing must take upon itself the organization of strike committees in the work of preparing for and directing strikes. The strike committees must be elected at general or delegate meetings of the workers. The strike committees must prepare for and direct the strike, despite and against the reformist leaders. In their work to prepare for and direct the strikes, the R.I.L.U. supporters in Korea must be guided by the decisions of the Strasbourg Conference and of the Fifth Congress of the R.I.L.U.

12. The skilful combination of legal and illegal work is one of the conditions of successful activities of the left wing. The left wing must organize workers' circles, trade union circles, evening schools, and other such legal organizations. It must, however, be borne in mind that these auxiliary organizations cannot be substitutes for the trade unions.

13. Japanese workers play a big part in the most important industries and largest enterprises in Korea. A considerable part of the Japanese workers form an imperialistically inclined labor aristocracy, and not infrequently the Japanese workers belong to fascist and imperialist organizations. This does not imply that

the R.I.L.U. supporters must refuse to carry out the most difficult task of freeing the basic masses of the Japanese workers from the influence of the bourgeoisie. The R.I.L.U. supporters in Japan must extend all possible assistance to their Korean comrades. The revolutionary workers of Japan and Korea must act in a united front in the struggle for the defence of the Chinese revolution and the Soviet Union, for the overthrow of Japanese imperialism.

14. The Chinese workers likewise occupy quite an important part in Korea. Japanese imperialism and the national reformist bourgeoisie strive to fan national hatred between the Korean and Chinese workers, utilizing the latter as scabs. The left wing must organize the Chinese workers, educate the Chinese and Korean workers in the spirit of international proletarian solidarity.

15. A most urgent task of the left wing is to set up a trade union press, to publish leaflets, factory papers, popular pamphlets, posters, etc., to throw light on the life of the workers, to give form to the demands and leadership to the class struggle of the Korean proletariat.

16. All these tasks can be accomplished if the left wing boldly and determinedly follows the line of forming its rank and file organizations at the factory, of carrying out the united front from below, promoting and training workers' cadres for leading positions, of creating broad trade union activities. The left wing must become the organizer and leader of the economic struggles for the everyday needs of the workers, must organize and mobilize the working masses for the struggle against Japanese imperialism, for the agrarian revolution, to fundamentally improving the position of the working class in Korea.

17. The left wing must maintain the closest possible connections with the R.I.L.U., the Pan-Pacific Trade Union Secretariat, and through these with the entire international revolutionary trade union movement, in particular, with the revolutionary trade union movement of Japan and China.

Item 36: The Labor Movement of Korea after the Fifth R.I.L.U. Congress[1]

The Korean labor movement during the period under report can be characterized by two basic features: the further upsurge of the strike wave in face of the deepening economic crisis, and the crystallization of the left wing of the Korean trade union movement. The ever-intensifying attacks of Japanese imperialism and the native bourgeoisie, which has served to worsen still more the already miserable conditions of the Korean workers (the lengthening of the working day to 15-16 hours, wages cut by 30-50 percent, over 200,000 unemployed), gave rise to the development of the strike movement in Korea. The number of strikes, particularly lately, has greatly increased. Whilst in 1930, 70 strikes were waged involving 15,000 workers, which was a record figure for the history of the strike movement in Korea, we see that 60 strikes were waged only during the first half of 1931, with 12,000 participators. More and more fresh strata of the Korean workers are rallying to the fighting front—the agricultural laborers, the building workers and women workers. The strikes acquire a more and more obdurate character. Clashes frequently occur between the strikers and police. Strike committees are formed, picket-lines and demonstrations organized which can be explained by left wing influence. Facts have been recorded of joint manifestations with the unemployed (Inch'ŏn), with Japanese workers (Mokp'o) and Chinese workers (Ch'ŏngjin):[2] In result some strikes ended in complete or partial victory for the workers (dockers— Ch'ŏngjin, chemical workers—Hamhŭng, food workers—Inch'ŏn). However, instances

[1] This is a rare document and is available only in English. The author of this document is not known, but it is assumed that he is a Korean who knew a great deal of the Korean labor union movement. This document is available in *Eastern and Colonial,* vol. IV, no. 10-11 (November-December, 1931), pp. 8-10.

[2] These are all names of large cities in Korea. Exact reference to these towns is not clear, for Inch'ŏn is not known for its unemployment particularly, nor Mokp'o for the Japanese workers and Ch'ŏng jin for the Chinese.

are not rare, when the readiness of the strikers to fight turns into passive forms of struggle, as hunger strikes, etc., which still bears witness to the spontaneity of the movement and the insufficient revolutionary leadership.

The Fifth R.I.L.U. Congress and the September Resolution of the Executive Bureau marked the beginning of the activity to collect our forces and to organizationally reinforce the influence of the left wing. The R.I.L.U. adherents carried out this work, setting up revolutionary trade union opposition groups inside the reformist unions of transport workers, metal workers and printers, as well as preparing the organization of revolutionary unions among the unorganized workers in those branches of industry where no trade unions had existed (trade union groups among the chemical workers).

The left wing succeeded in achieving these results by approaching more closely the everyday struggle of the working masses. Work was carried on for setting up factory committees and for convening delegates' meetings. A number of strikes were headed and organized during which strike committees and picket-lines were set up (P'yŏngyang, Pusan, Hamhŭng, Inch'on). Some work has begun for organizing the unemployed. Under the leadership of the lefts, the unemployed committee in Inch'on rendered support to the strikers, putting obstacles in the way of the strike bearers.

However, the tempo of our work and the growth of the left wing lags behind the leftward trend of the working masses and their growing militancy. The Korean proletariat is still very weakly organized. The workers of such an important industry for Korea as mining industry are still wholly unorganized. Work for organizing the chemical workers has only begun. Most of the organized workers are in the ranks of the Korean Federation of Labor, headed by reformists, the left wing still has very little influence over them.

Along with objective difficulties, due to the colonial regime in the country (illegal conditions of work, continuous repressions and arrests of activists of the revolutionary trade union movement, which wrested 400-500 active organizers of the revolutionary trade unions from us in July last, stirring national differences between the toiling Japanese, Koreans, Chinese, etc.), the lagging behind of the left wing is due to a number of mistakes made by it in the field of leadership of economic battles, in its attitude towards arbitration, and also mistakes of an organizational character.

The left wing has not always strained sufficient efforts to head the discontent of the masses and to develop it into organized action. Most of the strikes broke out spontaneously. The strike of the 600 women textile workers in Hamhŭng and the 400 women textile workers in Seoul, the strike of about 1,000 dockers in Ch'ŏngjin, and a number of other more or less important strikes, despite the readiness of the strikes to fight, had not been duly supported by the left wing and went off without its participation. Insufficient work was carried out for exposing the reformists. Concrete facts of betrayal on the part of the reformist leaders from the Korean Federation of Labor were weakly used, at the time when the whole activity of the latter was openly directed to substitute the class struggle with class collaboration (the coordination of the reformist leaders and the police in the question of suppressing the P'yŏngyang strike, the trecherous role played by them in a number of other strikes).

Simultaneously with lagging behind the growing activity of the masses, some mistakes of a sectarian nature were made. The left wing, instead of carrying on energetic and systematic work inside the Korean Federation of Labor and other reformist trade unions, set up its own dwarf-like trade unions, often quite parallel to unions already existing, which led to these to be turned into isolated from the workers, narrow sectarian organizations.

The ranks of the left wing are still numerically weak, however there can be no doubt about it that it is steadily growing and developing. By continuing to extend and reinforce its influence organizationally, on the basis of heading the growing activity of the Korean proletariat, the left wing is bound to mobilize the wide working masses and rally them to its ranks, organize them in its militant organizations and lead them to battle against Japanese imperialism and the national bourgeoisie.

Item 37: Letter of the Pan-Pacific Labor Union Secretariat to the Supporters of the Union in Korea[1]

Dear Comrades:

The Pan Pacific Labor Union Secretariat, after discussing the problems concerning the conditions and duty of the revolutionary labor movement, recognizes the need to call several important problems to the attention of the Korean working class at present stage.

1. The present economic panic in Korea is a part of Japanese and world economic panic. The Korean economic panic is worsening because of the Japanese imperialistic policy and internally chronic agricultural crisis that is the remnant of the feudal serf system. The process of land grabbing and peasant bankruptcy is rapidly increasing. Besides, the condition of desperate Korean workers is getting worse. The panic has caused the closure of many factories and significantly increased the number of the unemployed (one out of three workers in Korea was forced to the streets). This was followed by 30% to 50% reduction in wages and one to two hour extension in working period. At the same time the suppression of the revolutionary movement is greatly intensified, and the arrests of four to five hundred revolutionaries and barbaric interrogation and sentencing of the arrested are becoming a part of the ruling system of Japanese imperialism in Korea. Paralleling with the institution of the emergency laws to place the nation under emergency alert following the occupation of Manchuria and to change Korea as a base for imperial plundering, the revolutionary labor movement is under the heavy pressure of the ruthless militarists. In an effort to escape the economic panic by increasing the

---

[1] This document is the directive of the Secretariat of the Pan Pacific Labor Union to the supporters of the Union in Korea. It was issued from Shanghai in October 1931, and is often referred to as the October Theses. It seems obvious that the directive was originally written in English, but the original English version is yet to be located. This document is available only in Japanese, and this English version is a retranslation from the Japanese. See the Japanese version in *Intanashonaru*, Vol. VI, no. 8 (June, 1932), pp. 72-75.

workers' burden and in fear of the loss of their share of the plunder from the Korean people as a result of the outbreak of a revolution, the Korean bourgeoisie is compromising with the Japanese imperialists under the motto of autonomy and resists the national liberation movement. The Korean bourgeoisie is used as tools of the Japanese imperialists in their scheme to send troops to Manchuria. They have assisted and participated in the provocative attack in the Manbo-san incident, and led the attack on the Chinese in Korea. Thus, in effect, they have directed the energy of the masses toward national friction, and at the same time they have deviated the attention of the workers from the struggle against their chief enemy, the Japanese imperialism. The national bourgeoisie embelish themselves with such phrases as "revolutionary" and "anti-imperialism" to preserve their dignity in the national liberation movement. They attempt to separate the workers from the class struggle and bring them under their influence by utilizing such methods as organization of national reformist conciliatory labor unions and incorporating those labor masses who follow them into their own organization such as *Ch'ŏndo-kyo* and *Shin'gan-hoe.*

2. In connection with the worsening living condition of the laboring masses and intensification of the oppression against them, the revolutionary struggle and the mass movement are gradually growing. In the stages of anti-imperialist and revolutionary struggles, the Korean proletariat is emerging as a vanguard of the struggle. The Korean masses are meeting the all out offensive of Japan and the national bourgeoisie with positive resistance. The peasant movement that resists not only the landlord but also the Japanese police (in Hongwon and Tanch'ŏn) is gradually developing into a large scale.

The wave of the strike struggle is rapidly rising, particularly in recent years. There is a marked increase in number of strikes, and their scope is widening gradually to include all working masses. Peasants (Yŏnghung) and working women are advancing as a new company of the Korean proletariat in the strike struggle. They have organized demonstrations for the striking groups and many occupy the vanguard position of the struggle, directly confronting the police. Thus the strikes are intensified, became doggedly and also became a persistent fight. Fightings have been staged between the striking groups and the police. The result of the enthusiastic participation of the left wing gave expression to the strength and cooperativeness of the striking groups in many strikes. In those strikes where joint efforts of the Japanese and Chinese laborers (Makinojima and Ch'ŏngjin) are developing, the more complete methods are devised and used. These are the organization of the strikers' groups, picket group, and the demonstration of the strikers.

However, most of them are still small scale strikes, bursting out spontaneously. The discontent of the workers concerning the strikes weaken the power of the strikers, losing the energy for direct struggle and thus forcing them to take such negative methods of struggle as hunger strikes. Although it is the expression of great self-sacrifice and firmness of the workers, it is also the very reason that invited the failures of most of the workers' strikes. What is the basic reason for the failure? The reason for not winning even a single victory by the Korean proletariat in strikes is not only the treasonable acts of the national reformist leaders and brute forces of the police, but also the inadequate preparation for the struggle and organization of the Korean proletariat.

The Korean proletarian organization is as yet weak, but there is almost no organization in the most important industries in Korea such as mines and chemical industries. Despite the fact that women workers as a great Korean proletarian force, suffer from the ruthless exploitation and feel more deeply the fear and oppression of the Japanese imperialists, the rate of organization is extremely a small percentage. The majority of the organized workers are in the Korean Federation of Labor [Chosŏn Noch'ong] which is led by the national reformists who are the tools of the national bourgeoisie. The national reformists are gradually becoming a weapon of the bourgeoisie against the proletariat. All their activities are geared to replace the class struggle with class compromise.

They are waging their treasonable activities through forced mediation, compromise, and other similar methods that preclude the continuation of struggle. Especially the national reformists are giving comforts to the bourgeoisie and welcome the police mediation which is non-peaceful and oppressive measures. The treasonable activities of the leaders of the Korean Federation of Labor were made clear in numerous strikes: such as the stopping of P'yongyang strike by the leaders of the Korean Federation of Labor in cooperation with the police, the refusal of the branch office of the Korean Federation of Labor to join the Shinhung miners' strike, the eventual breading of the strike in cooperation with the factory owners, and numerous other similar incidents. The only force under such circumstances that possesses the strength to organize the Korean proletariat and can stage a definitive struggle against the Japanese imperialism and its plunderers is the left wing of the Korean labor union movement, but the left wing is still weak. The growth of the left wing falls short of the Korean proletariat's positiveness. The wishes of the Korean working masses to develop their struggle and to create the leftist trends in the working class should free the working masses from the influence of the national reformists for the left wing, and make it possible to include masses organizationally, and create favorable conditions to bring these about.

3. The decision of September 1930 issued by the Executive Bureau of the Profintern and the Secretariat of the Pacific Labor Union had pointed out the duty of the supporters of the union to organize the left in the Korean labor union movement and unite the wide range of laborers for the class struggle. The supporters of the Profintern and the Pacific Labor Union Secretariat began their struggle for the realization of this duty, and they have accomplished some results in their struggle at the Profintern Congress. The organization of the union groups among the chemical and metal workers, the usage of such auxiliary organization as *Ch'in'u-hoe* [Friends Association] that combined the workers without regard to nationality, organization of leftist groups in all industrial sectors, activities to organize representative group and factory committee, and others. All these activities prove that the process of organizing the left wing has begun. The supporters of the left wing have

fought for strikes (P'yŏngyang, Pusan, and Inch'ŏn). At Inch'ŏn the Committee of the unemployed under the direction of leftists prevented the breaking of strikes. The activities to organize the unemployed are the evidence that the left wing is getting closer to the working masses's side.

4. Despite the fact that the supporters of the left wing have achieved numerous results, it should be pointed out honestly that they were not able to accomplish numerous tasks that confronted the left wing. Their shortcomings in the activities are the following:

First was the inability to organize the masses' discontent and transform it to organizational struggle. The majority of the strikes were in primitive form. In all such strikes as those of women textile workers in Pusan and Hamhŭng and the strikes of water front workers in Ch'ongjin, the will of the workers to struggle was expressed but organizational and political leadership of the supporters of the left wing was insufficient. The weakness in the left wing leadership, the lack of systematic struggle and forced mediation together with the treasonable policy of the national reformists, have assisted the factory managers in deceiving and breaking the ranks of the workers and helped attack the progress of the strike movement (workers in rubber, grain, and textile factories). Thus the efforts of the P'yŏngyang workers were not utilized to enlarge the fighting front, but those places where workers advanced with cooperative self organization the strikes turned out to be victorious for the workers (Inch'ŏn rice mill strike).

Second, the supporters of the Pan Pacific Labor Union Secretariat did not fully recognize the importance of the activities within the Korean Federation of Labor and other reformist mass labor unions. The decision of the Executive Committee of the Profintern made it the foremost duty of the supporters of the Profintern and Pan Pacific Labor Unions Secretariat in Korea to win over the low class masses and unite them with the left wing. The only way to win over the masses to our side is to shake hands with them and to work with them and also to expose the truly antagonistic picture of the national reformist leaders' policy through daily struggle and experience.

However, despite the fact that the supporters of the Profintern must stage a strong mass struggle within the national reformist labor unions and organize the opposition group to their revolutionary labor unions, they have not as yet liberated themselves from the factional tendency, and they tend to organize isolated labor unions. Such steps have only invited a tendency to mechanically transplant a narrow factional labor unions apart from the masses where there is no working masses surrounding the left wing, and ultimately brought the division of the working masses from the left wing.

5. The supporters of the left wing must clearly liquidate all of their past mistakes and shortcomings and at the same time must prepare for a new struggle and victory of the Korean proletariat based upon their past experience. Only through enlargement and strengthening of their organizational influence in the working masses and also through leading the growing desire of the Korean workers for struggle, can the left wing make progress and lead the wide range of the masses, because the masses come to recognize those who truly fight for their benefits only through the process of the struggles. The left wing must carry out the following duties:

A. The supporters of the left wing must have closer relationship with the leadership of Korean proletarian struggle and their preparatory works. They must systematically prepare the strikes by making detailed demands that are detailed which can easily be understood by the masses on such matters as wages, working hours, dismissals, and other working problems, and arouse interests of the masses in collecting strike funds. The demands regarding strikes must be widely discussed by the participation of all the workers in a factory, and if the mass struggle is prepared, the conference of all strikers should be held, and then a strike struggle committee should be elected consisting of those workers irrespective of the organized or the unorganized or women workers who proved that they are the struggling elements in the fight against the capitalists. At the same time the strikers must prevent the national reformists, the running dogs of the capitalists, from infiltrating the strike committee. The national reformists are doing everything they can to break the strikes utilizing such methods as the forced mediation of police, arbitration of the chamber of commerce (in Wŏnsan strikes) and others. At the same time, in order to avoid a situation where the strikers are left without strike leaders when some members of the strike committee are arrested, there must be a few comrades of the strike committee that are left behind to form a successor committee so to provide continuous strike leadership in place of the arrested comrades. All works of the strike committee must be continued by the successors of the strike workers. During the strikes all activities of the strike committee must be periodically reported to the strikers' conference.

The left wing must directly participate in all strikes that occur spontaneously, and expend all energy to bring the strike under their leadership. In order to attain this objective, the left wing must attend strike conferences by sending labor representatives to the striking workers, participate in the picket lines, organize and assist the joint demonstration movement, raise a good suggestion through the leadership organ of the strike [strike corps], and must ultimately reorganize the strike corps into a strike committee which is composed of members elected by the entire strikers. The left wing must not take a negative attitude even in those strikes in progress under the direction of the national reformists. The left wing must strive for an organization of a united front of all striking workers, separating them from the influence of the cohorts of the treasonable national reformists, and must strive to take the strike leadership into their hands through the method of electing the strike committee.

The supporters of the left wing must hold key positions not only in the organization of the preparatory committee and the strike committee but also in the organization of the picket group and self-defense corps. In many cases the accomplishment of the struggle is closely related to the alacrious activities of the picket groups. The picket groups should be organized by the experienced and fighting comrades, receiving assistance from women and youth groups. Especially young women workers must be drawn into the struggle. It is necessary to organize a joint demonstration movement of the striking workers and workers of other factories, and collect money and food stuffs from the workers, peasants and the poor people in the cities. The victory of the struggle of the workers can be assured only when they advance under the united front from below under the leadership of the left wing.

The supporters of the left wing must expose the true picture of the treasonable national reformists with detailed facts—the plans to lead the strikers into compromise, the destruction of the direct methods of struggle, the suggestion of forced mediation in cooperation with the factory owners and police and others. The left wing must place a special emphasis on explaining the futility of utilizing the negative form of struggle (starvation league, etc.). They must explain the strikes that use such methods, and must awaken the strikers to change their methods to direct struggle (picket groups, the mass demonstration movement).

B. The unemployment and the general increase of the unemployed masses have firmly established the duty of the left wing supporters to lead the unemployment movement. A committee of the unemployed must be organized in the area where the unemployed are concentrated and unite the unemployed masses. The committee of the unemployed utilizing the methods or organization and the process of struggle must fight for the following:

   a. Free distribution of rice, clothings, and fuel.

   b. Exemption from house rent.

   c. Payment of support in equal amount to the wages of the unemployed during the period of unemployment.

   d. Payment of full pay to the workers who are half-employed.

   e. Institution of unemployment insurance system financed by the factory owners and the government, etc.

The committee of the unemployed should organize sections in accordance with each problems (accounting, rent, labor union, cultural and educational section, and others), and must select devoted elements to lead each section.

Paralleling with this, all unemployed workers must be drawn into the path of class struggle, while organizing a united front of the employed and the unemployed. Not only the oppositions against the dismissal, half-unemployed work week, and shady labor practices, an effort should be made to assure organizational support for every unemployed worker with the coorperation of the unemployed and the employed. In the event of pressure to the unemployed individually, such as the eviction from non-payment of the house rent and water bills, the resistence must be resolute. Determined struggles must also be waged against the merciless exploitation of the unemployed masses by the Korean Government-General and their agents under the guise of the unemployment relief, the so-called unemployment relief projects. The unemployed workers must be assisted by organizational methods, their daily life reformed, and be assured of the support of the employed workers. The organization of the united front of the employed and unemployed workers is the most important prerequisite to success of the economic struggle and anti-unemployment struggle by the workers.

C. Special attention should be paid to the question of drawing women workers into the revolutionary labor unions. The rate of organizing women workers is still low. This is due to the fact that the fighting corps, a section of the proletariat, was considered non-responsive in front of the advance by the factory owners. In view of the fact that the wages of women workers were lowered, that the numbers of women workers dismissed became large and that the showing of their direct participation in the strikes is strong, it is wrong to be lax in organizing women workers by advancing such reason as the impossibility of carrying out the duty to draw women workers into the union. In order to successfully incorporate women workers into the fighting ranks of the working class, there should be organized a women section that can responsibly carry out the activities of the revolutionary working men, and a special meeting of working women in factories, lecture sessions and conferences should be called to disucss poignant problems that directly concern them.

D. At the same time, the left wing must organize youth groups in the revolutionary labor unions, and enlarge their influence within the working youth organization and consolidate the projects of the working youth, utilizing the methods of drawing the working youth into the revolutionary labor union organizations. The project to win over the working youth must be carried out by organizing the leftist group within the youth athletic groups. At the time of a strike, demand conditions especially beneficial to the working youth must be pointed out.

E. A serious attention should be paid to the problems concerning the formation of a fighting united front of foreign workers (Japanese and Chinese workers in residence). A strong and enduring project should be developed to incorporate all workers regardless of their nationality eliminating nationalistic friction into all out struggle against the capitalists' advances and for the benefits of the proletarian class, and oppose the policy of the bourgeois which propagandize patriotism and cause friction among the people of nationalities. On such incident as the Japanese government's conspiracy to attack the Chinese workers, the left wing must correctly explain such policy of Japanese imperialism to the workers, and on the one hand inspire the rage to fight against such attacks by distributing the leaflets and public notices, while on the other hand organize together with Chinese workers the fighting self-defense corps and support the Chinese workers.

F. The decision of the Profintern Secretariat pointed out the growth of favorable conditions for organizing the labor-farmer league under the direction of working class. The conditions necessary to bring about proletarian influence and leadership of farmer's revolutionary struggle are the organization of farm laborers and the direct action of the laborers who return to farms. However, the supporters of left wing are yet to do anything toward this direction. The realization of the definitive change toward this direction is one of the most important duties of the left wing. The supporters of left wing must pay special attention to the problems of their liaison with the peasant groups, the formation of the labor-farmer united front, and close mutual support to fight against the landlord and imperialism of the capitalists.

G. The important prerequisites to a successful establishment of the revolutionary labor union in Korea is to shift the center of the labor union activities to the factories. The basic form of the revolutionary labor union movement is a union group within the manufacturing factories and small scale enterprises. The factory group that has large membership is to elect three-man executive bureau for leadership and the group that has small membership is to elect a group representative. The factory groups must be established in the factory where they work and not in the residential districts, and they must maintain contact with the regional organization of the unions. The reorganization of the left wing labor unions based on the factories must be developed to prepare for and execute the strikes and daily activities of the labor unions. Especially at the time of the strikes and other proletarian mass movement, recruitment of new members to the union group must be carried out energetically.

Only through energetic and constant recruitment, the present factional conditions in the left wing labor unions, in the labor union groups, and in the opposition faction (those revolutionary opposition factions against the national reformism) could rapidly be overcome. The supporters of the left wing must have a definitive change to draw widely the organized laborers from the national reformist unions and unorganized laborers into the labor union groups. Especially, a special attention should be paid to the organization of women and youth—the textile and chemical industries. The factory group, the opposition group and the left wing labor unions should be established on democratic principles. The leadership organs must discuss all important problems before the wide range union members, and from the important conditions in strengthening the left wing labor unions is to eliminate bureaucracy and command ideas from the top leadership. In daily operations the left wing labor unions must operate on the basis of factory representative conference that is the organ of the united front from below, the factory committee which is elected by all workers in the factory, and the committee for struggle that is organized when there is discontent among the laborers.

In a transitional stage of organizing the factory committee, the revolutionary representatives can perform the task. Elected by the working group representatives, they must be elected in much smaller ratio than the election ratio of a factory committee election. The organization of a revolutionary representative group is the best method to mobilize and unite the working masses for the struggle to destroy all oppressive systems of the police and to present necessary demands of the workers. The left wing labor unions must utilize all legal and semi-legal possibilities, and must have legal organizations as their base (labor club, *Sangjo-hoe* [Mutual Assistance Association], atheletic groups, evening schools for the workers, campaigns to eliminate illiterates, picnic clubs, fishing and hunting clubs, labor sightseeing groups, and others). The left wing labor unions and the united front organs from below must stage the most determined struggle to exist legally and at the same time must draw a wide range of workers into this struggle.

H. In order to emancipate and win over the masses of the Korean Federation of Labor and other national reformist labor unions from the influence of the national reformists, the left wing of the Korean labor union movement must develop a direct actions and organize a revolutionary opposition group within the national reformist groups. For this, the left wing must quickly begin to organize their groups within the labor unions of the national reformists. This group must unite not only those workers designated by the left wing supporters but also those who are partially or completely discontented with the policy of the national reformists, and the group must include all the union members of the national reformists from those who refuse to struggle for their own demands to those who support the demands that we propose.

The left wing must exploit discontent of the workers against all treasonable activities of the national reformist leaders that avoid the struggle for the workers' benefits and against every discontent of the laborers in the national reformist labor unions and the policy of compulsory mediation and compromises by the national reformists to bring worse situation to the workers; the left wing must definitively expose the activities of national reformist leaders. The left wing should also be widely used for the purpose of leading the masses to the opposition group within the labor union. Each revolutionary group must have platforms which express all basic demands, written plainly and easily comprehensible to even the least educated.

The left wing must first begin to organize the revolutionary opposition groups within the national reformist labor unions, uniting the workers engaged in land and sea transportation, textile, and printing industries. The revolutionary opposition group, regardless of the numbers with which the group was organized, must not immediately separate themselves from the union. Conversely, the revolutionary opposition group must struggle for their legal existence within the union, and must develop a struggle to win over the majority of members and to take over the leadership of the lower organs.

I. By developing organization work and instigating the masses within the enterprises, and by holding workers' conferences and widely organizing the labor unions with leadership capabilities, the left wing can create conditions for organizing independent labor union. Some progress of the left wing with the chemical workers, organization of a few union groups within the chemical factories, lack of a labor union inclusive of all chemical workers, and some others, all these point to the fact that the left wing must set an immediate and detailed task to organize a union or workers in chemical industry under the leadership of the left wing, and must initiate a labor union from this conference, establish a group, and adopt acting platform. All possible methods should be employed to organize legally the left wing unions, and wide range of masses must be mobilized to struggle for the union's legal existence.

Paralleling with the chemical workers' union, the Pan Pacific Labor Union Secretariat assignes the detailed duties to the left wing to develop activities among the mine workers, to organize a union group within the mines and mine stations, to write up the demands of the mine workers, and to propagandize consolidation of labor unions. When the duties are successfully carried out, the left wing can begin to organize a labor union for the revolutionary miners. The tendency to organize a narrow factional revolutionary labor union based not on the masses must definitely be eliminated. We need a true mass group, not a union in name only. At the same time we must struggle against any plan to interfere with the participation of workers in labor unions or union groups. In order to become a member of the revolutionary labor union or union groups, these laborers and women laborers can become members who wish to struggle for their demands regardless of their nationality or political views.

J. There must be a wide-range of self-criticism from below in instituting a democratic labor union and moving the main force of activities to the factories, but the self-criticism is to strengthen the revolutionary labor union movement and the left wing union organizations. Despite these, however, the unprincipled factional criticism, in truth a distortion, has given hinderance to all projects of the left wing and destroyed our union. The unprincipled factional struggle in Korea is a reflection not only of the influence of petty-bourgeois elements in the laboring class but also of the polished methods of the Japanese imperialists in destroying and weakening the revolutionary labor unions. The left wing must explain in detail the harmful effects to the laboring class, to those laborers who are deceived and drawn into the unprincipled factional organizations. The left wing must explain the fact that the Left Wing Labor Union Council Preparatory Committee in Korea is a factional group, and the present plan to organize a Left Wing Labor Union Council in Korea is premature.

Self-criticism from below, cooperate leadership, and the definitive change in leadership and preparation for economic struggle and national liberation struggle, all these must be done with maximum speed by carrying out all duties given to the present left wing and by recommending those new and able leaders and organizers from the union members and lower masses who are not bound by factional fightings. Whosoever wants to oppose the factory owners and imperialism and wants to join the rank of Profintern supporters must be incorporated into the left wing labor union which is based upon the class, fighting for a quick liquidation of factional groupings and definitively denying the traditional factional struggle.

Thus the projects for a mass organization on the basis of class struggle must forcefully be carried out. The membership in the Profintern and Pan Pacific Labor Union Secretariat requires fidelity to their daily tasks, institution of organizational and tactical principles of international revolutionary labor union movement both in theory and practice. This means above all, the denial of unprincipled distortion, conspiracy, factional activities, and an attempt to truly and devotionally enforce the decisions of the Profintern and the Pan Pacific Labor Union Secretariat.

K. The left wing has done little on the problems of labor union publication. The publication is an important weapon for propagating class benefits and influencing the masses. All publication activities must proceed in the form of liaison with the wide range of masses, establishment of the distribution network, financial assistance, reports from the districts and its reply, and others. Special attention must be added to the organization of a factory newspaper.

L. What has been pointed out above is the clearest presentation of the problems concerning the ability of every possible activity that confronts the left wing. The lack of nucleus elements is still a shortcoming of the left wing of the Korean labor union movement. Those few basic nucleuses of officers are breaking up by the continuous arrests. To select officers from the low level workers and to educate them through lecture and study groups are the immediate duties confronting the revolutionary labor union movement, and they are the true assurance of the success of a labor movement.

M. In order to mobilize the working masses around them, the left wing must present the following demands:

a. Opposition to the lowering of wages and extension of working hours. Institution of raise in wages and its weekly payment and eight-hour work system.

b. Payment of equal wages for the same work regardless of sex, age, and nationality.

c. The social insurance paid for by the factory owners and the government for the insurance of the unemployed, the handicapped, the sick, and the unfortunate.

d. Opposition to a dismissal.

e. Establishment of insurance on women and youth workers.

f. One day paid holiday every week, two weeks per year for adult and one month rest per year for the minors.

These demands must be related to such conditions that have general political character:

a. Right to strike, assurance of right to establish a revolutionary organization. Freedom for assembly and publication.

b. Immediate release of all political prisoners.

c. Withdrawal of Japanese armed forces from Korea and Manchuria.

d. Support of the Chinese revolution, etc.

N. In the common struggle to oppose the Japanese imperialism and Kuomintang reactionaries, the left wing of the Korean labor union movement must definitively oppose all conspiratory activities and all propaganda that attempt to instill friction in an effort to fruitfully unite the forces of Sino-Korean workers, and organize and strengthen the revolutionary united front. And also the left wing must organize a mass movement to oppose the Manchurian occupation, oppression against the revolutionary and anti-imperialism movement in China, and the preparation of war against the Soveit Union. Only through a joint progress of the Japanese, Korean, and Chinese workers, the Japanese reactionaries can be overturned.

Comrades: The Pan Pacific Labor Union Secretariat fully understands that there are many difficulties in carrying out the duties stated above. The difficulties emanate from the fact that the comrades must fight under the condition of cruel police terrors and also due to the fact that there are relatively small number of comrades in the ranks because the comrades have just begun the true work of consolidation. On the matter of strengthening the already established relationship between the Secretariat and the left wing of the Korean labor unions, we firmly believe that comrades will on the one hand quickly overcome all the shortcomings and on the other will win a victory with the firm unity of the wide range of working masses under the banner of the left wing in the struggle against Japanese imperialism and the exploiters of the mainland.

October 1931
Shanghai, The Pan Pacific Labor Union Secretariat.

Item 38: Directive of the Communist Youth International Concerning the Korean Communist Youth Association[1]

To the Members of the KCYA.

Dear Comrades:

1. The intensifying crisis of Japanese imperialism precipitated by the world economic crisis, is dealing a very severe blow to the colonial economy of Korea that suffers from the rule of Japanese imperialism, and the Korean working masses bear the burdens of the deepening crisis of all aspects of Japanese imperialism and of the corresponding agricultural and industrial chaos in Korea.

In an effort to find a way out of the chaos, the Japanese imperialists and their allies in Korea, the bourgeoisie, the landlords, and the usurers, are shifting the burdens of their chaos to the shoulders of working masses. The attack on the standard of living of the working masses is now naturally spreading throughout Korea. The chaos has greatly intensified the impoverishment of the peasants and the process of land loss. The increasing debt of the Korean peasants reached 500 million yen, and according to the official statistics of the Government-General approximately 1.5 million peasant households are suffering from the debts resulting from the excessive taxes, the payments to the usurers, and other debts.

The living condition of the working class has also deteriorated significantly, and while the wages of workers are lowered by thirty to fifty percent, the working hours are increased by one to two hours. Furthermore, because of the closure of

---

[1] This is a directive issued by the Executive Committee of the KIM (Kommunisticheskogo Internatsionala Molodezhe) to the KCYA in January, 1932. It is assumed that the document was originally written in Russian, but the Russian version is, so far, not available. This English version is a translation from the Japanese version which is available in *Kōtō Keisatsu-hō,* nos. 2 and 3 (n.d.), n.p. It is also available in *Chōsen minzoku tokuritsu undō hishi* (Tokyo, 1959), pp. 641-50.

various enterprises one third of the workers are roaming the streets. Today in Korea some 100,000 persons are without employment, do not receive relief funds, and are literally on the verge of starvation.

As a result of the economic panic, the working youth also received a severe attack, and the national, political and economic oppressions, accompanied by the opening of a war in Manchuria by the Japanese imperialists, have intensified. The Japanese imperialism, in its war against the Chinese revolution and the Soviet Union, transformed Korea into its base on the continent, and further intensified the severe terror against the revolutionary movement in Korea. The worsening of the living conditions of the Korean working masses and the severe oppression against them are arousing the workers' revolutionary ferment and the growth of dissatisfaction and discontent.

In contrast to the sufferings caused by the crisis in the Capitalist systems, the working masses in the Soviet Union are gaining splendid results in their establishment of socialism, and the Soviet Union is solving the nationality problems in accordance with Leninism, still more, continuing the unending struggle against imperialism to emancipate the colonies. These events tend to revolutionize the working masses in Korea.

Spontaneously rising labor strikes and peasant disputes are increasing, and the poor of the cities on the Nationalist movement front, particularly the students, are participating in them. While the labor, peasant, and student struggles show tenacity, the Communist organizational leadership on the struggle of the working masses is totally lacking, and because of this the struggle stops at very low level and the struggle for natural growth always ends in defeat.

With the intensification of revolutionary movement, the position and the duty of each class are more clearly expressed: the landlords and the usurers who endeavor to retain the condition of feudalistic exploitation of the Korean peasants, are becoming faithful allied soldiers of Japanese imperialism, absolutely obeying the orders of Japanese imperialism, and the Korean bourgeoisie (compradore bourgeoisie, industrial bourgeoisie, commercial bourgeoisie) who maintain liaison with the

large land owners and Japanese imperialism, are not participating in the decisive struggle against Japanese imperialism nor
in proposing a radical land platform.

Fearful of a successful revolution by workers and peasants,
the Korean bourgeoisie are rushing to the camp of the
imperialists, and they are using "leftist terms" against Japanese
imperialism, but this does not mean that they will discontinue
their plottings to divert the attention of the working masses
from the revolutionary struggle for Korean independence and a
revolutionary solution to the land question. On the contrary,
we must expect such plottings to continue.

Hereafter, the elements of anti-imperialism revolution and
land revolution in Korea are proletariat, working peasants, and
their ally, the poor class of the city, and these, of course, grow
under the leadership of the proletariat. Accordingly, the
decisive duty of the Korean Communists and the Communist
youths is to win the hegemony of the proletariat leadership in
the Korean revolution and firm and permanent struggle.

2. Suffering from the deepening crisis, the aggravation of the
working youth is intensifying in rapid tempo, and its duty in
the revolutionary struggle is increasing rapidly. The struggle to
win over the youths is particularly intensifying, and the
Japanese imperialists and their running dogs are busy in the
so-called youth's "thought guidance." And the national reformists, the running dogs of imperialism, take pains to destroy
the struggle of the youth, utilizing revolutionary words and
advocating the natural growth struggle.

Because of the weakness of the Korean Communist Youth
movement, the lack of direct exposure to the class enemy's
deceptive policies and the lack of firm leadership in the
spontaneously growing youth struggles, the treasonable and
deceptive policies of the national reformists are gaining results.

The present Korean Communist Youth movement is confronted with serious crisis. The present Communist group in
Korea is the organic sectional organization that has no link with
the working youth masses. These Communist groups are not
organized to struggle for the daily demands of the working
youth and also not performing the role of leadership. The

Communist group is not mobilizing the youth through such struggle under the slogans of anti-imperialist struggle and land revolution, and majority of youth struggle is conducted without the Communist Youth group and its leadership.

Although the influence of communism on working youth masses is undoubtedly growing, the organizational imbalance in the Korean Communist Youth movement is due to the fact that several Korean Communist youth organizations have fallen into the opportunistic mistakes and to the misinterpretation of the KIM's directives. In other words, the severe factional struggles which for many years disturbed the unity of the Korean Communist Youth movement originate from the misinterpretation of the KIM directive. There is no doubt that the Japanese police is advocating such unprincipled factional fightings.

The cause of factionalism, first of all, is isolation of the working youth for whom the various Communist organization is struggling, and the general lack of peasant youths in working youths and the predominance of intelligentsia and petty bourgeois youths in the rank and file of the Communist youths attest to this fact. However, there is a lack of bolshevik self-criticism within the rank and file of the Communist Youth (CY).[2]

The KIM has pointed out to the Korean Communist Youth groups that the future movement cannot be continued under such conditions, and the Korean CY members must strengthen their rank and file organizationally and ideologically and must struggle definitively, and in order to form a strong massive Korean CY, it is necessary, hereafter, to wage a more direct struggle. The Korean CY groups must develop bolshevik self-criticism, drastically liquidate their mistakes and short-comings, and at the same time make detailed plans to win over the vast youth masses, first of all the working youth masses, to the rank and file and to the side of the CY.

The CY groups, in the struggle to win over the youth masses, must develop a direct struggle to reject the opportunistic

[2] Reference here is to the organization, the Korean Communist Youth Association (KCYA), or at times referred by the KIM as the Communist Youth League of Korea.

misinterpretation of KIM's line. The attention of the Korean CY groups should be focused on a determined struggle against the right wing. Those who tolerate the manifestation of the right wing, deny the leadership role of the proletariat in the Korean revolutionary struggle, evade incessant struggle against the enemy youth groups, misunderstand the role of the national reformists and at the same time take conciliatory attitudes toward them, and plan to organize surface organization (Proletariat Youth League), underestimating the significance of the secret CY organization and conducting the surface movement, must be mercilessly rejected.

The "rightist sentiments," particularly sectarianism of the Korean CY groups, and the isolation of the Communist Youth groups from general working youth masses (the "leftist sentiments"), and others, must be resolutely rejected. The leftist sectarianism that create fence and wall between the youth and CY groups, has become an important obstacle in winning the wide range of working youth masses over to the side of the CY. If one wishes to win the working youths over to the rank and file of the CY and unless one wages a direct struggle against those leftist opportunists who do not know how to win over against sectarian ideologies and practices, it is impossible to massively lead the Korean Communist Youth movement.

3. The Korean Communist youths! In order to win over the masses and to reestablish a mass oriented Communist youth movement, it is essential for the working youth to participate on a comprehensive basis in the revolutionary movement for the emancipation of the Korean people. The CY members should always make the working youths understand that only under the leadership of the Korean proletariat, the Korean workers, peasants and their allies, and the poor people in the cities, can they struggle directly against Japanese imperialism and struggle directly against the bourgeoisie and the anti-revolutionary landlords who aid Japanese imperialism thereby gaining victories in the anti-imperialist revolution and the land revolution.

The CY members must incessantly expose with positiveness of the bolshevist the national reformists who do not wage a direct struggle against Japanese imperialism and its protectors, the landlords and bourgeoisie, and advocate only peaceful method and gradual reforms as though that can emancipate the Korean people.

The CY members must develop especially strong and unyielding struggle, opposing the autonomy movement led by the national reformist who separate the working masses from the revolutionary struggle of true national liberation. The autonomy movement is in fact a manifestation of the policy of deception instituted by Japanese imperialism and is designed to strengthen the fortress of Japanese imperialism in Korea. The Korean CY organizations must gain control of leadership even in those movement that have wide range and detailed demands in all movements of workers, peasants and student youth that aim at the national liberation. In leading and winning the spontaneously growing struggle of the youth who oppose the oppression of the people, the CY organizations not only gain sympathy of the youth but also improve the political consciousness of the youth in the process of the struggle. It is necessary to quicken the process of anti-imperialist revolution and the land revolution. The important task that confronts the national emancipation movement in Korean laboring masses is to struggle against the imperial Japan's troop dispatch to Manchuria.

The CY organizations must expose the adverse propaganda of imperialists and their running dogs that troop dispatch to Manchuria is to protect the Korean peasants. The fact that the Japanese troop dispatch to Manchuria, supported by the bourgeois landlords and the national reformists, surely increases the severity of national oppression in Korea and results in more serious political and economic oppression should be widely pointed out to the working youth masses. The Korean CY members must explain the fact that the Japanese imperialists' dispatch of troops to Manchuria is directed against the Chinese revolution and the Soviet Union, the enemies of imperialism and Japanese imperialism, and at the same time it must also be emphatically explained to the working youth masses that it is an important duty of the Korean working masses in the struggle to oppose Japanese imperialism so as to give total support to the Chinese revolution and to truly protect the Soviet Union in the rear of the imperialists' military activities. The working youth masses of Korea possess common class interest with the Japanese, Chinese, and Taiwanese working masses, and it must be strongly emphasized to the working youth masses that unless the Japanese, Chinese, Taiwanese and Korean working masses form a united front, it is impossible to overthrow the Japanese imperialists bourgeoisie and the landlords in Korea.

The Korean CY organizations must develop a wide-range struggle of the working youth masses to oppose the Japanese imperialists' troop dispatch to Manchuria and the imperialists' preparations for a new anti-Soviet war, and to support the Chinese revolution, and to win the Korean independence. In order to accomplish these purposes, the youth must be organized for demonstrations and strikes, and they should be urged to refuse to transport all military goods and the mobilized troops that pass through Korea.

4. On the mobilization of working youth masses under the slogan of anti-imperialism revolution and land revolution in Korea, the CY organizations must develop daily struggle for a partial demand to reform the living condition of the workers and peasants and student youths, and strive to link this struggle to win the partial demands with the basic struggle. The Korean CY members must take special care to organize and lead the economic struggle of the working youth.

The CY organizations should inspect carefully the condition of working youth in each region and factory, and make a detailed platform of a partial demand, and in the detailed platform of the partial demand such issues as the reduction of working hours, increase in wages, special protection of young workers, paid vacations, prohibition of child labor, same wage for the same work must be the basic demands of the CY.

The CY organizations must actively struggle against the plan to separate the youth benefits from the general benefits of the working class, and thus link the struggle of the working youth with that of the adult workers.

The CY organizations must attract the working youth and apprentices into the general workers' struggle. They should attempt to add special demands of the youth and the apprentices to the general demands of the striking workers, and the fact that the youth workers must support the demands of the youth must be widely propagated to them. And an attempt to have a representative of the youth to participate in the strike committee should also be made. This is clearly a necessary item to be included for youth's benefit in the demand items of the striking workers. The fact that many working youths and apprentices are working in each enterprise in Korea is a favorable factor in the struggle to win their demand items.

Thus, in preparation for the youth initiated struggle, the CY organizations must first make a detailed platform of the struggle, disseminate it widely to the youth, and lead the youth to have the adult workers participate in the youth struggle. In other words, the youth struggle should be transformed into a general struggle of the adult workers, and a sympathy strike organization for the workers in neighborhood enterprises must be planned. The CY organizations must endeavor to link the struggles of the employed and the unemployed working youths. It is necessary to organize a mass movement of the unemployed workers and the unemployed working youths to attract the unemployed working youth to the struggle of the employed working youth. Under the leadership of the Communist Party Red Labor Union and the CY, a committee of the unemployed workers should be organized, and a struggle to give jobs and unemployment subsidies should be developed with such conditions as exemption from the house rent during the period of unemployment.

In the region where there is no Communist Party and the Red Labor Union, the CY should themselves organize an unemployed workers' committee. In the region where the Red Labor Union is established, the CY organizations must organize an economic struggle of the working youth in close liaison with the Union. However, in each case the CY organization must assure the general workers of their independent leadership in the strikes.

The CY organizations must pay special attention to the question of developing a daily task of the labor union. In Korea, there was an attempt to organize a special youth labor union, but this is very dangerous because this tends to isolate the youth movement from the general struggle of the working class. The youth must organize only a general labor union together with the adult workers; and in order to protect the benefits of the working youth, a youth section must be organized within the general labor union.

The basic duty of the Korean Communist youths on the works within the labor union is to have all the working youths to participate in the red labor union movement and strengthen them generally. Because of the extreme inadequacy and organizational weakness in the cell network of the Red Labor Union in Korea, all Korean CY members must thoroughly participate in the works within the Red Labor Union. The CY organizations must carry out a slogan, "each Communist Youth member must become a member of the labor union and become a devoted element of the union." Thus, first of all, an effort should be made to attract all CY members into the labor union.

The CY members must take initiative in organizing the Red Labor Union, and also organize an opposition faction within the national reformist labor unions. Showing such initiative by the CY organizations is especially important in the regions where there is no Communist Party organization. The basic duty of the CY members within the national reformist labor union is to develop their daily task within the union, expose with detailed examples the role of betrayal played by the leaders of the national reformists, and to win the working youths organized within the national reformists labor union over to the rank and file of the Communist youths and to the side of the Red Labor Union.

5. In order to overcome the serious backwardness of the Communist movement in comparison to the development of the peasant youth revolutionary movement, the Korean CY organizations must consider a positive countermeasure. The important duty of the Korean CY members in farm villages is to aid the Communists by developing and leading peasant revolutionary struggle for non-payment of tenant fees and taxes and other partial demand items.

The CY members under the leadership of the Communists must develop a mass peasant movement with all their effort, and help organize a revolutionary peasant committee and an opposition faction within the existing national reformist peasant union. The CY members must expose with detailed examples the apostatic characteristics of the national reformists, and thus develop a struggle to reject any influence of the national reformists on the peasants and youths. The CY members must become initiators and leaders of the revolutionary struggle of the peasant youths in order to meet every demand (reduction of taxes, reduction of tenant fees, institution of free elementary education) to reform the living conditions of the peasant youths.

Through such struggles the peasant youths should be mobilized under the slogans of land revolution and anti-imperialist revolution. The CY members should organize *iacheika* [cell] of the CY with peasant working youths, poor peasant youths and middle class peasant youths who participate earnestly in the revolutionary peasant movement, and strengthen the influence of the Communists in the peasant youth masses. The CY members should develop a mass youth organization in farm villages and struggle to establish a youth section in the peasant union, and organize and lead every cultural and economic peasant youth groups (such as clubs, night schools, and sports clubs).

With the daily growth of the struggle leadership of the peasant working youths, the Korean CY members under the Communist leadership must carry out within a short period of time the task or organizing a peasant labor union which is one of the important duties in farm villages.

The CY organizations must lead the revolutionary struggle of the student youths such as the struggle to oppose the assimilation education, the struggle for freedom to organize a student association, and the struggle to oppose academic customs. It is the duty of the CY members to incorporate the student youths generally in the Korean national emancipation front, but the student struggle should also be linked to the struggles of the peasants and the poor in the city.

On the preparation of toiling peasants and student youth struggles, the CY organizations must incorporate working youths in accordance with the struggle platform of the CY and must widely utilize the gradual united front. The CY organizations must reflect in detail the mood of different youth classes in each different circumstances, but must not yield the theoretical position of the CY, and regardless of the political views and religious and reformists organizational affiliations, it must present the detailed demands that can unite all working youths, thus strongly demanding them to develop a struggle. In leading such struggles, an action committee must be organized inclusive of wide range of youth masses struggling under each circumstance, and only through the organization of a unified joint struggle of all working youth under the slogans of the CY, it is possible to gradually win over the youths under the influence of enemy organization. Only through this process, it is possible to make the youth understand the duties of the class struggle and national liberation movement.

Positive struggle must be made against the apostatic leaders of the enemy youth organizations and against any attempt to alter the united front and strategies of the true CY struggle network into a right opportunism by all sorts of accommodation and compromise.

6. It is an important duty of the Korean CY organizations to fully exploit the possibilities of legal movements in the illegal operations, link them generally and to organize around the CY the legal and illegal mass assistance organizations that can link the wide range of working youth masses. Mass organizations which are not Communist organizations can also perform the function of concealing the secret tasks of the CY which is a secret organization. Every organization whose work is of revolutionary character, such as anti-imperialism league, red sport workers' self-defense corps, youth club, self-study association, night school (crusade against illiteracy), student groups that have a Marxism study section, is to become auxiliary machinery together with the peasant union youth group. There are comrades in the Korean CY who oppose the organization of all legal auxiliary organizations with the excuse that it is easy

for "not fully revolutionary" youths to join the legal organizations, but such leftist tendency must positively be rejected.

Such a plan to replace secret organization, the CY, with such a legal organization as "the proletariat youth league" should also be positively rejected. Considering the fact that the outrageous police terror is severe, it is impossible for the revolutionary organization to exist legally in Korea. However, regardless of "the proletariat youth league," it is possible to organize with condensed minimum platforms, but to reduce the youth's revolutionary movement to an inevitable minimum, is to yield the youth movement to the demands of the bourgeois and the landlords. In other words, this is clearly falling into liquidationism.

In order to attract the working youth masses into the revolutionary struggle by organizing and utilizing the legal and surface organizations, the Korean CY organizations must neither lose their independence nor reduce their direct mass works. It is dangerous to lose the independence of the CY or to lose the leadership in the youth's revolutionary struggle because of that.

However, to operate within the auxiliary organizations and develop it by utilizing such operation is to strengthen the direct operation of the CY, and the CY must incorporate the efficient elements of the auxiliary organizations into the rank and file of the CY and insist incessantly on political leadership of the mass organization.

7. The incessant struggle against the enemy youth organizations and particularly "leftist" enemy youth organizations that use spurious revolutionary conduct to deceive the working youth masses, is necessary in order to strengthen the influence of the CY organizations on the working youth masses and to assure the transformation of the CY to a mass organization.

Because of the clearly expressed reactionary characteristics of the enemy organizations, there is a widespread leftist feeling among the Korean CY members who consider it unnecessary to operate within the enemy organizations, but as a result of such a "leftist" operational directive, the Korean Communist organizations has made their positions disadvantageous on the dissolution questions of the *Shin'gan-hoe* and the Youth Federation and committed an important political error. The mistakes of the CY members lie in their inability to understand the true meanings of the dissolution campaigns of the *Shin'gan-hoe*, an organization initially began by the national reformists under the direction of the Japanese imperialists, and the Youth Federation.

Because of the growth of dissatisfaction against the leadership of the national reformists within the *Shin'gan-hoe* and the Youth Federation, the dissolution was thus to ease the worsening circumstances. The CY members opportunistically supported the dissolution of the *Shin'gan-hoe*, and failed to expose the class deceiving policy to the youth masses, furthermore the CY members did not develop a campaign to win over the youth masses in the *Shin'gan-hoe* and the Federation of Labor. As a result, the dissolution of *Shin'gan-hoe* and the Youth Federation undoubtedly benefited the Japanese imperialism and the national reformist running dogs.[3]

The Korean CY organizations must not avoid the work within the enemy youth organizations and must struggle mercilessly. In order to operate within various enemy youth organizations, such as the Youth Federation, *Ch'ŏndo-kyo* Youth Friends' Party, *Kŭn'u-hoe*, Young Men's Christian Association, Young Men's Buddhist Association, the most efficient elements of the CY members should be dispatched.

The duty of these dispatched CY members is to organize the opposition group within it and to destroy the organization by utilizing such methods as separating the most progressive elements from them. The CY members must expose the true entity of the national reformist leadership by giving detailed examples of their apostatic roles and their avoidance of struggle for the benefits of the working youths. By such exposure

---

[3] It is obvious that the KIM was not aware of the circumstances surrounding the founding and dissolution of the *Shin'gan-hoe*. The organization was not founded under the direction of the Japanese imperialists, and although it is true that the CY members failed to win over the youth members of the *Shin'gan-hoe*, it was dissolved by the Communists at the opposition of the national reformists.

campaigns together with propaganda of the purposes and duties of the CY, the working youths of the enemy organization must be won over and led into the rank and file of the CY organizations.

8. Unless the Korean CY organizations positively strengthen their rank and file, it is impossible to solve the problems arising under the current situation in Korea and the complicated tasks directed by the KIM. The KIM demands the Korean CY members to develop unyielding bolshevik self-criticism within the bounds of secret preservation, to courageously point out the weakness and mistakes of their organizations, and to study a detailed policy to correct the weakness and errors.

The Korean CY members must examine how the leadership elements of the CY organizations put in practice the directives of the Fifth Congress of the KIM concerning the rank and file organization of the Korean CY and the liquidation of factionalism.

Each Korean CY group must thoroughly execute all directives of the KIM, maintain a true liaison with their working youth masses, truly lead the youth struggle, and define each CY group's affiliation to the Korean Communist Youth Association based on the KIM's directive in the struggle to establish a mass CY association. The level of struggle by the CY masses in opposition to the factional forces that interfere with the mass CY organization should be improved, and the factional forces must be mercilessly driven out of the leadership.

Those who are incapable of leading youth's daily revolutionary struggle and those opportunists who evade the duty of leadership, must be driven out of the leadership. The working youth, the peasant working youth, and the poor peasant youths who participate in the strikes and peasant struggles must be boldly promoted to the leadership. If such a step is carried out, it will be possible to purify the officers of the leadership and strengthen the Korean CY organizations, and also to hasten the CY's process of change toward the mass organization.

The CY organizations must strengthen the new *iacheika* organization operation, but these should first be organized in the big enterprises and the developing regions of the peasant movement. At the same time the existing *iacheika* must be strengthened. The majority of the Korean CY organizations can not even keep an elementary secret. Thus the KIM is pointing out the fact that the ability to keep the secret in promoting the work is one of the decisive tests of the fighting power of the secret organization, the CY organization, and at the same time cautions to pay special attention to preserve secrets and develop a struggle against the propagator.

Examine the present situation of the secret work and at the same time inspire the new members to undertake secret work. The violators who do not strictly observe secret preservation must be punished severely and at times should be expelled from the ranks of the CY. In Korea where the police terror is severe, the CY members must recognize the fact that to be negligent on maintenance of secrecy is clearly tantamount to select apostasy, but the KIM is clearly stating here that maintenance of secrecy does not mean to weaken the relationship between the CY members and the working masses.

The Korean CY organizations must liquidate factionalism within the rank and file of the Korean Communist Party, must assist the Korean Communists in reconstructing the party's regional organizations, and continuously introduce class conscious and most energetically trained CY members to the rank and file of the Communist Party.

The Korean CY organizations must widely discuss the directive of the Executive Committee of the KIM, rectify their errors by relentless self-criticism, and make detailed policy to transform the scattered organizations into the masses' Korean Communist Youth Association that can lead the struggle of the working youth under the slogans of Korea's future anti-imperialism revolution and the land revolution.

Executive Committee of the Communist Youth International
January 1932

C. THE KOREAN PARTICIPATION, 1933-35

Item 39: Platform of Action of the Communist Party of Korea[1]

The Japanese imperialists, since the actual seizure of our country (1905) and its conversion into their colony, basing themselves on their economic and political domination, have not ceased to plunder and oppress our toiling people. The Korean toilers live in the condition of slaves, deprived of any right to decide independently the question of their fate and [to] govern the country. The entire political power is concentrated in the hands of the Japanese Governor-General, who has at his disposal the army, the police, the gendarmes, the courts, the jails, the reservist league, etc., and whose duty is in the interests of Japanese robbers to oppress and plunder the Korean people. "Koreans must either submit to our laws or die." (Terauchi). The White Terror is raging in the country and the slightest attempt to protest against the violence of the Japanese imperialists is crushed by military force. Special laws exist to suppress the national liberation movement—the decrees of 1907,[2] the laws on the preservation of public order and the law on dangerous thoughts, etc. All the political and economic life of the country is managed to derive profit for Japanese

---

[1] This platform was prepared by a group known as the Initiatory Group, an organization yet to be fully identified. Judging primarily from the content of this document, this group seems to have been a group headed by Han Wi-kŏn who led the Sixth Incident. The document was circulated in early 1934, and it is assumed that it was written in English by a Korean. This document is available in English in *Inprecorr,* Vol. XIV, no. 11 (February 23, 1934), pp. 303-05 and no. 14 (March 2, 1934), pp. 355-58. A Japanese translation was made from this English version.

[2] Reference here of the decrees of 1907 is not clear. The original English version reads "the decrees of 1907 of the Taishō governor," but this apparently is a mistake, for there was no Taishō governor and the reign of Emperor Taisho did not begin until 1912. The Japanese version indicates the decrees of 8th year of Emperor Taishō which is 1919. However, the decrees of 1919 were relatively mild as a consequence of the March First Uprising compared with the decrees of 1907 which were more stringent.

imperialists and increase the national oppression of the Korean people and treat it as a lower nation—as is seen in the creation of special organs for Koreans, the prohibition to use the Korean language, inequality in wages. Privileges and rebates are reserved for the Japanese, while for Koreans there exist plenty of hindrances, etc.

The Japanese imperialists have converted our country into a market for their goods, a source of cheap raw material and labor, a place for capital investment and a strategic military point in the Far East.

The Japanese imperialists are holding back the development of our country. They control the national economy of our country and maintain the feudal relics, especially in the villages.

Owing to the domination of the feudal exploiters and Japanese imperialism, native industry develops very slowly and in a distorted way, and only to the extent permitted by the interests of the Japanese imperialists. Native industry consists of small workshops adapted to the primary manufacture of agricultural raw material for Japan. The share of native capital in industry is insignificant and is chiefly concentrated in light industry. Native capital plays a subordinate role to Japanese capital.

The same is seen in commerce (out of 1,547 commercial undertakings, 1,263 are Japanese or combined Japanese-Korean). The Japanese policy of national discrimination, so far as taxation, excise, credit, etc. is concerned, is clearly to be seen both in industry and trade. The urban petty bourgeoisie—artisans, handicraft men and small traders—suffer very much from this. Unable to bear the burden of the taxes and the competition of the protected Japanese capitalists, they are being rapidly ruined. Most of them become unemployed paupers.

The Korean working class suffers most of all. It lives in a condition of slavery. On the average the workers work 13 to 16 hours a day and get beggarly wages. They get about half of what the Japanese worker, and even the Japanese youth, get for equal work. Wages vary between 10 and 70 *sen* per day, which is far from sufficient to support a worker and his family. Their wives and little children are therefore compelled to work. The women and children are subjected to the most brutal exploitation. Wages are not paid in full or on time. In all factories workers suffer from the system of fines, deductions, "presents" to the foremen, compulsory "savings," delays in the payment of wages, payment by checks instead of money, which are later exchanged for money at 30 to 40 per cent below nominal, etc. Among the seasonal and building workers, etc., where piece work is in operation, the workers are robbed by the foremen, *shitauke* [subcontractor], *oyakata* [boss], etc. At the time of unemployment the Korean workers are doomed to death from starvation, the threat of which compels them to submit to the worst forms of exploitation and slavery of the moneylender and speculator.

The Korean workers suffer from chronic mass unemployment, constantly increasing, with the complete absence of any assistance from the government and the employers. The Korean workers have no rest days. There are no labor laws. In the factories a prison regime exists and the workers are at the mercy of the employers and their agents. The unsanitary conditions of the workers' houses and the complete absence of safety devices lead to tremendous growth of sickness and accidents at work, for which neither the employer nor the Japanese oppressors take any responsibility. The women textile workers and the workers employed on work "for assisting the poor" are particularly exploited.

The poor development, which is a result of the subjugation of our country, renders the lot of the Korean intellectuals extremely wretched. They cannot find employment and therefore are compelled to walk about unemployed or to take the shameful hireling path of becoming officials in the Japanese military occupational regime, and thus be utilized to oppress and plunder the Korean people.

Japanese capital in Korea is almost entirely used to plunder the Korean people, especially the peasantry. The Japanese agricultural and irrigation companies, money leagues, big landlords (latifundia and plantations), plans for increasing the sowing of rice, etc., are, in the hands of the Japanese colonizers, powerful means to drain super-profits out of the country while the Japanese colonization forms the foundation of the military occupational regime in the country.

The Japanese imperialists own the best land, forests and unoccupied land in the country, control agriculture through the banks, companies (Eastern Colonization Co., Shokusan Ginkō, finance companies). They maintain simultaneously the domination of feudal-landlord landownership that leads to greater exploitation, ruin and oppression of the peasantry, chiefly the poor. The insignificant development of capitalism in agriculture connected with the domination of Japanese imperialism does not improve the conditions of the peasants but on the contrary makes it worse and increases their dependence on the Japanese imperialists and their allies—the Korean landlords, money-lenders and speculators.

Low monopolist prices of agricultural products, high tariffs and the compulsory distribution of seeds, and fertilizers at high prices, etc., are a scourge for the Korean peasants. The Korean peasants are compelled to hand over their produce to the Japanese imperialists at the existing low monopolist prices, less than half of the market prices, while they are forced to take Japanese goods at prices increased three or fourfold. The peasants are crushed by all kinds of taxes and exactions. In our country there are 52 different kinds of exactions, of which eleven are in the form of direct taxes. The land tax has increased from 1919 to 1933 by 60 per cent. Local taxes for the upkeep of the apparatus of the governor-generals are growing and have increased during the last twenty years forty-three times, while the head tax had increased 240 times in eighteen years.

The Japanese imperialists have ruined our villages. The peasants, especially the poor and middle peasants, cannot bear the burden of the taxes, exactions and rents, and are rapidly being ruined. The ruined peasantry is either compelled to remain in the villages as enslaved tenants or to flee to Manchuria, where they again become serfs of Japanese and Chinese satraps. Some are forced to go to the towns where they remain unemployed or sometimes hire themselves as workers in

Japan, where they are subjected to the most cruel exploitation and are forced to play the role of strike-breakers. If they remain in their villages they have to try to cultivate new land, though as soon as they start they are again driven out by the Japanese imperialists. The land of the ruined peasants passes into the hands of the Japanese companies and Korean landlords, who possess over 54 per cent of all the ploughed area. The Japanese companies and the Korean landlords do not cultivate the land themselves, but rent it out to the peasants on unbearable conditions. Rent in kind dominates in our country and amounts to 50-80 per cent of the harvest. In addition to rent, the tenants have to pay land and water taxes to the landlord and for seed and fertilizers. They pay the same amount of rent in years of bad harvest. The recently introduced law on rent conflict does not improve the position of the tenants. It legalizes the existing oppressive conditions and entirely defends the interests of the landlords.

As a result of the mass ruin of the Korean peasantry, the central figures in our villages are the poor peasants, who form over 50 per cent of all the peasants. Most of them live in perpetual want in years of good harvest as well. The harvest of the poor peasant does not remain for his own consumption, and very often does not even suffice to pay rent. Failure to pay rent in time brings often the confiscation of the whole harvest and property of the peasant and deprives him of tenant rights. When bad years come, then the peasants are doomed to death from starvation.

The middle peasants, who form a relatively small section of the peasants, are in a very difficult and poverty-stricken situation. Most of them are being ruined and turned into poor peasants, and only a small number of them become kulaks. The middle peasants are also oppressed by all kinds of taxes and exactions, including the water tax for the irrigation company. The middle peasants of Korea live in constant danger of being ruined for not paying rent and taxes in time. Owing to agrarian overpopulation, caused by the policy of the Japanese colonizers, and owing to the increasing poverty, most of them have already become semi-tenants and are being turned into poor peasants.

The agricultural laborers are in specially difficult conditions. Owing to the domination of pre-capitalist forms of exploitation, which is the result of the weak development of capitalism in agriculture, the agricultural workers are subjected to unheard-of exploitation. Although they are workers like the town workers, they work unlimited hours. They have the most varied duties to perform, working as household servants as well, receiving 20 to 25 *sen* per day, which is about 1/5 of the wages of Japanese workers.

In addition to being plundered by the Japanese imperialists, the Korean peasants are severely exploited by the Korean landlords, rich peasant exploiters, moneylenders and speculators who are supported by the whole existing system. Poverty drives the Korean peasants, especially the poor peasants, to accept every kind of slavery and oppression by these parasites. The present total indebtedness amounts to 700 million yen.

In our country, owing to the robber policy of the Japanese colonizers, based upon landlord ownership, agriculture is on the downgrade. During the last ten years it has not emerged from a state of chronic agrarian crisis. The position of the Korean peasants and toilers is getting worse year by year.

Since the present world crisis, especially since the Japanese invasion of China, the condition of the Korean toilers has greatly deteriorated. Japanese imperialism, torn to pieces by the contradictions of the growing crisis, tries to find the way out of it by increased reaction, fascism, and an attack on the standard of living of the toiling masses of Japan and its colonies, by a new imperialist war and intervention in the U.S.S.R. The war in Manchuria has already ruined and worsened the position of the toilers of Korea, Japan and China. The real purpose of the war is not the defence of the Koreans in Manchuria, or improvement of the life of the masses of the people in Korea and Japan, as is falsely stated by the Japanese imperialists and their lackeys. It is an attempt to get out of the deep crisis by forcibly seizing new territories and plundering new millions of people. This war will bring new sufferings and evils for the toilers of Korea and Japan. Since the war of Japan in Manchuria, the urban petty bourgeoisie and the peasants, especially the poor and middle

peasants, have been greatly ruined. Every day the property of
the toilers and the peasants is sold by auction because they are
unable to pay taxes, debts, rent, etc. Besides this the Japanese
imperialists, under the pretence of "emergency times," prohibited the export of Korean rice to Japan, imposed high tariffs
on lentils from Manchuria, made the subscription to government loans compulsory, etc., which are additional forms of
robbery of the toiling masses.

The wages of the Korean workers have fallen by 32 per cent
during the last year and the working day has lengthened by one
to two hours. At the same time unemployment is growing, not
only owing to the closing of factories, but as the result of the
reduction in the number of workers because of the greater
exploitation of those who remain and as the result of the
replacement of adult workers by low-paid underaged youths.
The number of unemployed at the present time amounts to
700,000 which is over 50 per cent of the number of workers in
the country, while there are six million starving peasants. The
toilers of town and village are being ruined in masses, the
unemployed Koreans are being forcibly sent back from Japan,
and refugees from Manchuria are concentrating in large numbers
in the country.

The Japanese imperialists not only do not help the Korean
toilers, who are starving and unemployed, but on the contrary
take advantage of their helpless conditions to engage them as
cheap labor on the construction of military works in the
country. There the workers are subjected to a prison regime.
And all the expenses for this are again transferred to the toilers
of Korea and Japan.

In connection with the crisis and the war of Japan in
Manchuria, the reaction and terror have increased against the
revolutionary movements of the toilers of Korea and Japan.
Workers' and peasants' organizations are suppressed, the anti-
popular laws are reinforced. Strikes of workers and conflicts of
peasants are suppressed by the police and the army. Thousands
of revolutionaries are pining and dying in the jails.

While the masses of the people are starving and facing ruin,
Japanese imperialism makes every effort to support the Korean

aristocracy and landlords. It has introduced the rice law, which gives help to the aristocracy.

The Korean bourgeoisie, in spite of their different status from that of the landlords and their contradictions with Japanese imperialism, are more and more adapting themselves to the system of the colonial regime. Their contradictions with Japanese imperialism are contradictions arising from the monopolist possession of the right to exploit and plunder the masses of the Korean people, and above all, the workers. Although Japanese imperialism appropriates tremendous profits and the surplus product squeezed out of the toiling masses of Korea, the Korean bourgeoisie also have the possibility of exploiting the Korean workers.

The noose on the neck of the Korean people is drawing tighter and tighter. This will continue as long as the Japanese imperialists rule in our country.

Only the revolution of the Korean toilers in alliance with the Japanese and Chinese toilers can save the Korean people from the yoke of the Japanese imperialists. For the complete destruction of the unbearable slavery of the Korean toilers it is necessary to win the independence of Korea by the revolutionary overthrow of the economic and political rule of Japanese imperialism. It is necessary to raise the banner of the national liberation revolution, which by its character will also be anti-feudal and anti-imperialist, directed against the rule of the Japanese imperialists and landlord ownership. The agrarian revolution (bourgeois democratic) forms the axis of the national liberation revolution of the Korean masses. For the struggle against the oppressors and the victory of the revolution, it is necessary to organize the struggle of the revolutionary forces of the country, forming a united national revolutionary front against the Japanese imperialists and their allies.

In our country there is not a united nation, but there are classes which are not all interested in the revolutionary smashing of the existing system and regime.

The Korean landlords who plunder the Korean toilers under the protection of the Japanese imperialists and who are their allies, against whom the revolution will be directed, are in the camp of the imperialists, are struggling and will struggle against the people's revolution.

The position of the Korean bourgeoisie is somewhat different. Objectively, it is in their interests to get rid of Japanese rule, and establish their own rule so as to plunder our people as monopolists. This circumstance puts them against the Japanese imperialists. But at the same time, being considerably connected with Japanese capital directly and indirectly, with landed property and usury, they fear the revolution of the toilers, which will destroy all landlord ownership and money-lending capital and will destroy imperialist and feudal property. Therefore, they manoeuvre between the revolution and imperialism and take up a national reformist position. They try to strengthen their position by reforms, utilizing for this purpose the national liberation movement of the masses. On the other hand, they try to take advantage of the contradictions and conflicts between Japanese imperialism and its competitors so as to bargain for better conditions for themselves.

In March, 1919, at the time of the highest rise of the opposition to Japanese imperialism, the Korean bourgeoisie tried to limit the anti-Japanese movement among the masses of Korea, orienting them on Versailles and the U.S.A. But when the mass movement against their will began to grow into an armed revolt, the Korean bourgeoisie, fearing the revolutionary revolt of the masses, betrayed their struggle and accepted the reforms of 1919.

The position of the Korean bourgeoisie in the succeeding years is characterized by ever-greater capitulation to the Japanese imperialists and desertion of the national revolutionary front. The determining factors of their political position are: (1) the growth and development of the peasant movement in the country; (2) the rapid growth of socialist construction in the U.S.S.R., which is rousing ever new sections of the toiling masses of the whole world, including the toilers of Korea, in the struggle against their enslavers; (3) the Korean bourgeoisie have drawn their conclusions from the great Chinese revolution which not only sweeps away the foreign imperialists but also the native exploiters.

In the present conditions of crisis and the growth of the revolutionary movement of the toiling masses in Korea, the Korean bourgeoisie have linked up their fate with Japanese imperialism. The contradictions between the bourgeoisie and the toilers of the country have become the chief ones which determine their political positions. They are trying in every way to slur over the contradictions between them and Japanese imperialism. This explains their defence of the robber war of Japan in China, their support of the open plunder of the toiling masses of Korea, and the struggle against the revolutionary movement.

The support of the Japanese imperialists by the Korean bourgeoisie at the time when the imperialist powers, above all Japan, are waging or preparing a new imperialist war and intervention in the U.S.S.R., the basis and stronghold of the world revolutionary movement, shows that the bourgeoisie has no desire and is unable to carry on the anti-imperialist struggle.

The path of the Korean bourgeoisie is the path of systematic betrayal of the national liberation struggle of the Korean toilers. In future, they will do everything to disrupt this struggle. All the bourgeois political organizations, such as *Ch'ŏndo-kyo,* the group of the paper *Tong-a ilbo, Chosŏn ilbo,* etc., have taken this line already.

The Korean bourgeoisie, in spite of their reformism and treachery, have not lost their influence on the Korean toilers. And the possibility of maneuvering once more and betraying their struggle still exists. They try to keep control over the national liberation movement of the Korean people through their agents, such as the group of the journals *Pip'an, Shin dan'ge,* etc., which by using "left socialist" phraseology, try to win over the toiling masses, above all the workers.

Under these conditions the historic task of the complete liberation of the Korean people from the Japanese yoke and the carrying on of all revolutionary democratic changes can be carried out, as was shown by the experience of the October Revolution in Russia and the Chinese Revolution, only by the revolutionary struggle of the Korean toilers under the leadership of the working class and in alliance with the Japanese and

Chinese toilers. The working class of Korea is the only consistently revolutionary class. It has already entered into the struggle against its enslavers as an independent social force (Wŏnsan strike). Its struggle is growing year by year and at the present time already contains the elements of a counter attack. If the struggle of the workers is properly combined with the struggle of the peasants against the landlords, which is rapidly increasing also, it will form the basic link for leading the Korean toilers in the approaching revolutionary struggles.

In order to organize the working masses, to crystallize the proletariat as a special class force which realizes its special class interests, able to lead the national liberation movement, in order to bring about the revolutionary alliance of the working class and the peasants under the leadership of the proletariat, in order to liberate the Korean toilers from the influence of national reformism and correctly direct their revolutionary struggle, the working class needs its proletarian Communist Party.

The Communist Party of Korea is the Party of the working class, the final aim of which is to bring about socialism and then the complete Communist society. It struggles for the socialist path of development, for the complete destruction of all exploitation and oppression of man by man. At the present bourgeois democratic stage of the development of the Korean revolution, it fights for the complete independence of Korea, for the establishment of a Workers' and Peasants' Soviet government in it, for the liquidation of landlord ownership.

The only government which can look after the interests of the majority of the Korean population—workers, peasants and toilers in general—is the Workers' and Peasants' Soviet government. The Soviets, formed in the course of the revolutionary revolt of the toilers, under the leadership of the proletariat, as the organ of revolt and the overthrow of Japanese rule, are the only genuine organ of power, elected by the workers, peasants and toilers, able to carry out the confiscation of the land of the landlords, confiscation of the enterprises of the imperialists and the fulfilment of the basic interests of the toiling masses.

Taking this position, the Communist Party of Korea puts

forward the following chief slogans for the present bourgeois democratic stage of the Korean revolution:—

1. Complete State independence, by the violent overthrow of Japanese rule. The abolition of all government debts, the expropriation and nationalization of all the Japanese factories, banks, railways, sea and river transport, plantations and irrigation equipment.

2. The establishment of a Workers' and Peasants' Soviet government.

3. The confiscation, without compensation, of all the land, forests and other property of the landlords, monasteries, governor-generals, officials and moneylenders, handing them over to the toiling peasants. The annulment of all oppressive agreements and all the debts of the peasants to the moneylenders, banks, money leagues and companies.

4. The 8-hour day and a radical improvement in the conditions of labor, the increase of wages, introduction of social legislation, insurance against accidents and sickness and State provision for the unemployed.

The Communist Party of Korea, struggling for these basic demands, expresses the interests of the masses of the people. The carrying out of these demands will create the prerequisites and ensure the further development of our country in the direction of the construction of socialist society, with the aim of developing the mass revolutionary struggle of the toilers, at the same time putting forward a series of partial demands, the struggle for which will help to mobilize the masses for the revolutionary revolt for the independence of Korea.

The Communist Party of Korea declares that the only way to win the complete independence of Korea is the path of the revolutionary struggle of the broad masses, carried to the point of a nation-wide armed revolt against Japanese rule.

The partial demands put forward by the Communist Party of Korea differ in principle from the "partial" demands of the Korean bourgeoisie and their political organizations. Our demands are completely linked up with the tasks of the revolution, the struggle for which will help to mobilize the masses for the struggle against Japanese imperialism, while their slogans have the aim of bringing about the autonomy of Korea within the system of Japanese imperialism and to avert the armed revolt of the entire toiling masses against Japanese imperialism. The Korean bourgeoisie put forward partial demands in their own class interests. The Communist Party of Korea puts forward partial demands in the interests of the workers, peasants and urban poor.

A great danger for the victory of the Korean revolution is the fact that the toiling masses of the country still have illusions about *Ch'ŏndo-kyo* and other so-called national organizations. They have not understood that these are the class organizations of the Korean national reformist bourgeoisie which oppose the basic interests of the toiling masses of Korea. The Communist Party of Korea declares that it will mercilessly expose all shades of national-reformism and especially the autonomist trends led by the leaders of *Ch'ŏndo-kyo*. The exposure of and struggle against the national-reformists is one of the main tasks of the Korean Communists. Only a merciless struggle against national reformism will make it possible to win the working and peasant masses away from them and mobilize them under the banner of the Communist Party for the struggle against Japanese imperialism. Only the revolutionary struggle against imperialism can liberate the toilers from the influence of national-reformism.

In the struggle for the toiling masses, the Communist Party of Korea calls on all the Korean Communists: —

1. To make full use of legal and semi-legal possibilities for wide actions and the mobilization of the masses under revolutionary slogans, always exposing the treacherous role of national-reformism, exposing the bourgeois conciliatory front and calling on the masses to form the united workers' and peasants' front from below on the basis of concrete revolutionary demands and actions.

2. To develop mass revolutionary actions and the struggle of the working class for political and economic demands, the mass refusal of the peasants to pay taxes, exactions, rent, debts,

mobilizing and preparing the toiling masses for the revolutionary struggle against imperialism.

The Communist Party of Korea calls on all honest revolutionaries in Korea to rally under its slogans for the struggle against Japanese imperialism. While welcoming the loyalty and self-sacrifice which they show, it declares at the same time that the liberation of the Korean toilers cannot be won by the individual terroristic acts which they carry out. It points out that the path of the Korean revolution is the struggle and the revolutionary revolt of the broad masses under the leadership of the Korean proletariat. The supporters of individual terror do not see and do not understand the connection between the agrarian revolution, the struggle of the proletariat and the overthrow of Japanese rule. They do not see and do not understand that it is not the individual struggle of isolated heroes but only the revolutionary mass struggle which can liberate our country from the yoke of imperialism.

The Communist Party of Korea, in view of the special and urgent danger of a new imperialist war and armed intervention in the U.S.S.R., especially since the robber war of Japan against China, the war which is the beginning of the new war and preparations for invading the U.S.S.R., calls on all its supporters to widely organize the anti-war struggle of the masses of Korea, linking it up with the everyday struggle for their interests. At the present time the struggle against imperialist war and the defense of the U.S.S.R., the stronghold of the revolutionary movement, is an inseparable part of the struggle for the national liberation of Korea. Our struggle against war, in defense of the U.S.S.R., must be accompanied by a merciless struggle and exposure of the position of all national reformists, including the "left" groups like *Pip'an, Shin dan'ge,* etc., the Japanese socialists who advocate Pan-Asianism.

a. General Demands

1. The expulsion of the Japanese troops, the abolition of the police and the gendarmes, the disbanding of the Reservist

Union, the general arming of the toilers.

2. The immediate liberation of all political prisoners.

3. Unlimited freedom of speech, press, assembly, conscience and combination for the toilers and the repeal of all laws directed against the people.

4. The destruction of privileges of rank, etc., and the complete equality of all citizens irrespective of sex, nation and religion.

5. The repeal of the assimilation policy in regard to education. Free general education in the native language under the control of the toilers.

6. The establishment of free government help for the population in cases of natural calamity.

7. The abolition of the system of monopolist prices on agricultural products.

8. Free medical treatment for all the toilers.

9. The election of judges and officials from among the toilers and the right to recall them at any time at the demand of the majority of the toilers.

b. Special Workers' Demands

The Communist Party of Korea, in order to organize the broad masses of the working class and give them mass education to defend the everyday struggle of the toiling masses of our country, calls on all class-conscious workers to concentrate their efforts on the strengthening of the left-wing of the trade union movement. The Communist Party of Korea considers it necessary to organize mass class trade unions, above all among the factory workers. They must become regularly functioning mass organizations, acting in the spirit of the class struggle. It is necessary to isolate and expel the reformist leaders from the trade union movement and simultaneously to organize factory committees in the enterprises, the railways, docks, mines, etc.

The Korean Federation of Labor, basing itself mainly on the semi-feudal guilds of porters, seasonal workers and fishermen, and led by the national-reformists and the petty bourgeois elements, by repudiating the revolutionary class struggle has become a weapon for crushing and disrupting the struggle of the workers for the benefit of the exploiters. The Communist Party of Korea will carry on systematic everyday stubborn work in the reformist unions with the aim of winning the working masses to the side of the revolutionary trade union movement and isolating all the reformist leaders from them.

The Communist Party of Korea will struggle against the government trade unions, which are agents of Japanese imperialism among the workers. At the same time, on the basis of the united front from below, it will organize joint actions for the defence of the legal and material interests of the workers to improve their condition and do its utmost to form a fighting Korean centre of the labor movement. To carry out these tasks, the Communist Party of Korea thinks it necessary to form groups of supporters of the left-wing in the reformist unions and to organize class trade unions, above all, in the factories.

The Communist Party of Korea calls upon all its supporters to organize the movement and struggle of the unemployed, to form committees to fight for regular relief at the expense of the government and the employers, to hold demonstrations and carry on a joint struggle together with the organized workers for the partial demands of the unemployed—monthly relief, free supply of fuel, light, etc., by the local municipalities, etc.

The Communist Party of Korea calls on all the workers to help and take part in the formation of trade unions of farm workers. The struggle for the complete abolition of all pre-capitalist relations, compulsory and contract labor, deprival of rights and the unheard-of exploitation of the agricultural proletariat is one of the chief tasks of the struggle against imperialist rule.

The Communist Party of Korea, realizing the importance of bringing the foreign workers in Korea (Japanese and Chinese) in the united front with the Koreans, calls on its supporters to make every effort to attract and organize the basic masses of them on the side of the revolutionary trade union movement, to carry on a joint struggle for everyday needs and to develop the spirit of international proletarian solidarity and the united front against Japanese imperialism.

The Communist Party of Korea especially emphasizes that, realizing the hard conditions of the Chinese workers in Korea, it will struggle against every attempt of the imperialists and the national-reformists to destroy the united front and the class solidarity of the proletariat of the two countries by provoking and instigating national antagonisms.

The Communist Party of Korea will carry on a struggle for the following demands of the working class of Korea:—

1. For higher wages, for reduced working hours. Against the lengthening of the working day, for the 8-hour day and the 6-hour day in industries injurious to health and the mining industry.

2. Against wage-cuts, for the establishment of a compulsory minimum wage on the basis of the minimum cost of living for a worker's family. The prohibition of the payment of wages in kind or in checks. Against delays in the payment of wages, for weekly payment. The complete prohibition of fines, compulsory savings, "presents" to foremen in the factories. Double payment for overtime.

3. Equal pay for equal work, irrespective of sex, age and nationality.

4. Against police supervision in the factories, the abolition of the system of overseers. The prohibition of compulsory contract labor, the abolition of the barrack system and searchers. For the introduction of control over engaging and dismissing workers through workers' committees.

5. A weekly rest day and a yearly vacation of two weeks for adults and a month for youths, with full pay.

6. For complete state social insurance against unemployment, sickness, accident, disablement, old age, orphanage at the expense of the government and the employers on not less than the minimum cost of living.

7. The provision of overalls at the expense of the employers not less than once a year, and for miners and workers in industries injurious to health not less than twice a year.

8. The building of houses and baths for the workers at the

expense of the employers and the government, under the control of workers' committees, and fixing of rent through them. The organization of clubs, reading rooms, clean dining rooms, etc., in all factories at the expense of employers and managed entirely by the workers themselves.

9. Against the fierce exploitation of the home workers. The payment of home workers on a level with workers in factories.

10. The abolition of the system of contractors. For the election of the independent organizers by the workers and the signing of agreements. The abolition of the system forcing workers to buy their own tools.

11. Against dismissals, for insurance for the unemployed at the expense of the government and the employers. For the free distribution of rice and relief equal to the minimum cost of living. The abolition of all forcible deductions from wages under the pretense of supporting the unemployed.

c. Peasant Demands

The Communist Party of Korea will fight:—

1. For the confiscation, without compensation, of all the land and estates, forests, fishing grounds and pastures of the landlords, money-lenders, companies, governor-generals, and their transfer to the peasant masses for their use through peasant committees.

2. For the nationalization of the entire system of irrigation, the complete annulment of all the debts of the peasants to the irrigation companies and the establishment of peasant control over irrigation systems through peasant committees elected by the toiling peasants.

3. For the lowering of rent; against the eviction of peasants and tenants from their accustomed places and against deprival of the right of tenants to rent land, no matter what form it takes.

4. For the complete abolition of all taxes and exactions from the peasants who have suffered from natural calamities, and the establishment of special taxes on the landlords to give

help to those who have suffered from floods, droughts, etc.

5. For the immediate confiscation of the rice reserves of the governor-generals, the Japanese and Korean landlords, to be freely distributed among the starving peasants and those who have no seed for sowing.

6. For the complete abolition of all privileges, particularly the abolition of the system of sub-renting, and criminal prosecution for sub-renters.

7. For the complete abolition of the debts of the peasants to the landlords, money-lenders, companies, money leagues, irrigation companies and their agents.

8. The Communist Party of Korea, with the aim of disorganizing the rule of the Japanese and to develop the revolutionary attack on it, calls on the peasants and farm workers to hold all kinds of demonstrations, to refuse collectively to pay contributions and taxes and to refuse to carry out the orders and decrees of the government organs and their agents.

9. The Communist Party of Korea calls on all peasants to struggle against the confiscation of the harvests and property of the peasants for the non-payment of taxes, rent, debts, the education of their children, etc.

10. Against police supervision in the evening courses and for the repeal of the law prohibiting evening courses.

11. The Communist Party of Korea calls on all its supporters to help to organize delegate meetings of tenants, to work out general demands and to carry on joint activity in their struggle.

12. The Communist Party of Korea will struggle for every demand of the peasants which is directed against the rule of Japanese imperialism, the landlords, money-lenders, etc.

13. As a slogan for agitation among the peasants and as a means of giving the greatest consciousness to the peasant movement, the Communist Party of Korea thinks it necessary to organize peasant committees to carry on a struggle for bringing about all the revolutionary democratic changes in the interests of liberating the peasants from the oppression of Japanese imperialism and its feudal allies.

14. The Communist Party of Korea calls on the agricultural

workers to organize independent trade unions, to combine with the town proletariat under the banner of the Communist Party and to elect representatives into the peasant committees.

d. The Struggle for the Interests of the Urban Petty Bourgeoisie

The Communist Party of Korea calls on the small toiling strata of the towns to support the revolutionary struggle against the Japanese rule, the landlords and the money-lenders. The Korean bourgeoisie and their organizations, *Ch'ŏndo-kyo,* etc., by making a compromise with Japanese imperialism, not only betray the interests of the workers and peasants, but also of the broad strata of the urban petty bourgeoisie (artisans, handicraftmen, street traders, etc.).

Only the complete destruction of Japanese rule can radically improve the conditions of life of the broad masses of the urban petty bourgeoisie, handicraftsmen and the city poor.

The Communist Party advocates tariff autonomy to defend the national industry against ruinous imperialist competition.

The Communist Party of Korea struggles for the annulment of all money-lenders' debts which enslave the urban poor. It struggles for the abolition of all direct and indirect taxes, excise and other kinds of taxation of the wages and small earnings of the ruined handicraftmen, employees, etc., and for their replacement by progressive taxes on all the incomes of the capitalists, rentiers, banks, inheritance, etc. The Communist Party of Korea struggles for all revolutionary measures which serve the interests of the proletariat and which are directed towards improving the conditions of the urban poor.

The Communist Party of Korea calls on all *paekjŏng* (pariahs) to form a united revolutionary front with all the toilers of the country against Japanese rule and the landlord system. The Communist Party of Korea struggles for the complete abolition of all forms of slavery (social, cultural, etc.) and for the equality of the toiling pariahs with all the toilers of our country.

e. The Liberation of Women

The women of Korea are in a state of slavery, suffering from feudal relics, economic, cultural and legal inequality. They have no right whatever to decide their personal fate and are compelled to live a pitiful existence without the right to participate in social life.

The position of women workers is specially hard. Exploitation and the conditions of labor for working women, who form 30 per cent of the factory workers, is really unprecedented in its inhumanity and robber character. The slavish position of women in Korea is the result of the existence of enormous feudal relics in the entire social system of the country, which is jealously guarded by Japanese imperialism.

The Communist Party of Korea points out that the bourgeois feminist organization, like *Kŭn'u-hoe,* etc., do not carry on a real struggle for the liberation of women. The Communist Party of Korea calls on the masses of women to join the general revolutionary struggle of the toilers of Korea under the leadership of the Communist Party for the overthrow of the system which supports the slavish position of the Korean women. Only in alliance with the toilers and in the fight against Japanese imperialism can the toiling women of Korea obtain their freedom.

The Communist Party of Korea calls on all women workers in the factories and women farm laborers in the villages to join the class trade unions and carry on an untiring struggle against all kinds of reformists, including *Kŭn'u-hoe.*

The Communist Party of Korea fights (A) for the complete abolition of night work for women and the prohibition of all women's labor below ground (in the coal mines, etc.) and in all industries which are harmful to women's health; (B) for the abolition of national and sex inequalities in wages, putting forward the demand for "equal pay for equal work"; (C) for complete social, economic and legal equality for women; (D) for exemption from work and full wages for two months before child-birth, and two months afterwards and free medical treatment and medicine. The formation of children's nurseries at the expense of the employers in all factories and enterprises, with women workers to care for the small children and rooms for feeding them and the reduction of the working day for nursing mothers to six hours a day.

f. Demands of the Youth

The Communist Party of Korea calls on the revolutionary proletarian youth to restore the Young Communist League (Y.C.L.). In the conditions of terror and barbarous oppression, the Y.C.L. of Korea as an illegal organization must carry out directly and through a number of auxiliary legal and semi-legal mass organizatons (youth sections in the trade unions) the task of organizing the broad strata of the working, peasant, and revolutionary student youth under the banner of the Communist Party.

The Y.C.L. of Korea, as the assistant of the Party, has the special task of organizing the toiling youth under the banner of Communism. The Y.C.L. of Korea must act as a political organization, subordinating all forms of the struggle and the organization of the masses—economic, cultural, sport—to the interests of the political struggle, to the interests of the overthrow of imperialist slavery and the winning of the independence of Korea and the establishment of the Workers' and Peasants' Soviet Government of Korea.

The Communist Party of Korea, while declaring that the national reformist youth leagues—the Korean Federation of Youth and the religious organizatons of youth—cannot struggle for the everyday interests and the final aim of the oppressed and exploited Korean working youth, calls on all the supporters of the Communist Party to carry on persistent work to win over the revolutionary toiling youth in the national-reformist leagues to our side, so that by putting up a revolutionary struggle inside their organizations against the reformists the revolutionary youth will be drawn into the organizations of the Y.C.L. of Korea and the organizations under its leadership.

To protect the interests of the toiling youth and to develop their revolutionary activities for the national and social liberation of the toiling masses, the Communist Party of Korea fights:—

a. For the limitation of the working day to 6 hours for the youth between 14 and 16 years, and the prohibition of the employment of children under 14.

b. General compulsory free education in the native language up to the age of 14. The supply of food, clothing and school necessities for children at the expense of the government. The introduction of vocational teaching of children at the expense of the government and the employers. The abolition of Sunday schools for children and the freedom of organization of children's Communist groups of Young Pioneers.

c. A yearly paid holiday of six weeks for young workers.

d. Equal pay for equal work.

e. The abolition of all those systems in industry and agriculture that help to oppress and exploit the youth.

f. State support for the unemployed youth that ensures the minimum cost of living.

The Korean toiling youth can realize the above demands only under the leadership of the Communist Party of Korea and only if they carry on a merciless struggle against Japanese imperialism and national reformism and against all those who confuse the toiling youth.

Conclusion

The Communist Party of Korea, by putting forward its program of demands for the Korean revolution, calls on the toiling masses to rally under the revolutionary banners of the Party and to carry the struggle to the point of the successful winning of State power and the establishment of the revolutionary-democratic dictatorship of the workers and peasants in the form of Soviets.

The Communist Party of Korea declares that the successful fulfilment of the tasks of the anti-imperialist and anti-feudal revolution opens up the possibility that with the support of the

international proletariat and, above all, the workers of Japan
and China, and the class struggle of the exploited masses of our
country, our revolution through a number of stages will develop
into a Socialist revolution, and thus create the prerequisites for
the reconstruction of our country on socialist lines. In this
struggle the Korean people are not alone. In the U.S.S.R.
socialism is achieving victory after victory, which strengthens
the basis of the world revolutionary movement. The Korean
people have allies in the international proletariat and, above all,
the working class of Japan and China. Japanese imperialism
oppresses not only the Korean people. The toilers of Japan and
China are under its yoke and are also struggling against Japanese
imperialism. Therefore the victory of the national liberation
revolution of the Korean toilers is only possible by their joint
struggle with the Japanese and Chinese toilers against the
common enemy—Japanese imperialism. The workers of the
world are struggling to overthrow international imperialism and
destroy the entire capitalist system which is passing through a
general crisis. As the E.C.C.I. pointed out, the end of capitalist
stabilization has come. We are at the turning point in the
development of the general crisis of capitalism, at the moment
of transition to a new cycle of revolutions and wars.

The attack of capital brings the growth of the stubborn
resistance of the international proletariat and the colonial
people against their enslavers.

The revolutionary front of the world proletariat and the
colonial peoples is growing and strengthening day by day in
spite of all the cunning of the imperialists and their agents, the
reformists and social facists.

But for carrying on the struggle and to achieve the victory of
the Korean revolution, the Communist vanguard of the proletariat of Korea, the leader and organizer of the toiling masses
of our country, is necessary. The formation of a centralized,
disciplined ideologically united mass underground Communist
Party is now the basic and long matured task of the revolutionary liberation movement of the country.

To carry out this aim, the Communist Party of Korea exerts
every effort to form a united monolithic ideologically firm

fighting mass underground Party which will be able to rouse and organize the struggle of the Korean masses against the Japanese imperialists.

The Communist Party of Korea states with pride that it considers itself as a part of the organized international Communist Movement, a section of the Communist International.[3] The Communist Party of Korea calls upon all the advanced workers and the revolutionaries who are loyal to the cause of the working class to join the ranks of the Communist Party which is being formed to fight for the historic tasks of the Korean revolution. Owing to the oppression of the Japanese rule and terror the Communist Party can exist and develop only as an underground organization that utilizes all legal and illegal forms in order to develop mass struggle and to win the toiling masses for the struggle to establish the revolutionary democratic dictatorship of the proletariat and the peasants at the first stage of the Korean revolution.

The Communist Party of Korea is forming its Party organizations and groups in all towns and in all the factories and mines of the country.

The Communist Party of Korea will organize the working class and the basic masses of the peasants under the banner of the Korean revolution, and in spite of all difficulties and sacrifices will carry the struggle of the toiling masses to the point of complete destruction of Japanese rule and landlord ownership so that then, together with the world proletariat, it will be able to move ahead to the building up of a socialist society in our country and throughout the world.

Long live the independence of Korea!

Long live the working class, the leader of the toiling masses!

Long live the revolutionary uprising for independence, land, freedom and bread!

Long live the revolutionary alliance of the toilers of Korea, Japan and China in the struggle against Japanese imperialism!

Long live the Communist Party of Korea!

Long live the Comintern—the leader of the world revolution!

Long live the world proletarian revolution!

---

[3] Consider this statement with the rumor of the alleged expulsion of the KCP from the Comintern.

Item 40: To All Factory, Mill and Village Communist Groups in Korea[1]

Dear Comrades:

Our country is one of those countries in which there is not yet a recognized Communist party. This is explained exclusively by the severe factional struggle among the Communists which in our country has taken on an entirely unprecedented and monstrous form.

The factional struggle excluded every possibility of training the members of the party in the spirit of a principled policy. It dulled the party spirit, destroyed the discipline of the party, broke up the unity of its ranks and undermined the authority of the party in the eyes of the workers and peasants, drawing them away from positive work. The Korean Communists, absorbed by factional conflicts, were not occupied with the organization and the leadership of the struggles of the workers and peasants for their economic and political interests, they did not wage a struggle against national reformism, and did not aid the development of the national liberation movement of the toiling masses. As a result of the factional disintegration, the heroic work of individual honest comrades, unconditionally devoted to communism, was almost entirely destroyed.

The further the factional struggle developed, the more hideous was the character that it assumed until it directly merged with the provocative activity of the Japanese gendarmerie and police. The Japanese imperialists ably utilized the factional contradictions of the various groups and corrupted a number of Communists. In the full swing of the factional struggle conditions were created in which provocateurs and

[1] This document was also prepared by the Initiatory Group in 1934. There are two versions of the document in English: the English version presented here is from the *Inprecorr,* Vol. XIV, no. 48 (1934), pp. 1,265-66; there is a slightly different version in English in the *Communist International,* Vol. VII, no. 9 (May 5, 1935), pp. 420-24. These two English translations might have been made from the original document either in Russian or in Korean, but neither version in its original language is, so far, available.

spies could absolutely freely penetrate the ranks of the Communists. And in a number of groups they played a leading role (the Kim Ch'an, Hŏ Il, Chang Il-sŏng cases, etc.).[2] Some of the most devoted revolutionaries were lost as a result of the activities of these spies, and they fomented the factional struggle with the aim of weakening and disintegrating the ranks of the Communists and discrediting them before the toilers.

This shows that all the factional groups without exception, regardless of what they are called and when they arose, played and continue to play the role of marionettes in the hands of the Japanese police.

The Comintern, taking all this into account, was compelled to disband the Communist Party of Korea by a special decision in December 1928. This decision demanded the liquidation of all factions and at the same time pointed out the path to the formation of a new, genuine Communist party as the vanguard of the toiling proletariat.

The formation of a centralized, disciplined, mass underground Communist party with a single ideology is the main and basic task of the revolutionary movement of the Korean toilers. The chief elements of which the Communist party, with iron discipline and with Bolshevist principles of conspiracy, should be formed are the advanced workers and peasants who have come forward during strikes, demonstrations, peasant conflicts and other forms of mass struggle against their class enemies.

To our regret, we have not yet got such a party although there are all the grounds for its formation. The working class of Korea, the party of which must be the Communist party of Korea, has already written a number of brilliant pages in the history of the class struggle in Korea. It is sufficient to recall the Wŏnsan general strike and a number of other strikes which took place during the past few years, in order to be convinced that

[2] The precise cases involving these men are not clear, but Kim Ch'an fell into the group advocating the liquidation of the Communist movement within Korea in favor of the joint activities with the Nationalists. Hŏ Il was instrumental in the factional struggle of the third party, and Chang Il-sŏng is one of the leaders of the group that advocated the total liquidation of Communist activities.

the workers of our country have the desire and the determination to struggle against their class enemies.

The absence of a genuine Communist party holds back the development of the struggle of the Korean toilers, especially the struggle of the Korean workers against Japanese imperialism and its allies.

The absence of such a party is felt particularly now when a new wave of the revolutionary movement of the masses of the people is developing in the country. The present situation in Korea is characterized by the fact that the entire policy of Japanese imperialism is summed up in its trying to adapt our country to the needs of the imperialist wars of pillage. Japanese imperialism, striving to extricate itself from the crisis at the expense of the toiling masses, is more and more intensifying the oppression and exploitation of the masses of the people. On the other hand, it is savagely preparing a war against the USSR—the bulwark of the world revolutionary movement. In consequence of this, the situation of the Korean toilers, which is already miserable enough as it is, is becoming constantly worse. Unemployment is increasing, the peasantry is being ruined on a mass scale, particularly the poor peasants, and an army of poor peasants consisting of many millions is being formed. To all this there is added the fact that the robber war of Japan in China has already ruined millions of toilers. The Korean bourgeoisie, which more and more proceeds along the path of capitulation to Japanese imperialism, also comes forward in the struggle against the masses of the people. Under these conditions, only the Communist party of Korea can ensure the successful development of the struggle of the Korean workers and peasants against the existing order and for the complete independence of Korea, for the abolition of the land-owning rights of the landlords, for the eight-hour day, for a radical improvement in the conditions of the workers, and for the establishment of the workers' and peasants' Soviet power. There are no other paths. Only the Communist party of Korea can correctly lead the struggle of the working class and ensure its hegemony in the national liberation struggle against Japanese imperialism.

We, an initiatory group of Korean Communists, conscious of the importance and the responsibility of the given historical moment, set ourselves the task of forming a united Communist party for organizing and leading the struggle of the Korean toilers. We appeal to the Communist workers in the factories and mills and to the Communists in the villages, to whom the interests of the Korean revolution are dear, to respond to our call. We, proposing a platform of action for the Communist Party of Korea, call upon all Communist workers and Communists in the villages to fight for those demands which are set out in this platform and, taking an active part in this struggle, to organize themselves into Communist groups in the enterprises and in the villages.

Thanks to the firm and undeviating anti-faction line of the Comintern, a considerable part of the factional groups have been exposed before the toilers. But there are still remnants of factional groups which, in connection with the growth of the workers' and peasants' movement, strive to penetrate into their midst in order to continue their rotten factional struggle. For this reason the process of forming Communist groups in the factories, mills, docks, villages, on the ships, railroads, and other places of work, should be accompanied by a severe struggle against all factional groups and factionalists. The factionalists should be exposed and driven out of our ranks. The rage of the masses should be directed against them. Under the present conditions, when factional groups without exception and every factionalist is objectively a tool in the hands of Japanese imperialism for the purpose of disintegrating the revolutionary ranks, they should call forth in us justified disbelief and lack of confidence with regard to their political honesty. We must show exceptional vigilance with regard to all these varieties of provocateurs. The admission of any former factionalist into the Communist groups that are to be newly organized in the enterprises and villages can only be decided after he has shown his devotion to the cause of the revolution, not in words, but in deeds in the revolutionary struggle.

Only in this way, by organizing and rallying together the most advanced workers and peasants in Communist groups directly in the enterprises and the villages, at the same time isolating and exposing the factionalists, will we be able to organize a genuine Communist party, worthy to bear the high name of a section of the Communist International.

We, the initiatory group, boldly state that notwithstanding any of the artifices of the factionalists, the agents of Japanese imperialism in the ranks of the workers, notwithstanding their attempts to frustrate again the endeavor to form a Communist vanguard of the Korean proletariat, we shall overcome all difficulties and attain our aims with the aid of the newly organized Communist groups of workers and peasants. We are entirely able to liquidate the factional groups and to rally the best Communist elements from the workers and peasants in the towns and villages.

Long live the Communist Party of Korea!

Long live the Comintern—the General Staff of the world revolution!

Down with the factional struggle, the instrument of the Japanese imperialists in disintegrating the ranks of the revolutionary movement of the Korean toilers!

Item 41: Duty of the Korean Communists in the Anti-Imperialist War[1]

Comrade Ercoli [Togliati] related in his report that the imperialists are preparing a new imperialistic war, specifically, an anti-revolutionary war against the U.S.S.R., and he has proposed many new duties for the various Communist parties and organizations in the anti-war struggle. Imperialist Japan is now one of the leading nations in the preparation for the war. The Japanese imperialists have already attacked China and have continued the war for the past four years. Because the Chinese people do not want to become slaves of the Japanese imperialists, a hundred thousand laborers have already been killed, kidnapped, or oppressed, and this cruel exploitation is now fast reaching the Korean people. Therefore, I want to speak on how Japanese exploitation in China reflects upon the present condition of the Korean people.

The Japanese imperialists are exploiting every possible means to utilize Korea for their present war and for the preparations for the anti-revolutionary war against the U.S.S.R. Korea has a special significance to the Japanese imperialists, not only as their colony, but also, due to its geographical location, as a strategic fortress in the Pacific military campaign.

The Korean peninsula was the strategic fortress for the Japanese imperialists' territorial expansion to the Asian continent and the Soviet Far East, as well as to China, and it has now continued to be their strategic fortress. In order to make Korea their strategically important fortress, the Japanese

[1] This document is a speech delivered by Kim Ha-il at the Seventh Congress of the Comintern in July 1935. It is assumed that the document was written in Russian because the speech was delivered in Russian. The document, however, is not available in Russian in its entirety. Only an extract of a few paragraphs from Kim's speech is available in Russian. The document is available in both Japanese and Korean in its entirety. See the Japanese version in *Shisō ihō,* no. 14 (March 1938), pp. 97-110. The Korean version is available in a pamphlet entitled, *Pan Cheguk chuǔi chŏnjaeng e issŏsŏ ǔi Chosŏn kongsan chuǔi-ja dŭl ǔi immu,* (Moskva, 1935).

imperialists not only made Korea their colony, but also installed all kinds of military instruments without hesitation. The Japanese imperialists have occupied Korea by bayonett, but all these aggressive wars were conducted under the sweet words of "Korean independence" or "Protection of Korea." They fought two wars, the Sino-Japanese War of 1894 and the Russo-Japanese War of 1905, under these mottos. As a result of these wars, several hundred thousand Korean laborers were poverty stricken, becoming slaves, and Korea became a Japanese colony. Despite these facts, the Japanese Imperialists still use these excuses in the aggressive war against China; in other words, they say that they are fighting in Manchuria to preserve the rights of Koreans there. No matter how much they try to conceal their true objectives, the Japanese imperialists' aggressive wars of the past ten years, including the war conducted in China today, have exploited the Korean laborers and impoverished them in an unprecedented manner, and this is continuing. The Japanese imperialists cannot hide their exploitation and enslavement of Korean laborers, no matter what method they use.

The Japanese imperialists, suffering from economic chaos and the ever increasing contradictions of their system, attempt to free themselves from the chaos by exploiting the laboring masses of the Japanese Capitalist state and its colony. At the same time they have exploited and oppressed several hundred thousand laborers by attacking China. The Japanese aggressive war in China exploited several hundred thousand of the laboring masses in Manchuria, Korea and Japan, which did not solve the contradictions that the Japanese wanted to solve, but only intensified their difficulties. This war has deepened the contradictions between the laboring masses in Japan, Korea, and Taiwan and the Japanese imperialists, and is rapidly approaching the path of war against the U.S.S.R., the fatherland of all the proletarian laboring masses of the world.

The victorious establishment and progress of socialism in the U.S.S.R. points out the way to free the hundred thousand oppressed laboring masses from their cruel shackles, and has aroused the masses to fight against their oppressors. The Japanese Imperialists are trying to escape the present situation only through war, and, in order to continue the war in China and to prepare an aggression against the U.S.S.R., Japan is endeavoring with all of its strength to utilize Koreans, under such mottos as "total mobilization" and "emergency," to strengthen its military might. In order to utilize Korea militarily, the Japanese imperialists try to strengthen Korea as a strategic fortress; in order to use Korea as a supplier of materials, they dig up all the rich natural resources of Korea; and in order to use Korea as a safe region, they influence Korean social opinions. First of all, they do not mention the increase of standing arms in all the military branches, but only mention the increase of two or three divisions of infantry. They are building an air transportation network that links Korea and Manchuria, and they also are building new chemical factories, airfields, training fields for anti-aircraft guns, and military ports in Korea. Among these is a port in Najin, the most important naval base near Manchuria, which connects with northern Japan, and a new road and railroad that link northern Korea with Manchuria and the U.S.S.R. At the same time they settled Japanese military veterans in this region. This military build-up is in progress under the name of relief for the poor, but they exploit the laborers mercilessly and put them to forced labor, leaving large concentrations of peasants starving and unemployed. The Japanese imperialits are widely developing new mining facilities and are improving the presently operating coal and gold mines, as the owners of these mines. Realizing the lack of oil production in their country, the Japanese are trying to solve their oil problem with liquors produced from rice shipped largely from the rice warehouses of Korean landowners and the Korean Government-General, since oil is vitally needed for their airplanes and fleets. Although there are six million starving people in Korea, this rice is not used for the relief of these people, but rather is consumed in preparation for the anti-revolutionary war against the U.S.S.R. The Japanese imperialists are preparing for the war with a cruel exploitation of the Korean masses. Most of the funds used in waging the war against China and in preparing an armed aggression against the U.S.S.R. were obtained as the result of the exploitation of the

Korean masses in various forms of forced labor and by all kinds of taxes and other charges. The Korean masses are in a desperate situation even without these levies, but as a result of this exploitation their situation is worsening every day. There is no need to elaborate on the Japanese exploitation of Korean laborers during the period of economic chaos; it is easy to see their atrocities by the reduction of wages, reduced fifty to sixty percent compared with those of 1927, and the extension of working hours from thirteen to sixteen hours. During the period of economic chaos, Korean laborers were receiving wages two or three times lower than those of comparable Japanese laborers, but today the difference has been increased to three or four times. The number of unemployed laborers is increasing daily and today about half of the Korean laborers are unemployed. But they are not receiving any kind of relief from the government or the industries. Thus, in order to save themselves from starvation the unemployed are fast becoming slave laborers of the usurers and gamblers.

The Korean peasants are also in similar difficulties. The Korean economic chaos has merged with the gradual agrarian chaos resulting from the Japanese rule and the remnants of Korean feudalism. Korean agriculture was not able to escape the general agrarian chaos of the last twenty years. Aside from the increase in taxes and other charges, the tenancy fee alone has increased some twenty percent. This amounts to more than eighty percent of the total harvest. On top of this, there has been a series of floods and other disasters in both the northern and southern parts of Korea every year.

The Korean farm villages are literally starving, and, without any relief from the government, several millions of the peasant masses are maintaining their basic existence with the roots of herbs and the bark of trees. Recently even this was exhausted in many regions and the peasants have only water as food, and have even organized a water association. Although under such adverse conditions, they must still pay all kinds of taxes. Because the peasants cannot pay the assessed taxes, they are performing forced labor in construction projects termed "relief of the poor."

This administration that ruins the peasants has a great impact on the masses. The law called "Farm Ordinance," together with the Korean landlords and the Japanese imperialists, ruins the peasants and the lower class people in the cities as well. In order to meet the assessed taxes, the small merchants and artisans and the small industrialists are putting their possessions and houses on the auction block every day, and the lives of the intelligentsia and the college students are no better. The Japanese imperialists' thievery war against China is worsening their condition daily. The Japanese thieves' economic exploitation of the Korean masses is parallel to their political pressures. Therefore, the Korean laborers have become slaves without rights. All atrocities and pressures on the Korean laborers are carried out by the military organizations. The small improvements and reforms after the March Uprising of 1919 have become nothing more than a subject of conversation. The white terror is evident in Korea, and laws against the masses are rapidly changing to measures suppressing the revolutionary movement and they have even devised a law to put to death those who participate in the national liberation movement. The police, particularly the border police have been expanded and are rapidly becoming military affairs, and many new jails have been built. Labor, peasant, youth, and other social organizations are disbanded, and if there is any sign of opposition by laborers to the bureaucrats of the Government-General, they are quickly suppressed and the more direct ones are jailed. During the economic chaos alone, some 10,000 Korean revolutionaries were jailed. These are the results of the twenty-five year rule of Korea by the Japanese imperialists. When the Korean masses were temporarily suppressed, the Japanese declared to other imperialist nations that the Korean people are enjoying "culture," "progress," and "happiness." We declare here on this platform that our Korean people do not need such culture as that professed by the Japanese imperialists, and that we can no longer bear the unbearable oppression and exploitation of the Korean people. The Korean people know well the false and hypocritical declarations of the Japanese imperialists. The Japanese imperialists are trying to occupy Manchuria and make it a second Korea. Their promise of happiness to the Manchurian laborers is nothing more than their pledge to enslave and exploit them. This is already seen in Manchuria in the Japanese actions of exploitation and oppression of the Manchurian laboring class. The Korean laborers living in Manchuria know these Japanese imperialists well and have already started to fight against the Japanese, together with the Chinese laborers, under the Chinese Communist Party, so that the Koreans can expose the true meaning of the Japanese claim that their war in Manchuria is to "protect the Koreans." We praise the courageous struggle of the Chinese laborers.

Because the Japanese imperialists are suppressing the Korean laborers both nationally and politically in Korea, the anti-Japanese feelings of the Korean masses are intensifying daily, and their effort to fight against their enemy become more courageous. The Korean masses not only do not want to hide and endure the oppression of the Japanese thieves, but also they cannot hide and endure any more. Therefore, the struggle of the Korean masses must grow and be exposed. The history of the Korean revolution during the past seven years is filled with revolutionary incidents and progress. Recollection of the past several incidents involving the Korean laborers will suffice to prove how powerfully the revolutionary struggle of the Korean laborers grew under the cruel circumstances imposed by the Japanese imperialists. In the development of the Korean labor movement there are such significant and decisive developments as the courageous struggle of the Wonsan laborers in the general strike of 1927, and the mass peasant rioting incidents in northern Korea, with ten thousand peasants participating, and also the general student strikes against schools throughout Korea; these are proofs of our struggle. Not a day passed without a report in the bourgeois newspapers of a struggle by some revolutionary organization. Just to review several months of this year, we can point out the general strikes in June at Inch'ŏn, where some ten thousand laborers participated, and in July there was a general strike at the Kyŏmŭip'o military factory, where some twelve hundred laborers participated. There were more than seven thousand cases of peasant disputes.

Thus, laborers' general strikes not only grow in number, but also advance in characteristics, with the change of the labor strike movement to a general mass movement. Together with this the Korean peasant movement also grows, but in most cases the tenancy disputes have a tendency to end in a riot. The peasants are destroying the warehouses of the landlords and burning the bonds of debts, and in some villages the peasants have refused to pay the tenant fees and taxes. They have formed a non-payment-of-tenancy-fee-and-tax league, have distributed leaflets to commemorate various memorial days, and have joined the general strike of the laborers with peasant disputes. But the growth of the struggle of the Korean peasants and laborers was without proper leadership. The reason for this is that there were no adequate Korean Communist activities in the Korean national revolutionary movement. We must realize that the Communists are not leading the national emancipation movement against the Japanese imperialists. We have fallen from the vanguard of the movement and have stayed in one corner. This facilitated the Japanese imperialists to a certain extent in suppressing a certain portion of the revolutionary movement. This situation has provided the Japanese imperialists and their agents the opportunity to propagate the Japanese reactionary fascist ideology, Pan Asianism, and to arouse the enmity of Korean laborers against the Chinese and that of Chinese laborers against the Koreans, but this no doubt was to gain a favorable opinion in Korea for their plundering war in China. The failure to gain results from propagating Pan Asianism in Korea is clearer to see than the light of fire. But we do not mean that the national reformists and the pro-Japanese elements cannot temporarily lead the masses into such dangerous adventures if the Korean Communists fail to expose the schemes of the Japanese imperialists for preparation for war.

Under the present circumstances the Korean Communists have a duty to oppose a war that brings oppression, unhappiness, and fetters for the Korean masses. We must create circumstances that would bring a quick end to the war by using methods to transform and enlist the Korean laborers to the war of national emancipation.

Comrade Ercoli has correctly pointed out our duties for the struggle for peace. We can struggle for peace as well as for our emancipation. For Korean laborers there are problems either in breaking away from the increasingly unbearable oppression by joining the war against the thieving Japanese imperialists or in remaining permanently in a condition of slavery. The Korean masses already are hopeful of not remaining as slaves of the Japanese imperialists; thus, our duty is to organize correctly the revolutionary strength of the masses and to lead them to the path that opposes imperialism and the war. We must make Korea, the "safety region" of the Japanese thieves, a revolutionary rearguard of the world revolutionary movement.

We must use the struggle to oppose the war and the struggle for peace as levers to raise the struggle for Korean National emancipation. We must link the struggle of the Korean laborers and the conditions for economic, political and national demands.

We must utilize all available means, every contradiction between the Korean bourgeois and the Japanese imperialists, for this struggle. The Korean bourgeoisie, who had taken a deceiving attitude concerning the Japanese war in China have recently changed somewhat to a different direction. How should we interpret this? The Korean bourgeoisie predicted at the outset of the war that our economic chaos might be eased a little bit by the Japanese war in China, and that their condition might be bettered by the Japanese plunder of Manchuria and the laborers in Manchuria. They thought that they might get some concessions from the Japanese imperialists and also they thought that a slightly better market condition within Korea might result from this, but their predictions and expectations all came to naught.

Japan had solidified its position in Korea after the occupation of Manchuria, and this no doubt had some influence on the Korean bourgeoisie, but the hopes of the Korean bourgeoisie to colonize the "vast market" in Manchuria and to improve "Korean industries" came to naught.

The Japanese imperialists had even discussed Korean autonomy prior to the occupation of Manchuria, to gain the favor of the Korean bourgeoisie, but there is no talk of this any more.

The Japanese imperialists' war did not ease the contradictions between the oppressors and the Korean laborers, but rather intensified and deepened it.

The occupation of Manchuria that resulted from the cooperation of the Korean reformist bourgeoisie and the Japanese imperialists did not ease the contradictions between the Japanese imperialists and the Korean national reformist bourgeoisie, but rather intensified these contradictions. The Korean bourgeoisie led their movement in the hope that they might lead the revolutionary movement of the Korean masses onto the path of the National Reformists, to better their lot in accordance with the struggle and the growth of the Korean national emancipation movement.

The Korean national reformists did not forget the influence that the struggle against the Japanese imperialists had on the masses.

Comrades:

The duty of the Korean Communists rests in direct participation in the national revolution in opposition to the Japanese imperialists. The duty of the Korean Communists is to struggle for proletarian hegemony in the anti-Japanese struggle, by expanding the struggle for the political-economic benefits of the masses, utilizing all revolutionary movements. The Korean Communists can then organize the all-national anti-Japanese front and unite all anti-Japanese forces to fight against the Japanese bandits. Here is the main duty of today. Only the Korean masses, as part of the international proletariat, can perform the great task given to us by the Communists.

By mobilizing the masses to struggle against the war and for peace, we can fruitfully lead our national emancipation struggle. Under the present circumstances, we must wage a struggle opposing the anti-revolutionary war, under the slogans of "Protect the USSR," "Protect the Chinese Revolution," and "Down with the Japanese imperialists," and we must know clearly that this is one of the important sections of the national emancipation struggle of the Korean masses. If we do not fight for anti-war, it is impossible to widen the struggle of the Korean masses for liberation. The struggles against the war of the Japanese imperialists, and the struggles to protect the USSR and the Chinese Soviet are struggles to strengthen the basis of the world revolutionary movement. Therefore, we must link these struggles with the daily demands of the Korean masses.

We, the Korean Communists, must understand that this is an important duty and responsibility, and that in order to carry this out we must make fundamental changes in our method of operation. Our party has recently escaped several dangers, and in the past the party was divided time and again by criminal and unprincipled internal factional struggles. Only through the path of the Comintern's anti-faction principle were we able to expose our factional groups as enemies to the Korean masses and laborers. And only through the Comintern's line were we able to call upon the laborers and peasants, train new cadres and establish the basis for the re-establishment of a Communist party. We have defined our objectives in the Korean Communist Party action platform, and with this platform we must drive out all factional groups that are agents of the Japanese imperialists and close our ranks. Under the present favorable conditions, in which the masses are conscious of the increasing need for struggle against the oppressors of the people, the fundamental duties of the party are to solidify our ranks to influence the masses with Communist ideology and to make the party grow, as the laborers and peasants begin to realize that regardless of the outcome of the war, the war is bringing increased fear and hardships to them. We must attempt to popularize this increasing consciousness of our people. For this we must first march at the head of the Korean national emancipation movement, and enlist the intelligentsia of the national revolutionary struggle to our party. We must make it known that the Korean Communist Party is the only political party that can lead the Korean masses in their struggle for emancipation. We must raise high the banners of the national struggle and of the emancipation of Korea from the Japanese plunderers. In order to attain this, we must eliminate completely and decisively all the factionalism that was the fundamental obstacle in gaining the laborers.

Until now, we, the Korean Communists, were not able to perform our task in the national emancipation struggle of the Korean laborers. We merely stayed in a corner and did not jump into the reformists organizations that included the masses, and we led only organizational efforts to form factional groups in opposition to the national reformists organization. We must understand clearly that if we do not cooperate with the national reformists in their organizations and yet expose their leadership and their tactics and strategies, it is impossible to win over the laborers and peasants organized in the national reformists organizations. We must work with endurance and firmness within the reformists organizations to contact the masses and to organize small, true labor unions. We must work to attack the lies and expose the national reformists by giving detailed examples, but in practice, this was difficult and we have been denying our duty to perform this task. In order to perform the great duty of the Korean Communists we must organize the masses to oppose the Japanese imperialists in their war in China and in their preparation for war against the U.S.S.R. For this we must utilize all lawful and unlawful methods of struggle. In this connection, the present problem is to organize an anti-imperialist national revolutionary united front. We must clearly understand that the fundamental enemy at the present stage of our revolution is Japanese imperialism. The Korean masses must be mobilized to struggle against this enemy. We can gain the masses to our side by organizing an anti-imperialist national revolutionary united front and enlisting that part of the national reformist bourgeois group that has anti-Japanese feelings, by exposing the other national reformists, and also by correctly declaring the national emancipation slogans. The Anti-Imperialist National United Front must include all those people who hope to fight against the oppression of the Japanese imperialists by opposing the war. Only an anti-imperialist national united front with a wide base can successfully fight our enemies. We can establish proletarian hegemony only in this united front. This is the most important condition to our revolution and social revolution, necessary to bring success to our anti-feudalistic land reform and social revolution and to reject the Japanese oppression completely. We must courageously present the national political and economic demands of the Korean masses by organizing the Anti-Imperialist United Front.

The Korean Communist Party must gain the confidence of the Korean people by struggling for the Korean masses in their future struggle, and the party itself can truly become the party of the masses only through this process. We must constantly struggle to oppose the rightists in our ranks and the bourgeois nationalists, and also to eliminate the factionalists, as a means to develop the national emancipation struggle of the Korean laborers. The organization of the Anti-Imperialist National Revolutionary United Front is definitely not to be allowed to weaken the proletarian party and the labor organizations. Furthermore, we must not forget for a moment that our ultimate objective is to establish a Communist society of proletarian dictatorship. Therefore, the Korean Communists must struggle for pure Marxist and Leninist principles; we must oppose the Capitalists, wars, and the national reformists, and we must organize the Korean Proletarian National United Front by opposing the Japanese imperialists. This is to ensure our relationship with the masses and to develop the broad opposition of the masses to the Japanese imperialists.

Comrades:

The Korean laborers are not alone in fighting against the Japanese imperialists. We know the constant and unending courageous struggles of the Japanese Communist Party and the Chinese Communist Party. We have promised at the Seventh Congress that we will transform Korea, the rearguard of Japanese imperialism, into a rearguard of the world revolution, under the direction of the Comintern and with the assistance of the revolutionary laborers of Japan and China. In this struggle we must also aid the struggling Chinese laborers, who struggle against Japanese attempts to make Manchuria a second Korea.

In this struggle we must also support the fatherland of the world proletariat and the oppressed, the USSR, and we must attain our emancipation. Long live the united revolutionary effort of the Chinese, Japanese and Korean laborers in struggling against the Japanese imperialists. Long live the Comintern, the command of the world revolution. Long live our great Stalin, the Chief of the world proletariat.

PART IV

THE ACTIVITIES ABROAD

1930-44

COMMENTARY

The Activities Abroad, 1930-44

THE COMMUNISTS failed to sustain a working party within Korea, and after the collapse of the fourth party many leaders again fled abroad. The party reestablishment movement and the regional activities of the 1930's were often conducted by those who intermittently returned to Korea to a particular region to perform a specific task. As early as the second party in 1926, the Korean Communist Party established various bureaus abroad, including a liaison center in Shanghai and bureaus in Manchuria and Japan.

The activities of the bureaus were seldom coordinated by the party in Korea. Although the Manchurian General Bureau was active during the late 1920's and early 1930's, the bureaus abroad, including the Manchurian General Bureau, was ultimately dissolved so their members could join the local Communist parties in their respective regions. The Korean Communists under the direction of the foreign parties did little to advance the cause, or prepare for the future, of the Korean movement. They shared much the same fate as the Chinese and the Japanese parties. Toward the latter part of the 1930's a group of Koreans in nearby Yenan reorganized the Korean Communist youth and fought the Japanese in China on the side of the Chinese Communists. This Yenan group continued its activities until the end of the second World War.

Little is known about the documents pertaining to the various bureau activities abroad. The bureau produced only a few documents and none concerning the relationship between the bureaus and the parties within Korea, such as the issuance of a particular directive, have been found. More importantly, documents dealing with Korean participation in the Chinese and Japanese parties are very scarce. Except for a few documents of the Manchurian Provincial Committee of the Chinese Communist Party which are concerned with the Korean Communists in Manchuria at the time of their cooperative Communist undertakings, as yet there are no documents of any importance available on the relationship between the Korean Communists and the foreign parties.

Some of the documents in this section deal with the declaration issued by the Korean Communists abroad dissolving their bureaus to join their respective local Communist parties. Much of the arguments advanced to justify the dissolution of the bureaus utilize the principle of "one party, one country," and the Korean "extensionism". There is no document available, expounding the theoretical foundation of these ideas. Abundant propaganda materials particularly from the Japanese Bureau are available, but most are statements and restatements of denouncing Japanese imperialism and glorifying their movement. Thus they are of little value and are omitted here. The documents presented here deal with: A) the Manchurian General Bureau, B) the Japanese Bureau, and C) The North China Korean Independence League (the Yenan group in north China). The liaison center in Shanghai, established in April 1926, was dissolved shortly thereafter, and the leaders joined the Fanan district Committee, Kiangsu Province, of the Chinese Communist Party. No material concerning this center, of its dissolution and subsequent participation in the Chinese Communist Party, is presently available.

A. *The Manchurian General Bureau, 1930*

The most active of the bureaus abroad was the Manchurian General Bureau (MGB). The Tuesday Association group, the Seoul-Shanghai group, and the M.L. group all participated in it at various times, and at some time commanded the Bureau. The activities of these groups caused what are known as the first, second, and the third Chientao Communist Party incidents. However, the factions later retreated into separate regions in Manchuria; the Tuesday Association group to northern, the Seoul-Shanghai group to eastern, and the M.L. group to southern Manchuria. They continued their independent activities until the early 1930's, when they joined the Manchurian Provincial Committee of the Chinese Communist Party.

Only a few documents pertaining directly to the bureau activities are available; for example, the records (the Japanese police version) of the executive committee meetings from October 28 to August 31, 1927 of the MGB, the Tuesday Association group meetings. which were uncovered at the time of the first Chientao Communist Party incident. Although they are informative on the activities of the MGB, they are merely the records and minutes of the meetings and do not contain substance of importance. They are consequently omitted here.

There are also a few propaganda materials sent by the MGB to the Korean nationalists in Manchuria, at the time of the first Chientao Communist Party incident, appealing to them to join the Communists in advancing the Korean revolution. Most of these items were initially written by the Tuesday Association group and were well received by the Nationalists. But as the Communist activities became more dangerous and more Communist groups appeared to make inroads on the Nationalists region in southern Manchuria, the Nationalists reacted adversely and at times violently to the Communists. For example, the Nationalists held a mass meeting to criticize the M.L. group and their activities and issued a proclamation calling for the destruction of the Communists in Manchuria. Numerous texts of this nature are available, but they are all of little value and are not included here.[1]

The documents in this section represent only the last phase of the bureau activities, partly because of the general lack of documents of value during the operation of the bureau and partly because the rapidity of the rise and fall of the bureaus made difficult, even given the several groups operating in Manchuria, sustained activities by the Bureau.

There are records of several manifestos written in 1929, shortly after the Communists in Manchuria received the

[1] See the various documents under such titles as "Proclamation of the Mass Meeting to Criticize the M.L. group." For the documents of the MGB to the nationalists see their various declaration, including the one entitled "Declaration of the Manchurian General Bureau of the Korean Communist Party." Full texts of these documents are available in the *JFMA*, reel SP 86 (sp. 205-4), pp. 9,736-59.

December Theses of 1928, but full texts of these declarations are unavailable. They generally vow renewed efforts to reestablish the party within Korea. Most of their independent Communist activities ended when they issued a dissolution declaration, dissolved their bureau, and joined the Manchurian Provincial Committee of the Chinese Communist Party in 1930.

The first such dissolution declaration was issued by the M.L. group on March 20, 1930. From the text of this by the M.L. group declaration (item 42) the decision to dissolve the bureau was apparently reached as early as September 20, 1929, at the tenth plenum of the Manchurian General Bureau. The declaration attacked the very foundation of Korean Communist activity in Manchuria by stating that the root of all mistakes by the Korean Communists in Manchuria was the extension of the Korean Communist Party to Manchuria in public opposition to the Chinese Communist Party. It is clear from the text that there was a significant controversy over the dissolution of the bureau and the termination of independent Korean Communist activities in Manchuria. The M.L. group was the first group to advocate the dissolution and to condemn what they called Korean "extensionism" in Manchuria. Objectively the absurdity of the arguments advanced to justify the dissolution, both "extensionism" and the principle of "one party, one country", are obvious. This becomes even clearer when they are compared with the reasons advanced for the dissolution of the Japanese Bureau. One startling aspect of this document is the statement that the group (the M.L. group) opposed the Bureau activities in Manchuria as early as 1927. This is an obvious contradiction because the M.L. group began their activities in Manchuria in 1927.

In an effort to facilitate the dissolution of all groups and to encourage their entrance into the Manchurian Provincial Committee, the Korean Communist League in Manchuria was organized temporarily. The declaration of this group (item 43) is introduced here. The extent of cooperation by other groups in this League is not clear although it seems to have been dominated by the Seoul-Shanghai group. The M.L. group had issued their dissolution declaration earlier, while the Tuesday

Association group never did declare their dissolution. The League also indicated several different arguments for the dissolution but also to assist Korean entry into the Chinese group. After some two months operation, the League issued the dissolution declaration (item 44). This declaration refers to a critical evaluation of the Manchurian General Bureau which was written in July 1930, but along with seven other items that the League is reported to have written it is not available.

In contrast to these groups, the Tuesday Association group in northern Manchuria was warned by the Manchurian Provincial Committee, the Ning-an prefecture, of the Chinese Communist Party in an open letter (item 45) giving the Koreans specific warnings and instructions. They specifically directed the leaders to submit written statements pledging to abstain from factional struggles and to join the Chinese Communists as ordinary members and not as leaders. The majority of the Tuesday Association group, however, did not issue any official dissolution declaration and did not join the Chinese Communists in Manchuria. The Manchurian Provincial Committee often made appeals to the Korean laborers and peasants to join the Chinese Communists. However, there were difficulties in their joint activities and Korean participation dwindled to a small contingent after the massive arrests of Koreans in the fourth and fifth Chientao Communist incidents.

The Manchurian Provincial Committee accomplished little and terminated after its last chairman Han Shou-kuei was arrested in 1936. There are two important documents on the Manchurian Provincial Committee. The first is a directive, commonly known as the January Directive, issued on January 26, 1933 by the Central Executive Committee of the Chinese Communist Party to the Manchurian Provincial Committee. The directive analyzed the anti-Japanese struggle in detail, gave instructions on how to combat the Japanese, and specified the duties of the Chinese Communists in Manchuria. The second, a follow-up to the first, was issued on February 22, 1934, and is commonly known as the February Directive. It reviewed the accomplishments of the previous year and made a detailed evaluation of the Chinese Communists in Manchuria. The

January Directive is entitled "Condition in Manchuria and the Duty of our Party," and the February Directive "Letter to the Manchurian Provincial Committee." Both documents deal primarily with the Chinese Communist activities in Manchuria. Properly considered documents of Chinese communism, they are omitted here.[2]

There are other important documents on the Manchurian Provincial Committee, such as a letter from the Comintern to the comrades of the Kitung Bureau of the Manchurian Provincial Committee. It is a detailed evaluation of various aspects of Communist activities in the region east of Kirin under the control of the Kitung Bureau. The letter is important because it is perhaps the only one so far available which was sent to the Manchurian Provincial Committee by the Comintern.[3] There are other less important documents, such as the three-month plan of the Manchurian Provincial Committee, an operational plan from January to March of 1935. These latter have no specific relevance to Korean participation or to Korean activities in Manchuria and so are omitted.

B. The Japanese Bureau, 1931-32

In contrast to the Manchurian General Bureau, the activities of the Japanese Bureau were smaller in scale and shortlived. Only one incident of significance, the 8-29 incident, marked Korean Communist activities in Japan. The Korean Communists engaged in numerous publication ventures and produced a large number of leaflets, pamphlets, proclamations, and literary writings, but these seldom had direct relevance to Bureau activities. Except for a few pamphlets which came from the *Musanja-sa*, a literary group of Korean Communists in Japan,

[2] The full texts are available in both Chinese and Japanese. See the Chinese text in microfilm in the journal, *Toucheng*, no. 44, first published on June 9, 1933. See the Japanese text in *Manshū kyōsan-hi no kenkyū*, supplement pp. 4-29. The text is also reported to be available in an organ of the ECCI of the Comintern in the issue of December 1, 1935, but this text is yet to be located.

[3] See the extract of this letter in Japanese in *Manshū kyōsan-hi no kenkyū*, Supplement, pp. 47-58.

most of the writings are propaganda materials designed for a particular memorial day or a minor incident which may or may not have had relevance to the Bureau as a whole.

The complete publication activities of the Bureau are not known, but some pamphlets that the *Musanja-sa* published are available. These are mostly the work of one man, Ko Kyŏng-hŭm. Ko led the last phase of the Japanese Bureau under the direction of Han Wi-kŏn in Shanghai but was later arrested and interned. His writings include eight articles, four each in pamphlets entitled "Zen-ei borusheviki-ka no nimmu" [The Duty of Vanguard Bolshevization] and "Chōsen mondai no tame ni" [For Korean problems.] There are other pamphlets of similar content, such as "Chōsen zen'ei-tō tōmen no mondai" [The Problems Confronting the Korean Vanguard Party] jointly authored by Kwang-u and Ch'ŏl-ak (Han Wi-kŏn and Kim Kyŏng-jae), both leaders of the fourth party. These are mostly statements and restatements concerning the unsuccessful revival of the fading Communist cause and lack a concrete program for, or support of, the Korean Communists in Japan.

Most pertinent is a factual essay by Ko, "How did the Korean Communist Movement develop in Tokyo." An informative account of the Bureau, Ko apparently wrote the document in jail under duress and generally the facts are so presented as to give the impression that they were answers to innumerable specific questions by police interrogators. The contrast between his writing in this short account of the Bureau and in his earlier publications by the *Musanja-sa* is so striking that one cannot but assume that his writing was under duress.

The documents presented here, much like those of the Manchurian General Bureau, deal with the dissolution of the Japanese Bureau and its aftermath. The dissolution declaration of the Japanese Bureau (item 46) was written in October 1931, a year later than those of the Manchurian General Bureau, and is a short, simple declaration stating the dissolution of the Bureau. Quite conspicuous is the absence of any mention of either the much heralded principle of "one party, one country" or Korean "extensionism" in Japan. The declaration remarked on the natural growth of cooperation between the Japanese and

Korean toiling masses, finding their common movement and mission as a laboring class beyond national limitation. Given this context, this document is very important because it confirms the absence of a central controlling organ of the party within Korea on the issue of dissolution of bureaus abroad and, more importantly, because the attempted justification of dissolution of the bureaus abroad was really a futile effort to justify a seemingly natural development. The dissolution of the bureaus abroad appears to be nothing more than an effort to alleviate the operational difficulties of the Korean Communist abroad.

In Japan, also, there were some who advocated the maintenance of an independent Korean movement. These Communists, headed by Kim Ch'i-jŏng and Kim Tu-jŏng, organized a group known as the *Nodong Kegŭp-sa* and published a journal, *Nodong kegŭp*. The next document presented (item 48) is a declaration issued by this group in June 1932, sometime after the dissolution of the Japanese Bureau. The declaration called for unity among all Koreans in Japan under their leadership, and stressed the importance of the Korean movement in Japan, including the publication of their journal. It is evident from the declaration that the major concern of the group was not so much maintaining a separate Korean Communist group in Japan apart from the Japanese party as it was the perpetuation of some Communist activities by the Koreans. Some of the leaders of this organization later ventured into Korea in an unsuccessful attempt to revive and reestablish the party within Korea.

There are virtually no documents, or none so far available, emanating from the Japanese Communist Party on the Korean Communists in Japan during this period. There are a few insignificant declarations by the Japanese Communist Party concerning the Korean Communists, such as a declaration by the Central Executive Committee entitled "Duty of the Japanese Proletariat and the Development of a Revolutionary Movement in Korea" and a few decisions by local committees affecting the Koreans in Japan, such as the "Decision Concerning the Kansai District Committee of the Japanese Communist Party." These were sent to the Japanese Communists to point out their duties in cooperating with Korean workers in regions where they were numerous. These and other declarations concerning Koreans were issued to mark particular occasions. For example, the two cited above are dated August 20 and August 30, 1932, respectively, and were issued in conjunction with the observance of Korean Humiliation Day (August 29), the day Japan annexed Korea. The joint operation of the Korean and Japanese Communists in Japan accomplished little beyond sporadic and minor terrorist activities and propaganda publishing.

C. The North China Korean Independence League, 1941-44

The Communist activities of the bureaus abroad, both alone and under foreign parties, ultimately shared much the same fate as the Communists of respective regions. The only Korean group that sustained independent Communist activities abroad until the end of the World War II was the North China Korean Independence League, the NCKIL, commonly known as the Yenan group. There are three important facts that must be clarified about this group. The first is that they did not begin their activities until sometime after both other bureaus abroad and the movements within Korea failed. Thus, they attracted many who could manage to join the group in China, including some Nationalists. The second is that the common appellation of the group, the Yenan group, is misleading because their main center of activities was not in Yenan but along the frontlines of the Japanese attack in north China. They also operated at times behind the Japanese line conducting subversive activities. The third is the fact that although this group ultimately retreated to Yenan, this was not until 1944, and their relationship with the Chinese Communists, which is suggested by their name, is not fully understood. From presently available sources it is difficult to assume that a cordial relationship of any significance existed between the Koreans and the Chinese Communists in Yenan. If there was such a relationship it had to be confined to a period of less than two years.

The NCKIL was first organized as a youth group appealing to

the Korean youths in China, nationalists and Communists alike. Since they were mostly stationed near the fighting fronts against the Japanese, the activities of the NCKIL were more military than political. Although they did succeed in indoctrinating those Koreans who joined them from the Korean Volunteer Corps, a Nationalistic military group in China, the majority of their activities consisted of assisting the Chinese Communists in whatever little fighting they did against the Japanese in north China. Many leaflets were written by this group appealing to the Korean students and soldiers in the Japanese army to defect to the anti-Japanese cause, but documents pertaining to the League itself are scarce. Documents dealing with the relationship of the Koreans and the Chinese Communists in Yenan, if they exist at all, and in whatever language, are yet to be uncovered.

The first documents introduced here (item 48) are the manifesto and platforms of the North China Youth Federation, the predecessor of the NCKIL. This organization was founded in Shansi Province near the border of Honan Province on February 10, 1941, by two Koreans, Mu-jŏng and Ch'oe Ch'ang-ik, influential Communists who later led the League in China and who also assumed important positions in North Korea. Because of Mu-jŏng, who was said to have been attached to the Eighth Route Army of the Chinese Communists, the Youth Federation was often reported to have some ties with that army. However, there is no concrete evidence to this effect.

The declaration is an appeal to Korean youths in China and is far more anti-Japanese in sentiment than pro-Communist. It should be noted that the appeal is primarily an effort on the part of the Communists to attract and secure Koreans from the Nationalist independence movement to their federation. The six-point platform that accompanied the declaration is as non-commital to the Communist cause as it is to the anti-Japanese cause. There are a few documents of this federation available that make a direct appeal to the Nationalists, such as the letter entitled "To the Korean Compatriots in North China," which was circulated among some 100,000 (?) Koreans who lived in China. This letter, first published in the Federation journal *Korean Youth,* makes a direct appeal to Koreans in north China to support their cause. Although the participants and the leaders of the Federation were undoubtedly Communists, their non-Communist appeals are obvious in two other documents: one to the Nationalists is entitled "For the Korean People's Liberation Movement," another to the Chinese people and their leaders, including both Chiang Kai-shek and Mao Tse-tung, is entitled "The North China Korean Youth Federation Expresses Respect for the Chinese People."[4]

The Federation was dissolved in favor of the North China Korean Independence League (NCKIL). The founding Congress of the League was held in Lo prefecture near the border of Honan and Shansi provinces on August 15, 1942, exactly three years before the end of the World War II. In view of the eleven men elected to the Executive Committee of the North China Korean Independence League and their subsequent activities in Yenan and North Korea after the liberation, it is undoubtedly a Communist organization although the program, declarations, and platform of the League (item 49) are conspicuously mild on propagation of the Communist cause. A partial explanation perhaps is their effort to make a broader appeal to recruit nationalists to the League.

The next two documents (items 50 and 51) are from the Korean Volunteer Corps of mid-China and north China. These documents yield two important facts. First, the operation of the NCKIL was primarily military. Second, the mid and north China branches of the Korean Volunteer Corps, which was officially the military group of the Korean National Revolutionary Party in Chungking under the Nationalists, were strongly in support of the League. Later there was some migration of revolutionaries from Chungking to join the Communists in the north. The appeals were not only made to the Korean Nationalist revolutionaries but also to Koreans in the Japanese army in north China. For a propaganda statement to these Koreans by the League, there are many leaflets giving the

---

[4] See the complete texts of these documents in Japanese, *Tokkō geppo* (April 1941), pp. 99-101.

instructions on surrender procedure. They were successful in some cases and those who defected to the Communists side later made public statements which the Communists circulated widely. These statements are available but omitted here.[5] Perhaps study of the Chinese Communists in Yenan during the early 1940's would yield some documents clarifying the relationship of the Korean Communists in Yenan with the leadership of the Chinese Communists.

[5] See the texts of these statements in Japanese. *Tokkō geppo* (November 1943), pp. 105-06.

PART IV

DOCUMENTS

Items 42-51

A. THE MANCHURIAN GENERAL BUREAU, 1930

Item 42: The Dissolution Declaration of the Manchurian General Bureau of the Korean Communist Party[1]

Laborers and Peasants in all Manchuria! Communist Comrades in all Manchuria! Representing the will of 430 members of our party, we declare to you the revolutionary dissolution of our only organization, the Manchurian General Bureau of the Korean Communist Party, as follows:

Comrades!

The Manchurian General Bureau of the Korean Communist Party was first organized in Manchuria in the Spring of 1926 by the Central Committee of the Korean Communist Party when it was organized in Korea as a section of the Comintern. During the last five years, under the organizational leadership of the party, the Manchurian General Bureau has constantly performed revolutionary struggles by courageously and systematically countering the barbaric oppression of the truly evil and anti-revolutionary white terror. In spite of the fact that the advances of the reactionary elements of those national and social fascists and members of the Sino-Japanese ruling class (Kim Ch'an, Shin Il-yong, Kim Tong-kŏl, and Ch'oe Tong-uk)[2] resulted in the imprisonment of nearly 200 comrades and produced 31 casualties and other sacrifices, the Manchurian General Bureau had always insisted on truly benefiting the laborers and peasants against the robbery, oppression and exploitation of all the bourgeoisie and landlords, and had struggled to bring about ultimate victory and daily benefits and to truly represent the masses by adding more people. However, at the same time, due to the lack of thorough Bolshevization of

---

[1] This document is the dissolution declaration of the M.L. group issued on March 20, 1930. Undoubtedly this document was written in Korean, but it is available only in Japanese. See Utsumi Haruichi, *Manshū kyōsan-tō undō gaikan* (Dairen, 1935), supplement.

[2] These men are apostates and Nationalists who cooperated with the Japanese in suppressing the Communists.

our party and the weakness of the proletarian forces in Manchuria in general, we committed not a few mistakes. The continual factional prejudices that accompanied all of our activities, the misunderstandings among the leadership concerning the united front, our inability to clearly link the struggles against the forces of the national fascist organizations, such as *Kungmin-pu* and *Hanjok Yŏnhap-hoe,* with the struggles of anti-imperialism and anti-feudalism particularly against the landlords, and our inability to incite a mass struggle in support of the Soviet Union, particularly last year at the time of the war to take the East China Railway, these were some of the more important mistakes.

The fundamental root of all such mistakes was the extension of the Korean Communist party organization into Manchuria and the maintenance of a racially separate organization in public opposition to the Chinese Communist Party. We must clearly recognize and understand this. Therefore, since we recognize this mistake, it is our most immediate task to fight definitively to abandon our organization.

Comrades!

Originally, the Communist party organization, the organization of a proletarian vanguard party, is based upon the principle of "one party, one country." This is because only through such a principle can we assure the ultimate and definitive victory.

However, Manchuria is a semi-colony and a part of China; it is a part of the Chinese revolution and one of the important operational regions of the Chinese Communist Party as well. The Korean laborers and peasants who reside in Manchuria are suffering from the unlimited suppression and exploitation of the Capitalists, landlords, and usurers because they reside in Manchuria. However, their miseries are not due to the fact that they are Koreans, but rather it is due to the fact that they are peasants and workers. Furthermore, the unhappiness that they suffer is not suffered alone, for the Chinese workers and peasants equally suffer such unhappiness. Under these conditions, the masses of the Korean workers residing in China have come to realize that the mere "independence of Korea" is not sufficient to emancipate them from the stubborn Capitalistic and feudalistic oppression and exploitation.

On the contrary, it has become clear that only through the victory of the Chinese land revolution can their own emancipation be attained. Therefore, the Korean workers and peasants in Manchuria must unite with the Chinese workers and peasants. They must struggle to establish a Soviet Government and fight for a representative congress of the peasants, workers, and soldiers; they must overthrow the political power of the Capitalist class, the Kuomintang and the bourgeois class and they must overthrow imperialism in China.

Because this is the only course leading to emancipation and the only way for the workers and peasants in Manchuria to struggle, the Korean Communists in Manchuria must be reorganized under the banner of the Chinese Communist Party, in accordance with the principle of "one party, one country" and on these economic and political bases. Thus, the organization of the various factions extended from Korea must be dissolved fundamentally. Of course, it is not that there was no realization of this fact among us in the past. Especially, we have not only advocated direct participation in the Chinese revolution, but we have also sternly raised a banner against the issues of Korean "extensionism" since 1927. However, it was extremely idealistic, and the issues of "extensionism" began under the pretext of Manchuria being a special region of the Korean Communist Movement.

Specifically, we were not aware of the fact that the Chinese Communist movement had its own organization. As a result, the original split of the Chinese and Korean Communists, who must now be united under one banner, was maintained and continued, and the only leading Bolshevik forces of any significance were in fact scattered. Therefore, among the workers and peasants of China and Korea, who must necessarily be united, racial barriers and national prejudices separated the people. Especially, the lack of a balanced development between the Communist comrades involved in, on the one hand, the proletarian class struggle of the Chinese in the cities and, in, on the other hand, the peasant struggles of the Koreans in the villages, indicates the greatest shortcomings.

Therefore, in accordance with the demand for the internal development of the movement and considering all of the objective conditions in recent times in Manchuria, the false principle of Korean "extensionism" can not exist, for they fall into a condition of stagnation and can not progress.

Thus, at the tenth enlarged plenum of the Manchurian General Bureau, on September 20, 1929, the Korean Communist movement in Manchuria has resolved definitively to reorganize as a section of the movement within the Chinese Communist Party. Pursuant with the fundamental spirit of the plenum and also in accordance with the overwhelming demand of the entire membership, we began to progress toward our reorganization within the Chinese Communist Party by the dissolution of our organization.

Comrades! The Communist movement in Manchuria must change its direction. At this solemn moment, we have seen the raising of the following views.

1. First, there is the contention that it is still too early to dissolve our organization. Proponents of this idea say that it is not wise to join forces with the Chinese Communist Party before the reestablishment of a section of the Comintern in Korea and, further, that it is not advantageous to join the Chinese Communist Party in Manchuria at this time because the Chinese Communist forces in Manchuria are weak. In accordance with this observation, if the forces of the Chinese Communist Party in Manchuria are in fact weak, we, as Communists, have a duty to expand and strengthen them; in contrast, if we were to use such a fact as a reason for abstaining from joining, we would, in effect, be committing a crime of opportunism. Thus, as long as there are Korean Communists in Manchuria, Koreans must join the Chinese Communist Party and it is of no consequence whether a separate Korean Communist Party is established in Korea or not. This contention of premature timing is nothing more than a device for the opportunists to hide themselves.

2. A second contention is that all the past organizational apparatus of our party should be maintained, and we should adhere only to the policies of the Chinese Communist Party. This contention is an anti-bolshevik position that does not abandon Nationalistic racial bourgeois concepts.

We must forcefully and mercilessly carry out theoretical and political struggles against all such reactionary contentions. At the same time we must yield all our tasks unconditionally to the Chinese Communist Party, and, after the dissolution of our organization, all Communists must join the ranks of the Chinese Communist Party as individuals, after thorough revolutionary investigation and inspection by the Chinese Communist Party. Since there is no section of the Comintern in Korea and since we are told not to join the Chinese Communist Party as a group, we must join the Chinese Communist Party in this way [as individuals] through solemn struggle.

Comrades! All Communist comrades that belong to the various factions! We are signaling bolshevik progress with the following slogans, which show us the way and the correct attitude for success.

1. The Korean Communists in Manchuria must withdraw from the Korean movement.
2. Abandon the Korean "extensionist" organizations in Manchuria.
3. Dissolve all factions.
4. Join the Chinese Communist Party as individuals.
5. Struggle to assist the Korean revolution.
6. The Korean workers and peasants in Manchuria can be emancipated only under the leadership of the Chinese Communist Party.

Long live the Chinese Communist Party.
Long live the Communist International.

Manchurian General Bureau of the Korean Communist Party
March 20, 1930

Item 43: Declaration[1]

1. Due to the necessity of internal development and to the change in objective conditions, the Korean Communist movement in Manchuria must abandon the Korean "extensionism," which is nothing more than a remnant of the past movement of various thought groups, and the Korean Communists in Manchuria are confronted by a new phase in which we must join the Chinese Communist Party in response to the practical demands of the class struggle.

The Korean Communist movement in Manchuria, with a history of nearly a decade, has lost several hundred thousand vanguard fighters to the poisonous militarists of imperialism, but our spirit is undaunted, and we have continued to struggle ceaselessly. The strengthened, mass-participation Korean Communist Party reestablishment movement, with unified vanguard ranks, has been developing step by step together with the heroic struggle of the bolshevised Chinese Communist Party. Especially, the recent revolutionary struggle of the Korean workers and peasant masses that spread heroically throughout Manchuria under the leadership of the vanguards indicates clearly the great development of the Chinese revolution, together with the enlargement of Soviet political power in southern China.

2. The Korean Communist movement in Manchuria is developing a new phase. We must organize a new organization to meet the new struggle of our new phase. The past Korean Communist movement in Manchuria was a mere extension of the movement in Korea. The mainstream of this past movement in Manchuria was merely a thought propaganda movement, reflecting the inevitable mutual class relationship of Korea and

---

[1] This declaration was issued by an interim organization known as the Korean Communist League in Manchuria on June 24, 1930. It is assumed that the declaration was written in Korean by the leaders of the League including Yun Cha-yŏng, Ch'oe Sŏng-ch'il, Ch'oe Hwan and Yi Kyŏng-sŏp. This document is, however, available only in Japanese in *JFMA,* reel SP 86 (sp. 205-4), pp. 9,820-27.

Manchuria. However, during more recent years, we have developed a serious all-out class struggle against the capitalists, landlords and militarists and against the rule of imperialism. At this point the object of the struggle of the Korean Communist movement in Manchuria is not only the same as that of the Chinese Communist Party, but its practical political struggle can not effectively be carried out without receiving the leadership of the Chinese Communist Party.

3. In the midst of this rapid development of the Korean Communist movement in Manchuria, there appeared publicly numerous opportunistic arguments:

a. The first is that we must join the Chinese Communist Party in theory, but must maintain organically a separate organization. This is nothing more than an effort to maintain Korean "extensionism" and a tendency toward opportunism. This is nothing more than a petty bourgeois conceptualism that merely hoped for such ideas, but failed to understand the actual practice of class struggles.

b. The second is the argument advanced in the newspaper *Chŏkki* [Red Flag], that calls for an unconditional dissolution of each group. We can not join the Chinese Communist Party as a group, but we must have a transitional organization to facilitate the Korean Communists joining the Chinese Communist Party, thus avoiding any irregular entrance into the Chinese Communist Party. The insistence on dissolution without detailed views on the organizational life of the Communist prior to his joining the Chinese Communist Party is an advocation of the dissolution of the party.

c. The third is an argument to transplant the various factions organically into the Chinese Communist Party by adhering to the remnants of the several factional organizations, as advocated by impure elements. This is the main element of bourgeois popular learning that attempts to separate the process of organization from that of the struggle.

d. At the extreme, there are reactionaries who wish to steal the name of the Chinese Communist Party in order to utilize it as a tool of their factional struggle.

4. A certain struggle requires a suitable organization. Thus,

the Manchurian section of the Korean Communist Party reestablishment movement has established a Korean Communist League in Manchuria as a transitional organization, in order to bolshevise the Korean Communist movement in Manchuria and to correct the most important theoretical mistakes of Korean "extensionism". This organization is necessary because there is a severe factional struggle in the ranks of the Korean Communists in Manchuria and inferior organizational training and a low standard among its members. With this organization we declare ourselves ready to enlist the more energetic Communists and Korean working masses in Manchuria under the leadership of the Chinese Communist Party, by a complete cleansing of the ranks of the Korean Communists in Manchuria, by overcoming reactionaary and opportunistic tendencies and, ultimately, through bloody struggle against the darkening forces of the Capitalists. The Korean Communists in Manchuria and its more energetic elements must join the Chinese Communist Party with its correct theoretical and practical routes of struggle. Only through participation in the struggle under its leadership will we be able to accomplish the Chinese workers' and peasant revolution by downing imperialism and the Kuomintang military cliques and thus accomplish the world revolution.

a. Oppose Korean "extensionism."

b. Oppose the transplantation of factions into the Chinese Communist Party.

c. All workers and peasant masses join the Chinese Communist Party under their leadership.

June 24, 1930
Korean Communist League in Manchuria.

Political Theses were written on the following subjects:

1. The world situation and the Chinese revolution.
2. The current condition of the Chinese revolutionary movement.
3. Special characteristics of the present stage of the Korean Communist movement in Manchuria and our present tasks.

4. Criticisms of the Manchurian section of the Korean Communist Party reestablishment movement and of various other groups.

5. The Chinese Communist Party and the Korean Communists League in Manchuria.

6. Important slogans of the League (16 items).

7. Current duty of the League.

Duty concerning tactics and strategy.

Duty concerning political organization.

Duty concerning the winning of the laborers and peasant masses.

Duty concerning the labor movement.

Duty concerning the peasant movement.

Duty concerning the Soviet movement.

Duty concerning the military movement.

Duty concerning the youth movement.

Duty concerning the women's movement.

Duty concerning the MOPR movement.

Duty to struggle against patriotic halucinations.

Duty to struggle against reactionary Nationalists.

Duty concerning the United Front.

Item 44:   Dissolution Declaration[1]
   [extracts]

In the rapid development of the class struggle to put an end to capitalism, this League, in accordance with the correct directive from the Chinese Communist Party, declares its dissolution, having completed its fundamental duties as expressed in the declaration and political theses dated June 24.

The most important shortcomings that hindered all fronts of the past Korean Communist movement in Manchuria were the non-liquidation of the remnants of Korean "extensionism," the thought organizations filled with petty bourgeois intellectuals and the destructive repetition of unprincipled factional struggles. After the Comintern theses of December 1928 concerning the Korean question, the Manchurian section of the Korean Communist Party reestablishment group was established on September 1, 1929, asserting theoretical and practical unity under the slogan of fundamental change and liquidation of factionalism by dissolving all past factional organizations, and in December of the same year its organ, *Manju noryŏk-ja shinmun* [Manchurian Workers' Newspaper], was first published, at which time it was declared that the Korean movement in Manchuria must in principle be a part of the Chinese movement. The fact that it began an unprecedented disintegration of the past factional organizations was certainly a step forward.

However, the idea to liquidate factionalism by the Korean Communist Party reestablishment group failed to proceed beyond its subjective hopes, and in essence the group became merely another faction, indistinguishable from the others in its composition and in its method of struggle. It was not only

---

[1] This declaration is the dissolution declaration of the Korean Communist League in Manchuria issued in August 1930. The Communists of this League were the members of the Seoul-Shanghai group in Kirin province. The full text is yet to be located. The declaration was written in Korean, but the extracts are available only in Japanese. See *JFMA*, reel SP 86 (sp. 205-4), pp. 9,862-70.

unable to bring about the fundamental change, but it also failed to establish the new forces needed to lead the laborers, and the remnant organizations of Korean "extensionism" continued to exist. Thus, on June 24, this league was organized as a transitional organ, by which the more earnest of our Communists, through bloody class struggle and self-criticism, as well as by reexamination of the ranks and the abandoning of the past Korean extension organs, would join the Chinese Communist Party.

However, the theoretical basis of joining the Chinese Communist Party is not an idea created independently by this League, but was insisted on by all factions in accordance with the developments in objective conditions and the internal changes in the Korean Communist movement in Manchuria. Even under such conditions and despite the correct direction, there remain reactionary elements who attempt to transplant their factions, thinking only of their own self-importance and great dreams, and who publicly and privately continue the factional struggles. Such unpleasant events have been significant obstacles to each ardent Communist. However, these lies, instigations of the worst kind, shameless slanders, and destructive plans were overcome. The July declaration of the Chinese Communist Party concerning the Korean Communists is the most solemn criticism and most correct directive of this historical class struggle.

With its unconditional acceptance of direct support for this declaration, this League came to understand more clearly the correctness of its theoretical and historical directions, and an opportunity to rapidly conclude its past duties, and decided on dissolution. Thus all ardent Communists must reject the miserly petty bourgeoisie and the craze of the factional leaders and their running dogs, who promote nothing but destructive factionalism, slander and bad propaganda, and go to the workers and the peasant masses and prove themselves through bloody struggle as brilliant class warriors under the direct leadership of the Chinese Communist Party.

Come all ardent Communists under the banner of the Chinese Communist Party.

Destroy all unprincipled factional struggles, slanders, and instigations.

Long live the Chinese Communist Party.

The Korean Communist League in Manchuria, August 1930.

Item 45: Open Letter to the Korean Communists in Manchuria from the Manchurian Provincial Committee of the Chinese Communist Party[1]

The Korean Communist Comrades in Manchuria!

Today, the world revolution has sharpened to an extreme, and the world wide economy of the Capitalists has fallen into a deeply chaotic situation, while the number of unemployed workers is increasing with great speed. In order to solve their market problems, the imperialists are openly preparing for a large war in order again to divide the colonies, and at the same time they are preparing to attack the Soviet Union directly and thus destroy the headquarters of the great world revolution and suppress the world revolution as a whole.

The proletarian classes of all countries have launched fierce revolutionary activities—strikes and demonstrations—under the influence both of the Soviet Union and of the threat of unemployment and economic difficulties. Fierce revolutionary movements are bursting out in such colonial countries as India, Annam, Korea, and Taiwan, and bloody armed confrontations are everywhere. The developments of the Chinese revolutionary movement are marked by the rising of the urban workers against the white terror of the Kuomintang's military cliques, the spread of direct armed confrontation everywhere, the institution of agrarian land revolution, the increasing development of the Soviet districts, and the enlargement of the Red Army by the unlimited increase in the defection of Kuomintang soldiers and the Kuomintang military cliques. Such fierce and enlarged revolutionary movements are shaking the whole world and this together with the success of the Russian Five-Year Plan gives an absolute threat to the imperialists. The third period of the world revolution is about to unfold before us in detail.

---

[1] This letter dated July 1, 1930, with a seal of the Ningan Committee of the Manchurian Provincial Committee of the Chinese Communist Party was issued to the Korean Communists in northern Manchuria, the Tuesday Association group. This letter was written in both Chinese and Korean, but it is available only in Japanese in *JFMA,* reel 404 (S.9.4.5.2-31), 624-37.

China is the drill ground of the imperialist's war effort, and at the same time it is the weakest link in the iron shackles of the imperialist's effort to control the world; thus, the beginning of the Chinese revolution is the beginning of the whole revolution. At present, when the struggles of the two great world revolutionary classes are sharpened, the Communists, who themselves have responsibility as revolutionaries, must rise and participate directly in the activities of the revolution. The Communist movement is the world revolutionary movement, and thus the Communists must in principle necessarily participate in the revolutionary activites of the places where they reside. In the past, Korean Communists in Manchuria generally acted in accordance with the Korean independence movement to attain Korean independence. This means that they neglected two important enemies that confront us, the imperialistic Chinese Kuomintang military cliques and the Kuomintang bureaucrats, landlords, and capitalist class, and that they attempted to conduct the Korean revolutionary movement in China. This is an absolutely mistaken idea. The Korean Communist movement has a long history, but due to the shallowness of their class consciousness and the low level of their political understanding, they have ceaselessly continued their unprincipled and anti-political factional struggles without gaining recognition and guidance from the Comintern. The attempt to utilize the anti-revolutionary organs, such as *Chŏng-ŭi-pu, Shinmin-pu, Tonghyang-hoe,* and others, without recognizing their true enemies, indicates truly that they have forgotten their political mission. Without a fundamental liquidation of such unprincipled and anti-political factionalism. It is not only difficult to perform revolutionary duties, but also it is in reality an obstacle to the revolution. The Manchurian Provincial Committee of the Chinese Communist Party, in accordance with the position of the Comintern for the benefit of true revolution, advises the Korean Communists in Manchuria to liquidate completely the idea of factional struggles, to join the Chinese Communist Party, participate in the Chinese revolution, as well as to plan and strengthen the organization, and thus to promote political and action unity in Manchuria.

We hope that the Korean Communists will solve without fail the following problems before they formally enter the Chinese Communist Party.

1. According to the Comintern's principle, the Korean Communists in China must join the party of their residence, the Chinese Communist Party. However, in order to join the Chinese Communist Party, we require that the Korean comrades recognize the platforms of the Chinese Communist Party, follow the tactics, strategies and decisions of the party, obey the rules and regulations of the party, participate with due diligence in the operation of the internal party organizations, and participate in reality in the Chinese revolution.

2. Since the organization of the Korean Communists in Manchuria has neither an independent platform nor the recognition of the Comintern, the Chinese Communist Party recognizes this organization as a mere assemblage of Communists and not as a formal brother party, and thus declines to incorporate into our party all those who belong to the various organs. Instead of resorting to the Comintern's rule of transferring the party register of each Communist, we have decided to establish a party branch in various places to incorporate individually those comrades who have renounced their factional affiliation.

3. Because we recognize the fact that, pursuant to their class position, the poor peasants and tenant farmers of every faction are the revolutionary masses and the middle-class peasants are our immediate allies, the introduction of these comrades into our party, regardless of their past factional affiliation, is based upon the principle of equality, and we will admit those who have a correct political concept of the party and revolutionary courage.

4. Those leaders who have a history of factional affiliations shall be admitted to the party only after close observation and inspection indicates that they have abandoned their factional concepts and have shown signs of diligence in the actual movement. Even after admission to the party, those who maintain factional ideas and engage themselves in factional

struggles or similar activities shall, upon verification, be expelled from the party immediately.

5. In order to establish a strong and unified party, it is necessary to adopt fighting principles and to abandon peaceful all-inclusive methods. We recognize the importance of the liquidation of all unprincipled anti-political struggles, for the benefit of our true revolution. In accordance with the principle of the solution of factionalism in the Chinese Communist Party, particularly among the various factional organs of the Korean Communists, we must transform unprincipled diversionary movements and anti-revolutionary struggles into perfect political struggles. Such struggles are not only necessary and important, but also upgrade the political standard of the party and strengthen class consciousness, assuring the correct road to revolution.

The above items are truly important principles that solve the problems of the admission of the Korean Communist comrades. In accordance with the above principles we hope that the Korean comrades will cease the unprincipled and anti-revolutionary factional struggles and join our party. Anti-revolutionary factionalism is the enemy of the Korean Communist movement and an obstacle to revolutionary operations in Manchuria, and therefore we have even decided to eliminate several centers in Manchuria. Because the solution to this problem has a significant meaning for the Chinese and Korean revolution, we can not ignore this problem. We hope that the Korean comrades do not fall into the mistaken paths of one or two leaders in Manchuria, and that they will attempt to understand the duty that confronts them.

Manchurian Provincial Committee of the Chinese Communist Party
Manchurian Provincial Committee of the Chinese Communist Youth Party
Ningan Committee of the Manchurian Provincial Committee of the Chinese Communist Party.
[Seal]
July 1, 1930

B. THE JAPANESE BUREAU, 1931-32

Item 46: Dissolution Declaration of the Japanese Bureau of the Korean Communist Party and the Japanese Section of the Korean Communist Youth Association[1]

To the Japanese and Korean laborers and peasants:

Our bureau and the Japanese section of the Youth Association were organized in 1926 as dispatch groups of the Korean Communist Party and the Korean Communist Youth Association in Japan, engaged in leading the Korean labor movement in Japan. The fact that the dispatch groups of the Korean Communist Party and of the Youth Association existed independently, without any organic link whatever with the proletarian movement in the region, was a reflection of the special objective conditions but undoubtedly was an anomalous situation. Therefore, these organizations had even from the time of their creation certain historical limitations and had historical precedents for their own dissolution for the sake of the proletarian movement of the region. However, before the question of dissolution was presented to us as an actual problem, our bureau and the Japanese section were destroyed in the midst of the rampage of white terror, and the dissolution problem, which should have come naturally, but did not, later became a reality with the natural growth of the toiling masses themselves, reaching the present condition of cooperation between the Japanese and Korean proletarian classes and the appearance of a wide class front.

This testifies to the fact that they have found trusted comrades in the process of practical struggle, realizing their common movement and mission as a laboring class, beyond narrow national limitations, and this must assure the end of the

[1] This declaration was issued in October 1931 jointly by the Japanese Bureau of the KCP and the Japanese Section of the KCYA. This document was written in Japanese as most of the materials of the Japanese Bureau were written in Japanese. It first appeared in Japanese in *Akahata,* December 23, 1931. There is as yet no Korean translation of this document.

historical duty of the bureau and make possible practical dissolution. However, because it was not possible for the bureau to carry out its duty of dissolution, due to the aforesaid conditions and the destruction of the bureau itself after the February Incident within Korea in 1926,[2] some sectors of the masses still did not understand that the dissolution of our bureau was a temporary phenomenon resulting from the pressure of our enemies, and some even had the illusion that the bureau still exists as a political leadership group. This is the very reason why we now declare our dissolution, despite the fact that dissolution should be carried out by a directive of the upper organs and according to the rules of the Party, for present conditions within the country [Korea] do not allow normal procedures. Therefore, except for those comrades who could not participate in the discussion of the dissolution decision, the decision to dissolve the bureau and the Japanese section of the Youth Association was reached unanimously.

The establishment and dissolution processes of our bureau and of the Japanese section of the Youth Association were decided by the objective conditions of the historical process; dissolution certainly is not in contrition due to our unhappy past, nor is it simply a liquidation of a mistaken direction, as some apostates allege. There will be an opportunity to discuss this in detail, the only remaining problems to be solved being the adjustments that must accompany the dissolution and our new direction of action. However, in this short declaration it is impossible to even present an outline of these problems. Suffice it here to say that the dissolution is not a settlement of our camp, but a conversion to a new struggle. Confronted with the last stage to find the class duty in all the revolutionary organizations of the Japanese and Korean proletariat, we are sending a firm handshake to those comrades who shared hardships with us in undertaking the tasks of the bureau and the Japanese section of the Youth Association, and who now suffer

[2] The reference to the February Incident of 1926 in Korea is an obvious mistake for the February Incident of 1928 when on February 2, 1928 32 leaders of the third party were arrested. See the details in D. S. Suh, *The Korean Communist Movement, 1918-1948* (Princeton, 1967), pp. 90-92.

in the jails of our enemy or are exiled abroad. Now we are dispersing from our ranks and go to various different places, but our brilliant revolutionary tradition and firm spirit in the struggles of our bureau will shine in our new front.

October 1931.
Japanese Bureau of the Korean Communist Party
Japanese Section of the Korean Communist Youth Association

Item 47:   To the Laborers, Farmers, and Working Masses on the Occasion of the Establishment of *Nodong Kegŭp-sa*[1]

Revolutionary laborers, poor peasants, working masses, and all comrades who are continuing to fight the hard battle to crush the ever increasing barbarous pressures of Japanese imperialism.

Imperialistic countries are confronted with economic and political crises and are breathing their last breath, and in contrast, the Soviet Union, the fatherland of the workers, has succeeded in completing its first five-year plan in four years and upon this firm basis the second five-year plan has been launched and is progressing successfully. The blood suckers of Japanese imperialism, the chief reactionaries in the Far East, are engulfing the cities of China in flames from land, sea and air, are slaughtering the masses, occupying Manchuria by force, and busying themselves with suppressing the Chinese revolution and preparing to proceed to the Soviet Union.

The all-out political and economic attack on colonial Korea, which occupies the most important and strategic position in the advance of Japanese imperialism to the Soviet Union, has been intensified, and they have not only plundered Manchuria but also suppressed the workers and peasant masses with an extreme barbarity of white terror. They have intensified the exploitation of the proletariat by transforming all industrial organizations to military use and war industries; they have produced an army of unemployed by depriving the peasants of their land; and they exploited the people to the last drop of blood and sweat and produced ten million starved masses.

[1] This document was written jointly by Kim Ch'i-jŏng and Kim Tu-jŏng who headed the organization, *Nodong Kegŭp-sa* [Laboring Class Group], in Korean in June 1932. The Korean version appeared first in their journal, *Nodong kegŭp,* but this version is, so far, not available. The authors later translated the document into Japanese with some minor corrections of the original Korean version, and they issued the Japanese version on August 15, 1932. This English translation was made from the Japanese version which is available in Japan, Naimu-shō, Keiho-kyoku, *Shōwa shichinenjū ni okeru shakai undō no jōkyō* (Tokyo, 1933), pp. 1,508-12.

The Japanese militarists are busily engaged in the preparation of an assault against the Soviet Union and the crushing of the Chinese Revolution by reinforcing two divisions in Korea, equipping these divisions with tanks, building military ports in Ch'ŏngjin, Sŏngjin and Unggi [Korean towns near the Russian border], constructing an airport in Lungch'ingtson [Yongjong in Chientao], purchasing fighter and bomber planes, extending the railways to the borders of the three countries [the Soviet Union, China and Korea], opening the roads in the border areas, secretly producing poison gas and ammunition in the Hŭngnam Fertilizer factory, instituting a steel mill in Shinŭiju (this was reportedly created near the border to facilitate the attack on the Soviet Union), and engaging in other insane activities.

At the same time, in an effort to frustrate the revolutionary struggles of the working masses of poor peasants and workers, the Japanese imperialist have strengthened the police force by adding two thousand additional men and establishing 42 additional police branch offices, dispersing a wide spy network in the ports of Pusan, Inch'ŏn, Wŏnsan, Ch'ŏngjin, and others, instituting a direct line of communication to the Korean borders, adding mounted police and purchasing 100,000 horses, generalizing the practice of the plain-clothes bureaucratic dogs carrying pistols, making an unlimited expansion of the jail facilities, expanding the thought police, instituting spy networks in factories and even village schools, etc.

On the other hand, in an effort to win over the reactionaries, the Japanese imperialists are bribing the majority of the Nationalist bourgeois and feudal landlords. Sweetened by this policy, the left and right national reformists are opposing the dissolution of *Shin'gan-hoe,* which would support the war effort, and cry out for a nationally united political party. One group of *Ch'ŏndo-kyo* (they have organized *Ch'ŏndo-kyo* peasant unions and all-Korean peasant unions deceiving tens and thousands of peasants and they have been acting as the most faithful dogs of the Japanese imperialists, but recently they have organized a conspiratory corps, a mixed organization of the Korean and Japanese bureaucratic dogs called the workers' party, in an effort to reach the as yet organized masses), the Buddhist Youth League, and Christian apostates are busily engaged in deceiving the working masses by organizing various national associations. At the same time, a certain group of degenerates, disguised as Communists by painting their faces with coal dust and using revolutionary words to incite the workers, are only serving as the faithful dogs of Japanese imperialism.

With this military and police oppression, as well as by other alienation measures, the Japanese imperialists are madly destroying the revolutionary organization of the workers and peasants; they are mobilizing all reactionary terrorist organizations, such as the youth corps, veterans' corps, firemen's association, the gendarms, the military and their dogs, and are further committing bloody white terror by imprisoning and murdering nearly 5,000 vanguards and 40,000 revolutionary workers and peasants. However, their madness has incited the huge masses wandering on the borders of starvation and suffering a barbaric oppression that may even surpass the barbaric treatment of cows and horses.

We have nothing but our chains to lose, and we have the world to gain. Our workers, poor peasants, and all the working masses, who are struggling against the merciless suppression of Japanese imperialism and who are bursting out of all dangers and difficulties, must carry on an even broader struggle in the factories, mines, villages, and ports.

Thus, following such unprecedented objective conditions, the toiling masses throughout the country are more in need of a revolutionary publication than of daily bread, a publication that would enliven the bloody struggle.

The greatest necessity for the mass and class publication is to enlighten the class consciousness of the masses, who are suffering barbaric exploitation in darkness and ignorance. Instead of instituting compulsory education in Korea, the Government-General of Korea, the branch office of Japanese imperialism in Korea, has abolished by force the educational facilities of the masses, thus leaving them in darkness and ignorance; even the evening class for the laborers and peasants, the youth, and others, have been abolished, numerous organs to exploit the masses have been instituted, such as the Oriental Overseas Company, various commercial banks, irrigation associations, forest guilds, many factories for the production of munitions, etc. The laborers are paid the lowest possible wage of fifteen or sixteen cents per day, or at times are not paid at all, and if any sign of rebellious attitude is detected, they are unconditionally imprisoned. Sometimes the Japanese imperialists try to use religion to crush the dissatisfactions arising from the hard life of the masses. We must stand in the forefront and enlighten the masses by exposing all oppressive and exploitative measures.

Second, we must eradicate the poisonous evangelic efforts and colonial slave education policies of Japanese imperialism. The Japanese imperialists are not only instituting a slave education for the naive children, but also are expending great efforts in reactionary evangelism to enslave the unconscious masses, mobilizing the Christians and Buddhists from the Japanese-Korean cooperation groups such as *Suyang-tan.* We must expose and destroy all this reactionary education and evangelism of Japanese imperialism.

Third, we must eliminate all reactionary publications of the national bourgeoisie from among the masses. The various organs of the national bourgeoisie, such as *Chosŏn ilbo, Tong-a ilbo,* and *Chung-ang ilbo* (publication of which was suspended for a lack of faithfulness as a dog of Japanese imperialism), and reactionary magazines such as *Haebang, Pip'an, Hesŏng, Samch'-ŏlli, Shin Tong-a, Shin Yŏsŏng,* and others, are spreading the poisonous elements to the masses, utilizing the opportunity created by total elimination of revolutionary publications. We must destroy all reactionary publications and arm the masses with Marxism and Leninism through our revolutionary publication.

Fourth, through propaganda we must mobilize the masses loitering on the verge of starvation and thus create a fundamental organization based upon materialistic foundations.

Fifth, we must fully understand the experiences and bloody struggles of the toiling masses, and expose the merciless tyranny of Japanese imperialism to the masses. For example, local labor strikes, peasant riots, and tenancy struggles were not known to other neighboring villages because of the breakdown in the communication lines of the bureaucratic dogs of Japanese imperialism. Consequently, an understanding of the lessons and experiences of the strategy of the struggle was not possible. At the same time, the Japanese imperialists are busy concealing the barbarous activities of their barbarous methods of investigation, which often resulted in murdering our revolutionary brothers. But we must gather together all the practical experiences of revolutionary struggle that arise in all corners of the country, and mobilize the masses for further political struggles by exposing the facts of the white terror of the Japanese imperialists.

Sixth, we must unify the intensifying struggles and numerous problems arising in the country. Due to the lack of publication activities, despite the fact that in some regions youth leagues are being dissolved in order to consolidate the youth guilds, other regions are establishing youth leagues. Another example is the indecision and aimlessness of the organizations in some regions following the dissolution of *Kŭn'u-hoe*. We must assist their activities with our publication.

Seventh, we must introduce fully the directives, teachings, and experiences of the international proletariat revolutionary struggles. All decisions and theses of the proletarian international organization must be widely introduced to the workers, and the laborers and peasants must be informed of all of the efforts of socialism, the construction in the Soviet Union, the Chinese proletariat's heroic revolutionary struggle under the Red banner, the anti-war struggles of the international proletariat, and the Japanese, German and other international proletariat's courageous struggles.

Comrades, laborers and poor peasants, and toiling masses! Lo, although the need for a revolutionary publication for the masses is predominent, publication and writing activities are not so prevalent that this life-giving water can be provided for the laborers and poor peasants. The pamphlets that are printed under such adverse conditions, as those printed in the mountains while hiding from enemy attack and eating the roots of herbs and the bark of trees, are not widely circulated, and the materials legally published in the completely isolated cultural atmosphere of today are not even meeting one-ten thousanth of the cultural needs of the masses. Thus, all propaganda activities are carried on only verbally by the leaders.

Should we abandon the publication activities demanded by the masses suffering from persecution, execution, and starvation? No, definitely not. We must meet the demand of the masses, regardless of how severe the persecution and how indifferent some opportunist elements are. In order to carry out such an important class duty, we have created *Nodong kegŭp-sa* amidst the bloody struggle of today, and a journal, *Nodong Kegŭp,* is to be published.

Our beloved comrades, laborers, poor peasants, and all toiling masses, we declare to you that we will carry out a revolutionary publication task, based on Marxist and Leninist principles, for the laborers, poor peasants and all toiling masses of Korea. In order to carry out such an important auxiliary class task, the *Nodong Kegŭp-sa* has decided to perform its proletarian revolutionary publication task temporarily in Tokyo, due to the difficult conditions currently prevailing within Korea. The reasons why the *Nodong Kegŭp-sa* has to be located in Tokyo are:

1. Even under the suppression of Japanese imperialism, in Japan it is relatively easy to attain legality in our struggle, compared to Korea, where the cultural boundaries are completely closed. For example, in Korea even a single message could not be read, a three-year sentence is handed down for a single handbill, and even the playful cartoon of a child receives a severe criminal judgment. But in Japan the revolutionary pamphlets are flowing to the masses like a flood.

2. Pamphlet publication and proletarian cultural activities are very much superficial in Korea, but in Japan, as in Germany, both proletarian cultural struggles and publication activities are most actively carried out.

3. The manuscript examination system in Korea leads to

confiscation of the entire article or deletion of enough of an article to change the meaning substantially before publication, if it ever is published, but in Japan the system used is merely an official presentation system.

4. From Japan, compared with other regions, distribution is the easiest.

5. For publication in Korea, the geographical location is extremely disadvantageous, and there is no printing press that can be effectively utilized in Korea. In contrast, Tokyo is not only geographically convenient, but also the utilization of printing presses is relatively easy.

Due to the above-stated conditions our publication activities must temporarily be centered in Tokyo. However, we must struggle on the one hand to establish the legality of our publication and, on the other, we must attempt to finalize our effort within Korea.

The *Nodong Kegŭp-sa,* though weak, pledges its full support and whatever sacrifices are necessary in carrying out the duty of this class struggle. At the same time, the laborers, the poor peasants, and all laboring masses must keep and support this organization that grew out of bloody struggles, and help it to grow under any and all adverse circumstances.

We again appeal to the Japanese proletariat. We hope that you will understand the circumstances that forced us to undertake publication activities in Tokyo, and that you will directly help and support our efforts.

Comrades, laborers, poor peasants, and all toiling masses, we must keep the revolutionary publishing house, *Nodong Kegŭp-sa,* and make it grow and protect it even under the most cruel of white terrors.

Guard with death the *Nodong Kegŭp-sa.*

Read, our friend, *Nodong Kegŭp.*

Long live the expansion and strengthening of the *Nodong Kegŭp-sa.*

Long live the joint revolutionary efforts of the Japanese and Korean proletariat.

June 1932, *Nodong Kegŭp-sa.*

Postscript: Our beloved comrades. We are very glad that the Japanese proletarian comrades are aiding and supporting our development. At the same time, at the request of our Japanese proletarian comrades, we are printing a translation of this declaration in Japanese, with minor corrections of the misprints in the original edition which appeared in the preparatory issue of the *Nodong Kegŭp*. Congratulations to the struggle of our comrades.

August 15, 1932, *Nodong Kegŭp-sa*.

C. THE NORTH CHINA KOREAN INDEPENDENCE LEAGUE, 1941-44

Item 48: Platform and Manifesto of the North China Korean Youth Federation[1]

Platform:

1. Unite the exiled Korean youths in all north China, and make them participate in the great task of restoration of our fatherland. Overthrow the Japanese imperialists' reign in Korea and establish as independent and free Korean national republic.

2. Support the anti-Japanese front of all the Korean people, and launch a war of Korean national liberation.

3. Struggle to protect the Korean people in north China, and give political, economic, and cultural benefits, particularly to the youth in north China.

4. Protect the Korean people, particularly youths, who are suffering oppression and maltreatment in the occupied areas of China, and must carry out an operation to secure their livelihood.

5. Oppose Japanese imperialism's invasion of China and directly participate in the anti-Japanese war in China.

6. Support the Taiwanese national liberation movement, help the anti-war movement of the Japanese people's revolution, and thus form an anti-Japanese united front of the Korean, Taiwanese, and Japanese peoples.

Manifesto:

We are the great Korean people. We have heroically struggled for the past thirty years despite the severe oppression of Japanese imperialism. The March First uprising of 1919 clarified

[1] This document was written in February 1941 at the time of the founding of the North China Korean Youth Federation, most likely by Ch'oe Ch'ang-ik who founded the Federation. The document was written in Korean, but available only in Japanese in *Tokkō geppō,* April, 1941, pp. 97-99.

the basic foundation and direction of our national emancipation struggle. The anti-Japanese struggle has continued since the March First uprising, and our resentment is endless at the memory of such righteous revolutionary leaders as An Chung-kŭn, Yi U-myŏng, and Yun Pong-kil,[2] who fell in succession after the fallen revolutionaries. Such great sacrifices are worthy of appraisal in the pages of the history of the Korean people's emancipation and such sacrifices are confusing our enemies. This further proves to the world the fact that the great Korean people will not perish and also that the Korean national emancipation movement will definitely develop.

We must struggle whole-heartedly to destroy the rule of Japanese imperialism in Korea and regain the emancipation and independence of the Korean people. In the past struggle, our people paid the price of sacrifice in precious blood, and we must not make these sacrifices and the spirit of our forerunners meaningless. Because the bloody struggle of the Korean emancipation movement originated in and inherited the teachings and revolutionary tradition of these great forerunners, this is not the autumn when the Korean people can count and hesitate, but rather it is the time when we are confronted with the important problem of our very existence.

We must continue a ceaseless and courageous struggle and eliminate and destroy Japanese imperialism. Our will to accomplish this task will not change even if the ocean dries up and stones become putrid. On this day of the founding of the federation of our thirty million compatriots and the righteous people of the world, we are reasserting our faith and determination to sacrifice ourselves for the great task of restoring our fatherland.

We must not forget the fact that the present world situation is in the midst of an important change. Even in the Far East this change is daily made apparent by the increasing difficulties and isolation of our enemies. The struggle of the great Chinese

[2] These are the martyred Korean revolutionaries. An Chung-kŭn is the assasin of the first Japanese prime minister Itō Hirobumi. An was captured immediately after the shooting, and was executed.

people has continued for three and a half years, and the more the enemy moves the deeper they fall into a bottomless hole. The difficulties of the enemy with the British and the Americans in the Pacific have increased, and the Soviet Union with all its national strength is aiding and strengthening the struggle of the oppressed peoples. These and all other visible and invisible threats are great obstacles to our enemy. The people's anti-war revolutionary movement within the enemy state is also growing daily.

When we review all these conditions they are seen to be beneficial to our Korean national liberation movement. During the past thirty years our thirty million Korean national compatriots, with sustained determination and perseverance, and our innumerable national heroes have spent their blood to erect a scaffold for the independence and freedom of our fatherland. The present situation is the best opportunity to drive out our enemy. Thus we must strive to attain the great national objective of restoration of our fatherland. We understand very well the anti-war movement of the Chinese people. This war has close, nondivisive, common relations with the Korean national liberation movement. Much earlier, after the 8-1-3 Incident,[3] when China was bursting out in anti-war efforts, our Korean compatriots participated actively and began to fight. Perhaps it is difficult for the Korean compatriots to understand, but the sought-after emancipation of the Korean people will be gained on the dawn when the Chinese people win victory through their anti-war efforts. However, the development of the Korean national emancipation movement lends great assistance to the Chinese anti-war movement. Korea and China share in common their life and death, glory and shame, and all disasters and difficulties.

We are appealing to all Koreans who are scattered in north China and all over China to help the Chinese anti-war effort effectively, and thus bring victory through common operations with the Chinese compatriots. We know that an important reason for the victory of Japanese imperialism is the unity of

---

[3] The incident referred to here is not clear.

the Japanese. We must participate in the Chinese national unity
and assist the Chinese as well as learn together with them, and
ultimately we will form a Korean anti-Japanese national united
front. We invite all those Korean revolutionary organizations
that agree with us, regardless of class differences, factional
affiliations, characteristics, and religious inclinations, to join us
in opposing Japanese imperialism and struggling to free our
nation.

We extend the greatest respect for the heroic struggle of the
various revolutionary organizations in the United States and
Korea, the Korean National Liberation Struggle League, the
Korean National Revolutionary Party, the Korean Provisional
Government. Especially we wish the unity of all these organizations to lead the Korean people in the struggle against the
Japanese. We understand bitterly that our past thirty-year
struggle has been nothing more than merely a sectarian struggle
of each organization. Today, patriotism and the will to unite in
the struggle are overwhelming among the people. We firmly
believe in the realization of our cherished objective in the near
future, and our scattered Korean youths in north China, in view
of their number alone, cannot be neglected, nor can their
sufferings under the cruel oppression of the enemies be
overlooked.

To mobilize and organize these youths and to participate in
the struggle of the great national liberation are the duties of this
Federation, and it is a responsibility that must not be evaded.
This Federation also has the duty and responsibility to destroy
the inhumane living conditions under the oppression similar to
that of beasts, to remove the sorrow resulting from the
impoverishment of our fatherland, to relieve the hardship of
wandering in North China, and to give cultural, economic, and
political benefits to our Korean youths.

We earnestly hope that every Korean youth, throwing away
personal interests, will become a member of a cell in our
people's struggle for the work of national emancipation and will
protect and foster the work of national emancipation.

We hope Korean youths who reside in North China will join
us and participate in our ranks. Furthermore, we must

organically link the revolutionary movement of Korean people all over the world and, with the direct action and full strength of our youth, initiate the emancipation war of all Korean people under the Korean anti-Japanese united front. A great future is promised for our Korean people, and in this great revolutionary history the Korean people have assigned a special task to the Korean youth.

We must respond with unending vigor to the wishes of our thirty million compatriots and with our united efforts hold high the anti-Japanese banner and accomplish the task of Korean national emancipation for the day of ultimate victory. This we respectfully declare.

Item 49: Programs, Manifesto, and Platform of the North China Korean Independence League [NCKIL][1]

I. The Executive Committee of the NCKIL:
    Kim Tu-bong, Mu-jŏng, Ch'oe Ch'ang-ik, Wang Chi-yon, Pak Hyo-sam, Yi Yu-min, Kim Hak-mu, Kim Ch'ang-man, Yi Ch'un-am, Chin Han-jung, and Ch'ae Kuk-bŏn.

II. The Programs of the NCKIL:
     1. a. Development of the armed revolutionary movement.
        b. Establishment of the bases of the armed revolutionary movement.
        c. Education of the revolutionary cadres.
     2. a. Prolonged and continuous operation against the enemy.
        b. Establishment of revolutionary bases in enemy occupied areas.
     3. a. Development of a unified Korean revolutionary movement under the principles of anti-Japanese operation.
        b. Enlargement of the Korean people's unification front.
        c. Establishment of an organization of the Korean people's unification front.
        d. Establishment of a close connection with the anti-fascist organizations east of Yenan.
     4. Participation in all kinds of anti-Japanese movements in the enemy-occupied areas in north China.
     5. a. Strengthening of internal unity.
        b. Cultural development of the ranks.

---

[1] This document was issued by the Executive Committee of the NCKIL on August 15, 1942. It is perhaps the work of Ch'oe Ch'ang-ik. It was written in Korean, but it is available only in Japanese. See Japan, Naimu-shō, keiho-kyoku, *Shōwa jushichinenju ni okeru shakai undō no jōkyō* (Tokyo, 1943), pp. 973-75.

III. Manifesto of the Congress of the Representatives, North
China Korean Independence League:

Revolutionary comrades within Korea, Korean compatriots
in north China, and all revolutionary organizations and armed
groups that are within and outside Korea:

Our representative congress expresses its respect for the
lofty revolutionary spirit, of each revolutionary organization
and armed group and of the people who ceaselessly struggle for
their own national emancipation under adverse circumstances,
and expresses its hope for their victory.

The convening of the representative congress strengthens
the forces of the Allied powers on the international scene, and
the new order of the post-war era is becoming apparent. The
preparations for the Chinese counter-offensive under extremely
difficult circumstances are progressing daily, and this indicates
that the defeat of the Japanese fascists initiated the barbaric
aggressive war, the Korean people have been deprived of human
materials and financial benefits, and have been living under
inhumane and insufferable living conditions, but the courageous
and righteous Korean people with lofty ideals have been
struggling tirelessly, following in the path of the fallen
revolutionaries, to carry on military struggles by overturning
military transportation cars and by destroying military establishments in an effort to aid the international anti-fascist
movement and the Chinese anti-war efforts to win the peace
and freedom of the post-war era. The Korean people will
emerge to clear away all darkened, impoverished, estranged and
enslaving colonial livelihoods, and will secure enlightened,
prosperous, free and sound nationally independent livelihoods.
We now face such a time; therefore, the representative congress
declares to all our compatriots and revolutionary organizations
the following:

1. We must enlarge our political influences, enforce our
revolutionary strength, strengthen internal cooperation by
disciplining ourselves, unite the armed ranks and all revolutionary organizations, and uphold the anti-Japanese struggles to

accomplish the Korean people's national emancipation.

2. Enlarge and strengthen the anti-Japanese national united front and accomplish national revolution. Our past independence movement suffered significantly from disunity, diversion, individual vs. collective struggles, and other factors. We must clearly learn the lessons that we pay for with our blood, understand our policy, realize the correct line of our revolution, and advance toward one ultimate objective by mobilizing all our efforts and strength.

3. We must struggle to protect the political, economic and cultural interests of the 200,000 Koreans residing in North China, and we hope that the Koreans in North China forget not the Korean spirit and participate in the revolutionary organizations and display their revolutionary spirit through armed revolutionary organizations.

4. Our immediate duty is to prepare a posture of total struggle by establishing a connecting link between the revolutionary organization within Korea and the revolutionaries outside Korea.

5. Because the Korean national emancipation movement coincides with world revolutionary currents, we are internationally connected as part of the international anti-fascist struggle, and we hope to accomplish Korean national emancipation. We firmly support the Eastern anti-fascist League, and, together with each anti-war organization in Japan, carry out anti-Japanese operations.

With a firm belief in our ultimate victory, we declare this to the international revolutionary leaders and to our compatriots.

IV. Platform of the North China Korean Independence League:

A. The League has as its objective the establishment of a Korean People's Republic by overthrowing Japanese imperialist rule in Korea, and it struggles to attain the duties listed below:

1. Establishment of democratic government by popular election with all people voting.

2. Assurance of freedom of speech, publication, assembly, organization, religion, thought, and occupation.

3. Establishment of a social system wherein the human rights of the people are respected.

4. Establishment of the equality of the sexes in livelihood, society, and in law.

5. Establishment of friendly relations with all freedom-loving peoples under the principle of self-determination.

6. Confiscation of all land and property of Japanese imperialists in Korea, nationalization of all large enterprises that have had close relationships with the Japanese imperialists, and distribution of land.

7. Establishment of eight-hour labor laws and assurance of the rights of laborers in society.

8. Abolition of the forced-labor systems and of miscellaneous taxes on the people, and establishment of a uniform tax system.

9. Establishment of a compulsory education system supported by the state.

B. The League, as a local organ to win Korean independence, must participate directly in the Korean revolutionary movement and must struggle to carry out the following duties:

1. In order to increase the revolutionary strength and to reform the masses, the League must directly participate in and lead the daily life of the masses.

2. The League must struggle to develop organizational discipline for the mass revolution.

3. The League must struggle in every direction to increase the political, economic and cultural benefits of Korean compatriots residing in China, particularly North China.

4. The League must struggle to consolidate and enlarge the anti-Japanese united front of all Korean people.

5. The League must struggle to establish a revolutionary military unit to develop the anti-Japanese struggle of all Korean people.

6. The League must oppose the Japanese imperialistic fascist's invasion of China, and participate directly in the Chinese anti-Japanese struggle.

7. The League must cooperate with each oppressed people's movement in the East and with the Japanese people's anti-war movement, and must support the world's anti-fascist righteous war.

Item 50: Fighting Platform of the Mid-China Company of the Korean Volunteer Corps[1]

1. The objective of this branch company at the present stage is to struggle for the fulfilment of the platform of the Korean Independence League.

2. This branch company will proceed to engage in armed propaganda activities among the Koreans residing in enemy occupied areas and will induce the Korean soldiers in the enemy armed forces to join us, thus expanding the military capabilities of our company to develop a direct armed struggle against the Japanese and to promote the Korean people's concrete emancipation struggle.

3. All anti-Japanese operations, including organizational, propagandistic, and educational activities directed towards the Koreans residing in mid-China, will be undertaken by this company, and we will strive to accomplish these tasks thoroughly.

4. Each member of this company, with diligent study of the revolutionary experiences of other nations, particularly those valuable experiences of the Chinese New Fourth and Eighth Route Armies, must become a paragon of the Korean independence revolutionary movement.

5. Each member of this company must study diligently the history of the Korean revolutionary movement, learn from its experiences and teachings, and must arm himself with a theoretical understanding of the Korean revolutionary movement.

---

[1] This platform was prepared by Yi Sŏng-ho, Kim Yun-dŏk, and Son Tal who were dispatched from the headquarters of the North China Korean Independence League to operate within the New Fourth Army in central China. It is assumed that the platform was written in Korean in early 1944, for it was in January 1944 the three men were dispatched to central China. The document is available in Japanese in *Tokkō geppò*, November 1944, pp. 73-74.

Item 51: Proclamation[1]

1. Oppose all Japanese conspiracies to destroy us: the crafty oppression and exploitation, the assimilation policy, the institution of a conscription system and many others. Our comrades must quickly unite under the banner of this Army and the NCKIL and participate in the Korean fatherland restoration movement.

2. In a special effort to protect and encourage Koreans residing in North China, the Chinese Eighth Route Army and Anti-Japanese Democratic Government issued a law specifying special treatment to Koreans: loans without interest to Korean merchants; similarly, to farmers the loan of land, cows, tools for agriculture, seeds, and houses; for others, assistance in getting employment; and for students, tuition-free schooling. We welcome our compatriots to join us in the anti-Japanese democratic bases and escape the living hell of the Japanese oppression.

3. Since the "Great East Asia Bank Notes" will soon be abolished, we hope our compatriots will exchange all Japanese bank notes into commodities and hide them to protect their interests.

4. All those who act as spies or running dogs of the Japanese conspiracy in instituting the "assimilation policy of Korean-Japanese unity, the conscription law, and the general usage of the Japanese language," and also those who attempt to destroy interests of our Korean compatriots and interfere with and destroy the operations of the Eighth Route Army and this Volunteer Army, must repent, because this Army will deal with these traitors severely in the near future.

[1] This proclamation was issued in May 1943 by the general headquarters of the Korean Volunteer Army in North China operating in the branch of the NCKIL headed by Yu Tǔng, a Korean Communist. This proclamation was numbered as the Proclamation No. 102. It is not clear what this number represents. The proclamation was written in Korean but available only in Japanese in *Tokkō geppō*, January, 1944, pp. 78-79.

5. To further the independence of our fatherland, Korea, this Army welcomes the return of the Korean soldiers and interpreters who are now serving the Japanese army. The way to surrender is to raise a white flag and say, "I want to participate in the anti-Japanese struggle," and everyone will be treated very kindly.

May 1943, General Headquarters of the Korean Volunteer Army in North China.

MAKE KOREA INDEPENDENT [2]

The victory of the world anti-fascist war is near. In the Russo-German war front, Germany is being defeated as the Russian counter-offensive is intensified. On the other hand, the Japanese forces are being isolated and defeated by the coalition forces of China, Great Britain, and the United States. And within the near future, a great counter-offensive by China, Great Britain, and the United States will definitely begin. With such changes in the world fronts, the possibilities for the independence of our Korean people have increased significantly, and the forces of the people's revolution within Japan and the anti-Japanese movement of the oppressed people in the East are gradually being reinforced. When the counter-offensive of the Chinese, British, and American forces begins, it will defeat the Japanese and Germans, and this will ultimately bring the independence of Korea.

1. All Korean compatriots residing in North China, participate directly in the independence movement of our fatherland.
2. Overthrow the Japanese fascist control of Korea, and fight

<hr>

[2] This document was issued by the branch of the NCKIL commanded by Kim Se-kwang in May 1943. The Corps was later commanded by Pak Hyo-sam and others who played an important role in North Korea after the liberation. The document was written in Korean but available, so far, only in Japanese. See the Japanese version in *Tokkō geppō,* January 1944, pp. 79-80.

to establish an independent and free Korean Democratic Republic.

3. Cooperate with the liberation movement of the oppressed Eastern peoples, particularly the Japanese people's anti-war revolutionary movement, and participate in the anti-fascist united front.

4. All Korean compatriots in North China, unite under the banner of the NCKIL and the Korean Volunteer Army of North China.

May 1943, Northwest Branch of Shansi Province, North China Korean Independence League.

PART   V

THE NORTHEAST ANTI-JAPANESE

UNITED ARMY AND THE KOREAN PARTISANS

1934-40

COMMENTARY

The Northeast Anti-Japanese United Army and the Korean Partisans, 1934-40

THE NORTHEAST Anti-Japanese United Army, the NEAJUA, was a Chinese Communist guerrilla army which operated in Manchuria during the 1930's after the Japanese established the puppet state of Manchukuo. This army played a relatively minor role in the Chinese Communist revolution taken as a whole. Since it operated underground during its entire operational period of some seven years, approximately 1933 to 1940, its military activities succeeded only in causing disturbances to the security of the Japanese rule in Manchuria. Some Koreans participated in this army, and although they did on occasion infiltrate into their homeland from their operational bases in Manchuria, neither the Korean participation nor the Sino-Korean cooperation resulted in any significant force. They were successful only in a few skirmishes against the Japanese garrison army in Manchuria. Before the beginning of the war with the United States the Japanese succeeded in suppressing the guerrillas through the use of numerous punitive expeditions. After losing several important leaders, the army moved to Khabarovsk in the Russian Maritime Province in early 1940 and remained there until the end of the World War II.

The Chinese Communists recognized the guerrilla activities of the NEAJUA, and, for example hailed Yang Ching-yü, who was killed in action in February, 1940, as a national hero. Others who were killed in action included the commander of the Second Army, Wang Teh-t'ai, and the commander of the Third Army, Chao Shang-chih. The leaders who survived the war did contribute to the Chinese civil war. For example, the late Chu Pao-chung served as a deputy commander to Lin Piao at the time of the Manchurian campaign; and Li Yen-lu, who was the commander of the fourth route army of the NEAJUA in its last phase of operation, is today a member of the Central

Committee of the Chinese Communist Party.

There are two important facts about this army especially relevant to the Korean Communists. The first is that those Koreans who participated in this army became the leaders in North Korea, including Kim Il-sông. The North Koreans are silent concerning their participation in the Chinese army, the NEAJUA, and glorify only Korean partisan activities against the Japanese. Nonetheless, from the available records of the NEAJUA, it is clear that they were a part of the Chinese army. The second is that these Koreans had no relationship with mainstream of Korean Communists either at home or abroad. As has been pointed out, the cooperation of the Koreans within the Manchurian General Bureau was confined to the Manchurian Provincial Committee, and even this cooperation came to an end in the mid-1930's. No Korean Communists of any importance participated in the NEAJUA ever held a significant position or participated in the Korean Communist movement, in Korea or abroad, before the end of the World War II.

The study of the NEAJUA has been important to two groups of people, with disparate purposes and at different times. The first, of course, are the Japanese who studied its activities in an effort to defeat them and maintain the security of Manchukuo. The second are the North Koreans of today. They study NEAJUA partisan activities in detail but not its participation in the Chinese army, and describe their anti-Japanese partisan activities in Manchuria as their contribution to the Korean revolution. They not only depict their activities as the major revolutionary undertakings, but also seek to discredit all other activities by Korean Communists. There are a few Chinese studies, primarily the reminiscences of participants such as Feng Chung-yun and a few works by Chi Yun-lung and Liu Pai-u, which seem to recognize the paltry nature of the undertakings that ended in defeat in Manchuria, especially when these are viewed in the context of the entire Chinese Communist revolution.

In an effort to "Koreanize" their participation in the Chinese army, the North Koreans claimed to have established a Korean organization in Manchuria known as the Korean Fatherland

Restoration Association in Manchuria, the KFRAM, in conjunction with their participation in the NEAJUA. This was also
done to propagate their leadership and Communist undertakings
by Koreans in Manchuria. A few original documents pertaining
to the KFRAM are available and are introduced here. The
documents in this section are divided into two groups: A)
documents of the NEAJUA, some documents of the second
army in which the Korean participation was concentrated and a
few documents pertaining to the relationship of the Koreans
and Chinese Communists in the army; and B) documents of the
KFRAM.

A. *The Northeast Anti-Japanese United Army, 1934-36*

Numerous documents are available concerning this army,
both in Chinese and Japanese, and they include various
proclamations, declarations, action platforms, slogans, operational principles, etc. The army itself underwent several
reorganizations with the regional army groups first united as the
Northeast People's Revolutionary Army in September 1933. It
was not until February 1936, that the NEAJUA was officially
created. At this time there were six army corps and two
guerrilla groups attached to the army. The first document, item
52, is a declaration issued when the NEAJUA was formed. It
stated that the various armies had been fighting the Japanese for
four years and that they were the arms of the Northeast
anti-Japanese Association and the national salvation movement.
The declaration was signed by six army commanders and two
guerrilla corps leaders, and was sent to various leaders in China,
including Nationalists.[1]

The present North Korean premier, Kim Il-sŏng, was a
division commander of the Second Army throughout the
reorganization of the Army. There were other Korean leaders in
other armies, such as Ch'oe Yong-kŏn in the Sixth Army and
the late Kim Ch'aek in the Third army. The largest Korean

---

[1] See other documents of similar nature in, among others, Hatano
Ken'ichi, *Chūgoku kyōsan-tō shi,* Vol. VI, pp. 387-89 and 754-55.

contingents were in the Second Army. The next two documents, items 53 and 54, are a letter circulated by the Second Army to various anti-Japanese detachments and a fighting platform of the Second Army. The numerical exaggeration of their forces in the letter of over 300,000 is obvious. Much stress is laid on the united efforts in their anti-Japanese struggle to attract the Communists and all others who opposed the Japanese in Manchuria. The letter is signed by Wang Teh-t'ai and Wei Chi-min, perhaps the two closest comrades-in-arms of Kim Il-sŏng. Both were later killed in action. They served in the Second Army under its first commander, a Korean named Chu Chin. The fighting platform, one of many such platforms of the various armies, is included here because it is the platform of the second army and because it was issued in 1934 when Chu was in command.[2]

The operation of the second army was often harsh in impact on the Korean residents in Manchuria, exacting materials and funds from them by questioning their loyalties. Threats and demands on the Korean villagers in Manchuria were common and the Communist "bandits" exacted heavily when the villagers failed to comply with their requests. Three such threatening notes are grouped as one, item 55. The notes make clear the punishments which accompanied noncompliance with the demands. One of these notes was issued by Ch'oe Hyŏn, now a general of the Korean People's Army and a ranking member of the Central Committee of the Workers' Party of Korea.

Korean participation in the Chinese army was not without difficulties. The joint activity of the Koreans and Chinese was seriously hampered by an incident known as the *Minsaeng-dan* Incident. The *Minsaeng-dan* was a Korean organization which sided with the Japanese gendarmes to undermine the Communists. The members of the *Minsaeng-dan* (later called *Hyŏpjo-hoe*) penetrated into the NEAJUA and sent some

---

[2] For a similar slogan, see one in as late as January 1940 in *Shisō geppō* (no. 67, pp. 181-99). This particular one includes a special slogan for the Koreans, stressing their support of the KFRAM, already defunct at this time.

operational information of the army to the Japanese. When the Chinese realized the Korean spies were in the army a mass purge of the Koreans was carried out, including many innocent Korean leaders and soldiers in the army. Items 56 and 57, directly concern this incident. Yi Sang-muk, who was one of the innocent leaders purged and who was once the head of the organization section under Wang Teh-t'ai, stated his complaints and reflected some of the feelings of the Koreans in the first of these documents. Subsequently, the Chinese, realizing the excessive treatment of the loyal Koreans, held a meeting and issued a declaration, item 57. Extracts from that declaration reflect a moderating attitude by the Chinese in an effort to regain the support of the Koreans, and admit that up to thirty percent of the Koreans purged may have been innocent. However, only a few were restored and cooperative efforts between the Koreans and the Chinese became more difficult.

B.   The Korean Fatherland Restoration Association in Manchuria, 1936-40

Because of the special emphasis the North Koreans place on the partisan struggles in Manchuria and because of their unending efforts to socialize the Korean public regarding their participation in the anti-Japanese guerrilla fightings, which they depict as the most important of the Korean revolutionary struggles, the meager nature of their true partisan activites under the Chinese leadership in Manchuria have received more appraisal than is warranted. However, since the partisan leaders who control the north Korean regime today trace every conceivable and at times genuine achievement in the North to the tradition of their partisan struggles, their revolutionary activities require closer scrutiny to clarify the facts that are known and recorded in the documents of the KFRAM, if not to refute their many claims.

Chu Pao-chung, one of the few Chinese leaders of the NEAJUA who survived the war, later became an alternate member of the Central Committee of the Chinese Communist Party and was invited by the Chinese government to a banquet

given for a North Korean military delegaton to China. Many
members of the delegation had been his subordinates in their
revolutionary days in Manchuria, and, as they reminisced on
their difficult days, Chu was cheered as the revolutionary hero
of the Chinese and Korean revolutions. Regardless of the high
praise for Chu, who died in 1964, and for other surviving
leaders of the NEAJUA who attained a position of importance
in Communist China, those of the NEAJUA who ultimately
became most famous are the leaders of North Korea, Kim
Il-sŏng and his partisans.

The partisans have built a huge museum in P'yŏngyang
extolling their revolutionary past, and have traced and retraced
their revolutionary bases in the woods of Manchuria, erecting
several monuments in Manchuria and Korea along the Tumen
and Yalu rivers. One of the wall pieces in the museum is a
document of the KFRAM, the Great Ten-Point Platform. The
north Koreans claim that it was written by Kim Il-sŏng, who
founded and became President of the KFRAM, and they even
have a painting in the museum portraying Kim's writing of the
Great Ten-Point Platform.

The original Great Ten-Point Platform, item 59, was written
on June 10, 1936 and was issued with two other documents,
the declaration of the KFRAM, item 58, and the by-laws of the
KFRAM, item 60. According to the original records, all three
documents were developed by a preparatory committee of three
men headed by a Nationalist revolutionary named O Sŏng-yun.
The refutation of Kim's writing of the platform is of little
importance when compared with the content of the platforms,
the declarations, and the by-laws as a whole.

The declaration of the KFRAM, which the North Koreans
have yet to make public, reflects most of the ideas and thoughts
of the authors, particularly O Sŏng-yun. The declaration praises
the patriotic but terroristic activities of the Korean national
revolutionaries by citing An Chung-kun, an assasin of Itŏ
Hirobumi, Yun Pong-kil's bomb throwing in China that killed
the General Shirakawa, crippled Mamoru Shigemitsu and others.
O himself is a well known patriot who undertook many terrorist
activities in China. One of the most audacious undertakings of

O was his attempt to assassinate Baron Tanaka Giichi. He was arrested but escaped and returned to Manchuria via Moscow. In view of the O's past undertakings, it seems clear that he authored the declaration.

The declaration strongly emphasizes the question of the Korean autonomy in Manchuria. This question is also taken up in the second point of the ten-point platform. The declaration stated that the task of attaining the Korean independence is the basic duty, but nevertheless the Koreans in Manchuria "insist first on the realization of autonomy for the Koreans in Manchuria." This definitely suggests that the KFRAM was in fact an organization that advocated little if any of the Communist cause the partisans fought for in Manchuria. These documents in general stress the importance of the autonomy of the Koreans in Manchuria and the restoration of the fatherland, but certainly none of the documents expresses even by implication the aspiration of the Communist partisans to bring about a Communist revolution in their fatherland.

It is evident from the texts of the documents that any effort to read into them, or to interpret and reinterpret, as the North Koreans do, anything that remotely pertains to a Communist partisan revolution seems futile if not absurd. These documents may be important to those Koreans in Chientao, Manchuria, who today in truth have achieved and enjoy the regional autonomy of the Koreans from the Chinese Communist regime. The documents are presented here not to refute the exaggerated claims of the partisans, but, more importantly, to raise the question of Kim's revolutionary thought patterns and ideology as manifested in these documents with his claim of authorship. If in fact Kim Il-sŏng did write the Great Ten-Point Platform, it reveals that the ideas of Kim are strongly anti-Japanese but not Communistic, patriotic but not proletarian, more terroristic than revolutionary, and that they stem more from the instigation of non-Communist Korean residents in Manchuria than from a theoretical exposition of the Communist future of his fatherland. That such thought patterns were held by Kim as late as 1936 will readily be denied by the North Koreans. As is clear from the documents, the writing is poor and is certainly not worthy of Kim's authorship.

The points advanced here are not intended to deny Kim and the partisans their relationship with the KFRAM. Some of their military undertakings were in fact conducted in conjunction with branch organs of the KFRAM; particularly well known is their cooperation with the Kapsan Operation Committee of the KFRAM. However, the KFRAM itself did not survive the Japanese punitive expeditions and not long after their establishment the Association became non-operational. A group of eight Korean partisans in northern Manchuria attempted to re-establish a branch of the KFRAM in June, 1939, and issued a letter to the Koreans there, item 61. Two of the eight men have been identified as the members of the Korean partisans in the NEAJUA, Sŏ Kwang-hae and Pak Kil-song. Recent North Korean studies on the partisan activities pay tribute to the martyred revolutionaries and their struggles, including Pak Kil-song.[3] This document is similar to some introduced earlier, being strongly anti-Japanese but not necessarily Communistic. This document and the three documents of the KFRAM are presented here to demonstrate that the KFRAM was, in fact, an organization not fit to be claimed by the Korean partisans in Manchuria as the vanguard organization of a great Korean Communist revolution.

The last document, item 62, suffers from many of the same problems of two previous documents, items 56 and 57: the problems of retranslation from the Japanese police extraction and translation of the original records. However, this document is important, even in this extracted and retranslated form, because it is the only document available that officially describes the last phase of the partisan operation. The document reveals their decision to engage in small unit operations

---

[3] Sŏ Kwang-hae was a political commissar of the first division commander Ma Teh, a Chinese, of the Sixth Army. According to recent studies in the North, Pak was once arrested for participation in partisan activities, but after his release he returned to his partisan groups and fought until his death. For the North Korean accounts of Pak, see *Hyŏngmyŏng sŏn'yŏl dŭl ui saeng'ae wa hwaltong* [The Lives and Activities of the Revolutionary Forerunners], (P'yŏngyang, 1965).

and admit the difficulties involved in large scale operations which, according to the partisans, became an "easy target for the Japanese punitive forces". The conference that produced this document was held March 13-15, 1940, coming after the death of their commander-in-chief, Yang Ching-yü on February 23, 1940. This conference marks the end of Korean partisan activities in Manchuria.

PART V

DOCUMENTS

Items 52-62

A. THE NORTHEAST ANTI-JAPANESE UNITED ARMY, 1934-36

Item 52: Declaration of the Establishment of the United Army of the Northeast Anti-Japanese United Army [NEAJUA][1]

We declare this to all the Chinese people and to all the soldiers of the anti-Japanese armed forces in the Northeast. In the name of autonomy and anti-communism, the Japanese imperialists have taken our five provinces north of the Yellow river; their talk of renewed Sino-Japanese cooperation is deceiving, for they are attempting to realize the annexation of all of China.

Recently, Japan again and again challenged the Soviet Union and, in collusion with Italy and Germany, is preparing for a war against Great Britain, the United States and France. Japan is planning on a military adventure and is certain to make a second world war, sacrificing the lives and property of 450 million Chinese people, transforming them into horses or cows and making them slaves of a ruined country.

Because every Chinese with passion and brains knows that there is no way for survival other than fighting the Japanese, there has been a general rise since last autumn of an anti-Japanese national salvation movement in all cities and ports throughout China. There have been few particulars, but the slogans, "fighting Japan means survival" and "not fighting Japan means death," express truly the unified thinking of all Chinese people. For the Chinese this is the autumn when all Chinese should organize a national army, and mobilize the people to declare war against Japan. This anti-Japanese national salvation movement is truly the key to the emancipation and free growth of the Chinese people and state.

[1] There are several documents of this nature, but this is the first declaration issued after the formation of the Northeast Anti-Japanese United Army. The declaration was issued on February 20, 1936 at a joint conference of the leaders of the first, second, and fifth armies. The document was written in Chinese, but only Japanese version is available in *Manshū kyōsan-hi no kenkyu* (Shinkyō, 1937), pp. 775-77.

Our people's revolutionary armies in the Northeast, the first, second and third armies, the anti-Japanese united army, the fourth, fifth and sixth armies together with all anti-Japanese guerrilla forces, have been fighting for four years to restore the territories of the Northeast to the Chinese fatherland.

Under the leadership of the anti-Japanese association of the northeast, we are now unifying our fronts of anti-Japanese armed comrades and anti-Japanese masses, and we vow to fight with guerrilla warfare against the Japanese imperialist policy of aggression.

In accordance with the outline of the national salvation movement throughout China today, we have organized the anti-Japanese armed forces and plan to strengthen and unify our activities. In order to establish our army we have abandoned our different names and have united under one command as the First, Second, Third, Fourth, Fifth and Sixth Armies of the Northeast Anti-Japanese United Army and the anti-Japanese regional guerrilla forces. As a unified army we declare the following:

1. The Northeast Anti-Japanese United Army is under the leadership of the Northest Anti-Japanese Association because there is a close relationship between the Army and the people's national salvation movement and politics.

2. All Communist compatriots and armed anti-Japanese soldiers, without distinction as to religion, beliefs, political grouping, social organization, sex, and wealth, must engage solely in anti-Japanese, national salvation activities. Our Northeast Anti-Japanese United Army supports the insistance of the Chinese Red Army on an anti-Japanese national salvation declaration of war against Japan with the support of all compatriots within or outside the country, regardless of their affiliation to political parties or factions.

3. The Northeast Anti-Japanese United Army prepares for the eventual organization of a national anti-Japanese united army and at the same time welcomes the participation of each anti-Japanese armed group in the Northeast in the Northeast Anti-Japanese United Army. Thus, as the government to

establish a command post of the Northeast Anti-Japanese United Army.

4. We welcome all the oppressed peoples, the Koreans, Mongolians, Taiwanese, and their organizations, to participate in the Northeast Anti-Japanese United Army. By forming a united front of weak nations against the Japanese imperialists' aggression, together with the anti-Imperialist Socialist neighboring state of the Soviet Union, with Britain, the United States, France, and all other anti-Japanese states, we must give aid and sympathy to the United Army.

5. Former spies of yesterday for our national enemy, Japan, today repent your past and surrender to our United Army with a pledge of future loyalty to the Chinese people; we welcome you to the ranks of our army, without question as to your past, for our future anti-Japanese efforts.

Dear compatriots!

The aggressive imperialist Japan is definitely not a strong country. It is merely a portion of their bureaucratic nobleman (landlords) and militarists who rampage. Confronted with the dangers facing international Capitalists, the Japanese imperialists exploit and oppress people in their own country, and, in an effort to steal markets, launch aggressive wars against other countries. Thus the Japanese imperialistic policy of aggression maintains them as parasites.

Our Chinese compatriots within and outside China must unite against this parasitic aggressive imperialism. In view of all history, past and present, east and west, and especially the recent struggle of the Ethiopian people against Italian aggression we firmly believe in the success and victory of the Chinese anti-Japanese national salvation.

February 20, 1936

Signed by

Yang Ching-yü, First Army Commander; Wang Teh-t'ai, Second Army Commander; Chao Shang-chih, Third Army Commander; Li Yen-lu, Fourth Army Commander; Chu Pao-chung, Fifth Army Commander; Hsieh Wen-tung, Sixth Army Commander; T'angyüan Guerrilla Corps; and Hailun Guerrilla Corps.

Item 53: Letter[1]

Dear Officers and Men of the Volunteer Army, National Salvation Corps, and Anti-Japanese Sanlin Company:

When the Japanese thieves occupied Manchuria with iron and blood, the patriotic comrades who did not wish to become slaves of a ruined country rose everywhere, organized various anti-Japanese armed bands, and undertook a heroic national revolutionary war, defeating the Japanese and Manchukuo army and making them retreat from their first and second great punitive expeditions. The Japanese and Manchukuo armies are making an extremely cruel advance against the anti-Japanese corps by launching a third punitive expedition on a large scale. However, the anti-Japanese people's revolutionary war is not weakened, but rather is enlarging and developing ceaselessly. The anti-Japanese corps of over 300,000 in the Northeast is always attacking military posts, destroying the enemy's transportation, military installations and military transport trains, and taking their arms, utilizing guerrilla tactics. The heightened consciousness of anti-Japanese ideas by the soldiers in the Manchukuo army is causing their continued defection. (Recently an entire detachment of the Manchukuo army defected to the People's Revolutionary army in Hunch'un). The anti-Japanese and anti-Manchukuo struggles of the people are heightening daily.

Because the various anti-Japanese corps in eastern Manchuria did not have a unified command and leadership, their activities were extremely diffuse and they did not have detailed and complete military plans. Politically unstable and lacking in

---

[1] This letter was issued by the commander Wang Teh-t'ai and leaders of the second army (Wei Chi-min and Liu Han-hsing) in June 1935 to the anti-Japanese guerrillas in Manchuria. The second army of the Northeast Anti-Japanese United Army had the largest concentration of the Koreans, and Wang and Wei were perhaps the closest comrades-in-arms of the North Korean premier and his partisans. The document was written in Chinese, but it is available only in Japanese in Hatano Ken'ichi, *Chūgoku kyōsantō-shi,* Vol. VI (1936), pp. 381-83.

determination, a few unashamed militarists, politicians, and running dogs have defected, surrendered and escaped, thus causing a partial loss to the anti-Japanese war and a temporary delay in the development of our national revolutionary war.

Now the Japanese-Manchukuo armies are attacking our anti-Japanese corps madly, utilizing all sorts of strategems and methods; they have concentrated ten thousand military forces, are utilizing all kinds of new weapons (airplanes, bombs, cannons, tanks, and poison gasses), and have encircled the anti-Japanese corps and even launched new guerrilla warfare.

By utilizing and buying the politically unstable and shallow-willed militarists, politicians and running dogs, they have tried to bring about disturbances in the anti-Japanese front and to drive the anti-Japanese united front. They have attempted to bring about conflicts among the anti-Japanese corps, thus attempting to speed our destruction. Economically, they are using a strict blockade strategy, establishing military posts, barracks and fortresses of cannon around the guerrilla districts, thus sealing off and cutting the economic routes of the guerrilla districts and preventing the anti-Japanese corps from receiving material assistances from the masses.

The past two or three years of valuable experience have taught us that the enemy is advancing by utilizing all kinds of assault strategies, by lies, provocations, alienation, and other methods. Each anti-Japanese corps has fought its own battles without a unified command and mutual contact, always receiving the enemy's attack directed at each unit. Furthermore, the politically unstable anti-Japanese corps were always deceived by the spies and running dogs of the militarists and, deceived by provocations and lies, they surrendered and even staged fights against their own comrades. These events have been important obstacles to the future of the national revolutionary war in the Northeast. The most immediate and important duty at the present stage of our anti-Japanese struggle is to unite the anti-Japanese corps in the Northeast and to organize a leadership of the anti-Japanese united army in eastern Manchuria, facilitating the anti-Japanese revolutionary war in east Manchuria by more effective organization and planning. By doing this we can drive out the Japanese thieves from the Northeast, restore the lost territories of China, and bring about ultimate victory. The platform of the anti-Japanese army is as follows:

1. To recover the lost territories by resisting the Japanese to their end, without surrender and betrayal.
2. Regardless of factional affiliation (the Volunteer Army, the People's Revolutionary Army, the National Salvation Corps, the Self-Defense Army, the Anti-Japanese Sanlin Company, the Hungchiang-hui, and others), party affiliation (the Communist Party, Nationalist Party or the Third Party), national origin (Chinese, Korean or Mongolian) and religious belief, to unite for the joint struggle for anti-Japanese national salvation.
3. To confiscate the property of the Japanese and their running dogs to meet the expenses of the anti-Japanese struggle.
4. To allow freedom of speech, publication, organization, assembly, and arming of the masses, and to join the masses for the united anti-Japanese National salvation struggle.

This army hopes that each corps will send representatives or communicate with us to discuss in detail the formation of a leadership group of the anti-Japanese united army in eastern Manchuria.

Meeting place and communication center is the headquarters of this Army.

June, 1935
Wang Teh-t'ai, Commander
Wei Chi-min, Political Commissar,
Liu Han-hsing, Chief of Staff.

Item 54: The Fighting Platform of the People's Revolutionary Army[1]

1. Japanese imperialism has dispatched its army and navy to Manchuria, stationed it here and established military barracks, airfields, railroads, wireless communication systems, ordinance depots, etc., planning to butcher the thirty million masses in Manchuria. Therefore, all people must oppose the Japanese policies, destroy their installations, and drive them out of Manchuria.

2. Incite the Manchurian army to revolt and assemble the soldiers under the banner of the People's revolutionary army; liquidate and kill the Japanese advisors and Manchurian traitors.

3. The tax system in Manchuria exploits the blood and sweat of the people, and the Japanese imperialists have confiscated the arms of the people and sapped their revolutionary resistance. They have forced on us the Japanese language and have paralyzed people's thought, and, by extending the railways, have made it convenient to murder our revolutionary comrades. Therefore, the masses must oppose taxation and all their laws.

4. Confiscate all property of the Japanese and Manchurian traitors, and use them for anti-Japanese operations and to meet the revolutionary expenses.[2]

5. Confiscate all arms and ammunition of the Japanese and Manchurian traitors and arm the revolutionary army and the general masses.

6. Mobilize the Masses and enlarge the guerrilla districts.

---

[1] This document is a platform of the Second Army which was written in March 1934 in Chinese. At the time of the writing, the commander of the Second Army was a Korean general named Chu Chin, and the document might have been simultaneously written in Korean as well. The platform is, however, available only in Japanese in *Manshū kyōsan-hi no kenkyū* (Shinkyō, 1937), pp. 166-67.

[2] Compare this article with the great ten-point platform of the Korean Fatherland Restoration Association in Manchuria, item 59. There are striking resemblance in many platforms of the NEAJUA. Kim Il-sòng claims that he has written the great ten-point platform of the Korean Fatherland Restoration Association in Manchuria.

7. The peasant committee is the real political organ of the villages and will be the basis of the future unified people's government; therefore, there must be a close relationship between the peasant committees and the revolutionary army.

8. Organize a unified front of anti-Japanese revolution among the workers, peasants, soldiers, students, and revolutionary military officers, and destroy the enemy's rear as well as main forces.

9. Oppose the Lytton Report, and unite firmly with the working masses of the Soviet Union and form a friendly alliance with them.

Item 55: Threatening Notes[1]

a. To the Heads of Tithings in Nich'iukou:

We have returned. We and our compatriots must unite and destroy the Japanese devils. Therefore, our compatriots must assist equally in the struggle for anti-Japanese national salvation; contribute guns if you have guns, people if you have people, money if you have money, and materials if you have materials. Especially we are advising the heads of tithings in your village to contribute fifty feet of satin, ten feet of yellow thin silk, fifty feet of cotton fabrics, ten balls of white thread, one copy of the Wenho [Mosquito Creek] map, and two sheets of copying paper. These must be submitted within five days as an expression of your loyalty to the anti-Japanese struggle. In case of non-compliance to this request, the people in your tithings are considered by our army as pro-Japanese, paying taxes to the Japanese, killing the Chinese, and ignoring the cause of the Chinese; and when our army comes to your village in full force to destroy the Japanese devils there will be numerous ways to take care of the people in your village. This is a special message and we do not wish any further words concerning this matter. The Second Division Command of the Northeast People's Revolutionary Army. The Second Division of the First Army of the NEAJUA.

[1] All three notes are the documents of the Second Army where the majority of the present North Korean leaders participated. Some phrases of the first document reappeared in the writings of the North Korean leaders including Kim Il-sòng. For example, "Contribute guns if you have guns, money if you have money, etc." The first note was found and reported by the Japanese police in April 27, 1936. The second note was written by Ch'oe Hyŏn, a ranking member of the Workers' Party of Korea and a general of the Korean People's Army in the North. The third note makes it clear the reprisals for non-compliance to these notes. Similar notes appeared in large numbers in 1935-36, but they are all in Japanese. See *Manshū kyōsan-hi no kenkyū*, (Shinkyo, 1937), pp. 213-17.

b. To All Householders of Sŏhwang-ku:

Because of the temporary difficulties in supplies in the region, the Chinese working masses are unable to submit grains. Therefore, we have been demanding and collecting the supplies from the masses of every national. Since it is truly unfair to the masses in general to collect the grains from them, you, the householders, must gather three and a half *sŏk* [approximately eighteen bushels] of corn, beans and other grains, and not even one grain less than ten catty of salt within two days, tomorrow and day after tomorrow, and send them to Soyuch'ŏn. If the supplies do not reach us within two days, you will be punished mercilessly.

Ch'oe Hyŏn, Chief Supply Officer, The First Division, The Second Army of the NEAJUA.

c. The Young and the Old of the Families in Tungfu and Everyone of the Wenchi Families, All Read the Following:

Five days ago this army kidnapped members of your families, but this is not to kill them. It is because we want to supplement the anti-Japanese war expenses of our army with a portion of your property. The killing is not our objective, but if you refuse to prepare the money and the goods, it is absolutely impermissible.

The big landlords are now assisting the imperialism, trusting the Japanese strength, and they exploit and oppress the people. Such cold-blooded animals unaware of patriotism and content with their slaves must rightfully be killed. Thus, if you do not belong to such group, you must come immediately and take care of the matters. We have ordered Tungfu families to bring within five days the underclothing of 150 items, and the fact that they are yet to comply is truly suspicious. This time, if you do not bring them by tomorrow noon, we will cut off ears of one of the kidnapped and will return him to your families, and if you do not comply within three days, we will cut off heads of all the kidnapped and return them to you. In short, if you love your money and goods you lose your men.

Quickly relate this to the Wenchi families. At the same time tell the families of Hsiu and Chi also that they must submit money and goods by tomorrow, and if they do not comply we will cut off the ears of the kidnapped before returning them.

Political Commissar of the First Group, First Division of the
    Second Army of the Northeast People's Revolutionary Army.

Item 56: To Dear Korean Comrades in Hunchün[1]

In the past we have done our best in the revolutionary fronts for the realization of ideals and for the workers and peasants and the Chinese Communists. But what has the Chinese Communist Party given us? Nothing but a poor name of reactionary elements. Now the Chinese Communist Party is attempting to deprive us of the record of our past struggle and efforts, and is incorporating them into their history. The reasons for the worsening of the situation arising from the *Minsaeng-dan* Incident are as follows:

1. All important officers were replaced by the Chinese.
2. All suspects of the *Minsaeng-dan* Incident are Koreans.
3. The Koreans were aroused by the severe punishment resulting from the Incident.
4. There is no effort on the part of the East Manchurian Special Committee to embrace the Koreans.
5. Inability to rely on the strength of the Chinese bandits.
6. Relative lack of progress in the revolutionary movement.
7. Neglect of the masses who are sympathetic to the Communists.
8. The Communist officers deprived us of the materials of the masses.
9. Parted from their families, many Communists were tired of life in the mountains and woods.

---

[1] This letter was written by a Korean named Yi Sang-muk, former secretary of the East Manchurian Special Committee. The letter was written in Korean and was sent to the Korean comrades on April 1, 1935, after the *Minsaeng-dan* Incident. It is available only in Japanese in *Manshu kyôsan-hi no kenkyū* (Shinkyō, 1937), p. 121.

Item 57: Concerning the Change of Direction and Rectification of Peculiarities in the East Manchurian Committee[1] (*extracts*)

According to the investigation of the delegate dispatched by the Manchurian Committee, the facts concerning the purges of the suspects in the so-called *Minsaeng-dan* Incident in Eastern Manchuria indicate a surprising number of errors in the purges, reaching up to thirty percent of the party enthusiasts, who were purged without adequate evidence. The punishments were also carried out in public in front of the masses, causing loss to the dignity of the party and arousing fear, complaints and grudges against all party organizations, thus creating an increasing number of desertions and resulting in giving the enemy materials for adverse propaganda. These are preludes to the destruction of our organization and to anti-revolutionary political change.

In the past we have interrogated, tortured and killed those who committed anti-revolutionary activities, on the basis of the opinions of our comrades. The fact that we have committed such errors in the process of the anti-*Minsaeng-dan* struggle has resulted in aiding our enemy's operations and in losing the trust of the Korean officers, and their withdrawal from anti-Japanese operations into operations to hurt Koreans for the sake of rewards is extremely discouraging to the Koreans. In view of this, it is clear that the Koreans are opposed to the Chinese officers, and such conditions have easily made Koreans suspicious of being connected with the *Minsaeng-dan.* What lessons must we learn from these experiences and what policy must we adopt? Even those who were expelled in the past but are not a running-dog of the Japanese and have maintained neutrality

[1] This document was reported by the Japanese police in Chientao on March 13, 1936. The document was first issued after a Sino-Korean joint conference held in 1935. The extracts presented here are only portions of the document which is not available in its entirety. The extracts are available in Japanese in *Manshū kyōsanhi no kenkyū* (Shinkyō, 1937), pp. 122-24.

must be approached; we must try to understand them and give them a duty to perform, so that we can investigate them through their operations.

We must not command them but rather try to explain things and ask their opinions. We must repeat these operations many times, and if we get assurance from our comrades we must notify the Special Committee and assign duties. To reenter the party, however, new references are required.

Those who were forced to join the *Hyŏpjo-hoe* should not have forgotten their revolutionary spirits. We must adopt a special method in our anti-*Hyŏpjo-hoe* policy to utilize such people for revolutionary operations in *Hyŏpjo-hoe* regardless of their membership in that organization. However, this must be a top-secret operation.

We are opposed to the *Hyŏpjo-hoe* because it is opposed to the revolution. Those who supported our revolution should welcome the opportunity to return to us from *Hyŏpjo-hoe.*

Comrades:

The *Hyŏpjo-hoe* is another variation of the *Minsaeng-dan,* and in truth continues the work of the *Minsaeng-dan.* The majority of the officers of the *Hyŏpjo-hoe* are traitors of the revolution, but we oppose the *Hyŏpjo-hoe* as an organization and do not oppose its revolutionary members.

Therefore:

1. We must continue a cordial relationship with the members of the *Hyŏpjo-hoe* who return to us and we must utilize them.

2. But we must pay considerable attention to their person, address, organization and secret operations.

3. When we transmit a message we must use a runner, and pay attention to the runner.

4. When they organize a self-defense corps or other organization with force, we must infiltrate into these organizations.

All the members of our party must understand all these conditions and carry on independent operations.

Interim Operation Committee of the East Manchurian Special
    Committee of the Chinese Communist Party.

B. THE KOREAN FATHERLAND RESTORATION ASSOCIATION IN MANCHURIA, 1936-40

Item 58: Declaration of the Korean Fatherland Restoration Association in Manchuria[1]

Let us fight for the true autonomy of the Koreans in Manchuria and for the reestablishment of a free and independent Korea! Brothers, sisters, and comrades of the proletarian class who reside within and outside our country! Our fatherland, the beautiful land of Korea that we have inherited from our forefathers, has been seized by our enemy, the Japanese, and it has already been twenty-seven years since our twenty million Koreans, who have a glorious history of five thousand years, became slaves of the Japanese. Under the unendurable Japanese policy of oppression, exploitation, and murder, carried out against the twenty million Korean people during these years, we have been kicked out of our homeland and are wandering on foreign soil, where too we have been mistreated, kicked around, arrested, and murdered. Our people's tragic situation of a slave life without a state, but with all the hardships of shedding sweat and blood, has placed us below the pathetic situation of domestic animals. After the occupation of Manchuria, as an excuse to industrialize Manchuria, the Japanese attempted to emigrate seven million Koreans to the plains of Manchuria in less than three years.

Such a plan by the Japanese is not intended to assure the livelihood of our people, but is to provide benefit for themselves by scattering the Koreans on the Manchurian plains enslaving them forever; it is intended to harm us in the midst of a whirlwind of wars to suppress the Chinese revolution and ultimately to attack the Soviet Union. The fate of our people,

---

[1] This declaration was drafted by a three-man initiatory committee of the KFRAM, consisting of O Sŏng-yun, Ŏm Su-myŏng and Yi Sang-jun. It was issued on June 10, 1936 in Korean. Although Kim Il-sŏng claims that he authored this document, he is yet to publish this document in its original Korean. It is, so far, available only in Japanese in *Shisō ihō,* no. 14 (March 1938), pp. 60-64.

particularly the Koreans in Manchuria, is in extreme danger. Our only hope at this time is to fight our enemy, and we can attain victory only through fighting them.

The patriotism and spirit necessary for the independence of our people is clearly indicated by their past and present activities. Lo, except for a few pro-Japanese factions, the people formed volunteer armies and fought bloody battles against the Japanese for three years after Korea fell, and the subsequent March First movement has astonished and attracted the attention of the whole world. There have been many fierce activities by the patriots and heroes of our country scattered in Manchuria, Shanghai, Peking, the United States and various places in Japan: particularly, the murder of Itō Hirobumi by An Chung-kŭn, the bombing of Governor-General Saitō by Kang U-kyu, the murder of General Shirakawa by Yun Pong-kil, the bombing of the Government-General by Kim Ŭi-sang, in addition to peasant disturbances, labor strikes and student boycotts in Korea. These activities and the Korean armed struggle in Manchuria are all holy struggles of the Korean people against the Japanese thieves, in order to attain our emancipation and independence.

These are the proofs that the Koreans with fierce fighting spirit and a plentiful spirit of independence will ultimately bring victory to our work of restoration of our fatherland. The sacrifices of a great many patriots, during these many years of unending activities by our heroes, have not yet brought about emancipation and national independence. One of the important causes is that there has been a lack of unity and mutual assistance under a unified policy and a lack of detailed planning of our national restoration movement. There has not been a close cooperation with other anti-Japanese nations and peoples and each unit has acted alone.

Therefore, in order to accomplish the duty of restoration of our fatherland and also to bring true autonomy to the Koreans in Manchuria, we declare to our compatriots within and outside Korea the following basic political platforms:

1. All Koreans, regardless of class, sex, position, faction, age,

and religious belief, must unite and fight the Japanese to restore our fatherland.

Our twenty-three million Koreans are suffering continuously under the oppression, exploitation, and mistreatment of Japan. Therefore, every Korean has a responsibility to fight for Korean national independence. We do not discriminate against anyone; the old and the young, the rich with their wealth, those who have food with their food, those who have skills with their skills, all twenty-three million Koreans must unite and mobilize to form the anti-Japanese restoration front, and if we face the Japanese with a united effort we can certainly accomplish our national emancipation and independence.

2. We must organize an army to fight for the true autonomy of the Koreans in Manchuria and for the restoration of the fatherland. Because Manchukuo, the Japanese thieves' running dog organization, and the traitors of Korea are our enemies, we must fight them by organizing all kinds of revolutionary armed mass organizations in addition to the struggle based on general fighting methods. We must plan and then incite a fierce battle, drive out the Japanese thieves from Manchuria and overturn Manchukuo. Only by establishing a government that assures the emancipation of the Chinese and Korean people can we realize the true autonomy of the Koreans in Manchuria, and thus facilitate the independence of Korea.

3. We fight for the realization of true autonomy for Koreans in Manchuria.

To accomplish the independence of Korea is our basic duty. However, the Koreans in Manchuria insist first on the realization of autonomy for the Koreans in Manchuria. At the same time we firmly oppose the false autonomy propagated by the Japanese thieves and their running dogs to deceive the people; we have a close relationship with the anti-Japanese masses and we will overturn the Japanese rule in Manchuria, thus bringing true autonomy to the Koreans in Manchuria and helping and participating in the holy task of restoration of our fatherland.

4. We must first solve economic problems in order to make progress in the task of bringing autonomy to the Koreans in

Manchuria and achieving our fatherland's restoration.
As to methods:

a. Unconditionally confiscate all property, shops, lands, factories, mines, and banks of the thieves.
b. Confiscate all property of the national traitors and their running dogs.
c. Receive special contributions for fatherland restoration from our wealthy compatroits.
d. Make a wide appeal to those who sympathize with and want to assist and contribute to our national emancipation movement.

5. The Korean Fatherland Restoration Committee in Manchuria is to be organized by representatives from all the patriotic organizations and anti-Japanese independence movement organizations within and outside Korea. Because this Committee is a leadership organ for leading the Korean autonomy movement in Manchuria and the Korean independence movement, and also because we have learned a lesson from our past when we lacked a leadership organ to unify and direct our various scattered activities abroad and at home, we insist on the establishment of a leadership organ, the Fatherland Restoration Association.
6. We must form a close alliance with nations and peoples who are sympathetic toward our true autonomy movement for the Koreans in Manchuria and our fatherland restoration movement, and must form a united front against our sworn enemy, the Japanese thieves.

In order to assure the victory of true autonomy for the Koreans in Manchuria and Korean independence, form a close alliance with the enemies of the Japanese thieves—China, Taiwan, Inner Mongolia—and with the oppressed peoples under the rule of Japanese imperialism. We declare to the whole world the necessity of destroying the Japanese thieves. We consider those peoples and nations which are sympathetic and willing to assist the Korean people's liberation movement as our friends, and we have no alternative but to consider those who assist and sympathize with the Japanese as our enemies.

Our patriots and compatriots! The six basic platforms stated above cannot be considered as all-inclusive of our work on fatherland restoration, but these are extremely important. Our compatriots who want to live as humans, together with all our compatriots who do not wish to live the slave life of birds and beasts! Discuss these platforms fully in the shops, barracks, railroads, newspapers, cities, schools, farms, mines, factories, and in all anti-Japanese organizations, and those who agree with these platforms help establish the Fatherland Restoration Association, and at the same time organize armed guerrillas. With the representatives from these organizations, there will be the first representative congress of the Fatherland Restoration Association to discuss the details of our movement.

Let us fight for the emancipation of the Korean people.

Let us fight for the true autonomy of the Koreans in Manchuria.

Long live the victory of Korean national liberation and independence!

The Initiatory Committee of the KFRAM
Signed by O Sŏng-yun, Ŏm Su-myŏng and Yi Sang-jun
June 10, 1936.

Item 59: The Great Ten-Point Platform[1]

1. All individuals and national organizations within or outside of Korea unite, and accomplish the emancipation and independence of the fatherland by fighting strongly against the Japanese thieves.

2. Firmly oppose the deceitful autonomy propaganda spread by the Japanese under their colonial rule; destroy our common enemy, the Japanese rule, with an elaborate alliance of the Chinese and Korean peoples, and realize the true autonomy of the Koreans in Manchuria.

3. Seize the property and arms of the Japanese and their Chinese and Korean running dogs, and organize all kinds of guerrillas to fight to the end for the autonomy of the Koreans in Manchuria and the restoration of our fatherland.

4. Confiscate all the property, including lands of the Japanese and their Chinese and Korean running dogs, and use them to meet the expenses of our anti-Japanese fight and also use a portion of them for the relief of the unemployed Koreans.

5. Abolish all petty and miscellaneous taxes, oppose the Japanese policy of economic monopoly, develop collectives in farming, and reform the daily life of the laborers, peasants,

---

[1] This platform is now available in many languages, but those versions in Russian, English and other western languages are the translations of the Korean version publicised by the North Koreans after the liberation of Korea. Although the North Korean version of the platform differs somewhat in wordings from the original platform, essential meanings of the platform are maintained. Of the sources dated earlier than 1945, only a Japanese version is available. The platform was no doubt written in Korean together with the declaration of the KFRAM, item 58, presumably by the three-man initiatory committee, but the original Korean version is, so far, not available. The English version presented here is a retranslation from the Japanese, and differ from the English version published by the North Koreans. See the Japanese version in *Shisō ihō*, no. 14 (March 1938), p. 64. Compare this with the North Korean version in Korean in Yi Na-yŏng, *Chosŏn minjok haebang t'ujaeng-sa* (P'yŏngyang, 1958), pp. 430-31. For a similar great ten-point platform written by Chon-Kwang, a close comrade of Kim Il-sŏng, on March 15, 1940, see *Shisō geppō* (Ministry of Justice), no. 77 (November 1940), pp. 129-76.

soldiers, youth, women, and all working masses.

6. Insure the freedoms of speech, assembly, organization, and all kinds of anti-Japanese struggle.

7. Oppose the slave education of the Japanese, institute free education, and establish a special people's school to enhance our national culture.

8. Abolish all military conscription systems of the Japanese among the Koreans and oppose participation in the wars of anti-revolution attacking the Russian and Chinese revolutions.

9. Oppose the white terror policy of arrest, internment, and killings under the all-inclusive Japanese laws, and free all political prisoners.

10. Ally closely with the peoples who treat the Koreans equally and at the same time maintain friendly relationships with the peoples and nations who, with good intentions, maintain their neutrality in the matter of the Korean independence movement.

June 10, 1936

Item 60: By-Laws of the Korean Fatherland Restoration Association in Manchuria[1]

CHAPTER I. Name of the Association.

Article 1. This Association is organized by the Koreans who reside in Manchuria who have anti-Japanese, Korean-independence ideas, and is named the Korean Fatherland Restoration Association in Manchuria.

CHAPTER II. Purpose of the Association.

Article 2. The purpose of the Association is to unite the compatriots who have anti-Japanese, Korean-independence ideas, and to fight the Japanese imperialist thieves to bring complete independence to Korea and to gain a true emancipation of the Korean people. In order to accomplish this purpose, the Association must fight to realize the ideas expressed in the great ten-point platform of the Association.

CHAPTER III. Membership and Admission to the Association.

Article 3. Anyone who agrees with the purpose of the Association and is willing to fight for the realization of the principles expressed in the great ten-point platform of the Association can apply, become a member, and participate in the Association activities, without regard to age, occupation, religion, wealth, and local faction.
Article 4. Admission procedures for the Association are as follows:

a. A group of individuals who want to join the Association

---

[1] The by-laws of the KFRAM was also written by the initiatory committee of the KFRAM and was adopted by the Association at its founding congress in either May or June, 1936. The document was written in Korean, but it is available only in Japanese in *Shisò ihò,* no. 14 (March 1938), pp. 65-69.

can apply jointly for membership and thus form their own branch organization of the Association.

b. Those who work in factories, schools, barracks, shops, or other collective organizations can apply for membership collectively with all or part of their members, and can become a branch organization of the Association.

c. Any number of people who recognize the purpose of this organization can organize a branch of the Association.

d. Whatever the mass organization, if they want to join the Association, they can join as an organization and become a branch of the Association.

With any of the above-stated methods, those who become members of this Association must be investigated and recognized by the higher organization of this Association.

CHAPTER IV. Organizational policy, the branches, and organizational system of the Association.

Article 5.

a. When there are more than three members of the Association in a factory, enterprise, farm, military barracks, store, or village, a branch organ is to be established, and this is the lowest basic organ of the Association. A branch organ can also be organized for the scattered unemployed and poor of cities and villages.

b. A branch organ with more than three members, but less than thirteen, shall elect a President of the organ; a branch organ with a membership of more than fifteen but less than thirty members shall elect a three-man committee and elect one of the committee members President of the organ; a branch organ with a membership of more than thirty shall elect a five-man, seven-man, or nine-man committee, in accordance with the membership, and elect a President from the committee or the branch organ.

c. When there is a large membership in a branch organ, the branch organ may organize a section, for example, a unit of a factory, class of a school, separate barracks of a military unit, or a sector of families in a village, in accordance with the necessity of the operational activities of the Association.

Article 6.

a. There shall be district organs above the level of the branch organs, and the district organs shall be organized with three or more branch organs.

b. A prefectural organ (or city organ) shall be organized above the district organs and comprise more than three district organs.

c. A provincial organ shall be organized with three or more prefectural organs.

d. The highest organ of the Association is the Congress of the representatives from all Manchuria, and its Executive Committee elected by the representative congress. The Executive Committee leads and oversees the entire operation of the branch organs and the Association.

Article 7.

a. The Committee organization at each level should use absolute democratic methods, and each branch committee shall be organized by the sectional congress or the entire representative congress, and the district committee shall be organized by the representatives of each branch committee.

b. The number of members for the committees at each level shall be decided in accordance to the actual situation at the time.

c. The Committee system shall be utilized by this Association, and the leader of the Committee shall be the President of the Association.

Article 8. Each branch organ with a membership of more than thirty and all organs above the level of district organs shall have the following officers in the Committee: i. Organizational Office, ii. Propaganda Office, iii. Office of General Affairs, iv.

Office of the Armed Force, v. Economic Office, vi. Judicial Office, vii. Youth Office, viii. Women's Office.

CHAPTER V. *Rights and Duties of the Members.*

Article 9. Duties of the Members.

a. Members of the Association shall participate in the monthly meetings and all other meetings, carry out the daily operational instructions, and follow the directives and the decisions of the Association.

b. Members shall voluntarily contribute monthly dues of three cents, to be utilized as operational expenses of the Association. (The unemployed and the poor are immune from this duty).

c. Members have a duty to propagate the ten great platforms of the Association and the political military aims of the Association, and also have a duty to recommend and introduce new members to the Association.

Article 10. Rights of the Members.

a. All members shall have the right to elect and to be elected.

b. Each member has a right to initiate ideas, to criticize the activities, to educate, and to lead the struggle to benefit the Association.

c. All members have a right to organize a branch organ and voluntarily introduce and recommend new members to their organs.

CHAPTER VI. *Temporary Secret of the Association.*

Article 11. The Association must protect the organs and its members in order to destroy Japanese imperialism and its slave rules and the organs of its running dogs. In branch organs and other organs where our operation is not as yet finalized, we must keep strict secrecy to protect our organizations from destruction by the Japanese and their organizations of running dogs.

Article 12. We must propagate the political claims of the Association widely to make them known to all our compatriots. (However, in those areas where the organizations are not as yet developed, the secrets must be kept strictly.)

CHAPTER VII. Rules and Punishments of the Association.

Article 13. Rules for the Members of the Association. Members should not operate individually, and any use of self-enlightened methods or any orders by force are absolutely forbidden. All problems of individual members should not be interfered with, except political problems concerning the anti-Japanese independence movement.

Article 14. Punishment of the Members of the Association. Any member who betrays us and conspires with the Japanese and their running dogs shall be punished and expelled; after reporting to the branch organ and through criticism of the sectional organs his activities should be made public to all members of the Association.

ADDITIONAL RULES: On Special Members.

Article 1. Special members are those who actively work in the Japanese organs and the organs of their running dogs, but who hate such a slave life without a country and truly sympathize with, cooperate and agree with the purposes and rules of this organization and want to undertake a portion of the operations of the Association. These special members must receive the special permission of the prefectural or district Committees.

Article 2. Organizational method for the Special Members.

a. When there are more than three special members in a regular branch organ, they can organize a special branch organ.

b. When a special member cannot, under a particular circumstance, leave his position, his place should be temporarily assured.

Article 3. Special Members must perform the following special operations:

a. Constantly furnish news of the enemy, particularly news concerning the enemy's plans to destroy the Association.

b. Rescue members and officers of the Association when they are arrested, utilizing all possible methods.

c. By using all kinds of methods, the special members must make it impossible for the command of the Japanese to destroy our operation, and must bring them to failure.

d. Special dues, 20 percent of their monthly salary, must be submitted to the Association regularly.

CHAPTER VIII.

These by-laws should immediately be put into operation by each branch organ, and if there is any unsatisfactory point, this must be communicated to the Association through the branch organ, and should formally be amended at the representative congress of all Manchuria. End of the By-laws.

Korean Fatherland Restoration Association in Manchuria.
Preparatory Committee of Eastern Manchuria, 1936.

Item 61: To the Korean Compatriots in Manchuria[1]

Dear Korean Compatriots in Manchuria!

Our nation, which continuously nurtured its people with over four thousand years of history, was ruined by the Japanese on August 29, 1910. Regardless of the strength of Japanese imperialism, if there had been no collusion by such national traitors as Yi Wan-yong and Song Pyŏng-jun, the annexation of Korea would not have been so easily accomplished.

Remember how pitiful has been the fate of the ruined people during the last thirty years and more. The politics of the thieves forced twenty million Koreans to an anti-Japanese political stage. The March First uprising in 1919 of all of the Korean people was a detailed reflection of the Japanese imperialists' thieving politics.

The solemn March First movement, which rose to throw off the shackles of the Japanese, was severely oppressed due to numerous internal and external shortcomings and disadvantages. The blood of the martyred comrades is painted in the villages and streets, and their intense hatred fills our heads.

Dear Korean compatriots! The fate of thirty million Chinese people in Manchuria on September 18 [1931] eight years ago was not different from that of the Koreans on August 29 [1910] some thirty years ago. Where is the difference between the harsh policy of the Korean Government-General and the righteous ruling front of Manchuria? There is a poisonous seed of destruction behind such ideas as the cooperation of Japanese, Korean and Manchurian, of friendship between Japanese and Koreans, and the ideas of great Asia. Their emigration policy of sending Korean peasants to Manchuria is a policy of expulsion

[1] This document was written by a committee of eight men on June 11, 1939. Their organization, called the Korean National Restoration Association in Manchuria, was similar to the KFRAM, but it was located in northern Manchuria. Among the eight men of the committee, two men (Pak Kil-song and Sŏ Kwang-hae) are eulogized by the North Korean leaders as their fellow partisans in Manchuria. The document was written in Korean, but it is available only in Japanese in *Tokkō geppō,* (August 1939), pp. 110-11.

and plundering, and the very lands you cultivate are farms for their serfs. To whom did you appeal when you left the warmth of your own country and crossed the river? The past Korean national liberation front has been a confrontation of the Socialists and those who purport mass movements, and the confrontations of the Nationalists and Socialists were nothing more than a suicidal movement. This is because they were poisoned by the Japanese policy of destroying Korea.

Repent and be self-conscious! The unruly political factional struggle will end in disastrous self-destruction. Because of our common enemy, the Chinese and Korean people must unite under the banner of anti-Japanese national salvation. Two long years of Sino-Japanese war have already elapsed and 400 million Chinese people have been mobilized for a prolonged war, and the fate of the present Japanese imperialists is daily approaching its end.

Victory and defeat in a war are decided by human beings. The lives of 1.6 million Japanese have already been turned into ashes in their aggressive war. The Japanese people's anti-war movement is progressing like a massive wave, and the Chinese anti-Japanese front is developing into an all-out counter-offensive. These sounds of great force make us excited.

Rise up, rise up with arms. In order to escape the oppression of Japanese imperialism unite with the Chinese people and develop a national liberation movement. Without repeating the mistakes committed by the past March First movement, wage a war to bring the last judgment to the Japanese imperialists. The day when the Japanese are kicked out of China is the day we begin the victory of Korean national liberation. In order to accomplish this the progressive elements of the Korean people in Manchuria must fight to establish a national anti-Japanese front of Koreans in Manchuria. Form a united front with the Chinese anti-Japanese movement, because the correct path to follow is to destroy the Japanese fascists to the end with a unified operation of the Chinese and Korean peoples. This is truly the traditional spirit of the great March First movement of the Korean people in Manchuria; it is the true method and the front to regain the self-determination of our people.

Dear Korean compatriots in Manchuria. Rise up, rise up with arms, and fight a death-defying battle to its end against Japanese imperialism. Establish a united front of the Korean national liberation front in Manchuria. Long live the victory of the Chinese and Korean national united front. Long live the victory of the Korean national liberation movement.

Preparatory Committee of the Korean National Restoration
  Association in Manchuria
Members:
Ku Se-rim, Chang Hung-dŏk, Chu Sŏ-bŏm, O Il-kwan, Sŏ
  Kwang- hae, Pak Kil-song, Yi T'ae, Ch'oe Ch'ong-su.
June 11, 1939

Item 62: Resolution¹

1. The fact that the party, in an effort to enlarge its party activities, has engaged solely in armed guerrilla activities since July 1936 is a grave error, and hereafter the party must deploy its main forces in operations to win the masses and to reorganize and rearrange the party, which is approaching the road to decline by being separated from the people.

2. Establish a regional operational section within the party and appoint Chŏn Kwang as its head. Several party members in good standing, with many years of experience, should be appointed to assist him in the operations among the masses.

3. At present, the operational section should be divided into Huatien, Panshih, and Chientao sections. Kim Chae-bŏm should be appointed head of the Huatien and Panshih sections and Kim Kwang-hak head of the Chientao section, and a few able members should be appointed to assist them.

4. The objective of the operation should be the peasants, but it should not be confined to the peasants only, and should be extended to any element and organization dissatisfied with Manchukuo, such as religious organizations, all lawful associations, night study groups, and even soccer associations.

5. The concentration and movement of a big company, as in the past, now provides an easy target for the Japanese punitive force; therefore, as a policy of the army, in the future the army should be divided into small units and should be scattered. Because of the Japanese punitive force's operation among the masses, the people in the guerrilla districts have since winter become distrustful of our army; thus, if possible, all small units should advance to the north and join the second and third armies.

¹This document is a resolution adopted by the Korean partisans of the First Route Army of the NEAJUA at one of the last meetings held in March, 1940. Although the circumstances surrounding the Japanese capture of this document is not clear, this document described well the last phase of the partisans' operation in Manchuria and stated their last retreat to Russia. The document may have been written either in Korean or in Chinese, but it is available only in Japanese in *Shisō geppō* (Ministry of Justice), no. 77 (November 1940), pp. 151-52.

COMMENTARY

After the Liberation, 1945-46

THE FOUR documents in this section are selected from many documents available on Communist activities during the short period immediately after the liberation in both north and south Korea, but they are somewhat incoherent. This incoherency reflects in part the diverse and dispersed Communist activities of the returned revolutionaries and of those reemerged within Korea. There were several factions that proclaimed the establishment of a Communist party. The Communists regrouped to found what they have considered a unified Communist Party in Seoul as early as September 1945. There were many problems which complicated the operation of the party, such as the occupation of the Russians in the north and the Americans in the south, the perpetual division of Korea, the operational difficulties of the Communists under the American occupation authorities, the relative indifference of the returned Communist revolutionaries toward cooperation with the leadership of the old Korean Communist Party (KCP), the problems in the coordination of the Communist activities in the north by the party headquartered in the south, and the difficulties in winning over and incorporating what were broadly termed leftist elements in both north and south.

In addition to these, the most immediate problem was the Communist participation in the first attempt by the Koreans to establish a government after the liberation. The leader in this attempt was a moderate leftist, Yŏ Un-hyŏng. Yŏ organized the Preparatory Committee for Korean Independence and later established the first Korean People's Republic. For these ventures he received support from some sectors of both Communists and Nationalists. Numerous documents relating directly to the republic are available; such as their declaration, platform, administrative policies, and the roster of the first cabinet of the republic. However, the republic was not recognized by the occupation authorities and was soon dissolved.[1]

Some supporters of the republic later formed a new political party known as *Inmin-tang* [People's Party], which became one of three major leftist parties in the liberated Korea. In addition to the Communist Party and the *Inmin-tang* there was *Shinmin-tang* [New Democratic Party], a party organized by the North China Korean Independence League (the NCKIL, the Yenan group) with its headquarters in the north. There are many documents pertaining to these groups, mostly their declarations, political platforms, and policy statements.[2] These documents are generally repetitious in nature and they contain statements expressing exuberance accompanied by strong hatred toward the defeated Japanese. These documents are always accompanied by a long list of names designating the party positions of the revolutionaries.

The first record of a document issued by the Korean Communist Party is as early as August 19, 1945, entitled "Ilbanjŏk chŏngch'i rosŏn" [on the General Political Lines] which is so far not available. The first available one was written by the chairman of the Party, Pak Hŏn-yŏng, on October 30, 1945 and is entitled "the Position of the Korean Communist Party."[3] The substance of this document is, however, a condemnation of some of the Communists who insisted on coalition by the Communists with the Nationalists in support of the institution of the Korean Provisional Government from Chungking in Korea.

There are a few documents issued by the KCP on particular issues or incidents, such as issued on the principle of the national united front and their public statement on the

---

[1] Full text of the various documents relating to the Republic are available in Korean, see among others, *Chosŏn haebang nyŏnbo, 1946,* pp. 83-39.

[2] Texts of these are available in many south Korean yearbooks. Perhaps the most authentic are the ones published shortly after the liberation. See *ibid.,* pp. 143-49.

[3] This particular document is a short seven-page handwritten document that condemned Ch'oe Ik-han, Yi Yŏng, Chŏng Paek, and others.

Chŏngp'an-sa incident.[4] These documents are short unlike most Communist documents, and to the point. They primarily discuss the position and sometimes the justification of the party on a particular issue. Surprisingly, no major statement of the party is available which discusses the general direction or policies of the party immediately after the liberation even when the operation of the Communist party was legal.

The first document, item 63, is from the north Korean branch Committee of the KCP, the P'yŏngnam Committee of the Korean Communist Party, and was issued in November 1945. It is a three-point statement of the party which accompanied its 23-point Action Platform. From the content of this document it is apparent that there was an earlier document, unavailable so far, which condemned the United States and Great Britain as well as the Korean bourgeoisie. The Communists reversed their position in the present document, admitting that they had committed errors in condemning the allies who liberated Korea. The document also refers to errors in the proposed land reform that would have confiscated all the lands of the big owners. It states that only those lands owned by the Japanese and pro-Japanese Koreans should be confiscated.

Although this document is perhaps more comprehensive than other documents available of the KCP, it is introduced here not so much to indicate retraction of Communist condemnation of the United States and Great Britain, as because the authors and the particular organization which produced the document played important roles in the development of communism immediately after the liberation. The P'yŏngnam Committee controlled the North Korean Branch Bureau of the KCP, although it was by means of assassination and systematic elimination of the leaders of the Committee that Kim Il-sŏng became the Chairman of the Communist Party in the north; some of those expressing the ideas included in the 23 point

---

[4] See for example the statements issued by the Communist Party in *Seoul Shinmun* on November 30, 1945. The *Chŏngp'an-sa* Incident involved the Communists in an affair of counterfeiting south Korean currencies. For the Communist statement on this incident see *Chosŏn haebang nyŏnbo, 1946,* pp. 242-51.

political platform later assisted Kim in the initial stage of his rule. Furthermore, under the leadership of Kim Il-sŏng, the North Korean Branch Bureau later formed a coalition with the Yenan group and eventually formed the ruling party in the north, the Workers' Party of Korea (WPK).

Despite the commonly accepted notion that the Russians masterminded the coalition between the Communists in the north and the Yenan groups, the coalition was actually initiated by the Yenan group, the North China Korean Independence League which changed its name to *Shinmin-tang*. This is made clear by the next document introduced, item 64, which is comprised of the reports of the two leaders, Kim Tu-bong of the Yenan group and Kim Il-sŏng. Kim Tu-bong stated explicitly that "the *Shinmin-tang* proposed a coalition," and that it was "received with sincerity" by the Communist Party in the north. The occasion for these reports was the preparatory conference for the founding of the North Korean Workers' Party (NKWP) in July 1946.[5] This is an important event because it marks the birth of the party which has ruled in the north for the past two decades and more. The South Korean Workers' Party (SKWP) was subsequently founded in the south and was united with the workers party of the north to produce the Workers' Party of Korea. However, the coalition of the two workers' parties came in June, 1949, after the NKWP had already held two of the four party congresses that were called in its more than two decades of existence. As the coalition came after the South Korean Workers Party had become inoperative in the south, it was more of an absorption than a coalition. The coalition did not occasion a party congress but was decided upon at one of the Central Committee meetings of the North Korean Workers' Party.

In the reports included here, Kim Tu-bong, who became the first chairman of the NKWP, made specific the reasoning behind the coalition when he stated that the Communist Party in the

---

[5] Subsequent to this conference, the first congress of the NKWP, the founding congress, was held from August 28 to August 30, 1946. This preparatory conference should not be confused with the founding congress of the WPK.

north "lacks the participation of the intellectual elements, and the *Shinmin-tang* lacks the inclusion of the laborers and peasants."[6] In contrast Kim Il-sŏng's report is a broad general statement, much like a typical Communist prolixity that says much of little substance, but his report ends with an expression of his firm belief that "within the near future several millions of the working masses will consolidate around the Workers' Party." This belief has been realized in the north.

The short declaration, item 65, was issued for the occasion. In terms of substance, the declaration is of little value, for it merely proclaims the coalition and little else. But, since the ruling Communist Party of the north traces its beginnings to this modest coalition meeting, this declaration deserves some attention.

The last document, item 66, is written by Pak Hŏn-yŏng, a Communist who is perhaps one of the few Korean Communists who entered the movement in the beginning and has lasted to participate in and was later purged by the North Korean regime. This document is concerned with the SKWP, which was formed on November 23, 1946, some three months after the formation of the NKWP. The primary reason for including this document is to give some indication of the circumstances surrounding the creation of the SKWP. It is often alleged that the formation of the SKWP was ordered by the Russians or the Communists in the north, but there is no evidence to this allegation.[7] It is also conceivable that since the coalition in the north was initiated by the *Shinmin-tang* (the Yanan group), the initiative for the coalition in the south also came from the *Shinmin-tang.* However, the last document demonstrates clearly that the coalition was proposed by the *Inmin-tang,* who organized the Korean People's Republic immediately after the liberation.

[6] According to the North Korean statistics, the NKWP had 366,339 members at the time of its founding congress in August 1946. They specified that of those members, 276,000 are from the Korean Communist Party while only 90,000 were the members of the *Shinmin-tang.*

[7] The closest to any documentary evidence of ordering the formation of the SKWP by the North is a report made by Ch'oe Ch'ang-ik on the last day of the First Congress of the NKWP, August 30, 1946, that there is a need for the Communists in the South to form a united party.

There is no logical explanation for this development, and the circumstances of the coalition still remain to be fully explained. The coalition of the three parties, the KCP, the *Shinmin-tang* and the *Inmin-tang* however, was a difficult task and the formation of the SKWP in effect produced splits in all the parties concerned. The Chairman of the SKWP, Ho Hŏn, was a moderate and under his leadership the Communists did little to advance their cause in the South. Ultimately all fled to the north. There are a few documents on the SKWP, most notably one by Pak Hŏn-yŏng called "the Manifesto of the SKWP."[8] Regardless of the verbosity and the lofty ideals expressed in the manifesto, neither Pak nor the SKWP had an opportunity to implement any of the ideas advocated in the manifesto.

Pak Hŏn-yŏng

Much like the Korean Communist movement itself, the life of Pak is filled with agonies and frustrations that ultimately ended in defeat. Pak served numerous jail terms and attained as high position as the chairmanship of the Korean Communist Party but was later purged and executed for his alleged treason against the Communist north. Pak was born on May Day, 1901, in Yesan county, Ch'ungch'ŏng Namdo. He received his elementary school education in both his home province and Seoul. He started to learn English at the YMCA in Seoul, but soon went to Tokyo for his schooling in 1920. Because of the lack of funds and difficult times in Japan, Pak stayed in Tokyo only a year, and left for Shanghai in 1921. Pak later related that during

---

[8] For the text of the manifesto see the organ of the Cominform, *For a lasting Peace, for a People's Democracy*, no. 12 (72) (March 24, 1950), pp. 3-4. It is also reprinted in D. G. Tewksbury, *Source Materials on Korean Politics and Ideologies*. It was not issued in 1950 as Tewksbury seemed to suggest, for the coalition of the South Korean Workers' Party came in June 1949 in the north. Pak Hŏn-yŏng, who was the chairman of the KCP, never held the chairmanship of the SKWP. For the documents dealing with the formation of the SKWP, see among others, *Chosŏn haebang nyŏnbo, 1946*, pp. 458-60. For the details of the development in the formation of the SKWP and the NKWP, see D. S. Suh, *The Korean Communist Movement, 1918-1948*, (Princeton, 1967), pp. 294-329.

his stay in Japan he was profoundly influenced by such Japanese Socialists as Sakai Toshihiko. However, it was at Shanghai where he was introduced to the study of socialism and participation in active Communist undertakings. He was introduced to the socialism study center in Shanghai operated by An Pyŏng-ch'an, and was reported to have attended the KUTV for a year in Russia. Pak was also registered at one time in a college of commerce in Shanghai, and continued to study English at the YMCA in Shanghai. Regardless of many different schools that Pak reported to have attended he had received at the most some two years of education in Shanghai and Russia, for he was elected by the Communists in China and was ordered into Korea in 1922. Pak was immediately arrested together with two of his comrades, Im Won-kŭn and Kim T'ae-yŏn, when entering into Korea on October 28, 1922. He served his eighteen-month jail term, and when released he worked for a newspaper, *Tong-a ilbo,* as its reporter.

Pak actively participated in the formation of the first Korean Communist Party, and became the first President of the Korean Communist Youth Association. He was arrested again in November 1925, but was temporarily released because he was said to have become mentally ill while serving his term. When he was released in August 1928, however, he fled Seoul to Vladivostok, and recuperated his health there with the assistance of the local MOPR organization. He was reported to have become a school teacher in Chientao and Vladivostok for a while, but he returned to Shanghai in 1932. The following year Pak reentered Korea but was immediately arrested again. He served another six-year sentence, but when he was released he began to reorganize the party within Korea. In the last wave of arrests in 1940-41, Pak was said to have narrowly escaped the arrest and fled to an obscure place in Kwangju where he stayed till the end of the war.

Immediately after the liberation of Korea, Pak emerged as one of the well known leaders of the Korean Communist movement, and was elected as the chairman of the Korean Communist Party. In the numerous encounters with the returned Nationalist leaders and the American occupation authority in the south, Pak lost much ground in the coalition of the leftists, and he made little or no effort to analyze the development in the north. At the time of the coalition of the leftists in the south, Pak was elected as one of two vice-chairmen of the South Korean Workers Party. When the Communist Party was banned in the south, the occupation authority issued a warrant for his arrest and he was forced to flee to the north.

Although he held several important positions in the north, such as vice-chairmanship of the Workers Party of Korea, Vice Premiership, and Minister of Foreign Affairs, Pak was not contented with the secondary roles he was playing in the north behind what he considered as a young man of little prominence, Kim Il-sŏng. The north Koreans claim that Pak and his supporters from the south instigated a coup against the government during the last phase of the Korean war, and after the cessation of the war in the Sixth Plenum of the Central Committee held on August 5-9, 1953, Pak was purged from the Party. Pak was later tried for his treason against the Democratic Peoples Republic of Korea. He was found guilty and was executed in December 1955. Among the numerous charges made against Pak, he was accused of being a spy of the Americans, and the Communists in the north cited his conversation in the south with numerous Americans including a few missionaries. Although a case can be made to clear him of his role as an American spy, his life and his Communist undertakings were exercises in futility. Pak was married to a fellow Communist female comrade named Chu Se-juk from Hamhŭng. Pak was also known as Kim Sŏng-sam and at times he used his Chinese name Wang Yang-yü.

Kim Tu-bong

Kim is regarded as one of the foremost Korean philologists. He has authored several books including one of the most popular Korean language texts, *Malbon*. Among many laureates that were conferred upon him during his life, perhaps the most fitting tribute is the doctorate in linguistics that was awarded to him in the north in 1948. Kim was born on February 16, 1889, in Kijang, Kyŏngsang Namdo. Among many Korean revolutionaries that Kijang produced, the family of Kim Tu-bong is the most famous. Kim is related to two other important leaders; Kim Yak-su (alias Kim Tu-jŏn) who presided over the founding congress of the Korean Communist Party in 1925 and also the first legislative body of south Korean government, and Kim Wŏn-bong who led the nationalist military movement in China commanding the Korean Volunteer Corps.

Kim's initial beginning of the revolutionary activities was with the Nationalists. After graduation from Pomyŏng and Chung'ang schools in Korea, Kim fled Korea at the time of the March First uprising in 1919 to Shanghai. He became a principal of a Korean school there named Insŏng school. He also organized a Korean philologers society named *I-ŏ-hoe*. As the Japanese oppression of Korea became intensified, the students of the Korean language were pushed into the revolutionary groups. Except for a brief participation in the Korean Provisional Government in Shanghai as a member of legislative council, his actual participation in the revolutionary movement is not until 1934 when he joined the Independence Party in China. There is a report of his study in Europe during the 1930's and also his voluntary participation in the Chinese Nationalist Army, but none of these can be verified. In China, however, he began working in 1934 with such Nationalist revolutionaries as Song Pyŏng-jo and Cho So-ang. He attempted to undertake an anti-Japanese struggle by mobilizing Korean students in Hopeh province, but failed. He returned to Chungking in 1939, but after a short unhappy stay there he joined the Chinese Communists in Yenan. He is reported to have become a principal of some Political Institute in Yenan, but his main activity was his creation and leadership in the North China Korean Independence League. Kim served as chairman of the League until the end of the war in China.

After the liberation of Korea, Kim, unlike other Communists who crowded the southern half of Korea, led his group to the north. He renamed his League as *Shinmin-tang*, and formed a coalition with the North Korean Branch Bureau of the Korean

Communist Party to found the Korean Workers Party. Kim was elected as the first chairman of the Korean Workers Party, and Kim Il-sŏng and Yi Sŭng-yŏp served as two vice-chairmen of the party. He held numerous political and non-political posts in addition to his chairmanship of the party. He was a member of the Presidium of the Korean National Democratic Front and became the first President of the Kim Il-sŏng University in 1946. He was elected to the First Supreme People's Assembly in 1948. When the north and south Korean workers parties merged, Kim was succeeded by Kim Il-sŏng in his party post, but he then became the President of the Presidium of the Supreme People's Assembly.

Kim has been decorated several times by the north Korean government beginning from July 1953 shortly after the Korean war when he received the award of "National Banner—First Class." He also sojourned to Europe and attended the celebration of 80th birthday of a German Communist, Wilhelm Pieck, in East Germany in 1955. Kim was reelected to his post in the Supreme People's Assembly each time, but his prominence gradually declined from the chairmanship of the party and assembly to a mere membership in the Assembly. Perhaps some of the reasons for his gradual decline can be attributed to his age, for he was in his late 60's, but he did not reach his 70th birthday when he was purged from the party in 1958.

Kim lasted much longer than most of the Communists who did not share the revolutionary past of Kim Il-sŏng, partially because he and his supporters from the Yenan group stayed aloof in the power struggle between Kim Il-sŏng and those Communists who supported Pak Hŏn-yŏng. After the third congress of the Workers Party in 1956, the Communists from Yenan unsuccessfully challenged Kim Il-sŏng. It is not clear how involved Kim Tu-bong was in this struggle, but the major force that made the challenge came from the Yenan group who supported Kim Tu-bong. He was officially charged with an anti-party, anti-revolutionary, and anti-government activities; and was purged. It is reported that Kim was sent to an obscure farm in the north as a common laborer.

Kim was also known as Kim Paek-yŏn in his revolutionary

days in Yenan, and Chu Teh-hai, a Korean in the Chinese
Communist regime representing the Koreans in Chientao, was
once a subordinate of Kim in Yenan.

Item 63:   Action Platform of the Korean Communist Party[1]

The enlarged plenum of the P'yŏngan Namdo Committee of the Korean Communist Party frankly points out the sectarian tendency in its political course due to the party's lack of correct understanding of the international situation, and after fervent criticism has decided the following:

I. Due to the lack of clear general understanding of international problems, the party has committed errors arising from a sectarian tendency, and has treated the historically progressive characteristics of the American and British allies ambiguously. In other words, the party stated in its platform to be friendly with the Soviet Union and other peace-loving democratic states, and decided to defend itself against the reemergence of imperialistic aggression.

Although these democratic states referred to in the platform are clearly the democratic states of Great Britain and the United States, they were not explicitly pointed out and were merely mentioned as democratic states. This is clearly an ambiguous way of handling the situation. Furthermore, defense against the reemergence of imperialistic aggression was clearly meant to be directed towards the aggressive characteristics of Great Britain and the United States. However, when recalling the roles the United States and Great Britain played during the past world war, it is an unshakable fact that these countries, together with the Soviet Union in a united front, destroyed the international fascist front and brought about the emancipation of the oppressed. Our Korea succeeded in its bloodless revolution by the driving force of the Soviet Union and by the contributions of Great Britain and the United States, and the revolution is now in the process of final completion. In such a context, these

[1] This document was issued on October 6, 1945. It is not clear who authored this platform. Hyŏn Chun-hyok who headed this group was assassinated on September 18, 1945. He was succeeded by Kim Yong-bŏm who also died soon after he assumed the leadership. This document is available in Korean in *Haebang ilbo,* November 14, 1945.

allied forces are our friends and we must realize that we must be friendly to these states. We are also supporters of the Potsdam Conference and at the same time must also become its practitioners. Complete liquidation of the remnant elements of international fascism and mobilization of an international democratic front are the basic articles of the Conference. In the articles of the Potsdam Conference, it is declared that those responsible for the war and the war criminals are to be punished severely. We must deeply understand that we must honor the above stated international commitment by wiping out the roots of Japanese imperialism and its running dogs and their representatives, which will mean maintaining friendly relations with all the allied nations, the Soviet Union, Great Britain, and the United States.

The fact we must clearly understand is that the Soviet Union is the ship of salvation that emancipated the Korean people and the United States and Great Britain are the victors of the war against the fascists. Therefore, we must make close ties with the allied countries of the Soviet Union, Great Britain, the United States, and China. We must endeavor to bring complete independence and emancipation, as well as freedom and happiness, to the Korean people, and at the same time we must resolve to get rid of all pro-Japanese Koreans and eliminate the Japanese imperialists from Korea as a preparation for the basic conditions of a proletarian revolution.

II. Concerning internal problems, we must form a united front of our homogeneous people, uniting all levels, all factions, and all anti-Japanese organizations within or outside Korea, and thoroughly purge the remnant elements of Japanese imperialism. Of course, the stage of the Korean revolution is the stage of bourgeois democratic revolution. After the thorough purge of Japanese imperialism there must be a land reform, and all the lands of the landlords must be confiscated and distributed to the peasants. But the present stage of the international situation requires us to purge thoroughly all Japanese imperialist elements.

Concerning our present struggle, we must prepare the way to

regiment and assemble the masses under the banner of our party, after realizing the unification of all mass organization of all parties, all factions, all organizations of all classes within or outside Korea. In other words, we can completely negate the excuse of our adversaries and their only propaganda material, which is their accusation that the Communist Party is interfering with the unification effort within the country, and at the same time this gives the masses time to understand the historical mission and righteousness of communism and prevents them from running to our enemy's camps, and we can expose the deceitfulness and reactionary characteristics of our opposition's camps. Only through these struggles can we expose the Capitalists' pro-Japanese face and can we detach the masses from their influence. When we have completely purged the remnant elements of Japanese imperialism, the land owners and the Capitalist class, the objectives of our struggle, cannot but be thrown off and wiped out.

III. Concerning the recognition of private property and private land, when in the past we advocated the control and confiscation of the land of the big land owners, it was due to a lack of correct understanding of the international situation. To purge the pro-Japanese elements was the correct political course and to unite with non-pro-Japanese national organizations was also correct. Then we must recognize private property and the private lands of the non-pro-Japanese groups. Therefore we must retract our statement in the land reform platform about control and confiscation of the lands of big landowners. Thus the amended platform is as follows:

Action platform of the Korean Communist Party.

1. Convene a people's representative congress and establish a People's Republic.
2. The people must unite to form a national union of all factions, organizations, and groups of all levels, and they must thoroughly purge the remnant elements of Japanese imperialism.

3. The people shall have freedom of speech, publication, assembly, organization, and religion, and men and women over twenty years of age shall have the right to elect and be elected.

4. Friendly relations should be established with the Soviet Union, the allied countries of Great Britain, the United States, and China, and all democratic countries.

5. Establish a universal military conscription system.

6. Confiscate and nationalize all means of production in industries transportation, mines, manufacturing factories etc., that were owned by the Japanese imperialists, pro-Japanese Koreans and all other reactionary capitalists.

7. Confiscate all facilities of Japanese imperialism and nationalize them.

8. Confiscate all the lands owned by the Japanese imperialists, pro-Japanese Koreans, and reactionary landlords, and nationalize them and distribute them free to the peasants.

9. The lands owned by the Japanese and the office of Oriental Overseas Affairs should be confiscated and nationalized. Distribute these lands to the poor peasants in accordance with their ability to cultivate them, and the tenant fee for the year is to be based upon the 3-7 system.

10. All means of production that are confiscated should be nationalized and administered by the laborers. All confiscated lands are to be distributed free to the peasants.

11. The production plans should be governed by national planning and production plans should be made in such a way as to increase production.

12. Korean industrialists and businessmen shall have free enterprise under the leadership of the people's political commissar.

13. Institute an eight-hour working system and establish a system of minimum salary to guarantee the livelihood of the workers (institute social security that includes the unemployed). The state guarantees the job of the workers and the unemployed.

14. Establish an iron rule of conscription.

15. Abolish immediately all colonial slave education, institute compulsory education, and revive the national culture.

16. Abolish all imperialistic taxes and institute an income tax that guarantees the income and livelihood of the people.

17. Invalidate all bonds issued by the Japanese banking organizations and usurers.

18. Institute social security to insure the sick, the old, and helpless people.

19. Abolish all semi-feudal slave systems of prostitution and the slave trade.

20. Reform the treatment of the cultured and the skilled.

21. Abolish all evil laws that infringe upon human rights, and abolish slave and forced labor.

22. Establish a national security system for unemployed workers and prohibit child labor.

23. Complete the institution of safety regulation in mines and other enterprises, and prohibit the excessive labor of women.

Item 64: Reports[1]

A. Report by Kim Il-sŏng

Comrades!

Today the unification of our parties has a historically important significance. The complicated and delicate state of affairs required a joint meeting of the General Committees of the Korean *Shinmin-tang* [New Democratic Party] and our Korean Communist Party. At this meeting we have agreed on our fundamental views and discussed the coalition problems of the two parties.

Democracy in Korea has developed under complicated situations. In North Korea, where the Red Army is stationed, the North Korean Interim People's Committee is already established, because the capabilities of the people are highly developed; all industries, railways, transportation, banks, etc. are rapidly being reconstructed. In the political, economic and cultural aspects of Korean society, the old feudalistic systems have been thoroughly abolished by the victorious completion of land reform, by the establishment of democratic labor laws and a tax system for agricultural products, by the establishment of laws concerning the equality of sexes, etc. The path to free development has been opened, and the material conditions for the establishment of a democratic Korea have been prepared. All these basic democratic reforms have been developed by the coalition of the laborers, peasants, intellectuals, and the working masses in North Korea, and there are already five million organized masses behind the democratic national united front. However, the democratic movement in Korea is facing

---

[1] These two reports were made by Kim Il-sŏng and Kim Tu-bong at the preparatory conferences for the founding of the North Korean Workers' Party held on July 29, 1946. These reports were written in Korean, and they are available only in Korean. See *Chosón haebang nyŏnbo, 1946* (Seoul, 1947), pp. 456-57. A similar statement made by Kim Il-sŏng under different title is also available in Korean in one of the earlier newspapers published by the north, *Chŏngro*, July 31, 1946.

the stubborn resistance of domestic reactionary factions. In this critical international and domestic situation, what shall we do? The domestic situation demands broader and more unified activities and we hope for a greater consolidation of the masses. This mass movement can be attained in the unification of the democratic parties of the working masses. We have agreed in principle to a coalition of the North Korean Communist Party and the Korean *Shinmin-tang* to form a unified workers' party of the masses. This is the most correct and necessary way. We have only a small number of the working masses that has potentially unlimited strength. Our tactics must not be merely a dead formula; they must change in accordance with new situations and circumstances.

Under such a situation, full-scale coalition of the two parties is the necessary direction. The members of both parties must understand the situation fully and must uphold the platform and policies of the workers' party with mutual understanding and acceptance. We firmly believe that within the near future several millions of the working masses will consolidate around the workers' party.

B. Report by Kim Tu-bong

We have assembled here today to discuss the problems of the coalition of the North Korean Communist Party and the Korean *Shinmin-tang*. Today, when we once again greet that historic day of August 15 in great, Red Army-occupied North Korea, we have instituted and are practicing the historic democratic tasks that we can be proud of throughout the world. But the reactionaries in South Korea rave in their death agonies, trying to colonize Korea once again as part of the foreign reactionary forces, interfering with national unification and destroying the democratic independence of Korea. In order to wipe out these reactionaries within and outside Korea, we must strengthen the democratic forces, and to this effort the Korean *Shinmin-tang* has come to the following conclusion.

1. The new situation requires new tactics and strategy and

the new tactics and strategy in turn require a new organizational system.

2. The new development of the Korean *Shinmin-tang* was greatly assisted by the friends of our party, the North Korean Communist Party. But in the process of the development of the Korean *Shinmin-tang* it was unavoidable to have some mutual friction, though it was very slight, and the shortcomings of the organizational systems of both parties can be pointed out. We can find the cause of such friction in the fact that the North Korean Communist Party lacks the participation of the intellectual elements, and the Korean *Shinmin-tang* lacks the inclusion of the laborers and peasants. In order to eliminate any such unnecessary separation and friction, the Korean *Shinmin-tang* proposed a coalition with the North Korean Communist Party.

This proposal was received with sincerity by the North Korean Communist Party, and we have come to have this historic meeting today. We must overcome the following points in carrying out this task:

a. We must make the members of both parties and the general masses have a correct understanding of the historic significance of the coalition of the two parties.

b. The coalition of the two parties is not to be interpreted as an absorption of one party by the other, but rather as an unconditional coalition based upon the historical necessity of the present stage.

Item 65:   Declaration of the North Korean Workers' Party[1]

The complex and delicate domestic and international situation requires wider alliances and a strengthening of the democratic forces of the North Korean working masses, who are the main force in and the basis of the establishment of a democratic Korea. In order to attain this purpose, coalition of the people's political parties which protect the interests of the working masses in North Korea is inevitably required. Confronting this critical situation, the Central Committees of the North Korean Communist Party and the Korean *Shinmin-tang* [New Democratic Party] have united the two parties and plan to organize the North Korean Workers' Party, and proclaim a struggle to realize the following tasks that confront us.

1. Promote the establishment of an independent and democratic Korean state.
2. Wipe out all reactionary forces and struggle to attain the mission of the Workers' Party.
3. Strengthen the land reform in North Korea and institute land reform throughout Korea; nationalize industry, transportation, banks, etc.; institute democratic labor laws.
4. Reconstruct the national economy and develop national industries, and rapidly upgrade the level of material living standards.
5. Develop the national culture and raise cultural standards.
6. Strengthen the friendship with the states that struggle for world peace and with peace-loving democratic states.

The mission of our North Korean Workers' Party will be to attain national independence, establish a truly democratic state, and make Korea able to participate with other advanced

[1] This declaration was issued on the last day, July 29, 1946, of the coalition conference. This document should not be confused with the more famous first manifesto of the WPK written in August 1946. This document is available in Korean in *Chosŏn haebang nyŏnbo, 1946* (Seoul, 1947), pp. 457-58.

countries in the struggle for world peace. We trust that all members of both parties will support the decision concerning the establishment of the Workers' Party, a decision reached by the Central Committees of the North Korean Communist Party and the Korean *Shinmin-tang*.

We trust that the members of the Workers' Party will make a sacrificial struggle for the realization of the mission of the party.

Item 66: The Coalition of Three Democratic Political Parties in South Korea[1]

The Korean Communist Party, the Korean *Inmin-tang* [People's Party], and the South Korean *Shinmin-tang* [New Democratic Party], which struggled and are still struggling courageously against all the reactionary forces for the independence of democratic Korea and for the benefit of the working masses in Korea, have decided on a coalition of the parties to strengthen the forces of the democratic national front and to consolidate the democratic forces to protect the benefits of the working masses. At the present stage of the development in Korea, the stage of democratic development, there has been a discussion among the leaders of the important parties which did not have significant differences in their action platforms for the working masses, to form one big coalition political party, but it has not materialized.

At the same time, in North Korea the North Korean Workers' Party has been formed for the benefit of the working masses by coalition of the North Korean Communist Party and the *Shinmin-tang;* I have pointed out the characteristics of this coalition as a consolidation and strengthening of the democratic forces in North Korea. The trend for a coalition that was prevalent in South Korea has been facilitated by the coalition of the two big political parties in North Korea, and several days ago the *Inmintang* proposed a coalition in the South. As a result of our party's careful consideration of the proposal, we have decided to accept the proposal in view of the general situation. Thus, at last the coalition and unification movement of the three great parties, the Communist Party, the *Inmin-tang,* and the *Shinmin-tang* is developing. This has an important and

[1] This document was written by Pak Hŏn-yŏng, the chairman of the Korean Communist Party, 1945-46, on August 6, 1946. Although it was no doubt written in Korean, the document was not published in Korean. It appeared only in Japanese in the journal of the Japanese Communist Party, *Zen'ei*. See the full text in *Zen'ei*, no. 13 (February 1, 1947), pp. 11-12.

epoch-making significance in the process of the establishment of a democratic state in Korea.

It is already almost one year since the Japanese imperialists were kicked out of Korea by the victory of the democratic allies. The democratic movement has developed rapidly throughout Korea. People's Committees, as organizations of the people themselves, by the creative will of the people sprouted like tender shoots after a rainfall everywhere in both North and South Korea. The Korean Communist Party, which waged a determined underground anti-Japanese struggle for the past several decades, is now advancing legally and the working masses are concentrating on its periphery. Other friendly democratic parties, the *Inmin-tang* and *Shinmin-tang,* were organized by the comrades who returned from abroad or emerged from their underground activities. Other democratic organizations of the workers, peasants, women, youth, cultural groups, and all sectors of society completed their organization, and several million organized masses south of the 38th parallel are united under the democratic national front. The democratic national united front is also organized north of the 38th parallel and through five million organized masses the political influence of democracy is penetrating widely among the people. Thus, within a short period of less than a year after the emancipation, our people, under the leadership of the Communist Party and other democratic parties, have completed the preparations for the establishment of a democratic provisional government in Korea as directed by the three-power decision.

When the Russo-American joint Committee to establish a democratic provisional government was convened in accordance with the three-power decision, these democratic forces throughout the North and South actively supported the joint committee and cooperated extensively with the works of the Committee. No efforts and sacrifices were spared in order to make clear the true intention of the three power decision, which is the correct decision for the independence of a democratic state in Korea. In spite of this, because of the right-wing schemes to oppose the three-power decision, the joint Committee was adjourned for an indefinite period. This is truly unfortunate for our people. Since then, the heads of the reactionaries did not repent opposing the three-power decision and have maintained the attitude of the anti-allied powers. Thus the important problem of the people's livelihood, requiring immediate solution such as land reform, labor laws, and economic reconstruction, the food and housing problems, the problems of inflation and others, have mounted, and our people have fallen into distress. The reactionary forces are trying to destroy the paths to world peace set by the three-power cooperation of the Soviet Union, Great Britain, and the United States, and are attempting to take the world and the human race into a new war.

At this time when complex and difficult domestic and international situations surround Korea, the three big parties, the protectors of the benefits of the working masses and the champions of the struggle for the true democratic independence of Korea, have as their basic action platforms the winning of democratic independence through the liquidation of the remnants of feudalism and the complete mop-up of all remnant forces of Japanese imperialism. We have earnestly practiced these action platforms. These three big parties are the parties centered around the workers, peasants, city dwellers, intelligentsia, and others. Therefore, coalition of the three parties is possible at the present stage with respect to platforms, practices, and organizations, and in view of the situation today it is necessary and correct. Our organization is not a mechanical organization, but an alive organization for practical struggle. The new situation requires new tactics and strategy and to require a new organizational system occurs not only in military affairs but also in political affairs. The complex and difficult domestic and international situations of today require the emergence of one big truly democratic party in the struggle to protect the benefits of our working masses. The coalition of the three parties is the expression in detail of this need. In other words, the domestic and international situation that surrounds Korea demands the unified action of a wider range of people and of the working masses and also a firm unity of the masses in general. The coalition of the three big parties that are the working people's party and the truly democratic parties is demanded to prevent the alienation, slanders, and schemes of the reactionary elements against our democratic camp. This coalition does not mean a singularization of all left-wing parties to make one party. Of course, it is necessary to have a multi-party system under the present circumstances.

Under the demands of the present situation our party has decided on this coalition for the democratic independence of Korea, for the progress of the people, and for the benefit of the working masses. In view of what might be called the independent revolutionary tradition of our party during the past several decades, is this not a significant change? However, because our party is the party of the working people, the patriotic party, and the party of democratic independence, we are not refusing any struggle to attain our purpose and are not refusing ány cooperation whatever. Our party's acceptance at this time of the coalition proposal of the *Inmin-tang* will be a good example to destroy with live facts the counter-propaganda of the reactionary group's accusation that our party is sectarian. Our party has always cooperated with parties that have the same platforms concerning our democratic duties and with those which faithfully practice them, and we are willing to cooperate at any time with such true democratic parties. The coalition of the three parties at this time will complete the leadership organ of the Korean people's great progress; it will establish the basis of Korean national unification and will develop the comprehensively blended special characteristics of the three parties. At the same time, it will be the great bulwark against all reactionary forces and be the vanguard standing at the head of the struggle. Thus, for the first time the establishment of a people's political regime by the people, which all our nationals are longing for, will make forceful and valiant progress.

We trust that the coalition of the three parties, which has such great significance, will receive the direct support not only of all our party members but also the party members of our friends' parties. Some of our compatriots who have been deceived by the leaders of the reactionaries, after criticizing the mistakes of these leaders, wish to join our party that is to be newly organized, the people's party, the patriotic party and truly the party for democratic independence. We will extend our hand to them and hope to cooperate with them in the struggle for the great task of building a free, wealthy, and democratic Korea. No matter how severe the storm, there always comes a time of clearing. Comrades! Let us dash on against the storm together, to fight for and win our historically inevitable democratic independence.

Only those events related to the Korean Communist movement are listed below. Some major events of the Nationalist movement are included only if they have relevance to the Communists. Numerous minor labor strikes and peasant disputes are included, for some of these were effected by the Communists. In an effort to study the revolutionary activities of Kim Il-sŏng in Manchuria in the 1930's, some of his partisan activities, important political and military campaigns claimed by North Korean historians, are included. Some obscure and fragmentary facts of the underground activities of the Communists are also included to give relatively detailed accounts of the Communist and leftist movement, but no attempt is made to cover the Korean revolution as a whole.

1917

March. A branch of the Russian Communist Party was established in Harbin and began propagating communism to the Koreans in Manchuria.

May. The First Congress of the Korean revolutionary organizations in Manchuria and Russia was held at Nikolsk-Ussuriisk.

August. The Korean Socialist Party was organized by Shin Kyu-sik. Shin organized this party to send representatives to Stockholm and to plead Korean independence.

1918

January 22. A Korean section of the Russian Communist Party in Irkutsk was organized by Nam Man-ch'un, and this section later became the basis of what is known as the Irkutsk group.

May. The Second Congress of the Korean revolutionary organizations in Manchuria and Russia was held in Vladivostok.

June 26. The first Socialist organization, the Korean Socialist Party, was organized in Khabarovsk by Yi Tong-hwi.

November. The New Korea Youth Corps was organized in Shanghai by Yŏ Un-hyŏng and Cho Tong-u.

1919

January. Strike was staged by the transportation workers at Sariwon, Hwanghae-do.

February 8. Several hundreds of the Korean students in Tokyo staged a demonstration. This demonstration later led to the March First uprising in Korea.

February. Strike of the workers at Korean Leather Company occurred in Yŏngdŭngp'o, Kyŏnggi-do.

March 1. Thirty-three of nationally prominent religious leaders demanded an independence of Korea from Japan, and issued a declaration of independence which led to the March First uprising, a nationwide resistance against the Japanese. The demonstration resulted in some 7,000 Koreans dead and 50,000 Koreans imprisoned.

March 2. The Korean Socialist Party in Khabarovsk convened a special meeting at New Korea Village in the outskirts of Vladivostok.

March 2-3. The third Communist International was found and its First Congress was held. One Korean participated.

March. Widespread demonstrations and riots continued throughout Korea including such incidents as a strike at Seoul Electric Company, the riots of the mine workers at Ch'ŏn'an, Ch'ungch'ŏng Namdo, and the brutal suppression and massacre of the people by the Japanese police in Suwon, Kyŏnggi-do.

April 25. Yi Tong-hwi moved the headquarters of the Korean Socialist Party from Khabarovsk to Vladivostok and renamed the organization as Koryŏ Communist Party.

April. Streetcar operators in Pusan staged a general strike.

May. The *Ilse-tang,* another socialistically oriented organization, was organized in Vladivostok by Chang To-jŏng and Kim Chin.

August 25. Krepknov who helped Yi Tong-hwi and the Korean Communists to organize their first party was captured and was executed at Omsk.

August 30. Yi Tong-hwi moved to Shanghai to join the Korean Provisional Government, and moved his Communist organization to Shanghai. Subsequently Yi became the first Premier of the Korean Provisional Government.

September 2. As a result of the March First uprising, the Japanese Governor General instituted what is known as the "Cultural Policy" to ease the discontentment of the Korean people, and under this policy numerous organizations and journals were allowed to appear.

September 5. At Irkutsk, a new Korean Communist organization, the All-Russia Korean Communist Party was organized by Kim Ch'ŏl-hun and O Ha-muk with the assistance of an agent from the Comintern named Shumiatsky.

December 2. A labor organization of the Koreans in the United States, the *Nodong sahoe kaejin-tang,* was organized in San Francisco by Yi Sal-um.

1920

March. Voitinsky is reported to have arrived in Shanghai and conferred with the Korean Communists, Yi Tong-hwi and Pak Chin-sun.

April 11. The first Korean labor organization entitled *Chosŏn Kongje-hoe* was organized by Pak Chung-hwa and Pak Ui-kyu. One of its founders, Ch'a Kŭm-bong, later became a head of the Fourth Party in 1928, but the organization in its early stage was dominated by the Nationalists.

April. Two important newspapers, *Tong-a ilbo* and *Chosŏn ilbo,* was first published.

May. An organization entitled *Ch'ŏlhyŏl-tan* was organized with sole purpose of destroying the newly created Korean Provisional Government in Shanghai.

July 17—August 7. The Second Congress of the Comintern was held in Petrograd and Moscow. Pak Chin-sun led the Korean delegation to this congress.

September 15. Mun ch'ang-bŏm, former Yi Tong-hwi's minister of transportation in the Provisional government and head of the Korean National Council, issued a declaration in support of the Communists in Irkutsk.

October. A group of Korean Communists in Shanghai led by Pak Chin-sun sent an agent named Yi Chŭng-lim to summon a Japanese Communist, Ōsugi Sakae, to Shanghai for the Propagation of communism in the Far East.

November. The Korean Youth Federation Association bringing together some 133 youth organizations throughout Korea with membership of over 30,000, was organized.

1921

January 10. Two Korean Communist agents, Kim Rip and Pak Chin-sun were reported to have brought funds from the Comintern to Shanghai, and with this fund the Korean Communist Party called a preliminary party meeting.

January 24. Yi Tong-hwi resigned his post as a Prime Minister of the Korean Provisional Government.

February. Mun Ch'ang-bŏm is reported to have concluded a secret agreement with the Russians in Chita.

May 10. The people's representative congress of the Korean Provisional Government was held and the Congress condemned the Communist Party.

May. The first party congress of the Korean Communist Party was held in

Shanghai, and the first manifesto and platforms of the party was issued.

May. Ōsugi Sakae, a Japanese Communist, came to Shanghai.

June 22–July 12. The Third Congress of the Comintern was held in Moscow. The Shanghai group represented the Koreans.

June 28. The Alexeyevsk Incident occured near the railway junction in Svobodny. The incident occasioned a military confrontation of the two rival Communist factions, the Shanghai and the Irkutsk groups.

June 29. The Irkutsk group organized a Korean Communist Youth Corps in Shanghai in opposition to Yi Tong-hwi.

July 20. Yi Tong-hwi left Shanghai for Moscow allegedly to plead his case on the Alexeyevsk Incident.

August 6. A branch organization of the Shanghai group was organized in Manchuria under the leadership of Yi Chung-jip.

September. More than five thousand transportation workers in Pusan staged a general strike demanding better working conditions.

September. A Nationalist leader, Ku Ch'un-sŏn, issued a declaration denouncing the Irkutsk faction and Mun Ch'ang-bŏm for his role in the Alexeyevsk Incident.

September 30. The Korean Revolutionary Military Government Council, the Irkutsk group, issued a reply, clarifying their role in the Alexeyevsk Incident.

November. A preliminary conference was held in Irkutsk for the Far Eastern Toilers' Congress under the direction of Shumiatsky.

November 15. The three-man investigation committee of the Comintern issued a statement on the Alexeyevsk Incident.

November. The Korean anarchists in Tokyo organized *Hŭkto-hoe,* some members of this organization later formed the first Socialist organization of the Koreans in Japan.

December. Mun Ch'ang-bŏm was reported to have concluded a secret agreement with the Russians in Siberia to help propagate communism and was said to have received three and a half million yen.

December. Nationalist leaders including Yi Pŏm-un and Kang Ku-u joined the Communists and pledged their support to the cause of communism after hearing the failures of the Washington Conference to solve the problems of the Far East.

1922

January 21–February 2. The First Congress of the Toilers of the Far East was convened. The Korean delegation composed primarily of the Irkutsk group represented the Communists.

January 30. A socialist organization called *Musanja Tongji-hoe* was organized in Seoul by Pak Il-byong.

February 8. Kim Rip was assassinated in Shanghai.

February. A general representative congress of the Korean Provisional Government was convened in Shanghai.

March 31. Two leftist organizations, the *Shin'in Tongmaeng-hoe* and the *Musanja Tongji-hoe*, merged to form a new organization, *Musanja Tongmaeng-hoe*.

April. Three important Korean Communists; Pak Hŏn-yŏng, Kim Tan-ya, and Im Won-kŭn, were arrested. They were returning to Korea from Shanghai to organize a Communist party.

April 22. The Comintern issued a directive to the Korean Communists on the Alexeyevsk Incident.

May 10. Yi Tong-hwi is said to have arrived in Moscow together with Pak Chin-sun and Wilhelm Pieck. Yi was reported to have met Lenin and discussed the Communist movement in Korea.

June. The secret agreement was said to have been concluded between the Korean revolutionary organizations and the Far Eastern government in China.

August. The Proletarian Youth Association was established.

October 10-15. The Irkutsk and Shanghai groups attempted a coalition of all Korean Communists abroad at Blagovshchensk.

October. The Korean Federation of Labor, *Chosŏn nodong tongmaeng*, was organized.

November 5–December 5. The Fourth Congress of the Communist International was held. There is no record of Korean participation.

November 17. The Korean Communists in the Russian Maritime Province and the Russian army in Vladivostok were reported to have concluded an agreement.

December. Some 1,500 peasants in Sunch'ŏn, Chŏlla Namdo, were involved in a tenancy dispute.

1923

January 3. The First National Representative Congress of the Korean Provisional Government was held in Shanghai.

March 24. The First Congress of the Korean Youth Association was held in Seoul.

April 24. *Hyŏngp'yŏng-sa* [Social Equality Association] was found in Chinju by a group of butchers.

May. Kim Chae-bong who later became the first chairman of the Korean Communist Party successfully entered Korea to organize a party in Seoul.

May 20. The Saturday Association *[T'oyo-hoe]* was organized by a group of Communists in Seoul.

June. *Puksŏng-hoe* [The North Star Association] was organized by the Korean leftist students in Japan.

July 7. *Shinsasang yŏn'gu-hoe* [The New Thought Research Association] was organized by a group of Communists in Korea.

August. Some 1,700 textile workers staged a general strike in Pusan.

August. Over one thousand textile workers staged a general strike in P'yŏngyang.

September. Kim Chŏng-kwan and nine other comrades were arrested entering Korea for the purpose of organizing a Communist party in Seoul.

1924

January. Over ten thousand peasants in Chŏlla Namdo staged an anti-Japanese demonstration.

February. The tenant farmers of Hwangju, Hwanghae-do, were involved in the tenancy disputes with Hŭngŏp Land Company.

February. Socialist students returning from Japan organized a leftist organization, Shinhŭng Youth League.

March. Over 2,700 workers of mill factories in some twenty places in the city of Kunsan, Chŏlla Pukto, staged a general strike.

April 17. The Korean Federation of Labor and the Korean Federation of Peasants merged to form a unified organization, *Chosŏn Nonong Ch'ong Tongmaeng* [Korean Federation of Workers and Peasants].

April 21. All Korean youth associations were united and organized the General Federation of Korean Youth.

May. *Tong'u-hoe* was organized for the leftist women in Korea.

June 17–July 8. The Fifth Congress of the Comintern was held in Moscow. No Korean participated.

June. Two important Korean Communists, Chŏng Chae-tal and Yi Chae-bok, were arrested entering Korea from Vladivostok.

September. Korean Peasant Union was organized.

November 19. The New Thought Research Association, *Shinsasang Yŏn'gu-hoe,* changed its name to Tuesday Association, *Hwayo-hoe,* that became the most powerful group of the Korean Communists.

November. The North Wind Association, *Pukp'ung-hoe,* was organized by the returned students from Japan. This organization succeeded *Puksŏng-hoe* and *Kŏnsŏl-sa.*

1925

January. The January Association was found in Tokyo by a group of leftist Korean students in Japan.

January. The Socialist Thought Research Association was established in Haeju, Hwanghae-do.

January 3. Strike was called by the transportation workers in Seoul.

April 17. The first Korean Communist Party was found in Seoul. Kim Chae-bong became its first chairman.

April 18. The first Korean Communist Youth Association was established in Seoul. Pak Hŏn-yŏng was elected to head the Association.

April. Cho Pong-am, a delegate of the Korean Communist Youth Association left Seoul for Moscow to seek recognition of the Korean Communist Youth Association in the Young Communist International.

June. The Korean Communist Youth Association sent 21 students to the KUTV.

June. Cho Tong-u, the official delegate of the Korean Communist Party left Seoul for Shanghai and for Moscow to seek admission to the Comintern.

June 11. The Mitsuya Agreement was concluded to curb the traffic of the recalcitrant Koreans from Manchuria.

July. The Korean Proletariat Artist Federation, commonly known as the KAPF, was organized. The Association declared its official founding date as August 23, 1925.

August 20. Cho Pong-am was reported to have gained the recognition of the Korean Communist Youth Association from the Young Communist International.

October. The Profintern, the Red International of Labor Unions, is reported to have sent 60,000 rubles to Seoul as a relief fund.

October. Over 700 transportation workers in Taegu staged a strike.

November 22. The First Korean Communist Party Incident occured in a border town, Shinŭiju, and as a result some 67 important Communist leaders were arrested.

November 27. Pak Hŏn-yŏng, the chairman of the Korean Communist Youth Association was arrested together with another Communist named Kim Kyŏng-sō.

December 19. Kim Chae-bong, the chairman of the Party, was arrested.

1926

January 3. Proletarian Women's League was organized in Seoul.

February. The Second Korean Communist Party was organized, and Kang Tal-yŏng was elected its chairman.

February. The Korean Communist Party was reported to have been admitted to the Comintern between the Sixth Plenum of the Executive Committee of the Comintern which was held in February and March and Seventh Plenum which was held in November and December of 1926.

March. Over three thousand workers in more than nine rice mills in Inch'ŏn staged a general strike.

April. *Chōng'u-hoe* was organized. This organization was initiated by the
returned students from Japan, attempting to rid all factional
affiliations and proposing "Change of Direction" of the Korean
Communist Movement.

April. Textile workers at Fukushima Spinning Mill staged a strike against
the Japanese management.

June 10. Mass demonstration, known as the June 10 demonstration,
broke out in Seoul. This demonstration was the beginning of the fall
of the second party. Chairman Kang and some 135 Communists
were arrested.

July. The Korean Communist Party and the Korean Communist Youth
Association established its Manchurian General Bureau of the
Korean Communist Party.

October 28. The Manchurian General Bureau of the Korean Communist
Party established an Eastern Manchurian Sectional Bureau.

November. After the fall of the second party, the returned students from
Japan began to organize the third party.

November 15. The *Chōng'u-hoe* declaration was issued.

1927

January 14. A new united front organization, *Shin'gan-hoe,* was organized, and the organization was formally announced on February
15.

April. The Japanese General Bureau of the Korean Communist Party was
established.

May 13. The so-called Kim Ki-jŏng incident occured. Some 1,000 men
attacked the police stations in T'ongyŏng, Kyŏngsang Namdo.

May 27. A women's organization called, *Kŭn-u-hoe,* was organized.

May 30. Seamen's riot broke out in Cheju island.

August 12. Group of farmers organized a league of non-payment of
tenant fees in Muan county of Chŏlla Namdo.

September. The Korean Federation of Workers and Peasants split into
two separate organizations, the Korean Federation of Labor and the
Korean Federation of Peasants.

October 2. The First Chientao Communist Party Incident occurred. The
Tuesday Association group suffered significantly and lost control of
the Manchurian General Bureau.

November 6. A secret organization of the leftist students in Taegu was
uncovered.

December. The Kaesŏng Communist Party Incident; an incident caused
by Kim Chŏng-hwan, a returned student from the KUTV, who
attempted to organize a party in Kaesŏng.

1928

February 2. The Third Communist Party Incident occurred. Kim Chun-yŏn and 35 other leaders were arrested, and the third party fell.

February. The Second Chientao Communist Party was organized by the North Wind Association group in Manchuria.

February. Student Communist leader, Kim Pok-jin, and the students in Seoul party cells were arrested.

February 27. The Fourth Communist Party was established under the leadership of Han Wi-kŏn. Ch'a Kŭm-bong was elected as its new chairman.

April. Pak Hyŏng-byŏng and his group of Communists were arrested in P'yŏngyang.

May 10. The Second Chientao Communist Party Incident occured.

June 17. Yi Yŏng and his group of Communists, members of the Ch'unkyŏng-won Communist Party, were arrested.

July. In Chŏng-sik and the Korean Communists in Japan established a section of their bureau in Kyŏto.

July 25. The Sixth Congress of the Comintern was held, and four Korean Communists representing two factions attended the Congress.

August 29. The mass arrests were made of the Communists in the Japanese Bureau as a result of what is known as the 8-29 Incident.

September 1. A resolution admitting the Korean Communist Party to the Comintern was passed in the Sixth Congress of the Comintern.

September 2. As a result of the Second Chientao Communist Party Incident, Kim Ch'ŏl-san and some 85 Communists were arrested in Manchuria.

September. Korean Communists in China decided independently to join the Chinese Communists. They joined the Fanan District Committee of the Kiangsu Provincial Committee.

October 5. The Fourth Korean Communist Party Incident occured, and Ham Myŏng-ch'an and some 175 Communists were arrested.

November 5. The Manchurian Provincial Committee of the Chinese Communist Party was established in Fengtien.

December 10. The Comintern issued a theses, commonly known as the December Theses, to the Korean Communists.

December. The Korean Student Communist Incident occurred involving students under the leadership of Ch'oe Sŏng-hwan and Yi Ch'ŏl-ha. Students boycotted the school by not attending classes.

1929

January 18. 1,600 union members of 32 local unions staged a strike for 82 days in Wonsan. This is what is commonly known as the Wonsan General Strike.

April 22. Yi Myŏng-su and the Communists who were involved in the Fourth Party Incident were arrested.

May. Secret agents from Manchuria who came in to Seoul to establish a party were arrested. An Sang-hun and 13 other agents were arrested.

June. The Korean Communist Party Reestablishment Preparation Association was organized under the leadership of Kim Ch'ŏl-su.

July 10. Yŏ Un-hyŏng was arrested in Shanghai.

July 10. The M.L. group of the Manchurian General Bureau was dissolved to join the Chinese Communist Party in Manchuria.

August. Kim Myŏng-si, a woman KUTV graduate, who worked in Shanghai under the Chinese Communists, was arrested entering Korea with other agents to reestablish the Communist Party.

September. Peasants in Kŏwŏn, Hamgyŏng Namdo, were involved in a tenancy dispute with the Oriental Development Company.

October. Tenancy disputes of the peasants in Fuji farm in Yongch'ŏn, P'yŏng'an Pukto, occurred. This is the first of series of tenancy disputes of this farm.

November 3. The Kwangju student incident occurred. This incident began purely as a student anti-Japanese demonstration, but it lasted almost six months, and imprisoned many important leaders of Shin'gan-hoe including Ho Hon and Cho Pyong-ok.

December 31. The Korean Communists in Manchuria organized an anti-imperialist league and led numerous riots.

1930

January 3-5. Mass demonstration led by the Communists took place in Chientao in support of the Kwangju student demonstration.

January. Myŏngch'ŏn Communist Youth Association Incident occurred under the leadership of Hwang Un-han.

January. Over 2,700 workers staged a general strike against a textile factory in Pusan.

January 9. Tanch'ŏn Peasant Union Incident involving 220 union members occurred. Kim Chae-kyu and some 75 members were prosecuted.

March 20. The Manchurian General Bureau of the Korean Communist Party issued its dissolution declaration.

April 13. The Third Chientao Communist Party Incident occurred, and Kang Sŏk-jun and some 68 Communists were arrested.

April 20. The leftist youth league members attacked the police station in Ch'ŏngjin, Hamgyŏng Pukto, demanding the release of the arrested Communist leaders.

May. Over 500 mine workers in Shinhŭng mines in Hamgyŏng Namdo staged a general strike.

May 28. The second Fuji farm tenancy disputes occurred.

May 30. The Korean Communists staged a massive and successful riot in several towns in Chientao. This incident is known as the Chientao May 30 Incident or The Fourth Chientao Communist Incident. 471 were arrested and 403 were later prosecuted.

June 8. Several hundred peasants in Chŏngp'yŏng, Hamgyŏng Namdo, were arrested for organizing a peasant union. Wŏn Hoe-kuk and some 73 leaders were prosecuted.

July 20. Over three thousand peasants in Tanch'ŏn, Hamgyŏng Namdo, rioted and attacked the police stations.

August 6. Two thousand workers staged a general strike against P'yŏngyang Rubber Company, which lasted almost a month.

August 30. The Seoul-Shanghai faction in Manchuria declared its dissolution in favor of joining the Chinese Communists.

September. Some 39 Communist leaders under the leadership of Yi P'yŏng-san were arrested attempting to reestablish a party. This arrest of the leaders is known as the Korean Communist Party Reestablishment council Incident.

September. A readers' association, leftist study group, was organized in Keijŏ Imperial University.

September 18. The Red International of Labor Unions, the Profintern, issued a directive to the Korean Federation of Labor.

November. Over two thousand peasants were involved in the tenancy disputes against Kowŏn Oriental Land Development Company in Hamgyŏng Namdo.

November. The Fifth Chientao Communist Incident that began from June lasted till November, involving the arrests of both Chinese and Korean Communists.

November. The organizational committee of the Seoul-Shinŭiju line of the Korean Communist Party Reestablishment Preparation Association under the leadership of Yi Sŏng-ch'ŏl was uncovered.

December 1. Red Yŏnghŭng Peasant Union Riot Incident occurred under the leadership of Ch'oe Su-ch'ŏl.

December. Hoeryŏng Communist Youth League Incident occurred and Kim Yŏng-jun and nearly one hundred Communists were arrested.

December 27. Shinhŭng Educational Research Association Incident involving leftist educators of both Japanese and Korean schools occurred.

1931

January. Andong Communist Group organization incident occurred in Andong, Kyŏngsang Pukto, and some 150 Communists led by An Sang-yun were arrested.

January.   Several anti-imperialism groups were organized in Seoul, but its
    leader Só Chung-sŏk and his workers in numerous schools in Seoul
    were all arrested.

January.   Red Labor of International Union in Korean Nitrogen Industries
    was uncovered and Kim Ho-pan and some twenty leaders were
    arrested.

February 13.   A group of Communists led by Kwŏn Tae-hyŏng returned
    from Shanghai to organize the Korean Communist Party Reestablish-
    ment Council. They held their first meeting, known as the first
    Yŏngdŭngp'o meeting, on February 27.

March 23.   The Leftist Labor Union National Council Preparation Asso-
    ciation was organized.

April 3.   Kwon Tae-hyŏng organized the Korean Communist Party Re-
    establishment Council, and held its meeting on April 10. This
    meeting is sometimes known as the Second Yŏngdŭngp'o meeting.

April.   The agents from the Manchurian Provincial Committee came into
    two Hamgyŏng provinces to organize the Korean workers in
    factories, but its leaders headed by Kang Mun-su and some hundreds
    of workers involved were arrested.

May.   Chŏng Chae-tal and a few Communists from the Fourth Party were
    arrested in P'yŏngyang, attempting to revive the local Communist
    organizations there.

May 16.   At the national convention of *Shin'gan-hoe,* the Communists
    successfully dissolved the *Shin'gan-hoe,* a united front organization
    that had some 141 branch offices and 39,410 members.

May 27.   Over two thousand peasants in Hongwŏn, Hamgyŏng Namdo
    staged a mass anti-Japanese riot, known as the First Hongwŏn
    Peasant Union Incident.

June.   A branch of the Pan Pacific Labor Union operating in the Hŭngnam
    Fertilizer Company in Hŭngnam, suffered its first arrest.

July.   Ko Kyŏng-hŭm was arrested, attempting to establish several
    anti-Japanese and anti-imperialism leagues.

July 26.   Kwŏn Tae-hyŏng and his associates in the Korean Communist
    Party Reestablishment Council in Taegu were arrested, and this
    resulted in a massive arrest known as the Sixth Korean Communist
    Party Incident.

August.   Ch'oe P'an-ok and some one hundred Communists organized the
    peasants in Yŏngŏm, Chŏlla Namdo, but they were all arrested.

August 5.   The proletarian literary organization was uncovered, and
    majority of its members were arrested.

September 17.   Hamhŭng Red Labor of International Union Incident
    occurred.

September 18.   The Japanese invaded Manchuria. The North Korean

historians claim this date as the beginning of the partisan activities of
Kim Il-sŏng who was then 19 years of age.

September 27. College students at Keijō Imperial University, both the
Japanese and Korean students, organized anti-imperialism league and
Red Friends Association.

October 26. The leaders of the Korean Internal Operation Committee
were arrested and their attempt to reorganize failed.

November. Cho Pong-am organized an anti-imperialism league of the
Korean Communists in Shanghai.

December. Agents from the Manchurian Provincial Committee came to
Seoul. Among these agents was Han Chŏn-jŏng who worked in high
schools and who was later arrested.

December 23. The Japanese General Bureau of the Korean Communist
Party issued its dissolution declaration.

1932

January. The Young Communist International sent a thesis to the Korean
Communist Youth Association known as the KIM's January Thesis.

January 18. The Manchurian Provincial Committee of the Chinese Communist Party moved its headquarters from Mukden to Harbin.

February 1. The Proletarian Science Research Center Incident occurred
in Taegu.

February 15. *Minsaeng-dan,* a Japanese police front organization of the
Koreans in Manchuria, held its founding congress.

March 16. Over three hundred peasants were involved in the Yangsan
Peasant Union Incident.

April. Kim Il-sŏng claims that he organized his first anti-Japanese people's
guerrilla bands in eastern Manchuria.

April 25. Kim Il-sŏng claims to have established a Korean Revolutionary
Army in Antu Province.

June 14. The Student Joint Committee was uncovered, and many
students of Hamhŭng's leading schools were arrested for their
involvement in the leftist movement.

July. A plan to organize a joint Red Labor Union of the Japanese and the
Koreans in Seoul was uncovered, and Kong Wŏn-ch'ang and Oba
Keimi were arrested.

July. Kwŏn Tae-hyŏng and some 500 Communists were arrested in and
near Taegu, marking the end of the Sixth Korean Communist
Incident.

September. The leaders of several leftist organizations in Seoul, including
Red Labor Union, the Anti-Imperialism League, and others, both
Koreans and Japanese (Cho Chŏng-rae and Wada Kenji), were
arrested in Seoul.

November. Kim Il-sŏng is reported to have begun to establish four guerrilla districts in Manchuria.

December. Kim Il-sŏng claims that he has organized and developed his guerrillas as an anti-Japanese People's Guerrilla Unit in eastern Manchuria. Kim also claims that the anti-Japanese partisan bases were established in northeastern part of Korea-China border and in all parts of Northeast China.

1933

January. Waterfront workers in Hamgyŏng Pukto organized red labor union under the leadership of Ch'oe Tong-hi. This is the first time the Communists attempted to organize the workers in the waterfront.

January 26. The Chinese Communist Party issued a directive to the Manchurian Provincial Committee. This directive is commonly known as the January Directive.

February. Communists from Japan, after the dissolution of the Japanese Bureau of the Korean Communist Party, entered Korea in an effort to reestablish the Communist Party, but its leader Kim Tu-jŏng and some 45 Communists were arrested.

April. Kim Il-sŏng claims to have had the first of several important military officers' conferences in eastern Manchuria. This one was held in Shiaowangts'ing of Wangts'ing Prefecture.

April. Kim Il-sŏng claims that they have created a People's Revolutionary Government in the guerrilla districts.

August. The First Army of the Northeast People's Revolutionary Army was established under the Chinese Communists in Panshih Province in which many Koreans participated.

October. Agents dispatched by An Kwang-ch'ŏn and a nationalist leader Kim Wŏn-bong in Peking, entered Korea and attempted to reestablish a working group of the Communists, but the agents and some 130 Communists involved were arrested.

October 4. Kim Tu-yŏng organized a Communist union of the educators in Kyŏngsang Namdo.

December. A Japanese educator at the Keijŏ Imperial University, Professor Miyake Shikanosuke, was arrested attempting to aid the Korean Communists in Seoul.

1934

February. The Chinese Communist Party issued a second directive, known as the February Directive to the Manchurian Provincial Committee.

February. The Second Army of the Northeast People's Revolutionary Army was established in Manchuria, and many Koreans participated in this army.

March. Kim Il-sŏng claims that the Korean People's Revolutionary Army was formally organized, uniting in Manchuria all units that were scattered in various regions.

June. United force of the Chinese and Koreans staged an assault on a town of Lotzukou in Manchuria.

July. Yi Ki-t'aek was arrested in Chŏlla Pukto. Yi propagated communism in an effort to revive the Communist activities.

1935

January. Chŏng Kil-sŏng and some thirty important Communist leaders were arrested in Taegu.

February. Yi Hong-kwang, a noted Korean woman general in Manchuria attacked the Korean-Manchurian border and infiltrated into Korea.

February. Kim Il-sŏng claims to have had the second important military conference at Tahongwae, Wangts'ing Prefecture in Manchuria, and it is reported that an extensive discussion on the problems of the Minsaeng-dan was debated at this conference.

February 23. Yi Tong-hwi, the founder of the Korean Communist Party, died.

February 24–March 3. The joint conference of the Chinese and Korean Communists was held at Taihuangkou to discuss problems resulting from the Minsaeng-dan incident.

May. Kim Il-sŏng claims to have had the third military officers' conference at Yoyŏng-ku, Wangts'ing Province, and stressed the united action of the Chinese and Korean military campaigns.

May. The Korean literary organization, the KAPF, dissolved itself.

June. Kim Il-sŏng claims to have staged a significant battle against the Japanese punitive expedition forces at Lohei mountain region of Tungning Prefecture.

July 5. Korean revolutionaries in China formed a united front organization, the Korean National Revolutionary Party. This party was primarily a nationalist party where some Communists in China participated.

July–August. The Seventh Congress of the Comintern was held, and Kim Ha-il represented the Korean Communists.

1936

January 3. Korean Communists who were disappointed in the joint Sino-Korean Communist undertakings in Manchuria detached themselves from the Chinese and organized a new group known as the Asŏng Communist Party under the leadership of Yi Chŏng-sik in Ach'eng, Kirin Province.

January. Communists in China who were disappointed by the Korean Nationalists began trek north to Yenan under the leadership of Ch'oe Ch'ang-ik and Mu-jŏng.

February. Kim Il-sŏng claims to have had the fourth and very important conference at Nanhu-tao, and as a result of this conference they began what they call their "long march" from Nanhutao to Tungkang which ended in May 1936.

May. Kim Il-sŏng held another conference when he completed his long march at Tungkang, the Tungkang Conference, and his guerrillas claim to have found a united front organization named the Fatherland Restoration Association.

May 5. According to Kim Il-sŏng, the Fatherland Restoration Association was found on this day. However, the documents of the Association indicate that the organization was not established until June 10.

June 10. The Korean Fatherland Restoration Association in Manchuria was established.

August 13. Over 2,500 workers at Kanebo textile spinning mills in Kwangju staged a general strike demanding better working conditions.

September. The fifth meeting of Kim Il-sŏng's military officers was held at Heishatzukou, Manchuria.

November. Kim claims to have fought and won a victory in the battle of Heishatzukou.

December. Kim Il-sŏng is said to have had an important meeting with Pak Tal from Korea at Samke, and planned his forthcoming infiltration into Korea, the Samke meeting.

December. A journal known as the *Sam'il wŏlgan* was first published.

1937

January. A branch organ of the Fatherland Restoration Association of Manchuria known as the Korean National Liberation League was organized in Kapsan, Hamgyŏng Namdo.

January. Kim Il-sŏng claims to have fought an important battle at Nun'am-dong and infiltrated into the town of Op'ung, Hamgyŏng Namdo.

May. Ch'oe Hyŏn, an important leader of the Korean guerrillas in Manchuria infiltrated into Korea in Musan county of Hamgyŏng Pukto.

June 4-5. Kim Il-sŏng and his guerrillas infiltrated into a Korean town of Poch'ŏnbo and scored a victory over the Japanese police. This venture is perhaps the best known and most widely publicized battle of Kim Il-sŏng.

June 30. Kim Il-sŏng claims to have fought at Kansambong, Changpai Province, Manchuria.

July 7. The 7–7 Incident occurred, and the Japanese army began to march into China.

July 28. The *Ilsim-tan* incident occurred in Hamgyŏng Namdo, and its leader Song Chu-dae and others were arrested. The *Ilsim-tan* was a local organization that propagated subversive ideas to young men in Anpyŏng, Hamgyŏng Namdo.

August. Kim Il-sŏng claims that the Korean People's Army held a mass meeting of both officers and men.

September 20. An ultra-leftist organization in Yŏngkwang, Chŏlla Namdo, was uncovered, and its leader, Cho Chu-hyŏn and some 130 men involved in the organization were arrested.

October 1. Kim Il-sŏng and his men infiltrated into a Korean town, Hesan, Hamgyŏng Namdo. During this raid some 223 men were arrested by the Japanese including Pak Kŭm-ch'ŏl, presently vice-premier of the North.

November 12. A few Communists established a study group and attempted to organize a peasant union in Mokp'o, but they were unsuccessful and their leader Kim Ch'il-sŏng was arrested.

November 14. Communists led by Ch'oe Kyŏng-ok and Kwŏn Yŏng-dae attempted to reestablish a Communist group in Seoul but all were arrested.

November 18. Several Communists led by Kong Wŏn-ch'ang and Pak Chin-hong also attempted unsuccessfully to establish a Communist group in Seoul.

1938

January 6. Yang Ho-wŏn and a few other Communists attempted to organize a Communist workers union in Samch'ŏnp'o, Chŏlla Namdo, but the leaders and some 130 workers who participated in the organization were arrested.

February 14. A few agents from the guerrilla company commanded by Kim Il-sŏng infiltrated into Kapsan, led by Hyŏn Chang-bong. Hyŏn, together with his comrade Ch'oe Sŏng-rak attempted to organize underground units of the People's liberation front in the region. Some 300 persons involved were arrested.

February 19. Korean artists and actors from Japan under the leadership of Kim Il-yŏng came to Korea to secretly propagate communism while they made their tour, but their plot was uncovered.

March 10. Several Professors at Yonhi College (Yonse University) led by

Yi Sun-t'aek and Paek Nam-un, one time Minister of Education in the North, conspired with a few leftist students led by Cho Un-sang, and propagated communism utilizing the Economic Research Society in the College and also organized a few readers' societies to study communism.

April 14. Kim Ik-sŏn, the Chief Justice of the North today, organized a Communist Anonymous Group in Seoul, and propagated communism. He has also directed his followers to infiltrate into factories to organize Communist cells.

July. Chŏngp'yŏng Peasant Union Incident occurred. This was the last of the series of peasant incidents of Chŏngp'yŏng Peasant Union.

August 22.–October 18. Ch'oe Yong-tal and several other important Communists including Yi Chu-ha and Kim Ho-pan attempted to infiltrate into the workers in Wonsan. They worked in various factories and railway workers organizations, and published a workers' paper known as *Nodongja shinmun*.

October 23. Japanese army occupied Wuhan, China, and the Korean revolutionaries there retreated to the hinterland. Some of the Communists who retreated later travelled north to join the Chinese Communists.

November. Kim Il-sŏng claims to have held an important meeting of his officers at Namp'aeja, known as Namp'aeja Conference in Mongkang Province.

1939

April. Kim Il-sŏng is said to have held what is known as Peitaching meeting with his officers and men.

May 18-22. Kim Il-sŏng and his men advanced once again to the Korean border and infiltrated the town of Musan and fought the Japanese police.

May. Kim Il-sŏng is said to have fought the Japanese at Ulkikang of Holung Province.

May. Wang Teh-t'ai, Kim Il-sŏng's immediate superior and the commander of the Second Army of the Northeast Anti-Japanese United Army died in battle.

August. Kim Il-sŏng claims that his forces fought the Japanese at Taesahwa, Antu Province, Manchuria.

December. Kim Il-sŏng claims that he and his men fought the Japanese army at Yukwasong, T'unhua, Manchuria.

December. The Japanese demanded the Koreans to change their surname to conform to the Japanese style.

1940

January. Kim Il-sŏng claims that the Korean People's Army advanced to Taemarokku, Holung Province, and fought the Japanese garrison army.

January. All Korean newspapers were banned by the Japanese and the Koreans were forced to use Japanese language in all official correspondence and common language in Korea.

February 23. The commander-in-chief of the Northeast Anti-Japanese United Army, Yang Ching-yü died in battle.

March. The Korean Communist Party Reestablishment Group incident occurred in Tokyo.

March. Kim Il-sŏng claims that his forces fought a battle at Hongkiha, Holung Province.

March 13. A meeting of the leaders of the First Route Army was held in Huanjen Prefecture in which Kim Il-sŏng participated.

August. Due to the frequency and intensity of the Japanese expeditionary forces, Kim Il-sŏng was forced to operate in a small unit operation. For this purpose a Hsiahapaling Conference was held in Mialing, Tunhua Province.

December. The Korean Communist group within Korea, known as the Com. Group was uncovered and many important Communists were arrested.

1941

January. According to the Japanese intelligence reports, Kim Il-sŏng and his forces retreated to Khabarovsk, and joined the already retreated Chinese forces commanded by Chou Pao-chung.

January 10. The North China Korean Youth Federation was organized. This is the beginning of the Yenan group.

June. Pak Hŏn-yŏng attempted to reestablish the party in Korea. Although he narrowly escaped the arrest, his effort was not successful.

August. The Korean Revolutionary Youth Cadet School was established in Tungko, Shansi Province.

1942

February. Chao Shang-chih, the Commander of the Third Route Army of the Northeast Anti-Japanese United Army, died. Chao had a close relationship with the Koreans, and he was married to a Korean girl and had a son from their marriage.

August 15. The North China Korean Independence League was established from the North China Korean Youth Federation.

October. Many Korean philologists were arrested in their involvement in an alleged revolutionary activity, the usage and study of Korean language.

1943

June 10. The Communist International dissolved itself. There was no Korean present at the time of the dissolution.

1944

March. Majority of the members of the North China Korean Independence League retreated to Yenan.

1945

August 10. Russian army landed in Korea at the ports of Unggi and Najin in Hamgyŏng Pukto.

August 14. In anticipation of the end of the war, the Japanese officials represented by Entō Ryūsaku conferred with Yŏ Un-hyŏng for the security of Korea and the safety of the Japanese after the end of the war.

August 15. The Japanese surrendered and the Koreans were liberated.

August 17. The Korean Independence Preparation Committee was organized by Yŏ Un-hyŏng.

August 17-18. Communist headed by Yi Yŏng and Chŏng Paek held a meeting to reestablish the Communist Party. They met at Chang-an building, and they are often referred to as the Chang-an faction. The Korean Communist Youth Association was also established. They met at Umi-kwan.

August 20. Pak Hŏn-yŏng revived his Com. Group and organized the Korean Communist Party Reestablishment Committee.

August 22. The Russian occupation forces arrived at P'yŏngyang, the capitol of North Korea.

August 28. The Russian forces occupied the city of Kaesŏng, south of the 38th parallel, but immediately withdrew from the city.

September 6. The Korean People's Republic was established by the Korean Independence Preparation Committee headed by Yŏ Un-hyŏng.

September 7. The American occupation forces landed in the southern half of Korea.

September 8. The Korean Communist Party Reestablishment Committee was formally organized under the leadership of Pak Hŏn-yŏng at the home of Hong Chŭng-sik in Seoul, and began to consolidate the Communists.

September 10. Several important Communist leaders headed by Yi Kang-kuk, Chŏng T'ae-sik, and Kang Chin held a conference with General Hodge.

September 11. The Korean Communist Party was formally established by a coalition of the Seoul Communist Group and the Chang-an group, and Pak Hŏn-yŏng was elected as its first chairman.

September 16. Kim Il-sŏng made his first public appearance in Korea and delivered a speech at a mass meeting in Haeju.

September 28. Hyŏn Chun-hyŏk, a Communist who worked closely with the Nationalists in the North, was assassinated.

October 10. Pak Hŏn-yŏng, the chairman of the Korean Communist Party, issued a policy statement of the Party.

October 11. General Arnold of the American occupation forces denied the legality of the Korean People's Republic.

October 14. The Russian authorities in the North held a mass meeting to welcome Comrade Kim Il-sŏng.

October 22. Yŏ Un-hyŏng dissolved the Korean Independence Preparation Committee and the Korean People's Republic and organized the party, *Inmin-tang.*

November 1. The North Korean Branch Bureau of the Korean Communist Party began publication of its party organ, *Chŏngrŏ.*

November 23. Students of Shinŭiju staged a mass riot against the Russian occupation forces and the Communists in North Korea. This riot resulted in 350 students wounded and over a thousand arrested.

December 17-18. Kim Il-sŏng took over the North Korean Branch Bureau of the Korean Communist Party.

December 27. The Moscow Conference announced the trusteeship plan for Korea.

1946

January 8. The Korean Communist Party issued a statement supporting the proposed trusteeship of the Moscow Conference.

January 26. Han Pin, the leader of the Yenan group, came to Seoul and organized *Shinmin-tang.*

February 8. The Interim People's Committee was established in North Korea, and Kim Il-sŏng became its chairman.

February 15. The Democratic National United Front was organized, and most of the leftist groups were united in support of the trusteeship.

April 24. Pak Hŏn-yŏng, the Chairman of the Korean Communist Party, conferred with General Hodge, the supreme commander of the occupation forces in the South.

May 4. A few officers of the Korean Communist Party were involved in what is known as the *Chŏngp'an-sa* Incident, the counterfeiting of the South Korean currency.

July 26-29. The North Korean Communist Party and the Korean *Shinmin-tang* held a preparatory meeting to found the Workers' Party of North Korea.

August 28-30. The North Korean Workers' Party was founded, and the Party held its first party congress.

September 4. Three major leftist newspapers; *Inmin ilbo, Haebang ilbo,* and *Hyŏndae ilbo,* were banned in South Korea.

September 8. Order was issued to arrest Pak Hŏn-yŏng in South Korea. In conjunction with this order, a leading Communist in the South, Yi Chu-ha, was arrested.

November 23. The Workers' Party of South Korea was officially declared in South Korea. Hŏ Hŏn was elected Chairman and Pak Hŏn-yŏng and Yi Ki-sŏk were elected as vice-chairmen.

BIBLIOGRAPHY OF THE DOCUMENTS

1. Agreement between the Korean Communist Party and the Asian Bureau of the Russian Communist Party [Koryŏ kongsan-tang kwa noguk kongsan-tang tongyang pisŏ-bu wa ŭi hyŏpjŏng].

   高麗共產黨과露國共產黨東洋祕書部와의協定

   Pak Chin-sun's agreement with the Russians. *The Japanese Army and Navy Archives (JANA)*, reel 128 (T1,193), 43,392-95.

2. The Russo-Korean Agreement [Nohan choyak].

   露韓條約

   Mun Ch'ang-bŏm's agreement with the Russians. *JANA*, reel 128 (T1,193), 43,359-60.

3. Agreement between the New Korean Government and the Russian Government [Shin-han chŏngbu wa nonong chŏngbu wa ŭi choyak].

   新韓政府와勞農政府와의條約

   The Korean Nationalists' agreement with the Russians. *The Japanese Foreign Ministry Archives (JFMA)*, reel SP 46 (sp. 151), 14-16.

4. Manifesto of the Korean Communist Party [Koryŏ kongsan-tang sŏn-ŏn].

   高麗共產黨宣言

   Yi Tong-hwi's Communist Party in Shanghai, May 1921. *JFMA*, reel SP 85 (sp. 205-4), 9,232-43. *JANA*, reel 123 (T1,186).

5. Platform of the Korean Communist Party [Koryŏ kongsan-tang kangnyŏng].

   高麗共產黨綱領

   Yi Tong-hwi's Platform of May 1921. *JFMA*, reel SP 85 (sp. 205-4), 9,232-43.

6. By-laws of the Korean Communist Party [Koryŏ kongsan-tang tanggwi].

高麗共產黨黨規

By-laws of Yi Tong-hwi's Party in Shanghai, May 1921. *JFMA*, reel SP 85 (sp. 205-4). Also in *JANA*, reel 123 (T1,186).

7. Income and Expenditure of the Korean Communist Party [Koryŏ kongsan-tang sujisŏ].

高麗共產黨收支書

Financial Accounts of Yi's Party in Shanghai. *JFMA*, reel SP 46 (sp. 150), 426-27.

8. Provisional Government Proclamation No. 1 [Imsi chŏngbu p'ogo che il-ho].

臨時政府布告第一號

Issued by Shin Kyu-sik and others on January 26, 1922. *JANA*, reel 128 (T1,193), 43,415-17.

9. The Socialist Movement in Korea [Chosŏn sahoe chuŭi undong]

朝鮮社會主義運動

Pak Chin-sun's account of the early Communist movement. "Sotsialisticheskoe dvizhenie v Koree," *Kommunist Internatsional,* nos. 7-8 (1919), pp. 1,171-76.

10. The Revolutionary East and the Next Task of the Comintern. [Hyŏngmyŏng jŏk tongyang kwa kukje kongsan-tang ch'ahu ŭi immu].

革命的東洋과國際共產黨次後의任務

Theses of Pak Chin-sun. *Communist International*, nos. 11-12 (June-July, 1920), pp. 2,315-20.

11. Declaration [Sŏngt'o-mun].

聲討文

Ku Ch'un-son's declaration in September 1921. *JFMA*, SP 46 (sp. 150), 46-58. Also in *JANA* reel 123 (T1,186).

12. Declaration of the Korean Military Government Council [Kŏryŏ kunjŏng ŭihoe sŏnp'o-mun].

高麗軍政議會宣布文

Mun Ch'ang-bŏm's reply to Ku's declaration, September 30, 1921. *JFMA*, SP 46 (sp. 150). Also in *JANA*, reel 123 (T1,186).

13. Decision of the Inspection Committee of the Comintern [Kukje kongsan-tang kŏmsa wiwŏn-hoe kyŏljŏng-sŏ].

國際共產黨檢査委員會決定書

Comintern's directive concerning the Alexeyevsk Incident. *JFMA*, SP 46 (sp. 150), 430-39. Also in *JFMA*, reel S 721 (S.9.4.5.2-30).

14. The Decision of the Executive Committee of the Comintern on the Korean Problem [Chosŏn munje e kwanhan kukje kongsan-tang chip'aeng-bu ŭi kyŏljŏng-sŏ].

朝鮮問題에關한國際共產黨執行部의決定書

Comintern's decision concerning the Alexeyevsk Incident, April 22, 1922. *JFMA*, SP 46 (sp. 150), 428-30.

15. Manifesto of the First Congress of the Toilers of the Far East [Che ilch'a kŭktong noryŏkja taehoe sŏn-ŏn-sŏ].

第一次極東勞力者大會宣言書

Available in English, Russian, German and Japanese. See among others: *The First Congress of the Toilers of the Far East,* (Petrograd, 1922). *Pervyi sezd revoliutsionnykh organizatsii Dalnego Vostoka,* (Petrograd, 1922).

16. The Korean Revolutionary Movement [Chosŏn hyŏngmyŏng undong].

朝鮮革命運動

Speech by Pak Kieng at the FCTFE. *The First Congress of the Toilers of the Far East,* (Petrograd, 1922), pp. 74-98.

17. The Asiatic Revolutionary Movement and Imperialism [Asea hyŏngmyong undong kwa cheguk chuŭi].

亞細亞革命運動과帝國主義

Writings of Kim Kyu-sik after the FCTFE. *Communist Review,* vol. III, no. 3 (July 1922), pp. 137-47.

18. The Mitsuya Agreement [Mitsuya hyŏpjŏng].

三矢協定

The full title of the agreement is "Agreement between the Chinese and Japanese Police Authorities Embodying the Principles to Regulate the Residence of Koreans in Chinese Territory." V. K. Wellington Koo, *Memoranda Presented to the Lytton Commission,* vol. I (New York, 1932), pp. 173-76.

19. By-laws of the Korean Communist Party [Chosŏn kongsan-tang tangch'ŭk].

朝鮮共產黨黨則

By-laws of the first party, April 1925. *JANA,* reel 102 (T625), 08790-806.

20. Slogans of the Korean Communist Party [Chosŏn kongsan-tang kuho].

朝鮮共產黨口號

Slogan of the first party related by Kim Ch'an. *Shisō geppō*, no. 4 (July 1931).

21. Hwang-san Reports [Hwang-san pogo-sŏ].

黃山報告書

Reports by Kang Tal-yŏng. *Shisō geppō*, vol. II, no. 8 (November 15, 1932).

22. Directives of the Comintern [Kukje kongsan-tang ŭi kyŏljŏng-sŏ].

國際共產黨의決定書

A short directive discussed during the fourth Party congress in 1928. *JFMA*, reel S 722 (S.9.4.5.2-30), Report of November 28, 1928.

23. Manifesto of the Korean Communist Party Reestablishment Preparation Association [Chosŏn kongsan-tang chaegŏn chunbi-hoe sŏn-ŏn].

朝鮮共產黨再建準備會宣言

Declaration issued on June 25, 1929. *Shisō geppō*, no. 6 (September 1931).

24. Political Programs [Chŏngdang kangnyŏng].

政黨綱領

Programs of December 20, 1929. *Lenin chuŭi*, vol. II, no. 1 (January 15, 1930), pp. 1-30.

25. Our League as a Regional Organization [Chibang jŏk chojik ŭrosŏ ŭi adŭng ŭi chojik].

地方的組織으로서의我等의組織

Chŏlla Namdo organization. *Shisō geppō,* vol. IV, no. 1 April 1934), pp. 39-41.

26. Platform of the Chŏlla Namdo League [Chŏnnam tongmaeng kangnyŏng].

    全南同盟綱領

    Yi Ki-t'aek's platform. *Shisō geppō,* vol. IV, no. 1 (April 1934), pp. 36-39.

27. Theses of the Chŏlla Pukto Movement [Chŏnbuk undong-non].

    全北運動論

    Kim Ch'ŏl-su's theses. *Shisō geppō,* vol. IV, no. 1 (April 1934, pp. 41-54.

28. Slogans of Pukch'ŏng Red Peasant League [Chŏksaek pukch'ŏng nongmin chohap kuho].

    赤色北青農民組合口號

    Slogan written by Han Sang-du. *Shisō ihō,* no. 2 (March 1935), pp. 50-51.

29. On the Training of Our Comrades [Tongji kyoyang ŭi charyo].

    同志敎養의資料

    Document prepared by Chu Yŏng-ha. *Shisō ihō,* no. 6 (March 1936), pp. 13-18.

30. Report [Sangshin-sŏ].

    上申書

    Kang Mun-su's renunciation of communism. *Shisō geppō,* vol. IV, no. 3 (June 1934), pp. 40-50.

31. Resolution on the Admittance of the Korean Communist Party . . .

into the Comintern [Chosŏn kongsan-tang ŭi kukje kongsan-tang kaip kyŏl-ŭi-sŏ] .

朝鮮共産黨의 國際共産黨加入決議書

The Korean Communist Party's admission to the Comintern, 1928. *Inprecorr*, vol. VIII, no. 83 (November 23, 1928), p. 1579.

32. Theses on the Revolutionary Movement in the Colonies and Semi-Colonies [Shingminji wa pan-shingminji e issŏsŏ ŭi hyŏngmyŏng undong-ron] .

植民地와 半植民地에 있어서의 革命運動論

Extract of the theses concerning only the Korean problems. *Inprecorr*, vol. VIII, no. 88 (December 12, 1928), pp. 1,659-76.

33. Resolution of the Executive Committee of the Comintern on the Korean Question [Chosŏn munje e kwanhan kukje kongsan-tang chip'aeng wiwŏn-hoe ŭi kyŏl-ŭi-so] .

朝鮮問題에 關한 國際共産黨執行委員會의

決議書

December theses of 1928. *Inprecorr*, vol. IX, no. 8 (February 15, 1929), pp. 130-33. Also in *Kegup t'ujaeng*, no. 1 (May 1929).

34. On the Korean Communist Movement [Chosŏn kongsan chuŭi undong e kwanhayŏ] .

朝鮮共産主義運動에 關하여

Otto Kuusinen's theses of 1931. *Revolyutsionnyi vostok*, no. 11-12 (1931), pp. 99-116.

35. The Tasks of the Revolutionary Trade Union Movement in Korea

[Chosŏn e issŏsŏ hyŏngmyŏng nodong chohap undong ŭi immu].

朝鮮에 있어서 革命勞働組合運動의 任務

Resolution of the Fifth World Congress of the RILU, commonly referred to as the September Theses, September 18, 1930. *Resolution of the Fifth World Congress of the RILU,* (London, 1931), pp. 152-58.

36. The Labor Movement in Korea after the Fifth RILU Congress [Che och'a chŏksaek kukje nodong chohap ch'onghoe ihu ŭi Chosŏn nodong undong].

第五次赤色國際勞働組合總會以後의
朝鮮勞働運動

Eastern and Colonial, vol. IV, no. 10-11 (November-December 1931), pp. 8-10.

37. Letter of the Pan Pacific Labor Union to the Supporters of the Union in Korea [Chosŏn e innŭn pŏmt'aep'yŏngyang nodong chohap pisŏbu chijija e taehan tong pisŏbu ŭi sŏhan].

朝鮮에 있는 汎太平洋勞働組合祕書部
支持者에 對한 同祕書部의 書翰

The October Theses, 1931. *Intanashonaru,* vol. VI, no. 8 (June 1932), pp. 72-75.

38. Directive of the Communist Youth International Concerning the Korean Communist Youth Association [Kukje kongsan ch'ŏngnyŏn tongmaeng ŭi Chosŏn kongsan ch'ŏngnyŏn tongmaeng e taehan chich'im].

國際共產青年同盟의 朝鮮共產青年同盟에

對한 指針

Directive of the Communist Youth International, January 1932. *Chosen minzoku dokuritsu undō hishi* (Tokyo, 1959), pp. 641-50.

39. Platform of Action of the Communist Party of Korea [Chosŏn kongsan-tang haengdong kangnyŏng].

朝鮮共產黨行動綱領

Platform of the Initiatory Group. *Inprecorr,* vol. XIV, no. 11 (February 23, 1934), pp. 303-05 and no. 14 (March 2, 1934), pp. 355-58.

40. To All Factory, Mill and Village Communist Groups in Korea [Chosŏn ŭi chŏban kongjang kwa chŏngmiso wa ch'onrak kongsan chuŭi tanch'e dŭl egye].

朝鮮의 諸般工場과 精米所와村落
共產主義團体들에게

The circular of the Initiatory Group, 1934. *Inprecorr,* vol. XIV, no. 48 (1934), pp. 1,265-66.

41. Duty of the Korean Communists in the Anti-Imperialist War [Cheguk chuŭi chŏnjaeng paegyŏk sang e issŏsŏ Chosŏn kongsan chuŭija dŭl ŭi immu].

帝國主義戰爭排擊上에있어서
朝鮮共產主義들의任務

Kim Ha-il's speech at the Seventh Congress of the Comintern. See the speech in Korean in *JFMA,* reel S 361. The Japanese version is in *Shisō ihō,* no. 14 (March 1938), pp. 97-110.

42. Dissolution Declaration of the Manchurian General Bureau of the Korean Communist Party [Chosŏn kongsan-tang manju ch'ongguk ŭi haech'e sŏn-ŏn].

朝鮮共産黨滿洲總局의 解体宣言

Dissolution document of the M.L. group in Manchuria, March 20, 1930. Utsumi Haruichi, *Manshū kyōsan-tō undō gaikan*, (Dairen, 1935), supplement.

43. Declaration [Sŏn'ŏn].

宣言

Declaration of the Korean Communist League in Manchuria, June 24, 1930. *JFMA*, reel SP 86 (sp. 205-4), 9,820-27.

44. Dissolution Declaration [Haech'e sŏn'ŏn].

解体宣言

Dissolution document of the Seoul-Shanghai group, August 1930. *JFMA*, reel SP 86 (sp. 205-4), 9,862-70.

45. Open Letter to the Korean Communists in Manchuria from the Manchurian Provincial Committee of the Chinese Communist Party [Chungguk kongsan-tang manju sŏngwiwŏn-hoe ŭi chaeman choson in kongsan chuŭija e ponaenŭn konggaejang].

中國共産黨滿洲省委員會의
在滿朝鮮人共産主義者에보내는公開狀

Letter of the Ning-an Committee to the Tuesday Association group, July 1, 1930. *JFMA*, reel 404 (S.9.4.5.2-31), 624-37.

46. Dissolution Declaration of the Japanese Bureau of the Korean Communist Party and the Japanese Section of the Korean Communist Youth Association [Chosŏn kongsan-tang ilbon ch'ongguk kŭp koryŏ kongsan ch'ŏngnyŏn-hoe ilbon-bu haech'e sŏngmyŏng-sŏ].

朝鮮共產黨日本總局及高麗共產青年會
日本部解体聲明書
Dissolution document of the Japanese Bureau, October 1931.
Akahata, December 23, 1931.

47. To the Laborers, Farmers, and Working Masses on the Occasion of the
Establishment of *Nodong kegŭp-sa* [Nodong kegŭp-sa ch'angnip e
chehayŏ nodongja pinsonong kŭp kŭllo taejung chŏgun e sŏn-ŏn
ham].

勞働階級社創立에際하여勞働者貧小農及
勤勞大衆諸君에宣言함

Declaration of Kim Ch'i-jŏng and Kim Tu-jŏng in June 1932. *Shōwa
shichinenjū ni okeru shakai undō no jōkyō* (Tokyo, 1933), pp.
1,508-12.

48. Platforms and Manifesto of the North China Korean Youth Federation [Hwabuk chosŏn ch'ŏngnyŏn yŏnhap-hoe kangnyŏng kwa
sŏn-ŏn].
華北朝鮮青年聯合會綱領과宣言

The Yenan group's first document by Kim Tu-bong and Ch'oe
Ch'ang-ik in 1941. *Tokkō geppō* (April 1941), pp. 97-99.

49. Programs, Manifesto, and Platforms of the North China Korean
Independence League [Hwabuk chosŏn tongnip tongmaeng ŭi sŏn-ŏn
kwa kangnyŏng].

華北朝鮮獨立同盟의宣言과綱領

Declaration of the Yenan group, August 1942. *Shōwa jūshichinenjū
ni okeru shakai undō no jōkyō* (Tokyo, 1943), pp. 973-75.

50. Fighting Platforms of the Mid-China Company of the Korean
Volunteer Corps [Chosŏn ŭiyonggun hwajung chidae t'ujaeng
kangnyŏng].

朝鮮義勇軍華中支隊斗爭綱領

Platform of the company led by Yi Sŏng-ho. *Tokkō geppō* (November 1944), p. 73.

51. Proclamation [P'ogomun].

布告文

The first one was issued in May 1943. The second one is by the Corps commanded by Pak Hyo-sam, Yi Ik-sŏng and Kim Ch'ang-man. *Tokkō geppō* (January 1944), pp. 75-79 and 79-80.

52. Declaration on the Establishment of the United Army of the Northeast Anti-Japanese United Army [Tongbuk hang-il yŏnhapkun t'ong-il kundae kŏnje sŏn-ŏn].

東北抗日聯合軍統一軍隊建制宣言

The first declaration of the NEAJUA on February 20, 1936. *Manshū kyōsan-hi no kenkyū* (Shinkyō, 1937), pp. 775-77.

53. Letter [Sŏhan].

書翰

Letter circulated by Wang Teh-t'ai in June 1935. Hatano Ken'ichi, *Chūgoku kyōsan-tō shi,* vol. VI (1936), pp. 381-83.

54. The Fighting Platform of the People's Revolutionary Army [Inmin hyŏngmyŏng-gun t'ujaeng kangnyŏng].

人民革命軍斗爭綱領

Platform of the Second Army under Chu Chin in March 1934. *Manshū kyōsan-hi no kenkyū* (Shinkyō, 1937), pp. 166-67.

55. Threatening Notes [Hyŏppak-mun].

脅迫文

Three short notes issued by the Northeast Anti-Japanese United Army. *Manshū kyōsan-hi no kenkyū* (Shinkyō, 1937), pp. 213-17.

56. To Dear Comrades in Hunchün [Kyŏngae hanŭn hunch'un hyŏn tangwŏn chŏgun].

敬愛하는琿春縣黨員諸君

Yi Sang-muk's letter, April 1, 1935. *Manshū kyōsan-hi no kenkyū* (Shinkyō, 1937), p. 121.

57. Concerning the Change of Direction and Rectification of Peculiarities in the East Manchurian Committee [Tongman tang ŭi pyŏngp'e kwakch'ŏng kwa nosŏn kaejŏng e taehayŏ].

東滿黨의病幣廓情과路線改正에對하여

Chinese and Korean Communists' statement on the *Minsaeng-dan* incident. *Manshū kyōsan-hi no kenkyū* (Shinkyō, 1937), pp. 122-24.

58. Declaration of the Korean Fatherland Restoration Association in Manchuria [Chaeman han-in choguk kwangbok-hoe sŏn-ŏn].

在滿韓人祖國光復會宣言

Declaration issued by O Sŏng-yun, Ŏm Su-myŏng, and Yi Sang-jun on June 10, 1936. *Shisō ihō,* no. 14 (March 1938), pp. 60-64.

59. The Great Ten-Point Platform [Shiptae kangnyŏng].

十大綱領

Issued together with the declaration, item 58. *Shisō ihō,* no. 14 (March 1938), p. 64.

60. By-laws of the Korean Fatherland Restoration Association in Manchuria [Chaeman han-in choguk kwangbok-hoe kwiyak].

在 滿韓人祖國光復會規約

By-laws of the KFRAM issued by the committee headed by O
Sŏng-yun. *Shiso iho,* no. 14 (March 1938), pp. 65-69.

61. To the Korean Compatriots in Manchuria [Chaeman chosŏn tongp'o
dŭl egye].

在 滿朝鮮同胞들에게

Propaganda leaflet written on June 11, 1939 by a committee of eight
men. *Tokkō geppō* (August 1939), pp. 110-11.

62. The Resolution [Kyŏl-ŭi].

決議

The decision of the Korean partisans at the meeting held in March
13-15, 1940. *Shisō geppō* (Ministry of Justice), no. 77 (November
1940), pp. 129-76.

63. Action Platforms of the Korean Communist Party [Chosŏn kongsan-
tang haengdong kangnyŏng].

朝鮮共產黨行動綱領

Platforms of the P'yŏngan namdo, October 6, 1945. *Haebang ilbo,* no.
7 (November 14, 1945).

64. Reports [Pogo].

報告

Reports by Kim Il-sŏng and Kim Tu-bong at the preparatory
conference held in July 1946. *Chosŏn haebang nyŏnbo, 1946* (Seoul,
1947), pp. 456-57.

65. Declaration of the Workers' Party of Korea [Nodong-tang sŏn-ŏn-sŏ].

勞働黨宣言書

The declaration of the preparatory conference held in July 1946.
Chosŏn haebang nyŏnbo, 1946 (Seoul, 1947), pp. 457-58.

66. The Coalition of Three Democratic Political Parties in South Korea
[Nam chosŏn e issŏsŏ sam minju chŏngdang ŭi haptong].

南朝鮮에있어서三民主政黨의合同

Pak Hŏn-yŏng's theses on the coalition of the leftist parties in the
south. *Zen'ei,* no. 13 (February 1, 1947), pp. 11-12.

GLOSSARY

The glossary contains the names of Korean Communists, their organizations, their journals, and a few other pertinent items to the study of Korean communism. Only a few non-Korean names are included, and these are marked with asterisks. One asterisk (*) indicates the item is in Japanese and two asterisks (**) indicate that it is in Chinese.

An Chung-kŭn	安重根
An Kil	安吉
An Kwang-ch'ŏn	安光泉
An Pyŏng-ch'an	安秉讚
Ch'a Kŭm-bong	車今奉
Chae-Man Han'in Choguk Kwangbok-hoe	在滿韓人祖國光復會
Chang Chi-rak (alias Kim San)	張志樂一名金山
Chang Il-sŏng (alias Shin Il-yong)	張日星一名辛日鎔
Chang Shi-u	張時雨

Chang Sun-myŏng	張順明
Chao Shang-chih**	趙尙志
Chayu-bo	自由報
Chayu-si	自由市
Chientao**	間島
Chita Hanjok Kongsan-tang Ŭijŏng-hoe	知多韓族共產党議政會
Cho Sŏng-ho	趙盛鎬
Ch'oe Ch'ang-ik	崔昌益
Ch'oe Hyŏn	崔賢
Ch'oe Ko-ryŏ	崔高麗
Ch'oe Nam-sŏn	崔南善
Ch'oe P'an-ok	崔判玉
Ch'oe Rin	崔麟

Ch'oe Sŏk-ch'ŏn (alias Ch'oe Yong-kŏn)	崔石泉一名崔鏞健
Ch'oe Sŏng-u (alias Tsoy Shen-u)	崔成宇
Ch'oe Wŏn-t'aek	崔元澤
Ch'oe Yong-kŏn (alias Ch'oe Sŏk-ch'ŏn	崔鏞健一名崔石泉
Chŏkki	赤旗
Chŏk'u Tongmaeng	赤友同盟
Chŏlla Namdo (Pukto)	全羅南道(北道)
Chŏn Chosŏn Nonong Ch'ong Tongmaeng	全朝鮮勞農總同盟
Chŏn-Ro Han'in Kongsan-tang	全露韓人共產党
Ch'ŏndo-kyo	天道教

Chŏng Chae-tal	鄭在達
Chŏng Paek	鄭佰
Chŏng'u-hoe	正友會
Ch'ŏngnyŏn Chŏnwi Tong-maeng	青年前衞同盟
Ch'ŏngnyŏn Yŏnhap-hoe	青年聯合會
Chŏngp'an-sa	精版社
Ch'ŏngsan-ron	清算論
Cho Pong-am	曹奉岩
Chosŏn Ch'ŏngnyŏn Ch'ong Tongmaeng	朝鮮青年總同盟
Chosŏn Ilbo	朝鮮日報
Chosón ji Kwang	朝鮮之光
Chŏson Kongsan-tang	朝鮮共產党

Chosŏn Kongsan-tang Chaegon Chunbi-hoe	朝鮮共產党再建準備會
Chosŏn Kongsan-tang Kongjak Wiwŏn-hoe	朝鮮共產党工作委員會
Chosŏn Minjok Chŏnsŏn Yŏnmaeng	朝鮮民族戰線聯盟
Chosŏn Minjok Haebang T'ujaeng Tongmaeng	朝鮮民族解放斗爭同盟
Chosŏn Minjok Hyŏngmyŏng-tang	朝鮮民族革命党
Chosŏn Nonong Tongmaeng	朝鮮勞農同盟
Chosŏn Sahoe-tang	朝鮮社會党
Chosŏn Ŭiyong-dae	朝鮮義勇隊
Cho Tong-u	趙東佑

Chu Pao-chung**   周保中

Chu Chin   朱鎭

Ch'ungch'ŏng Namdo (Pukto)   忠清南道（北道）

Ch'un'gyŏng-wŏn Kongsan-   春景園共產党
   tang

Chu Se-juk   朱世竹

Chu Yŏng-ha   朱寧河

Chwaik   Nodong   Chohap   左翼勞働組合
   Chŏn'guk   P'yŏng'ŭi-hoe   全國評議會準備會
   Chunbi-hoe

Feng Chung-yün**   馮仲雲

Fukumoto Kazuo*   福本和夫

Fuse Tatsuji*   布施辰治

Ha Ang-ch'ŏn   河仰天

Haebang Ilbo   解放日報

Hae-oe Yŏllak-so   海外連絡所

Haksaeng Kwahak Yŏn'gu-hoe	學生科學研究會
Hamgyŏng Namdo (Pukto)	咸鏡南道(北道)
Han'in Sahoe-tang	韓人社會党
Hanjok-hoe	韓族會
Han Pin	韓斌
Han Sang-du	韓相斗
Han Sŏl-ya	韓雪野
Han Wi-kŏn	韓偉健
Hesŏng	彗星
Hŏ Chŏng-suk	許貞淑
Hŏ Hŏn	許憲
Hong Myŏng-hi	洪命熹
Hong Nam-p'yo	洪南杓

Hu Pin**	許彬
Hŭkto-hoe	黑濤會
Hŭkno-hoe	黑勞會
Hwanghae-do	黃海道
Hwabuk Chosŏn Ch'ŏngnyŏn Yŏnhap-hoe	華北朝鮮青年聯合會
Hwabuk Chosŏn Tongnip Tongmaeng	華北朝鮮獨立同盟
Hwayo-hoe	火曜會
Hyŏn Chun-hyŏk	玄俊爀
Hyŏpjo-hoe	協助會
Ilse-tang	一世党
Ilwŏl-hoe	一月會
Im Ch'un-ch'u	林春秋

Im Hwa	林和
Im Wŏn-kün	林元根
In Chŏng-sik	印貞植
Inmin-tang	人民党
Kaesŏng Kongsan-tang	開城共產党
Kang Chin	姜進
Kang Mun-su	姜文秀
Kang Tal-yŏng (alias Hwang-san)	姜達永一名黃山
Kangwŏn-do	江原道
Kapsan Kongjak Wiwŏn-hoe	甲山工作委員會
Kegŭp T'ujaeng	階級斗爭
Kim Chae-bong	金在鳳
Kim Ch'aek	金策
Kim Ch'an	金燦

Kim Ch'ang-man   金昌滿

Kim Ch'ŏl-ju   金鐵柱

Kim Ch'ŏl-su   金綴洙

Kim Ch'ŏn-hae (alias Kim   金天海（金鶴儀）
    Hak-ŭi)

Kim Chun-yŏn   金俊淵

Kim Ha-il   金河一

Kim Il   金一

Kim Il-sŏng (alias Kim Sŏng-   金日成（金誠柱）
    ju)

Kim Il-su   金一洙

Kim Kang   金剛

Kim Ku   金九

Kim Kwang-hyŏp   金光俠

Kim Kyu-sik	金奎植
Kim Myŏng-si	金命時
Kim Rip	金立
Kim San (alias Chang Chi-rak)	金山一名張志樂
Kim Sŏng-t'aek	金成澤
Kim T'ae-yŏn (alias Kim Tan-ya)	金泰淵一名金丹冶
Kim Tu-bong (alias Kim Paek-yŏn)	金枓奉一名金白淵
Kim Tu-jŏng	金斗楨
Kim Ŭi-sŏn	金義善
Kim Yak-su (alias Kim Tu-jŏn)	金若水一名金枓全
Kim Yong-bŏm	金鎔範
Kim Wŏn-bong	金元鳳

Ko Kyŏng-hŭm	高景欽
Kongsan Ch'ŏngnyŏn	共產靑年
Kŏn'guk Chunbi Wiwŏn-hoe	建國準備委員會
Koryŏ Kongsan-tang	高麗共產党
Koryŏ Kunjŏng Ŭi-hoe	高麗軍政議會
Ku Ch'un-sŏn	具春先
Ku Se-rim	具世林
Kŭn'u-hoe	槿友會
Kwangju Haksaeng Sakŏn	光州學生事件
Kwŏn Yŏng-pyŏk	權永壁
Kyŏnggi-do	京畿道
Kyŏngsang Namdo (Pukto)	慶尙南道(北道)
Li Yao-k'uei**	李曜奎
Manju Ch'ongguk	滿洲總局

Manju Chosŏn'in Kongsan Chuŭija Tongmaeng	滿洲朝鮮人共產主義者同盟
Manju Nodongja Shinmun	滿洲勞働者新聞
Manju Noryŏkja Shinmun	滿洲勞力者新聞
Minjok Yuil-tang	民族唯一党
Minsaeng-dan	民生團
Miyake Shikanosuke*	三宅鹿之助
Mu-jŏng	武亭
Mun Ch'ang-bŏm	文昌範
Musanja Chŏnwi Tongmaeng	無產者前衞同盟
Musanja-sa	無產者社
Nodong Kegŭp-sa	勞働階級社

Nodong Kongje-hoe	勞働共濟會
O Sŏng-yun	吳成崙
Ŏm Su-myŏng	嚴洙明
Ōsugi Sakae*	大杉榮
Paek Nam-un	白南雲
Pak Chin-sun	朴鎭淳
Pak Chŏng-ae	朴正愛
Pak Hŏn-yŏng	朴憲永
Pak Kil-song	朴吉松
Pak Kŭm-ch'ŏl	朴金喆
Pak Mun-kyu	朴文奎
Pak Tal	朴達
Pak Yun-sŏ	朴允瑞
Poch'ŏnbo Chŏnt'u	普天堡戰斗

Puk Chosŏn Odo Haengjŏngguk	北朝鮮五道行政局
P'yŏng'an Namdo (Pukto)	平安南道(北道)
Sahoe Nodong-tang	社會勞働党
Sakai Toshihiko*	堺利彥
Sam'il Wŏlgan	三一月刊
Sano Manabu*	佐野學
Shinhŭng Ch'ŏngnyŏn Tong-maeng	新與靑年同盟
Shin'gan-hoe	新幹會
Shin Il-yong (alias Chang Il-sŏng)	辛日鎔一名張日星
Shin Kyu-sik	申奎植
Shin Sasang Yŏn'gu-hoe	新思想研究會
Shinmin-tang	新民党
Sŏ Kwang-hae	徐光海
Taehan Kungmin Uihoe	大韓國民議會

Taehan Nodong Sahoe Kaejin-tang	大韓勞働社會改進党
Toksŏ-hoe	讀書會
Tong'a Ilbo	東亞日報
Tonghak-ran	東學亂
T'oyo-hoe	土曜會
Tsoy Shen-u (alias Ch'oe Sŏng-u)	一名崔成宇
Tung-pei Jen-min Ko-ming-chŭn**	東北人民革命軍
Tung-pei K'ang-Jih Lien-chŭn**	東北抗日聯軍
Wang Teh-t'ai**	王德泰
Wei Chi-min**	魏極民
Yang Ching-yŭ**	楊靖宇
Yangdang-ron	兩党論
Yang Myŏng	梁明

Yi Chae-yu	李載裕
Yi Chu-ha	李舟河
Yi Chu-yŏn	李周淵
Yi Hong-kwang	李紅光
Yi Kang-guk	李康國
Yi Pong-su	李鳳洙
Yi Sang-jun	李相俊
Yi Sang-muk	李相默
Yi Sŭng-yŏp	李承燁
Yi Tong-hwi	李東輝
Yi Yong	李鏞
Yi Yŏng	李英
Yongjŏng-ch'on	龍井村
Yŏ Un-hyŏng	呂運亨
Yun Hae	尹海

INDEX